D0576221

HISTORY OF AMERICAN CITY GOVERNMENT

HISTORY OF AMERICAN CITY GOVERNMENT
The Colonial Period

By Ernest S. Griffith

DA CAPO PRESS • NEW YORK • 1972

Library of Congress Cataloging in Publication Data

Griffith, Ernest Stacey, 1896-
    History of American city government.
    Reprint of the 1938 ed.
    Includes bibliographies.
    1. Municipal government—United States—History.
2. Cities and towns—United States—History. I. Title.
JS309.G72   320.9'73   72-3615
ISBN 0-306-70526-5

This Da Capo Press edition of *History of American City
Government* is an unabridged republication of the first
edition published in New York in 1938. It is reprinted
by special arrangement with Oxford University Press, Inc.

Published by Da Capo Press, Inc.
A Subsidiary of Plenum Publishing Corporation
227 West 17th Street, New York, New York 10011

Manufactured in the United States of America

HISTORY OF AMERICAN
CITY GOVERNMENT

History of American
CITY GOVERNMENT
The Colonial Period

By ERNEST S. GRIFFITH

DEAN OF THE GRADUATE SCHOOL
THE AMERICAN UNIVERSITY

New York
OXFORD UNIVERSITY PRESS
1938

Printed in the United States of America

PREFACE

THE city is our most significant institution of local government. Yet it is worthy of note that its history has never been written. The author hopes some day to accomplish this task ; and the present volume, which deals with the Colonial Period, is accordingly designed to be the first of three or four volumes, which together will cover the political evolution of our cities.

In the preparation of this work, far too many have given assistance for me to hope to acknowledge their services individually. Chiefly, though, I would single out the staffs of various libraries, the state archivists, the city clerks, and those connected with the Historical Records Survey of the Works Progress Administration. It is a high privilege to pay especial tribute to Dr. Edna Vosper of the National Archives staff, who gave unstintedly of her time in reading the manuscript, making many suggestions for its improvement in form and content. To her, and to the many others who have rendered unselfish assistance, I owe a great debt of gratitude. Without them this study could not have been finished.

CONTENTS

7

HISTORY OF AMERICAN
CITY GOVERNMENT

INTRODUCTION

A CITY is a social organism extending its ramifications into segments of life far beyond the narrowly political. In spite of the growth of large scale industry, the city is still to some extent an economic entity. Even more strikingly it is and always has been a group in the sociological sense, with an ever more intricate internal pattern of milling sub-groups whose activities constitute the phenomena of its political and social life. It is at one and the same time a repository and a creator of our culture, a custodian of the past and an experimental dynamic in evolving new ways and institutions.

Its story from the early beginnings till the present time is still to be written in all its epic quality ; but, when it is written, it is not too much to predict that there will have been unfolded a force in our national life of very great magnitude and power. In fact, with the city's opportunities for creative activity, it is not too fanciful to suggest that, at least from the turn of the present century, the city has assumed the kind of dominant spiritual role which was once held by the now vanishing frontier.

A history of the governmental aspects of the American city, of which the present volume furnishes a beginning, has a more modest objective. This is to illumine the evolution of the political forms and practices, the political behaviour of our people, which found expression in our municipalities. That the juridical city did not and does not precisely coincide with the built-up, sociological, geographic, economic city should not blind one to the fact that these sociological and geographic and economic influences have been by far the most powerful of those motivating its political action.

This, then, is a history of the political city ; but it is a

11

history written with an attempt at an awareness of the interaction of the political with the economic and cultural. American city government did not develop in a legal vacuum, unpenetrated by unfolding forces from other segments of our culture. In turn, the political, governmental segment of our collective municipal behaviour was itself no will-of-the-wisp blown about without resistance by the gusts of an economic determinism. In its own right it was stimulus as well as response, a positive conditioning factor as well as a product of conditioning, an incorporator and forger of the dreams of a greater *Gestalt* for countless of its citizens.

In the colonial period, the sense of a time co-ordinate is relatively weak. Consequently, the material scarcely lends itself to chronological treatment. Changes in the size of the individual city played the most important role in municipal development. The small city of 1750 differed but little from the communities of similar size in 1650. Only the twenty-five years immediately preceding the Revolution brought alterations of attitude, and to some extent of function, sufficient to give much significance to a chronological approach. Hence the topical rather than the chronological approach has been deliberately chosen — a choice determined by the nature of the material itself. Such an approach makes the work more in the nature of a 'study' than a 'history' of colonial city government ; but in the final chapter, and where seemingly justified elsewhere, chronological elements have been stressed.

A word should be added concerning the sources used. With few exceptions, the charters are extant and have furnished the basis for most of the material dealing with structure. Enough corporations have preserved their minutes to make these a mine of material dealing with function, procedure, and issues. A list of the charters and minutes is included as an appendix to the present volume. Newspaper items concerned with municipal government were infrequent, but, where they did occur, were apt to be of unusual significance in any attempt at realism in appraising public opinion or the quality of the administration. Use has been made of old account books, petitions, maps, broadsides, and memoranda generally ; but those relating to city government are relatively rare and often inaccessible through their wide distribution among private collectors.

The official records of the several colonies have been used extensively, and are generally relatively accessible through the admirable policy of their publication under the auspices of state archivists or historical societies (see Appendix B). The laws and the minutes of the provincial assemblies and councils furnish the two principal bodies of source material of this type. Much of the actual appraisal embodied in the present work has consisted of a comparison of state records with actual conditions as revealed in the minutes of the city corporations themselves. The Board of Trade Journals and certain other British records and some private correspondence virtually complete the primary sources.

Mention should also be made of the multiplicity of secondary sources — for the most part consisting of local histories. Generally these were written with but little sense of the governmental or the political, but there were exceptions. Works such as Peterson and Edwards's study of *New York as an Eighteenth Century Municipality* and Scharf and Westcott's *History of Philadelphia* stand out as genuinely valuable contributions, although Scharf's tendency towards unsupported conclusions lessens the latter's usefulness. The best secondary sources dealing with the political development of each city have been noted in footnotes on pp. 425-38. Many of these works are actually of very little value. Of the more comprehensive studies, the pioneer works of Brown and Osgood in tracing the evolution and nature of local institutions belong in the category of the very best.

The author is perhaps most conscious of the shortcomings of the material he has been able to discover dealing with the finances of these early communities. It may be that there will never be found sufficient primary data for a really accurate and adequate portrayal of these finances. Similarly there are wide lacunæ in our knowledge of the issues, if any, which for extended periods agitated the municipal life of many of these communities.

The American city started as an outpost of a British institution. It was still British in 1775, but here and there changes were observable. Its own American tradition was formed between 1790 and 1870. Between 1870 and 1920 it rose to its dominant position in national life. The years since 1920 have been the city's 'age of administration.' It is into these divisions or periods that the history of American city government naturally falls. The present volume concerns itself with the first of these periods.

I

THE ENGLISH BACKGROUND

(A)

AN appreciation of its English background alone renders really understandable the early development of the American city. Itself English in origin, it was indistinguishable as to legal basis or function from the hundreds of similar boroughs of the seventeenth century scattered throughout the British Isles.

The development of the British municipal corporation prior to 1600 has been treated extensively and intensively by a number of historians.[1] It represented a 'contracting out' from some, at least, of the ordinary jurisdictions of the manor or hundred ; and often from those of the county as well. During Angevin days its growth was fostered by the sovereign as a counterpoise to the power of the barons. As such it was commonly associated with separate representation in Parliament. Customarily it obtained the right to commute the various fees due not only to the lord of the manor but to the Crown as well. For these privileges it paid an initial sum ; and it ordinarily was allowed to raise subsequent fees and dues by ways and means more or less of its own choosing.

Residues of this manorial origin were numerous even as late as 1600, in the form of manorial institutions such

1. Green, Mrs. J. R., *Town Life in the Fifteenth Century,* New York and London, 1925, 2 vol. ; Ballard, A., *British Borough Charters, 1042-1216,* Cambridge [Eng.], 1913 ; Madox, T., *Firma Burgi,* London, 1726 ; Maitland, F. W., *Township and Borough,* Cambridge [Eng.], 1898. For a different theory of borough origin, cf. Tait, James, 'The Origin of Town Councils in England,' in *English Historical Review,* vol. XLIV.

as court leets, court barons, and their derivatives.[2] In many boroughs there were considerable vestiges of the once powerful guild system, and in some of them the system itself survived — in form, if not in spirit.

By the fifteenth century the borough had also become a 'corporation,' and in 1600 it was this corporate aspect which juristically was the most prominent. Accordingly, it constituted not an area, a body of residents, or even an instrument of government, but rather a 'bundle of privileges.'

The earlier vigorous independence in internal affairs had, under the Tudors, been subtly undermined. By 1600 these municipal corporations had entered the era in which they were increasingly subject to national (and hence external) pressures.

The Tudors had been responsible for numerous new incorporations during their rule. These almost uniformly were 'close' in structure,[3] naming (and retaining through subsequent co-option) the sovereign's friends as the governing body corporate. In these municipalities, and also to an increasing extent in municipalities already in existence, further subservience was evidenced by the appointment of king's stewards. These officials gradually increased in influence and power over the internal affairs even of the most powerful incorporations, as the municipalities were compelled to carry out the national will in trade and fiscal and other matters.

2. Cf. Webb, B. and S., *The Manor and the Borough*, London, 1908, 2 vol., for a study of these institutions. As a generalization, one may consider that the court baron was the manorial institution dealing with disputes; while the court leet was the assemblage which tried criminals and transacted the manor's business. However, the two were by no means clearly defined, even in the early days, and latterly were often exceedingly confused.

3. By definition, a 'close' corporation is one that perpetuates its personnel by co-option, rather than by popular election.

By 1600 there were some hundreds of these British incorporations — usually, but not always, known as boroughs or cities. They possessed widely varying jurisdictions and even wider variation in internal structure. Some few of the more ancient among them claimed rights and privileges by prescription ; but, in the overwhelming majority of cases, such rights and privileges had been incorporated in a formal document or charter. While a few of these charters were seignorial in origin, for the most part they represented direct grants from the Crown. The majority appertained to areas which to-day would scarcely be termed urban. In a few places there had taken place an elaborate structural development often interwoven with the old guild. Such, in brief, were the British municipal corporations when the initial settlements were made in America.

(B)

Of more importance to the understanding of the colonial incorporations were the developments in England between 1600 and 1775.[4] This was the period in which the municipal corporation crossed the Atlantic and found permanent footing on American shores.

The Stuarts continued and extended the policy of the Tudors, in so far as control of the boroughs was sought as an instrument to consolidate power in royal hands. Under James I this policy revealed no new major developments ; and under Charles I many of the boroughs, particularly

4. For this period, cf. particularly the thorough study by Beatrice and Sidney Webb, *The Manor and the Borough*, 2 vol., upon the findings of which the present author rests heavily in this introductory chapter. Other useful sources are Madox, T., *Firma Burgi* ; Merewether, H. A., and Stephens, A. J., *History of Municipal Corporations*, London, 1835, 3 vol. ; Maitland, F. W., *Township and Borough* ; *First Report of the Commission on Municipal Corporations* (H. C. 116, 1835).

the more democratically constituted, indeed comprised one of the strongest factors in the growing success of Cromwell and his party. However, a few years after the Restoration, the King's Party under Charles II and James II took steps to see to it that any such treasonable attitude should be for ever banished. One after another of the earlier charters of corporations where subservience to the king was not absolute were delivered up, with or without a writ of *quo warranto*. The new charters which were substituted named king's supporters as members of the corporation, strengthened the Anglican element, and still further established the close corporation as the prevailing type. When the charter of London was forfeited in 1683, the backbone of resistance on the part of other municipalities was broken. Royal dominance became virtually absolute.

Charles II used the forfeiting of charters and the installation of new ones as a means of further establishing Anglicanism, and even more as a way of putting his own friends in power. James II made use of the same devices to restore Roman Catholicism. By this time, a large number of charters contained provisions permitting the naming of municipal officers by the Crown ; and James made full use of such provisions. Old charters continued to fall, and new (and often less democratic) documents were issued in their place. However, James's autocratic and pro-Catholic conduct in this and other matters was deeply resented and the throne was once again endangered. As one of his last acts before fleeing the country, James issued a proclamation restoring the earlier charters ; but this and other steps were too late. In the same year William and Mary ascended the throne at the behest of a triumphant Parliament.

The legal position of many municipal corporations

was by now exceedingly confused. Many boroughs by their own action resumed operations under the charters forfeited by Charles II and James II. Others continued under their new instrumentalities. A few, uncertain as to their existing legal basis, sought altogether new charters. Parliament itself increasingly took a hand in altering and amending, and even in the granting, of charters. Where such charters were granted, the fiction of royal prerogative normally was retained in the phraseology of the document. Yet so usual had the close corporation become, that it still remained the prevailing type in what might have been expected to be a more democratic age. Under Anne and the first two Georges, the retention of the close form was often a phase of the bitter national struggle between Whig and Tory. This form was useful as a device to assure election of members of Parliament sympathetic to those who were in actual control of the government of the day ; for the borough corporations frequently were units electing members of the House of Commons.

There was an additional reason for the close corporation and its tacit acceptance by the populace. By 1700 the obligatory service which had been among the residuals from the manorial epoch was largely superseded by paid service in the form of petty officials such as overseers, constables, surveyors. For the most part, these officials were under the direction of the vestries and county justices rather than the corporation.[5] Hence but little attention might be paid to the corporation by the inhabitants, and its 'close' nature remained unchallenged. Only in so far as mayor or aldermen were themselves justices of the peace did they normally find their actual governmental

5. Webb, op. cit., pp. 210, 403.

functions enhanced ; and then only as part of the nation-wide administrative system of 'local self-government' in the British sense of the term.[6]

During the entire eighteenth century, more and more the other functions of these boroughs became subordinate to their service as electoral bodies for a strongly partisan Parliament. Where considerable numbers of freemen still existed, bribery even of the basest sort was not uncommon. Many of the close corporations became scarcely more than preserves of those who desired further to entrench their power nationally. Regulation of trade no longer occupied its once major role in local affairs. The old court leet functions were also largely passing. Where it became necessary actually to administer some new municipal service (in the modern sense, such as paving, cleaning, lighting, etc.), the function was frequently not entrusted to the corporation itself. Instead, the device of the special commission or board was increasingly used. This still further divorced the corporation from actual effective liaison with the residents of its jurisdiction.

A few vigorous corporations stood out against the prevailing trend, and retained their integrity as well as their effectiveness. These were found fully as frequently among the close corporations as among the more democratic ; just as corruption and disintegration were found in both.

In general, except for the afore-mentioned, ill-advised attempts of Charles II and James II, changes such as there were took place gradually and anything but uniformly. Hence the baffling variety which characterized

6. In America, the term 'local self-government' is used to denote locally elected officials. In England, it merely implies administration by lay residents of the locality rather than by bureaucrats. These residents may be appointed or elected.

the English boroughs in their earlier existence was exaggerated by their subsequent modification. Survivals of every age and period there were ; and only in the light of such illogical and bewildering variety in England is the variety of form and substance in the Colonies explicable.

(C.)

Further illumination comes from a more detailed examination of the borough itself. For such an examination, except where noted, it is not particularly important to distinguish between 1600 and 1775 ; inasmuch as virtually every element to be considered was present throughout the period in one or more incorporations.

For our present purposes, it is not necessary to enter upon the complicated and at times controversial story of the precise origins of the various legal powers with which the several corporations found themselves endowed by 1600. Suffice it to say that by that date, and increasingly so in the subsequent years, the respective functions of the court leet, the court baron, the administrative courts of the county justices, the functions derived from the guild, the special endowments by charter — all had become confused and interlocked in the majority of the boroughs. Such confusion was reflected in the terminology of officialdom and the internal structure of the bodies corporate.[7]

None the less, it lends clarity to our subsequent analysis to distinguish broadly between the several major classes of corporate functions.[8] Four such classes, somewhat arbitrarily chosen, are (1) the judicial, (2) the corporate, (3) the urban, (4) the parliamentary.

7. Cf. Webb, op. cit., pp. 6, 8, 161, 200ff., *passim.*
8. Cf. Maitland, F. W., *Township and Borough*, pp. 38ff.

There were numerous activities which would be classi-
fied as 'judicial,' even in the more limited modern sense
of the term. The opportunity to have a court in one's own
locality was naturally valued in the days of primitive and
difficult transportation. The scope of the powers included
in the contracting out of manorial and county jurisdictions, which such an independent court involved, varied
enormously. By 1600 variation in the powers had run the
whole gamut from the attributes of a full-fledged borough
exempt altogether from the jurisdiction of the county
justices to those of the ephemeral borough or town whose
'mayor's court' was vested only with jurisdiction (and
then not exclusive) over the pettiest offence or civil
suit. Size bore no necessary relationship to such variations
in competence. They were accounted for, rather, by the
date of incorporation, the size of the fees paid, the whims
of the lord or the sovereign, and other more or less irrelevant considerations. Yet these distinctions of court jurisdiction were among the most important in any classification. In fact, the Webbs made the presence or absence of
the power to create its own justices of the peace the criterion as to whether or not a particular borough deserved to
rank as a municipal corporation at all, or whether it must
be considered in the inferior and nebulous category of a
'manorial borough.'

In the earlier days such 'liberties and franchises' had
normally been the subject of substantial payments ; and
their initial grant or enhancement was still customarily
paid for by aspiring municipalities — unless indeed it
happened to suit the purpose of the Crown to grant such
privileges without payment.

By 1600, all new incorporations were by charter. Customarily the jurisdiction of the courts thereby created
was accurately specified and subsequently adhered to with

considerable rigidity. Disputes concerning such jurisdiction seldom arose except in corporations claiming their rights by prescription, or under obscure earlier charters or charters of doubtful validity.

A second major branch of corporate life was that concerned with the management of corporate property. Originally this property consisted chiefly of the 'common land,' the regulation of which made up a large part of the more strictly administrative business of the corporation. These boroughs were still most often not urban at all in the modern sense ; but small collections of villagers (of whom some were freemen) enjoying the right of common.[9] With the growth of enclosures of commons many such bodies (in the absence of other corporate property) dwindled away or became almost wholly absorbed in their parliamentary functions. The possession of common land and other property tended inevitably to produce restrictions on the numbers of freemen. It was thus itself a factor in the increasing prevalence of the close corporation ; for those who already enjoyed this possession were reluctant to admit strangers.[10] If and when the borough's property came to be made up, not primarily of commons shared by the members of the corporation, but of land out on lease, of the right to certain fees, etc., the already evident separation was intensified between the members of the corporation and the unenfranchised general body of residents. Yet the latter group perhaps not unnaturally accepted such ownership by the close corporation as merely a part of the network of privileges and complicated ownerships which was characteristic of the England of the period. Thus the members of the corporation eventually and normally gave no account of their

9. Cf. Maitland, F. W., *Township and Borough*, p. 8.
10. Webb, op. cit., p. 407.

stewardship, if indeed they had not by this time lost sight of the original concept of stewardship altogether.

Hence the corporation as such came to have no necessary connection with a particular area. Indeed, it may never have had such a connection. For example, it might itself be the lord of the manor of another district.[11] It might, as with the City of London, exercise certain jurisdictions over the entire county. Conversely, within its own area, other bodies might also exercise prerogatives to-day associated with 'government'; and such a division of functions was not regarded as at all anomalous. Furthermore, some, or even a majority, of the freemen might be non-residents.

As a corporation, the borough had the right of succession and a seal — whether close or democratic. In its ownership of property, before the law, it was held to be indistinguishable from any private corporation. Such ownership became a surety for continuity in its other municipal functions.

The activities of greatest modern interest were derived, not from the borough's legal basis, but from the growth of urban life. This type of activity was almost entirely confined to larger municipalities. The line between these 'urban' functions and some of the more specific of the privileges granted by charter is not a sharp one. For the most part these peculiarly urban needs of the more populous areas were met by a mere extension of the terminology or devices of one or another of the other categories of functions. For example, it was originally under the guise of 'presentment' of obligations of the householder that sanitary regulations connected with cleaning the streets or hog rootings normally came before the 'court.'

11. Webb, op. cit., p. 279.

As time went on, the court inevitably began to issue instructions or ordinances of a more general nature in these matters. Hence these 'administrative courts' of the corporation in communities in which the corporation was actually a vital pervading force ultimately conducted the major part of the city's business. As the Crown and Parliament came also to utilize the justices of the peace for administrative purposes, so those corporations which had secured the right to create their own justices found their time well occupied with increasing urbanization. Eventually such powers usually forced the grant or assumption of the further power of rating or taxing the inhabitants to meet expenses.

In the same category of truly urban functions belong the markets and fairs. These were usually (but not always) specifically included in the privileges of the borough. Corollary to these were the petty market courts and the courts of piepowder which dealt with the many disputes arising at the fairs. More significant in the seaport cities were the frequent powers and privileges concerning exports and imports and the survivals of 'staple right' — though, apart from instances of ownership of wharves and docks, control of actual commercial policy had all but exclusively passed to the Crown.

In certain of the cities, the guilds were still surviving ; and in a few were even influential. Many of the truly urban communities had in the first instance purchased their freedoms through the agency and efforts of these guilds, which latter had subsequently in one form or another interwoven their own organization with the corporate organization of the town. For present purposes, it is not important to trace these intricacies ; but only to call attention to the fact that the regulation of local crafts was a frequent function of the municipal corporation.

By 1600 such regulation survived chiefly in the form of restricting to 'freemen' the practice of certain trades or of buying and selling. The status of freeman might indeed be acquired by purchase as well as by apprenticeship or birth and so was not necessarily undemocratic. The borough's activity in detailed regulation of the trades themselves was dwindling.

These rather miscellaneous functions have been grouped at this point under the general title of 'urban.' This is not because they were usually sharply differentiated legally from powers under one of the other categories ; but because in the seventeenth and eighteenth centuries they represented the equivalent of what to-day one commonly associates with the term 'municipal.' Even though these functions were ordinarily undertaken through the old legal forms and fictions, the fact of urbanization was none the less finding expression by forcing into its service institutions devised for an earlier age.

The role played by certain of the boroughs in the election of members of Parliament has already been mentioned, together with the increasing importance this role played in the diversion of municipal corporations from their original function. This, it will be discovered, had but little parallel in the colonial boroughs.

(D)

Of the internal structure of the English municipal corporation, rather less need be said. The 'powers,' not the 'constitution' or framework, were considered primary. Though the latter might indeed have been specified in detail in the charter, in actual practice the constitution was frequently altered by simple action of the corporation itself. This applied equally to the structure of the governing body and its officers, and the privileges and qualifications for 'freedom.' Hence the charters furnish a much less reliable guide than the minute book as to actual structure.[12]

In structure, as in powers, there were infinite variety and minute gradation among the various corporations. On the whole, the 'close' corporation with its self-perpetuating governing body increased at the expense of the more democratic type ; but the terms 'close' and 'democratic' were relative. The particular officers subject to election by freemen differed greatly from town to town, just as there was wide variation as to what constituted 'freedom' and what were its privileges. Yet the relatively democratic corporations were often among the outstanding, notably the City of London. In any event this type remained sufficiently numerous so that it was by no means exceptional. Under certain circumstances, usually local considerations, even Charles II granted democratic charters.[13] Isolated instances occurred later, ordinarily to replace existing charters.

The head of a borough was usually known as mayor. Other terms occasionally used were 'bailiff,' 'reeve,' 'head.' He might be undifferentiated from other members of the governing body of the corporation, except for ceremonial purposes. On the other hand, he might have special duties. In extreme cases he was virtually the administrator of the town, and combined the duties and responsibilities of many other offices.

The recorder normally provided the legal intelligence of the corporation, and usually also served *ex officio* as a justice of the peace.

The bailiff, or bailey, varied more than any other

12. Cf. Webb, op. cit., p. 367.
13. Cf. p. 195.

official. At times he (or they[14]) might be synonymous with the mayor ; but normally he was an officer who executed writs and performed other judicial or fiscal services. Other officers were innumerable in title, if not in function.

Aldermen, councillors, jurats, 'four and twenty' (together with the mayor and recorder) normally made up the governing body of the corporation. Sometimes this group was divided into two or even three categories, with or without differentiation of functions. In the full-fledged municipal corporation, those of the upper category (if two categories existed) were normally known as aldermen, and were *ex officio* justices of the peace. Here again there were numerous exceptions. In the larger communities, such bodies divided into committees for administrative purposes ; and in a few places each alderman was held responsible for a particular ward.

As regards the prevailing 'type' favoured in any particular period, it is possible to maintain the thesis that the colonial incorporations furnish a better guide than those of the mother country. The latter were normally cluttered with survivals of earlier peculiarities ; or subservient to the ulterior motives of the Crown. On the other hand, colonial incorporations tended to be simpler. In a sense, derived (as so many were) from local moves or the fostering tendencies of proprietors, the colonial charters represented a kind of sifting of those elements felt to be most worth preserving from the English experience.[15] Like other generalizations, this statement also suffers from numerous exceptions ; and it is sufficient once again to call attention to the outstanding fact of infinite

14. Occasionally there were two or more bailiffs.
15. Cf. p. 163.

variety among the British boroughs as to power and internal structure.

(E)

It is worth while finally to turn away from legal structure and internal construction and examine the borough corporations from one further approach. How did these bodies appear in England of the seventeenth and the eighteenth centuries to those various individuals who in one capacity or another were connected with them?

To the king and the Crown, the boroughs in the early part of the period unquestionably were still felt to be agencies to foster trade and commerce or instrumentalities to enhance the royal revenue. If and when they were hostile to the sovereign (or to the prevailing party), they were to be bent to his will or even crushed, if that were possible. To an increasing extent they were to be used primarily for his purposes — to reward his supporters, to enhance the prestige and power of his religion, to assure his policies a majority in Parliament. Thus the close corporation was inevitably the favoured device. In the latter part of the period there was little evidence that the Crown regarded the boroughs as in any real sense governmental or administrative agencies in a national hierarchy, except as the officers or members of the governing body of the corporation might be *ex officio* justices of the peace. This last prerogative made them an incidental part of the general administrative scheme.

To the members of the governing body, membership appeared increasingly as a vested right — something to which they were entitled by succession. Such membership frequently carried with it very considerable prestige and normally the deference of other residents, enhanced by ritual, pomp, and circumstance. It was thus usually possible to secure successors as vacancies arose, and keen was the competition for the mayoralty within. The perquisites in the form of fees were not inconsiderable. Much of the corporate revenue went for continual feastings. In 1600 there was still ample evidence of the survival of the originally strong concept of duties to be performed, coming down from the days of the court baron and the court leet ; but this attitude grew steadily less characteristic. Advantages of the grosser sort, in the form of sales of property, diversion of revenues, and receipt of bribes, became increasingly frequent, at the time when more and more the corporations found their municipal origin overshadowed by their subservience to national or party ends. Nor were the democratic bodies seemingly any better than the others in this respect. As to the close corporations, the management of property ran the entire gamut from a genuine and high sense of trusteeship in behalf of the community (as in Liverpool) to exploitation or outright theft.

The status of 'freeman,' while still prized, had been stripped of much of its earlier glamour. It still connoted certain privileges and immunities denied to others — residents and non-residents alike.

To such freemen as still survived in the close corporations, freedom most frequently appeared as a special privilege to carry on a trade, or (where voting privileges for members of Parliament were included) even as a means for a lucrative bribe for voting 'right.' It sometimes carried with it exemptions from certain fees, market or otherwise, or the right to be tried in a local court. In the democratic cities, where a freeman's voting privileges included the choice of members of the corporation, no generalization as to a sense of municipal responsibility is possible. It will be remembered that originally 'freedom' meant 'of the common.' This freeman's privilege of grazing (and other rights) continued in agricultural tracts and villages, and was highly valued.

Residents, apart from freemen, were more or less aloof. Towards the end of the period instances of questioning of the regime of special privilege did occur. Moreover, a non-freeman, if of the artisan or merchant class, usually could be counted upon to attempt to secure his 'freedom,' if the way were reasonably open. The number who secured such freedom was considerable only in communities where such accessions were needed to swing an election, or in those cities where one way of entry to the status of freeman was by apprenticeship. The residents in general probably enjoyed the pageantry of a municipal organization, but paid an indifferent respect to its decrees.

Parliament increasingly amended charters upon request, and towards the end of the eighteenth century was occasionally granting them. Yet for the most part, the party in power regarded these municipalities as objects for manipulation designed to insure its own continuance in office, and not as agencies of government. In this latter role they were neglected and ignored.

(F)

Such were the boroughs in England during the colonial period ; such were the main tendencies. Almost without exception these tendencies and characteristics found their parallel in the Thirteen Colonies, and were there to be understood and interpreted in the light of this English background. For these colonial incorporations were themselves but one part of the main stream of British municipal development, as yet differentiated in but relatively minor matters from their sister corporations in the mother country.

II

THE SOURCES AND LEGALITY OF
COLONIAL MUNICIPAL CHARTERS

A WRITTEN charter is to a city what a written constitution is to a nation. By it the city is endowed with powers. In its provisos are included the outlines of the framework of its government. However ·much charter and constitution may be modified by usage, none the less both stand as legal norms for their respective governments.

For this reason the political scientist instinctively commences his inquiry concerning any topic by asking, 'What is the law ?' For the student of the history of American municipal institutions such a beginning is likewise peculiarly appropriate, for in the Colonial Period it was the legal rather than the administrative or even the economic emphasis and approach which dominated men's thought forms concerning their municipal corporations.

In England, in spite of the presence of certain corporations claiming powers by prescriptive right, by and large the borough or city was a subordinate unit, a creature first of the incorporating agent and latterly of Parliament. The colonial boroughs were similarly constituted. Only the presence of an intermediary in the granting of charters differentiated their legal basis from that of boroughs of the mother country. Even though such an intermediary was necessitated by the fact of colonization, nevertheless these charters were deemed to rest upon the royal prerogative rather than upon independent powers of the afore-mentioned intermediary — be the latter governor, proprietor, or assembly. This fact cast the colonial borough in the legal mould of an English borough. Yet it is doubtful whether the king in person ever concerned himself with these colonial grants. Such concern as was evidenced on the part of England sprang from the Crown (i.e., the king-in-council), or from the various persons, boards, and committees which from time to time busied themselves about American affairs.

If, then, the governors, proprietors, and assemblies were the really significant agents in colonial incorporations, one may well start by an examination of the credentials of these intermediaries. These credentials, where they existed in specific or formal fashion, were found in the charters or patents of the various colonies or in the instructions to the governors. In the royal provinces, such governor's instructions, while frequent, were not in fact essential, and consequently some boroughs were chartered by governors on their own initiative. Inasmuch as all such acts were subject to review in England, not only the royal prerogative but also the wisdom of chartering was safeguarded.

No borough corporations were established in the chartered colonies of Massachusetts, Rhode Island, and Connecticut. The characteristic 'town' incorporations were issued under the authority of the assemblies within a few years of settlement. Some towns claimed (and apparently successfully) their corporate rights through long established usage. Differences of opinion as to their precise corporate nature still exist.

Though never exercised, the power to incorporate cities as well as towns was claimed by the assembly, at least in Rhode Island. This body in 1669, in connection with the incorporation of the town of Westerly, included the following clause : 'Considering the power by his Majestye given to this Assembly to order and settle townes, cityes and corporations, within such jurisdiction, as shall seem

meet.'[1] The charter itself (1663) was not quite so ex-
plicit, but did confer power 'to . . . constitute . . .
forms . . . of government and magistracye . . . and
. . . to . . . limitt and distinguish the numbers and
boundes of all places, townes or cityes.'

The grants or patents to proprietors furnished the legal
basis for a small number of city charters. The power to
incorporate cities and boroughs was normally included
in such a grant. For example, in the first charter of Carolina to Clarendon and his associates, the following clause
occurs : 'We . . . give . . . to them . . . full . . . power . . .'
to grant 'to the said cities, buroughs, towns, villages,
or any other place or places . . . letters of charters
of incorporation . . . with all liberties, franchises, and
privileges requisite and useful . . . ; and in the same
cities, buroughs . . . to constitute . . . markets.' No
charters apparently eventuated from this particular grant,
inasmuch as the elaborate 'Fundamental Constitutions'
devised by John Locke for the Carolina Palatinate never
went into full operation.[2]

In the grant to the Duke of York (1664), he was vested
with powers to establish 'all manner of orders, laws, directions, instructions, forms and ceremonies of government
and magistracy . . . ' He in turn granted Jersey to Carteret and Berkeley, and by them the power was promised
by concession to an assembly to 'erect, raise and build
within said Province . . . such . . . cities, corporations,

1. Field, E. (Edit.), *State of Rhode Island and Providence Plantations
at the End of the Century,* Boston, 1902, chapter by Wilson, G. G.,
'Political Development of the Towns,' vol. III, p. 54.
2. Only the most nominal efforts were made in the direction of even
those parts of the 'Constitutions' which seemed immediately desirable.
The entire scheme was soon abandoned, and a government was set
up more suitable for the simple conditions of the area. It bore scarcely
a trace of the original elaborate plan.

boroughs, towns . . . and then . . . to incorporate with such charters and privileges, as to them shall seem good, and the grant made unto us will permit.'³ This power was continued in the persons of the subsequent proprietors and by them vested in the assemblies in both East and West Jersey. Quasi-incorporations, as towns and possibly as boroughs or cities, eventuated from this grant for a number of places — notably Perth Amboy, Burlington, Newark, Woodbridge, Salem.⁴

In Maryland, St. Mary's (1667) was incorporated by 'Caecelius absolute lord and proprietary of the provinces of Maryland and Avalon, Lord Baron of Baltimore.'

In Pennsylvania, the charter granted to Penn by Charles II included authority 'to erect and incorporate Townes into Boroughes and Boroughes into Cittie.' Accordingly, the 'Frames of Government' which Penn gave the colony all contained the following clause : 'That the Governor and Provincial Council shall at all times settle and order the situation of all cities, ports and market towns in every county.' The grants of charters to Germantown (1689), Philadelphia (1691, 1701),⁵ and Chester (1701) eventuated.

In early Virginia, the Company also possessed such power 'to ordain forms of government,'⁶ and the interest-

---

3. *Documents relating to the Colonial History of New Jersey* (*New Jersey Archives*), Newark, 1880, vol. I, pp. 28-43. In 1677 similar jurisdiction was granted to the assembly of West New Jersey in Chap. XLIV of its Charter or Fundamental Laws.

4. Cf. pp. 43, 429ff.

5. The enacting clause of Philadelphia is worth quoting : 'at the humble petition of the Inhabitants and Settlers of this Town of Philadelphia . . . I have by vertue of the King's Letters, Patents under the Great Seal of England, erected the said Town and Burrough of Philadelphia into a City . . .'

6. Article XIV, Second Charter.

ing foundations of Bermuda City and other corporations
were the outgrowth.[7]

Last but not least among the proprietary colonies must
be noted the grant (1639) of Maine to Sir Ferdinando
Gorges.[8] This grant specifically included power to incorporate 'Citties, Borroughs and Towns,' and in 1640 or
1641 Agamenticus was duly chartered. Agamenticus was
probably the earliest English municipal corporation in
the Colonies that actually functioned as such.

The death or fall from favour of the proprietors often
left their borough charters in a precarious state. The corporation of Philadelphia was barely operating under the
1691 charter before Penn was deprived of his proprietorship in 1692. What subsequently happened, I have been
unable to ascertain ; but apparently Governor Fletcher
ignored the grant, and the corporation passed out of existence until its rechartering in 1701. The charter of Gorgeana was revoked in 1652 by the Massachusetts Bay Company.[9] The Company was perhaps taking advantage of
the fact that Cromwell was in control of England and the
royal prerogative was in abeyance. St. Mary's also found
its existence threatened when Maryland became a royal
province. The power to withdraw a charter apparently
belonged to the proprietor, should he see fit. Thus Governor Gordon (1726) made Newcastle once again a town,
after Governor Keith (1724) had made it into a borough.

(B)

The great majority of the Thirteen Colonies eventually

7. Cf. pp. 91-97.
8. Cf. Hazard, E., *Historical Collections*, Philadelphia, 1792-94, 2 vol.,
   vol. I, pp. 442-45.
9. For an interesting account of this episode, cf. Banks, C. E., *History of
   York, Maine,* Boston, 1931, pp. 186-194.

became royal provinces, for the proprietary and chartered forms for one reason or another proved unsatisfactory. While there were variations in detail, the normal type of such royal government included a governor and council appointed by the Crown, and an assembly more or less democratically elected. Strictly interpreted, it was deemed part of the royal prerogative that the governor or governor and council alone (as representatives of the king) might charter municipal corporations. Yet, in practice, the colonial assemblies did not completely fail in their attempts to share or even usurp such chartering power.

By and large, the charters were issued by the governor 'in the Royal stile' (i.e., in the name of the king). The reasons leading to such issuance may be reserved for separate consideration.[10] Theoretically, the governor, unlike the proprietor, did not act in his own behalf, though he often received an ample fee for exercise of his intermediary powers with the Crown. In practice, his action was usually final, whether or not instructions in his original commission delegated to him the granting of such charters. Even in instances where such commissions were much less clear than the proprietary grants, the charter usually stood. The commission of Andros (1686, 1688) may be cited by way of illustration. In it were specified 'full power to erect, raise and build within our Territory and Dominion aforesaid, such and so many forts, platforms, Castles, cities, boroughs, towns, and fortifications as you shall judge necessary and the same or any of them to fortify and furnish with ordnance, etc.'[11] This phraseology, which was military rather than municipal in its implications, was repeated in a number of subsequent

10. Cf. Chap. III.
11. In Thorpe, F. N., *American Charters, Constitutions, and Organic Laws*, Washington, 1906, vol. III, pp. 1863ff.

commissions.[12] Frequently the governor's authority to
incorporate cities was merely assumed ; and Governor
Seymour of Maryland (1708) was so unsure of his actual
powers that he preferred a compromise with the assembly
to having these powers put to a test before the then very
efficient Board of Trade in London.[13]

There is little gained at this point by a catalogue of
the numerous incorporations thus granted by these royal
governors.[14] Except for the small group of boroughs
which originated with the proprietors and the exceedingly doubtful ones set up by one or two of the assemblies,
they comprise all the properly designated boroughs and
cities of colonial days.

It is interesting to note the type of question raised if, as
occasionally happened, the legality of such charters was
challenged. Such challenges often illuminate the underlying procedures. The question of the seal, for instance,
was deemed important ; and the charter of New York
City granted in 1686 by Governor Dongan bore only the
seal of the Duke of York as proprietor, although it is
claimed that James II had sent over a new commission 'in
the Royal stile.'[15] Even the charter granted in 1730,
designed to confirm and add to the privileges and rights
of this earlier document — while it bore the seal of the
province — never was actually signed by either king or
governor ; and subsequently Governor Cosby unsuccess-

12. Cf. Davis, J. S., *Essays in the Earlier History of American Corpora-
    tions*, Cambridge, 1917, 2 vol., vol. I, p. 8 ; McBain, H. L., 'Legal Status
    of the American Colonial City,' in the *Political Science Quarterly*, vol.
    XL, pp. 177-200, esp. p.187.
13. Cf. p. 41f. Interesting light is shed upon these negotiations by MSS.
    in the 'Rainbow Papers' (Black Book, vol. II, pt. 2, no. 81 ; vol. VIII,
    pt. 1, no. 20), in the Hall of Records, Annapolis.
14. Cf. Appendix A for such a list.
15. O'Callaghan, E. B. (Edit.), *Documents Relative to the Colonial His-
    tory of the State of New York*, Albany, 1853-87, vol. V, p. 369.

fully raised certain doubts as to its validity on this account. It is possible that the 1686 charter may also have been somewhat suspect, in that it dated from the period in England when many charters were arbitrarily abrogated and new ones substituted.

Approval of the Board of Trade (or its predecessors) was also considered essential — or rather its disapproval was deemed fatal. Thus the 1722 'charter' of Charleston (S. C.) was disallowed, although passed by the assembly and approved of and asked for by the governor. In 1774 Governor Martin of North Carolina held up a re-incorporation of Wilmington in order first to consult the Lords of Trade, in accordance with a suggestion which the Board had previously made in connection with the charter of Campbelton (1772).

The Westchester charter granted by Governor Fletcher was also called in question, but apparently was allowed to remain. In this instance, the Earl of Bellomont had directed the Board's attention to the apparently excessive privileges granted such a minute corporation, and the Board commented, 'We have thereupon considered both his [Col. Fletcher's] commission and instruction, in which we do not finde any power given him to grant any charter of that kind.'[16]

The so-called corporations of New York and Albany of 1665 apparently rested upon the agreement and intention of continuing (under English forms) the powers and privileges extended to these municipalities by the Dutch. Thus they appear much more nearly municipal incorporations by usage than any others in the colonies and were not formal royal charters in the accepted sense.[17]

16. O'Callaghan, op. cit., vol. IV, pp. 427, 548.
17. This is indicated in the petition of New York City to Governor Dongan in requesting a new charter : 'That this Citty hath had and en-

(C)

The colonial assembly played a precarious and uncertain part in the chartering of municipalities.

While no question of principle was involved in the occasional resolutions requesting royal charters for certain localities, it was quite another matter when an assembly took it upon itself to 'confirm' or 'consent to' a royal incorporation. Those familiar with the general situation will remember how often governors and assemblies found themselves in conflict. The conventional picture is one of the tyranny of the former and the championing of popular rights on the part of the latter. Yet at least in some instances it was the governor who was on the side of fair play to the debtor groups, the Indians, the negroes, the masses generally, while the assembly might represent, for example, the entrenched position of a planter oligarchy.[18] Consequently the role of the various assemblies in municipal chartering and their quarrels with the governors were often a relatively minor episode in a larger quarrel.

In the instance of Annapolis, 1708, already mentioned, the assembly's refusal to admit the city's delegate and its insistence upon the necessity of confirmation forced Gov-

joyed severall ancient customes Priviledges and Immunities which were confirmed and granted to them by Colln Richard Nicholls the late Governor. . .' There follows the list, including those from the Dutch, and a request for their confirmation and certain others to be added 'by Charter from his Royall Highnesse.' The Albany charter (1686) read 'the town of Albany is an ancient town . . . and the inhabitants . . . have held . . . divers and sundry rights, liberties, privileges, etc. . . . as well by prescription as by grants . . . not only by divers governors and commanders in chief in the said province under his said Majesty, but also of . . . the Nether-Dutch-Nation . . . sometimes by the names of Albany ; sometimes by the names of schepenen of Williamstadt ; and sometimes by the name of justices of the peace for the town of Albany. . .' etc.

18. Cf. 329f. ; also Boyd, Julian, *The County Court in Colonial North Carolina,* 1926 (unpublished MS. in library of Duke University).

ernor Seymour to withdraw his original 'close corporation' charter and substitute a democratic one more to
the popular liking. This was perhaps not a clear cut issue,
because it will be remembered that the governor himself
was on doubtful ground, not having the appropriate seal
— but the compromise provided at least a working basis.[19]

There was more justification for the Act of 1691 of the
New York assembly, confirming the recently granted New
York City and Albany incorporations. The 1688 Revolution had just taken place in England, and the uncertainty arising therefrom as to the status of recent as well
as earlier charters apparently was also felt in the colony.
Hence we read that the Act was.'to quiet men's minds.'
Similar action with regard to a number of British charters had been taken by Parliament the year before, so
there was precedent.

Rather more gratuitously, the New York legislature
also insisted (1732) on confirming the New York City
charter of 1730. This act Governor Cosby asked the Board
of Trade not to approve. His request was granted on the
basis that the privileges extended were too liberal, rather
than on account of the assembly's action.[20] The Virginia
assembly in 1705 authorized the governor to incorporate
Williamsburg, and later confirmed the Norfolk charter

19. Seymour writes as follows : 'With the advice of her Ma^{tys} Councill
    I having granted a Charter to the Towne and Port of Annapolis . . .
    some troublesome persons not being satisfied therewith petitioned
    the late Convention, who were of opinion the Clause in my Commis-
    sion impowering me to erect Citys, Towns & Burroughs was not suffi-
    cient, and many of that Convention being returned to this Assembly
    were obliged to do somewhat to answer their Boasting in their respec-
    tive Counties — and for my part I would not think an Act of Assem-
    bly confirming that Charter any lessening to my Commission, many
    Acts of Parliament having been made in England for the like end
    . . .' (Remarks on Certain Acts of Assembly, MS. in library of Mary-
    land Historical Society.)
20. O'Callaghan, op. cit., vol. V, p. 956.

of 1736. The Williamsburg charter was not granted until 1722. In Pennsylvania, however, such tacit acquiescence even in this nominal measure of concurrent power was not forthcoming, for in 1704 the governor refused his assent to a bill to confirm the charter of Philadelphia. The question of prerogative thus raised apparently ended in a deadlock, and was complicated by the growing gulf between the proprietor and the assembly.[21]

The clearest examples of actual incorporations by the assemblies occur in East and West Jersey, where by agreement the proprietors actually delegated such power to the popular body — subject, however, to their confirmation in each instance. The 'incorporation,' for example, of Burlington took the form of one or more acts setting up a borough government and conferring appropriate powers.[22] The action of the South Carolina assembly in incorporating Charleston (at the instance of Governor Nicholson) was, as has been stated, annulled on other grounds. Governor Nicholson might have been influenced to some extent in allowing the South Carolina assembly to act in this fashion by the precedent established during his term of office as governor of Maryland, when the Maryland assembly had been allowed to incorporate the 'town' of Annapolis.

Apparently little question was raised as regards assembly action in the incorporation of 'towns.' This held true not only in New England, but also in numerous attempts in the provinces from Maryland south to foster town growth, and to utilize the town with its 'commissioners' as a means of developing and controlling commerce. Only when the term 'borough' was used and when (in

21. Shepherd, W. R., *Proprietary Government in Pennsylvania,* New York, 1896, pp. 298ff.
22. Cf. p. 429f.

certain instances) privileges more peculiarly associated with the royal prerogative were included, was a serious question raised of assembly competence.

The experience of North Carolina is particularly illuminating as representing the high point of independent assembly action ; even though, for the most part, its so-called 'boroughs' had little power save the privilege of electing a burgess to the assembly. The assembly incorporations of Bath (1715), New Bern (1715), and Edenton (1722) date from the proprietory period, and the act dealing with Bath also granted such representation to 'other towns now or hereafter built . . . to elect one burgess . . . Provided, that this election . . . shall not begin till such town shall have at least sixty families.'[23] Such incorporations continued after North Carolina became a royal province (1729) and included Wilmington (1738) and Brunswick (1745). Confirmation of the earlier action was forthcoming also in an Act of 1746.[24]

However, such independent action on the part of the assembly was doomed, as in 1754 the King in Council (on recommendation of the Board of Trade and Privy Council Committee for Plantation Affairs) disallowed acts which chartered the towns of Wilmington (1739), Edenton (confirming act, 1740), and Beaufort (1723), on the basis that chartering was a royal prerogative. Governor Dobbs also suggested the repeal of the act concerning Bath (1715) and the act of 1745 appointing markets for Wilmington, 'which is also the Prerogative of the Crown.' For the most part, on recommendation of the

23. *State Records of North Carolina,* vol. XXIII, p. 79. Chap. LII of the Laws.
24. Ibid., vol. IV, p. 457f. The Wilmington charter (1745) included market privileges and power to tax. At the request of Brunswick (a port rival) the Board of Trade (1740) considered for a time the advisability of revoking the 1739 Wilmington Act.

Board, new charters of incorporation were almost immediately issued to these towns by the Governor in the name of the Crown. Yet so much consternation and protest had resulted from this reassertion of the royal prerogative that supplementary instructions were issued (1755) to the governor to allow the acts to be repassed, excepting only the clauses allowing representation in the assembly. This power was still to be retained as a prerogative of the Crown.[25] But Edenton and New Bern continued none the less to send representatives on the basis of the overlooked act of 1715, which provided such representation for any town of sixty houses ; and a representative from Halifax was admitted in 1760 on the same grounds, over the protest of the governor.[26]

Charter incorporations by the governor and council followed (as normal in other colonies) for Halifax, 1757, 1760, 1764 ; Wilmington (in royal style), 1760, 1763 ; Salisbury, 1765, 1770 ; Hillsborough, 1770 ; Campbelton, 1773 ; Edenton, 1760 ; New Bern, 1760 ; Tarborough, 1772.

As far as the charters of Wilmington, Edenton, New Bern, Halifax (all of 1760) were concerned, the assembly rejected the bill for their confirmation.[27] This rejection was apparently accepted as final, except in Wilmington, for I have been unable to discover any trace of these charters having functioned. In Wilmington the charter

25. Ibid., vol. V, p. 405f. Cf. also Labaree, L. W., *Royal Instructions to British Colonial Governors*, New York, 1935, 2 vol., vol. I, pp. 108ff., p. 103f.

26. Ibid., vol. VI, pp. 245, 365, 538-41, etc. Cf. also Great Britain : *Journal of the Comnrs. for Trade and Plantations*, London, 1920-36, 12 vol., vol. XI, June 2, 1762, where it was stated that it was 'Unconstitutional to admit members without writs from his Majesty' and that the Act of 1715 concerning Bath could not properly be used to apply to Halifax and other towns.

27. Ibid., vol. VI, pp. 400, 495. Cf. below, p. 436f.

was reissued in 1763, confirmed by the assembly the following year, and seems to have operated for two or three years thereafter.[28] Martin (on what authority I do not know) claimed that the same favour was thereafter granted to New Bern, Edenton, and Halifax.[29] This was a period in which the assembly and the governor were striving to assert their respective prerogatives, and neither seems to have been wholly successful.[30] By 1770 all these boroughs appear again to have been under the jurisdiction of commissioners.[31] In 1774 Governor Martin wrote that the freeholders had surrendered the Wilmington charter and petitioned for a new one, which he had not yet granted.[32]

Hence, apparently to the very end, the North Carolina assembly was at least triumphant in a negative sense, to the extent that a charter did not go into operation unless there was a formal act confirming it. On the other hand, the governor won his point in so far as the actual issuance had to come from him. One cannot be certain, but it would appear that a working arrangement of granting, plus confirmation, was probably tacitly agreed upon about 1763 or 1764.

Assembly action in amending charters was far more

28. Ibid., vol. XXIII, p. 654f. (Chap. VII, 1764); cf. also vol. VII, p. 242, being a letter from the mayor to Governor Tryon.
29. Martin, F. X., *History of North Carolina*, New Orleans, 1829, 2 vol., vol. II, p. 174. Apparently at least this portion of his history was written inaccurately from memory.
30. The entire subject needs further investigation. Nash, F., *The Borough Towns of North Carolina* (N.C. Booklet VI, 1906), left many unsettled points.
31. New Bern, 1770, *State Records of North Carolina*, vol. XXIII, p. 832f.; Wilmington, ibid., pp. 866ff.
32. Ibid., vol. IX, p. 818. Letter to the Earl of Dartmouth. The surrender may have been as early as 1766 or 1767. Cf. ibid., vol. XXV, pp. 511ff. Waddell, A. M., *History of New Hanover County*, Wilmington, 1909, p. 193, gives the date as 1766.

successful, particularly in additions to powers already granted or modification of the internal municipal structure. Occasional disallowances did occur, but these appear to have been on the ground of inadvisability rather than of exceeding authority. For many decades prior to the Revolution the municipalities customarily went to their respective assemblies when finding themselves cramped as to detail. However, the Cornbury charter of New York (1708) used the more ancient method of formal grant through the governor as agent of the Crown to grant ferry rights and increased jurisdiction over the East River. To a considerable extent the Dongan and Montgomerie charters were also motivated by the City's desire for additional powers as well as to assure confirmation of those powers already existing. Yet New York City also added to or expanded its existing functions by acts of assembly concerning, for example, permission for a free school, power to raise funds for a night watch, rates for the ferry.

Of more significance as regards legal position was the confirming Act of the Maryland assembly covering the Annapolis charter of 1708, in so far as it actually curtailed in a number of respects the powers granted Annapolis in the charter itself. Among such restrictions were those limiting the jurisdiction of the mayor's court to the actual inhabitants, restricting the tolls to be charged at the fairs, limiting the pay of the delegates, and providing that the county court should continue its jurisdiction over the port.[33]

New York City also found its charter powers contracted as well as expanded by the colonial assembly. In 1746, over the protest of the City, the assembly broke the exist-

33. Laws of Maryland, Chap. VII, 1708.

ing monopoly of certain lawyers in practising in the mayor's court by throwing open such right to practise to other lawyers of the province.[34] Similarly, in 1771, the assembly took steps to break the monopoly of the city in the packing of flour.[35]

It is not necessary to go into further detail concerning amendments and additions to charters by colonial assemblies. The British Parliament was likewise by this time customarily amending the charters in England, and questions were no longer raised. Hence the British trend of the gradual ascendancy of Parliament at the expense of the king found its parallel in the colonies. In both, the form and fiction of royal prerogative as to the charters themselves were retained after the fact had disappeared.

It has already been noted that England's power of disallowance extended both to the edicts of the governors and to the acts of the colonial assemblies. Such disallowing was rare in matters which were concerned with municipalities. Where the power of disallowance was utilized, it ordinarily involved questions of prerogative alone, and only rarely considerations of advisability. Whatever the precise agency in England which at a given time might be entrusted with such supervision, the agency would normally hold hearings, and legal experts and other technical advisers would be asked for their opinions before the final decision was forthcoming.[36] A favourite device was a kind of provisional or 'probationary' allowance of the colonial act, with final judgment deferred in order to gain time and perhaps observe results. Policies

34. Peterson, A. E., and Edwards, G. W., *New York as an Eighteenth Century Municipality*, New York, 1917, p. 233 ; *Minutes of Common Council*, Jan. 7, 1745/6.
35. *Colonial Laws of New York*, Albany, 1894, 5 vol., vol. V, p. 198.
36. Cf. Russell, E. B., *Review of American Colonial Legislation by the King in Council*, New York, 1915.

naturally varied greatly with the zeal, conscientiousness, and ability of those 'advising the king' at a particular time. The precise 'committee' entrusted with such supervision varied. At various times the responsibility rested with special committees : a permanent board, 'Lords Commissioners for Foreign Plantations' (approximately 1634-1659) ; a sub-committee of the Privy Council (1660-1665) ; the entire Privy Council (1665-1670) ; a small salaried group, 'Council of Trade and Foreign Plantations' (1670-1674) ; the Lords of Committee for Trade and Plantations — a sub-committee (1674-1696) ; and finally the Board of Trade (Lords of Trade and Plantations) after 1696. This latter was made up of members of both Houses of Parliament and eight officers of state, who relied heavily on their legal advisers and (after 1768) on the 'Secretary of State for the Colonies,' who was their president and who became the real director. The supervision was most efficient from 1696-1712 and from 1752-1760.[37] Between these periods the supervision was lax, and it is noteworthy that the ascendancy of the North Carolina assembly took place at that time, only to be curbed in 1754.

(D)

Surveying the entire field of incorporation and amendment, one can recognize a moderate trend in the direction of an increased role on the part of the provincial assemblies. Yet down to the end the royal or proprietary prerogative involving the actual chartering was maintained intact, save only in the minor units of towns and villages. None the less, the activities of the assemblies in amending

37. Chitwood, O. P., *History of Colonial America,* New York, 1931, pp. 497ff.

and confirming as well as in fostering the municipal corporations must be regarded as a major factor in the subsequent assumption by these legislatures under statehood of the chartering function itself.

III

WHY COLONIAL CITIES WERE
INCORPORATED

THE ideology of the twentieth century is of little use in discovering why cities in seventeenth and eighteenth century America were incorporated. To-day one seeks an answer to a question of this kind in considerations of convenience or the necessities of government — or perhaps one probes more deeply and evaluates the causes, ordinarily geographic, which were responsible for urbanization in the first place.

For the most part the factors operating in colonial America were but remotely related to these modern considerations. In a way, the question of reasons for incorporation has been answered already in our analysis of the English background. The early settlers and their sponsors transmitted English institutions to the new world because they had been a part of their experience ; and the 'natural' thing to do was done. Under what circumstances was municipal incorporation 'natural' to Englishmen ?

One essential difference between the mother country and the Colonies must first be mentioned. In the Colonies for a hundred years the fundamental problems or questions concerned an idealized future rather than a realized present. In other words, incorporations at the stage at which they took place in the Colonies would for the most part have been considered premature in England. Yet in a land in which a civilization was in the making, it was not surprising that attempts at a speedy realization of that civilization should have included an institution such as the borough ; for without boroughs it would not

have occurred to men in those days that such a civilization could be built.

Why, then, was 'government' in the majority of the
Colonies anxious to have cities ? The term 'government'
is used advisedly and generically, for the efforts at fostering cities were equally associated with the proprietors,
the sovereign, the royal governors, and the popularly
elected assemblies. In point of time it represented a later
stage for the inhabitants of a given community themselves to seek incorporation.

Primarily, then, the reason for these earlier charters
appears to have been, as suggested, the thought that municipalities were inextricably associated with a 'developed' state. It is not surprising to find this attitude when
one considers how much towns like London and Amsterdam, or even lesser places such as Bristol, were the centres
of all the teeming commerce, craftsmanship, luxury,
pageantry, and alertness of the seventeenth century. It
was this commerce and its attendant growth of craftsmanship which coloured as well as determined the most conspicuous urban development of the time. Thus Governor
Culpeper of Virginia in 1680 announced that the king
was determined that there should be towns, as 'no nation
has ever begun a colony without them and none thrived
without their development.'[1] The 1680 Act and numerous earlier and later acts of the Virginia assembly were in
part attempts to carry out this intention.[2] In even more
specific terms this desirable association of incorporation
with the promotion of trade was expressed in the Burlington (N. J.) incorporating Act of 1692 : 'Not Any
Thing being of greater efficiency to promote Trade and

1. Quoted in Wertenbaker, T. J., *Norfolk*, Durham, 1931, p. 4.
2. Cf. p. 57.

Business in the said Town than the indult of such Privileges as may invite active and ingenious Men to resort thither and coinhabit therein and adventure their Stocks and Estates upon the issue of Providence in the way of trade.'[3]

The desirability of promoting the growth of an artisan class is also frequently expressed. Thus, in Risingh's Journal, describing the proposed Swedish city of Christenehamn (Del.), Risingh writes somewhat as follows : 'It was the intention to establish a staple town near the fort [Christina] and to cause the skilled workmen, such as shoemakers, blacksmiths, carpenters and the like to reside there. Here also manufactories of various kinds were to be founded and the harbor to be improved.'[4] The development of such craftsmanship was a dream also of the Virginia Company in its early incorporations : 'And for the better encouragement of all sorts of necessary and laudable trades to be set up and exercised within the said your cities or Boroughs' each artisan was allowed to fol-

3. Much the same thought is expressed in the Suffolk (Va.) incorporation of 1742 [also in Port Royal (Va.), 1745, Leeds (Va.), etc.] : 'Great numbers of people have lately settled themselves at and near a place called Constance's warehouse . . . which place is healthful, commodious, and convenient for traders . . . and . . . in case a town was laid out there, trade . . . would be greatly encouraged.' [Hening, *Statutes*, vol. V, pp. 199ff. (Chap. XXIII)].

In 1742, in incorporating Charlestown, the Maryland assembly included in the Act a declaration that 'the encouragement of Trade and Navigation is the surest means of promoting the Happiness and increasing the riches of every County.' (Andrews, M. P., *History of Maryland*, Garden City, 1929, p. 270.)

The royal grant to Newark (Del.), 1758, gave as the reason for acceding to the petition of the inhabitants, 'We, being willing to encourage trade and industry among our subjects.' (Conrad, H. C., *History of the State of Delaware*, Wilmington, 1908, vol. II, p. 497.)

4. Johnson, A., *Swedish Settlements on the Delaware*, Philadelphia, 1911, 2 vol., vol. II, p. 521.

low his trade and was to be allotted a house and four acres within the precincts.[5]

Specifically, why was incorporation thought to assist the growth of craftsmanship and trade ? Primarily because with incorporation were normally granted or associated monopoly privileges for artisans and merchants of the community. The advantages thereby obtained were thought to aid in the prosperity of the inhabitants. The consequent greater ease of control, particularly from the standpoint of taxation, was likewise a motive. These were the days of mercantilism, before the ascendancy of Adam Smith or the Manchester school. Confidence was complete both in the effectiveness of controls and in the conscious stimulation of commercial development ; and each direct and visible evidence of the effect of such stimulation naturally confirmed the authorities' belief in its essential soundness. That the granting of such monopolies and privileges to one town or one group might result in the stunting of a more vigorous and natural development elsewhere never occurred to the statesmen of the day — any more than it occurs to the advocates of tariffs or subsidies in our own day. The initial good was specific and obvious ; the ultimate harm was diffused and hence obscure. Town life as a 'way of living' was consciously favoured then, just as to-day subsidies to farmers and legislation favourable to 'independent' merchants are justified by appeals to the desirability of the type of life thereby fostered.

5. Instructions to Governor Yeardley, reprint in *Virginia Historical Magazine,* vol. II, p. 159f.
   The same thought was expressed in Wilmington (N. C.), 1739. 'Several merchants, tradesmen, artificers, and other persons of good substance having settled there ; and it having a good harbor,' the town was incorporated. (*State Records of North Carolina,* vol. XXIII, p. 133.)

This was not quite the full picture. It is only fair to the age to say that in part these port or staple towns were established in order to maintain the quality of the goods exported. Without some such control adulteration, mis-branding, and inferiority of quality would and did become rampant. With control, as for a time in New York City, the product (for example, flour) might establish a justly high reputation.[6] Sales and profits would increase, and a city's prosperity would rest upon a sound foundation.

Yet, for the most part, it was to control trade and derive revenue therefrom that governors and proprietors in particular promoted incorporations. This was especially true of port towns. In Maryland, for example, 'The Proprietor wished above all things the act establishing towns to be passed. To understand the opposition to this act it must be remembered that any man with a waterfront could have a landing of his own and load his tobacco directly from his plantation upon ships. By the act for towns no tobacco could be shipped except at these towns. Storage houses were to be provided and town officers of course received fees. To these towns the tobacco due from the taxpayers must be brought . . . The Lower House wished to name the places for these towns, but the Proprietor claimed that as his prerogative, and with entire justice, for it was especially mentioned in the charter.[7] This legislation was an attempt to accomplish what had hitherto been unsuccessfully tried in various proclamations by Calvert when he was governor.[8] Thirty-one (in-

6. Cf. Spencer, C. W., 'Sectional Aspects of New York Provincial Politics,' in *Pol. Sci. Quart.*, vol. XXX, pp. 400ff.

7. Sparks, F. E., *Causes of the Maryland Revolution of 1689*, Baltimore, 1896, p. 91.

8. Mereness, N. D., *Maryland as a Proprietary Province*, New York, 1901, p. 413.

creased by a subsequent Act to fifty-seven) such towns were laid out, but in 1694 these acts were repealed, and two towns only — Anne Arundel (Annapolis) and Oxford (or Williamstadt) — were given the monopoly as ports.[9] None of these attempts was really effective.[10]

In East Jersey the instructions of the Proprietors to Governor Lawrie were that 'as soon as can be Weekly Markets and Fairs, at fit seasons be apptd. at Perth Town, and that care be taken that Goods be not exported to New York or other Places but all be brought to Perth, as the Chief Staple, and that a Charter, with all necessary Priviledges and Jurisdictions be forthwith granted to that Corporation to encourage People to settle there.'[11] When the Proprietors (1702) surrendered their governmental power they asked that the ports of Perth Amboy, Burlington, and Cohanzie be established ports for ever, the ships not having to clear from any other port.[12] The charter of Perth Amboy (1718) stipulated that it was made a city because 'it is best situated for a place of trade and as a harbor for shipping preferable to those in the

9. Ibid., p. 414.
10. Cf. also Labaree, L. W., *Royal Instructions to British Colonial Governors,* New York, 1935, 2 vol., vol. II, p. 539, for a further attempt in Maryland in 1705. The same note was struck in the petition (1730) of New York City for a new charter — that these [earlier] rights and privileges had eventuated 'to the great Improvement of the Majesties Revenue and the sencible Increase of Navigation Trade and Commerce . . . whereby the said City is become a considerable Seaport and Exceedingly Necessary and useful to Great Britain in Supplying his Majesties Government in the West Indies with Bread Flour and other Provisions. (*Burghers of New Amsterdam and Freemen of New York* in *N. Y. Historical Soc.. Collection, 1885,* New York, 1886, p. 481f.)

This sentiment had been reduced nearly to a recurrent formula in Pennsylvania incorporations, 'for the . . . better regulation of trade therein.'
11. Scott, Austin, *Early Cities of New Jersey,* in *N. J. Histor. Soc. Collections,* 2nd ser., 1888, vol. IX, p. 161.
12. *New Jersey Archives,* vol. II, p. 405f.

provinces adjoining.' The incorporation of New Brunswick (1730) was forthcoming on account of its location,
'standing at the head of a fine, navigable river, and being
the most convenient place for shipping of the produce of
a large and plentiful country, lying on the back thereof,
and is the place of very considerable trade and commerce.' Similarly, Trenton (1746) was 'seated at the head
of the navigation of the River Delaware' and also had a
'large and plentiful country' as hinterland.

One final example may be cited, the most ambitious
attempt of all — the Virginia Act of 1680 which ordered
the institution of twenty new 'River Towns, Burghs, Sea-
ports, or Ports of Entry.' The towns were to derive support from warehouse fees and harbour charges, the use of
such warehouses being compulsory for the neighbourhood. 'All goods, English servants, Negroes and other
slaves and merchandize whatsoever that shall be imported
into this colony . . . shall be landed and laid on shore,
bought and sold at such appointed places aforesaid, and
at no other places whatsoever, under penalty and fore-
feiture thereof.'

Naturally, some regard was paid to location in these
attempts to foster the growth of ports and other cities.[13]
Yet the inexorable development of plantation civilization
scattered the population. Mere edicts were ineffective
among people unwilling to put themselves to the extra
inconvenience and expense involved in shipping from
or trading in such a limited number of places. This resulted, from Maryland southward, in the decrees being
either virtually ignored or repealed altogether. Only the

13. Cf. in this connection the early project in Massachusetts to found a
city 'Newtown,' which 'upon more serious considerations, it was not
thought so fit, being too far from the sea.' (Quoted from Woods,
New England's Prospect, in Jones, C. C., Jr., *Dead Towns of Georgia*,
Savannah, 1878.)

exceptional town thus incorporated really materialized, and then through 'natural' causes rather than through any artificially fostered economy. In the Middle Colonies, efforts of this character were somewhat more successful — although the recurrent failure of attempts to make Perth Amboy a rival to New York were all too evident.

It is thus fair to say that, first and foremost, the growth of towns was fostered in order to promote prosperity, trade, and commerce. From such a growth was to come increased revenue. The way chosen was incorporation, which included granting of special privileges and monopolies. At the same time, such incorporation and such monopolies made easier the control of trade and the consequent collection of revenue. Hence arose the fostering of corporate ports and towns in the proprietary colonies and royal provinces alike. As John Locke's suggested Constitution for the Palatinate put it : 'It being of great consequence to the plantation that port towns should be built and preserved ; therefore whosoever shall lade or unlade any commodity, at any other place but a port town, shall forfeit . . .'

(B)

In sharp contrast was the driving force behind William Penn. His attitude towards town life stands as perhaps the most noble concept of the period. We quote, not from Penn, but from Pastorius, who, as the founder of Germantown, had experienced the sincerity of Penn's attitude : 'William Penn will not give any man his portion separately, but all must dwell together in townships or towns, and this not without weighty reasons. Among these the chief is that in that way the children can be kept at school and much more conveniently brought up well.

Neighbors also can better offer each other loving and helpful hands and with united mouth can in public assemblies praise and extol the greatness of God.'[14] But Penn's attitude was not the usual one ; and, except for the earlier years of Germantown and perhaps one or two of the Quaker towns along the Delaware, its exemplification as a primary consideration on the part of the corporation subsequently set up does not seem to have been conspicuous.

Apart from these economic and altruistic considerations already mentioned, a number of special factors were responsible for individual instances of incorporation. It was quite usual to honour the capital city of each province with incorporation or special privileges. Burlington (1681) was declared to be 'the chief town and head of the province,' and 'the chief city and town therein' of West Jersey. Special privileges worthy of this dignity followed a year later and from time to time thereafter.[15] Perth Town in East Jersey was similarly treated — the council, courts and quarter sessions, and assembly were to sit there,[16] and 'A Charter, with all necessary Providledges and Jurisdictions, [was to] be forthwith granted to that Corporation.'[17] Repeated efforts by Virginia failed to foster James City, even by the grant of special privileges, such as a market and borough representation. The seat of government was finally moved to Williamsburg.

14. Pastorius, F. D., *Pastorius's Description of Pennsylvania, 1700* (Kimball, G. S. (Trans.), in Myers, A. C. (Edit.), *Narratives of Early Pennsylvania, West New Jersey, and Delaware,* New York, 1912).
15. Heston, A. M. (Edit.), *South Jersey — a History,* New York, 1924, vol. II, p. 638 ; Woodward, E. M., and Hageman, J. F., *History of Burlington,* Philadelphia, 1883, pp. 121, 123.
16. Instructions to Governor Lawrie, *New Jersey Archives,* 1st ser., vol. I, pp. 434ff.
17. Subsequent instructions, quoted in Scott, A., *Early Cities of New Jersey, N. J. Hist. Soc. Coll.,* 2nd ser., vol. IX, p. 161.

This city was planned in detail as the capital and soon after received a full-fledged royal charter.[18] Annapolis was the recipient of similar fostering care, and was well and deliberately planned as the Maryland capital.[19] A similar attempt of North Carolina to build and incorporate a capital (George City, the details of which were elaborately specified) was ultimately abandoned.[20]

In the seventeenth century superior military strength was frequently mentioned or implied as at least a contributory objective in the fostering of municipalities. In New Jersey, for example, in the grant to Berkeley and Carteret, 'forts, fortresses, castles' were mentioned as objects of incorporation alongside of 'cities, boroughs, towns.'[21] In the early Virginia incorporations, strength of situation was particularly essential on account of the threats from the Indians. Bermuda City was spoken of as 'our . . . most hopeful habitation whether we respect commodity or security.'[22] In 1622 men were asked for, 'skilful in the art of fortifications . . . for locating the chief city of this kingdom, if they shall find James City a place not fit or proper for that purpose.'[23] These early Virginia corporations actually served as military units as well as devices for government.

The desire to create 'pocket boroughs' in order to con-

18. Cf. Tyler, L. G., *Cradle of the Republic,* Richmond, 2nd edit., 1906, pp. 54ff., 59, 63, 73 ; Gulick, L., and Pollard, J. G., *Modern Government in a Colonial City,* New York, 1932, pp. 17, 21.
19. Norris, W. B., *Annapolis, Its Colonial and Naval Story,* New York, 1925, p. 31.
20. *State Records of N. C.,* vol. XXV, pp. 373ff.
21. The grant is printed in *New Jersey Colonial Documents,* vol. I, pp. 28-43.
22. Hamor, R., *A True Discourse of the Present Estate of Virginia,* London, 1615, p. 31.
23. Quoted in Brown, A., *First Republic in America,* Boston, 1898, vol. I, p. 462.

trol the assembly was apparently not entirely lacking, particularly in a province such as North Carolina where representation in the assembly was a customary perquisite of incorporation.[24] For example, it was specifically alleged that the incorporation of Hillsborough by Governor Tryon in 1770 was in order to provide a seat for his favourite, Fanning.[25] The erection of Orange County by the Earl of Bellomont and the granting to Albany of an additional representative in the New York assembly were perhaps actuated by similar motives.[26] Conversely, as has already been mentioned, it is probable that the desire on the part of the assembly to weaken the Catholic influence was responsible for removal of the Maryland capital from St. Mary's and its subsequent disfranchisement.[27] Whether or not the consequent addition of a friendly legislator was a factor in the willingness of Governor Fletcher to incorporate Westchester in 1696 must be the subject of conjecture, though Fletcher about this time was determined to gain control of the assembly.[28] Yet incorporation as a weapon to control the local assemblies was not a usual motive. The Colonies were at least spared the travesty of municipal interference to which the English boroughs and Parliament had been and were being subjected — first under the Tudor and Stuart Kings, and then in the later period, when a borough seemed designed

24. As a general policy, borough enfranchisement in North Carolina was pushed with a view to the strengthening of the otherwise virtually unrepresented commercial element in the legislature. Cf. p. 69.
25. *State Records of N. C.*, vol. VII, p. xxiv. (Vols. I-X were published as *Colonial Records of N. C.*, but for convenience the series will be referred to as a unit.)
26. O'Callaghan, E. B. (Edit.), *Documents Relative to the Colonial History of New York*, vol. IV, p. 621.
27. Scharf, J. T., *History of Maryland*, Baltimore, 1879, 3 vol., vol. I, pp. 345ff.
28. O'Callaghan, op. cit., vol. IV, p. 223.

not to manage its own affairs, but to assure the dominance in Parliament of a particular faction or party.

In New York State, a contributory motive of a governor must be sought in the recognized practice whereby he received substantial fees for the granting of charters.[29] Governor Dongan, for example, in 1686 had received £300 for his 'services,' and the city had financed this expense by the sale of lands.[30] The payment to Governor Montgomerie (1730) for the charter which bears his name was £1,000.[31]

Newcastle (Del.), 1724, probably received its charter on account of resentment at Philadelphia on the part of Governor Keith.[32] The charter was short-lived. Newcastle seems to have been peculiarly unfortunate in its incorporations, for the 1672 incorporation as a 'bailywick,' designed to make possible more orderly government, also had had but an ephemeral existence.[33]

The early Virginia incorporations under the Virginia Company deserve special mention.[34] To some extent the motivation of the incorporators must remain conjectural ; but it must be remembered that these incorporators were Englishmen, many of them Londoners, and municipal incorporation loomed large in their experi-

29. Ibid. vol. IV, p. 812. Except for Wilmington (Del.), I have been unable to discover similar instances of payment in other colonies. For the most part, these others were 'fostered' incorporations, and may not have been paid for — though such payment was recognized practice in England on account of the privileges involved, and in certain instances doubtless took place in the Colonies also (cf. p. 326f.).

30. O'Callaghan, op.cit., vol. IV, p. 812. Cf. also Gerard, J. W., 'The Dongan Charter,' in *Magazine of American History*, vol. 16, pp. 30-49.

31. Peterson, A. E., and Edwards, G. W., *New York as an Eighteenth Century Municipality*, pp. 218ff.

32. Keith, C. P., *Chronicles of Pennsylvania*, Philadelphia, 1917, 2 vol., vol. II, p. 681f.

33. Cf. pp. 434ff.

34. Cf. also pp. 91-7.

ence. 'Borough' and 'hundred' were interchangeable as units of representation, and as such were perhaps implicit in their design to grant a 'house of burgesses' to the new colony. As a company, they themselves were of course incorporated, and the power to incorporate seems also to have been theirs. Thus Bermuda City was their first actual corporation formally organized as such. It was not territorial in the sense of including the *residents* of the incorporated area, but was largely of English origin (many, perhaps most, of the incorporators still lived in England) ; and it was designed as a means of developing the area in question as the chief 'city' of the new province. The elaborate set-up of four chief 'corporations' with constituent boroughs was (except for the element of burgess representation) largely a paper scheme ; but it was apparently an instance — not unfamiliar in the England of the day[35] — of a 'hierarchy' of borough incorporations, probably ultimately designed to correspond to a hierarchy of courts with appropriate privileges assigned to each. Military and governmental motives were inextricably mixed up in this exotic framework, but real incorporations with full powers were apparently intended by these proprietors, who evidently aimed at founding a state at least in part urban. Thus at the Virginia Court (in England), on July 17, 1620, Sir Edwin Sandys proposed : 'of the particular government by way of incorporation for every city and borough [which was] to be for all of one and the same model uniformity, being not only a nourisher of amity, but also a great ease to the general government. . . . [The form was to be perfected by a committee] expert in the government of the corporation of London and other cities of the realm, who were to

35. Cf. Webb, B. and S., *The Manor and the Borough,* vol. I, pp. 32ff., 381.

frame out of the laws of those cities a form most fit for that people, namely : Mr. Robert Heath, recorder of London ; Mr. Robert Smith,' and three others.[36] But this was Virginia, not England, and the economic and geographic imperatives brought a civilization quite other than the urban, commercial, corporate type contemplated by its founders.

In their initiation, it is perhaps fair to say that incorporations in America were for the most part anticipatory, rather than consequential. In other words, they were primarily designed to aid in the creation of the kind of community which in England had resulted in a consequent grant of borough privileges. The Englishman of high rank in those days was nothing if not imaginative ; and in that imagination lay something of the secret of his genius and his success as a colonizer. That such imagination should include within its orbit prosperous and mighty cities in a land as yet virtually uninhabited was but to be expected. Colonial history was strewn with the wreckage of such hopes — Gorgeana, Joppa, St. Mary's, Bermuda City, Jamestown — to mention but a few of those better known. Yet some survived, and towns such as Annapolis, Norfolk, Wilmington, and even Philadelphia owe much to such fostering zeal.

(C)

The inhabitants' own urge to incorporate was later in its appearance.

Here, also, the chief factors were apparently economic, and to a considerable extent may be inferred from what has already been written. Incorporation, when it was sought, was generally sought in order to obtain special

36. Quoted in Brown, A., *First Republic in America*, p. 385f.

privileges which would not otherwise have been forth-coming. Frequent indeed was the desire on the part of a locality to be made a 'market town' with the consequent enhancement of local prosperity. Of a similar nature, but with far more colour and glamour attached, was the privi-lege of an annual or semi-annual fair. At these fairs peo-ple would gather from miles around to make merry as well as to buy, and appropriate fees were forthcoming to the incorporation. While the granting of such privileges was apparently not enough by itself to constitute a full borough incorporation, and while incorporated boroughs were not always granted such privileges, these were none the less the kind of special favours that stimulated the desire for incorporation. Normally the granting of such favours was considered to lie within the sphere of the royal prerogative. Thus Newark (Del.) in 1758 received royal 'letters patent, granting . . . the privilege of having fairs yearly, and one weekly market . . .'[37] In Camden (S. C.), such a grant (1774) was apparently deemed the virtual equivalent of a charter of municipal incorpora-tion.[38]

Even more important was the privilege of staple right or port monopoly, whereby all the hinterland could be counted upon to contribute its toll to the prosperity of the incorporators.

Of a similar nature was the desire of the merchants or artisans to establish a monopoly in their craft or trade over against 'foreigners' or pedlars. Incorporation made it legal to restrict such activities to 'freemen,' and also to control the standards and practices thereof. As one Thomas Hooten pointed out in connection with Burling-

37. Conrad, H. C., *History of Delaware*, vol. II, p. 497.
38. Kirkland, T. J., and Kennedy, R. M., *Historic Camden*, Columbia, 1905-26, 2 vol., vol. I, p. 13f.

ton (1677), such monopolies purported to promote growth and probably did ; 'the place I like very well : But if it be not made free, I mean as to the customs and govt., then it will not be so well, and may hinder many that have desires to come.'[39]

Another type of motivation showed itself in 1765 in a letter published in the *South Carolina Gazette*.[40] In this the writer asked for the incorporation of Charleston[41] so that forestalling and engrossing of firewood might be extirpated. A cord of wood was alleged to cost £5 (current money), while wages were only 30s. to 40s. a day. To deal with such abuses was a recognized power of a borough.

These functions of regulation and stimulation of trade were regarded as so important by the municipality of the period that more detailed consideration must be given to them later.[42] At this point it is desired merely to call attention to them as a factor — perhaps the most important factor — in the spontaneous moves on the part of inhabitants themselves towards incorporation. Government has ever been used by economic groups as a weapon to secure special favours ; and the seventeenth and eighteenth century colonial municipality was no exception.

There were other economic advantages. An increase of territory and of 'common' land was sought and obtained by the Albany charter of 1686.[43] Enhancement of land values, perhaps as a reward or consequence of earlier individual effort to develop an area, was apparently a factor in the moves to incorporate Wilmington (Del.)

39. Smith, Samuel, *History of the Colony of Nova-Caesaria*, Burlington, 1765 (Reprint, Trenton, 1877), p. 105.
40. Issue of Jan. 26-Feb. 2, 1765.
41. At this date customarily spelled 'Charles-Town.'
42. Chapter VI.
43. Weise, A. J., *History of Albany*, Albany, 1884, p. 197.

(1736),[44] Reading (1760),[45] Lancaster (1742),[46] and numerous Maryland towns.[47] How many other incorporations may have involved similar interests must remain conjectural. In the Lancaster charter one reason for the granting is given, 'the great improvements and buildings made and continuing to be made.' It was more bluntly put in Wilmington (Del.), 1739 : 'Whereas, our loving subjects, Joseph Pennock, William Shipley, Joshua Way, and others, freeholders and inhabitants of a tract of land . . . having been at great charge in purchasing of the said land, building of houses, removing their families, and making great improvements thereon, so that by their industry and expense it is at this time in a flourishing condition . . .' The said tract is to be erected into a borough and the freeholders and inhabitants are to be incorporated. In Westchester and Elizabeth the confirmation of land titles was involved.[48] In the 'commissioner' stage of town government, laying out of the land was a major activity of the governing body.[49]

Incorporation was also occasionally used as a weapon in the struggle with a commercial rival. Perth Amboy has already been mentioned in this connection, as has also Annapolis — though the rivalry of the latter with St. Mary's was as much religious and partisan as it was com-

---

44. Cf. Scharf, J. T., *History of Delaware*, Philadelphia, 1888, 2 vol., vol. II, p. 636.

45. Montgomery, M. L., *History of Berks County*, Philadelphia, 1886, p. 657f.

46. Riddle, W., *The Story of Lancaster*, Lancaster, 1917, p. 19.

47. Griffith, T. W., *Annals of Baltimore*, Baltimore, 1824, p. 12.

48. For Westchester, see its charter ; for Elizabeth, Minute Book of the Township, var. ; also Hatfield, E. F., *History of Elizabeth*, New York, 1868, var.

49. e. g. Minutes of the Commissioners of Tarborough, 1760-1793, esp. Jan. 24, 1761 ; Mar. 27, 1761 ; July 31, 1761. (MS., custody of N. C. Historical Commission, Raleigh.) For a brief description of this type of town government, cf. p. 85f.

mercial. Wilmington (N. C.) was engaged in a constant struggle with Brunswick. Its 1740 incorporation appears to have been strategic in nature ; and was bitterly fought by Brunswick.[50] Albany similarly fought the incorporation of Schenectady in 1765 as a threat to its special judicial and trade privileges — 'which We conceive would be a detriment to this City.'[51]

There were certain governmental as well as economic advantages pertaining to incorporation. As motives leading the inhabitants to desire such incorporation, these governmental privileges were most conspicuously operative under two circumstances : in the early period of paternalistic or autocratic government, particularly in New Netherland, and in the later period, where the desire for urban amenities produced in the inhabitants of certain places the nearest parallel to modern motivation which the colonial period offered. Of the first type was the move on the part of the 'Nine Men' of New Netherland in 1649 who petitioned the States General asking that the Company be ousted and that their town be given a suitable municipal government. They called attention to New England where 'neither patroons, nor lords, nor princes are known, but only the people.'[52] Another example is found in Germantown, which sought (1691 and later) to be independent of the court of Philadelphia County.[53]

50. *N. C. Records,* vol. IV, p. 457f. ; Waddell, A. M., *History of New Hanover County,* p. 191.
51. Letter from Corporation of Albany to the Governor and Council, Feb. 21, 1761, in Pearson, J., *et al., History of the Schenectady Patent,* Albany, 1883, pp. 427ff.
52. Quoted in Fiske, J., *Dutch and Quaker Colonies in America,* Boston, 1899 edit., 2 vol., vol. I, p. 218. Cf. below, pp. 223ff., for a fuller account of this and subsequent events leading up to the incorporation of New Amsterdam.
53. MS. Germantown Rathbuch, 1691-1706, in Library of Histor. Soc. of Pennsylvania. Cf. also Bolles, A. S., *Pennsylvania, Province and State,* Philadelphia, 1899, 2 vol., vol. II, p. 267f.

The convenience and privilege of separate and local courts counted heavily in favour of incorporation in the Colonies as well as in England, though evidence would mark it as a more influential factor in the case of the latter.

Separate representation in the assembly must have moved many North Carolina communities to seek incorporation ; for few privileges other than this were included in their acts of chartering. It was apparently deemed sound policy thereby to assure that commercial as well as agrarian interests were adequately represented in the assembly's deliberations.

For considerations such as an interest in law and order or in better government generally, or in the provision of municipal services, one must wait until the eighteenth century. Tangible evidence of such motivation in charter-seeking then multiplies,[54] for by this time one notes municipalities growing, not so much from paternalistic fostering as by natural evolution and the consequent increase of 'urban' needs. Thus Bristol (1718) inhabitants 'peticion' for a charter 'for Regulating their Streets and Preserving the better Order among the Inhabitants' ;[55] Wilmington (Del.), 1736, 'that they may be enabled to form and enact such ordinances for the regulation of the markets and streets and the cleansing and mending the streets and highways' ;[56] Elizabeth (which had found difficulties in conducting its town meetings), 1740, 'for the promotion of good order and the establishment of a

54. Note, however, instances such as the petition of the inhabitants of Jamestown for the right to make by-laws on account of the poor health conditions (cited in Tyler, L. G., *Cradle of the Republic*, p. 74).
55. *Minutes of Provincial Council*, vol. III, p. 49 (*Penn. Colon. Records*).
56. Quoted in Scharf, J. T., *History of Delaware*, vol. II, p. 636.

firm certain and peaceable government' ;[57] Burlington
(1733), for 'good and wholesome lawgiving amongst the
inhabitants themselves' ;[58] Schenectady (1765), 'to prevent disorders and excesses because of the influx of so
many strangers to this rapidly growing trading center.'[59]
All these statements strike on the whole a new, and one
might say an essentially modern note, indicating the
beginning of a subtle transition in men's minds from the
concept of a municipal *corporation* to that of a municipal
government. How far this change of attitude was also
taking place in the towns already incorporated will be
considered later.[60]

Such, then, were the motives of the inhabitants. Some
were laudable, some more questionable — but all of them
were understandable in the light of what incorporations
involved in England in the period in question. Desire for
a greater dignity and prestige obviously was also a factor,
and in this attitude also there was a somewhat blurred
copying of the institutions of the mother country.

In conclusion, it is illuminating to cite the examples
of Westchester and Gorgeana, incorporations in which
motives were both numerous and mixed. The examples
chosen are of microscopic towns, so that the theory of incorporation as distinct from its practice may be all the
clearer.

The motivation in the chartering of Westchester
(1696) included confirmation of land titles, the rights
of town government, the power to hold property in common, freedom from county jurisdiction in civil cases up

57. Scott, A., *Early Cities of New Jersey*, in *N. J. Hist. Soc. Coll.*, 2nd ser.,
    vol. IX, 153f. Cf. also Hatfield, E. F., *History of Elizabeth*.
58. Scott, op. cit.
59. Pearson, J., *et al.*, *History of the Schenectady Patent*, pp. 426ff.
60. Cf. pp. 266-76.

to £20, 'freedom' and guild organization (i.e., craft
monopolies), power to make by-laws, ferry rights,
markets, fairs, separate representation in the assembly.[61]
The borough had about twenty houses.[62]

Gorgeana, when incorporated in 1641, had a population of about 300, and enjoyed the following : aldermen
to be justices of the peace, court as the court of chancery,
attendant dignities, including 'serjants of ye White Rod,'
wharves, market, customs, by-laws, and all privileges the
great 'city of Bristol holdeth by their Charter of Incorporation.'[63]

(D)

One important question remains. Why was the desire for
borough incorporation so conspicuously lacking in the
inhabitants of the New England colonies ; and why, for
example, were towns as important as Charleston (S. C.)
and Savannah never incorporated ? The answer is reasonably obvious and completely understandable.

New England towns for all practical purposes were
already incorporations — of another sort, it is true, but
(from the circumstances of their origin) with equal or
greater privileges arising out of the original broad grants
of power under such Acts as those of 1636 and 1647.[64]
These made it possible for the towns to exercise in practice many of the privileges which were motivating factors
in so many incorporations in the other colonies. As to

61. As cited in the charter. Cf. Appendix B.
62. Letters of Bellomont to the Lords of Trade, Nov. 12, 1698 and Oct.
  17, 1700, reprinted in *N. Y. Colonial Records,* vol. IV, pp. 427, 719.
63. As cited in the charter. Cf. Appendix B.
64. *Laws and Liberties of Massachusetts,* 1648, Reprint, Cambridge, 1929,
  sec. on 'Townships.' Cf. the wording (1647), 'power to make such
  Laws and Constitutions as may concern the welfare of their Town.
  Provided they be not of a criminal but only of a prudential nature
  . . . and not repugnant to the publick Laws.'

local self-government, these people had it in full measure, and as yet they saw little or no reason for giving up their quite efficient type of town meeting for what might or might not be a more efficient borough government — even though the latter might appear to carry greater prestige. Besides, the notion that a municipal corporation was primarily 'government' was itself relatively new, and the current British notion that a corporation implied 'monopoly' or 'privilege' was still widely prevalent down to the Revolution.[65]

A paraphrase of the objections instanced in a Boston pamphlet in 1714 protesting against a mooted incorporation will serve to illustrate :

1. Fear of a monopoly in markets.
2. Duties collected in borough markets.
3. Cost of the prison, etc., macekeepers, sword bearers, clerks, recorder, chamberlain.
4. Fear of the close corporation, and objection to giving up the town meeting.
5. 'Paying for our Freedom, that was Free-born and in bondage to no Man.'
6. General suspicion that it would entrench the wealthy in power (n.b., the implication as to the class of those who were aldermen, etc., in towns such as New York and Philadelphia).
7. 'Don't change what is working well.'
8. Boston, being a county town, already had resident magistrates.
9. British towns sought incorporation, because otherwise (being under the county justices) they had

---

65. Yet very definite steps were taken in 1771 looking toward the incorporation of New Haven. Cf. Dexter, F. B., *New Haven in 1784* (*Papers of the New Haven Colony Hist. Soc.*, New Haven, 1865 — , vol. IV, p. 131).

no powers. Boston might do anything not repugnant to the laws of the Province.

10. A 'possibility of being reduced to manage but one
Trade' (i.e., shopkeepers and artisans who were
undertaking several trades would have to give up
the practice).[66]

Some at least of the vigorous local objections to the attempted incorporation of Charleston (S. C.) in 1722
were apparently traceable to a similar thought — that
those who would then be in power would be a small and
wealthy clique.[67] But the principal reason for inertia
in the matter of incorporation in Charleston (and perhaps in Savannah) was quite otherwise. Each of these
towns was the seat of its colonial assembly. Inasmuch as
the business of the colony as a whole was not too exacting,
the assemblies gave much attention to their capital's welfare ; and law after law was forthcoming in great detail as
the need arose. Furthermore, in Charleston, the agency
selected for municipal 'government' was not a formally
chartered corporation. Such government was entrusted
to a vestry (or vestries) — in accordance also with sound
English precedent — or to separate commissions.[68] As in
many English cities (and incidentally as in Philadelphia)
these commissions finally came to be the heart of the
municipal administration. They — not a corporation —
furnish the real parallel to our modern city government.

In some incorporations which failed to survive, the
opposition of independent planters or even of 'smugglers' was often sufficient to obtain a repeal of the monop-

66. Mathews, N., Jr., *Attempts to Incorporate Boston*, in *Col. Soc. Mass.
    Publ.*, vol. X, pp. 345-56.
67. McCrady, E., *History of South Carolina, 1719-1776*, New York, 1899,
    pp. 40ff.
68. Cf. pp. 246-50.

olistic concessions involved. For example, the opposition of certain of the planter group was expressed before the Board of Trade in 1707 in connection with acts settling ports. The arguments were advanced that such ports would draw off people from raising tobacco.[69] A few charters, such as that of Trenton, lapsed from sheer unsuitability to the needs of the community.

(E)

Municipal incorporations, whether fostered or sought for, represented deliberate acts on the part of a group or an individual. These acts were motivated variously, though economic considerations were most frequent. The ideas included in the concept 'borough' or 'city' in those days were other than the implications of such terms to-day. Technology and the development of ideas and the growth of democracy have brought other meanings and other forms, though the terminology of the old days is still largely retained. Primarily judicial, monopolistic, corporative — not administrative or governmental — were these communities at their inception. Not until well towards the Revolution does one see the dawn of a new motivation which to-day would be called truly *urban*.

69. Great Britain : *Journal of the Comnrs. for Trade and Plantations,* vol. I, Jan. 9, 1706/7. It was also pointed out that it would be unfair to allow such special privileges to the early settlers.

IV

THE INCORPORATIONS AND
THEIR CRITERIA

It would be desirable to limit the scope of the present study on the basis of some definite criterion as to what constitutes a city or borough. Particularly in a discussion of legal and structural aspects, it would be a distinct advantage to be able to say : 'This is an incorporated borough' or 'This is not.' Other studies of the colonial incorporations have attempted something of this sort.

Unfortunately, the closer and more detailed and thorough the examination, the less possible does it seem to be to draw any such hard and fast line. This is not surprising to any one familiar with the parallel or parent situation in England. There, as the Webbs have so well pointed out, the infinite variety of origins, the modifications that subsequently took place in usage, left a situation by the seventeenth century of almost microscopic gradations and variations in the charters — and even more in their actual operation.[1] Even when these ubiquitous authors had finally settled upon the ability of a given incorporation to create its own justices as the ultimate criterion of what constituted a borough, they still found it necessary to include a description of exceptions and modifications of this particular power. Then, too, one must not overlook the hundreds of English 'manorial boroughs' which, while not arbitrarily meeting the specific test proposed, none the less possessed one or more of the various attributes frequently associated with such incorporation.

It is, of course, possible to say of most of the colonial incorporated boroughs that they belong properly in our

1. Webb, B. and S., *The Manor and the Borough, passim,* esp. Chap. VI and pp. 381-3.

present discussion. It is equally possible to say of the majority of the towns that they do not so belong — except that, in the consideration of the functional development of urban areas, places such as Boston, Baltimore, or New Haven must inevitably be included. Between these two groups, however, lie many communities of which one is much less certain. Therefore, a consideration of two aspects of the problem is appropriate : first, possible criteria and, second, a place by place description of the situation as it existed, without necessarily attempting any *ex cathedra* ruling of whether or not a particular locality is or is not within the pale. In view of the multiplicity of details involved, such a description will be considered in an appendix.[2]

One must recognize at the outset that many towns, notably in New England, found themselves possessed of considerably greater powers and privileges than many of the boroughs ; yet they have been treated so ably and extensively by other authors that they need be mentioned here but incidentally.[3] The story of their evolution into more formal municipal institutions belongs not to the colonial period, but to the years 1785-1825.

It has always been part of the genius of Englishmen not to be too much preoccupied with logical distinctions or hard and fast categories in government ; but rather to allow institutions to develop as the needs arise — quite

2. Cf. Appendix A.
3. Cf. Sly, J. F., *Town Government in Massachusetts,* Cambridge, 1930 ; Channing, E., *Town and County Government in the English Colonies,* Baltimore, 1884 ; Adams, J. T., *History of New England,* Boston, 1927, 3 vol., vol. I ; Davis, A. M., *Corporations in the Days of the Colony* (*Colon. Soc. of Mass. Trans.,* vol. I, in *Colon. Soc. of Mass. Public.,* Boston, 1892 —) ; Hart, A. B. (Edit.), *Commonwealth History of Massachusetts,* New York, 1927-30, 5 vol., vol. II, chap. by Sly, J. F., on 'Geographical Expansion and the Town System' ; Howard, G. E., *Local Constitutional History of the United States,* Baltimore, 1889.

illogically, perhaps, but with that flexibility and adaptation to the conditions of the day wherein has lain much of their strength. Their institutions, like their poetry, have been intuitive rather than rational ; but because intuition, so called, is grounded in a rich experience, it has met with outstanding success in both these fields.

So these Englishmen in the Colonies likewise attempted to formulate no carefully defined categories, but developed their municipal institutions as the occasion offered — sometimes gradually, sometimes with a flight of the imagination which pictured things as they hoped they would be ; but always in the spirit of borough life and development as they had known it in their mother country. Hence, the variety of type and jurisdiction was very nearly as great in the colonies as in England, and deserves consideration in a similar vein.

(B)

Not that there did not appear certain imperfect criteria of municipal incorporation. For the most part these will be reserved for separate treatment, but it is useful to summarize possible bases at this point.

Population was not a criterion. In certain instances, as in Raleigh, Georgia, and perhaps the early Virginia incorporations, the charters were forthcoming before there were any white inhabitants at all. When incorporation was at its height between 1700 and 1750, places such as New Brunswick, Bristol, and the two Wilmingtons were granted full charters, though under 1,000 inhabitants ; while genuine urban centres such as Boston, Charleston, and New Haven — with ten or twenty times the number of inhabitants — remained under less developed forms of government. It was one of the complaints about Westchester that it had but twenty houses at the time of its incorporation.[4]

Nor did concentration of such population as there was within a given area furnish any test. In Westchester we read that 'every one has a plot of at least ten acres, which distances his neighbor from him.'[5] The city of Albany was one mile wide and thirteen and one half miles deep.[6] New Jersey boroughs had areas that were large enough for small counties.[7] Gorgeana, with a population of 300, covered twenty-one square miles.[8]

For the most part, one can expect a formal document, a charter, as a criterion of incorporation. Yet some corporations, for example, Burlington, were established by the assembly, and appeared by acts of the latter rather than by charters.[9] In the instances of James City, Perth Amboy, and perhaps Albany, the equivalent of borough incorporation — at least in modified form — seems to have been the result of a kind of accretion.[10] A certain few incorporations, apparently holding over from Dutch days, represented another more or less distinct type — minus any ordinarily recognized royal charter. Here and there are also found charters whose validity was at times successfully challenged. Should Newcastle in 1724, for example, be included in any rigidly narrow list which uses the existence of a charter as its criterion?[11]

4. O'Callaghan, E. B. (Edit.), *Documents Relative to the Colonial History of New York*, vol. IV, p. 427.
5. Dawson, H. B., *Westchester County during the Revolution*, Morrisania, New York, 1866, p. 1 (quoting a letter of Nov. 5, 1729).
6. Charter. Cf. Appendix B.
7. Scott, Austin, *Early Cities of New Jersey*, map (*N. J. Hist. Soc. Coll.*, 2nd ser., vol. IX).
8. Williamson, W. D., *History of Maine*, Hallowell, Glazier, Masters and Co., 1832, 2 vol., vol. I, p. 288.
9. Cf. p. 43.
10. Cf. pp. 88-91, 431f., 426f.
11. Cf. p. 435.

Full discussion of municipal powers and privileges must be reserved till later.[12] However, it is useful in our consideration of criteria to call attention to certain key powers customarily associated with borough incorporation.

One of the most valued privileges associated with such incorporation was the possession of local borough courts. These often were independent of county jurisdiction ; and varied in their powers from the pettiest of offences and civil suits to the full jurisdiction of justices in quarter session. Yet there does not appear to be any evidence that such powers were possessed by Chester or Lancaster or by the North Carolina boroughs, except Wilmington under the 1763 charter. The royal charter of Hillsborough, for example, granted as late as 1770, made no mention of courts.[13] On the other hand, certain New Jersey 'towns,' notably Bergen and Woodbridge, possessed courts of very considerable power. Bergen's court may have been a hold-over from Dutch days, but we read : 'a Town court by selectmen or overseers who used to be four or more as they please to choose annually to try small causes, as in all the rest of the towns.'[14] In Woodbridge, under the charter of 1669, the local justices were given the full power of county justices of the peace — or virtually as great an endowment as the most advanced borough of British or colonial incorporation.[15]

12. Cf. Chaps. V, VI, XI.
13. *State Records of N. C.*, vol. VIII, p. 216f.
14. Quoted in Van Winkle, D., *History of the Municipalities of Hudson County*, New York, 1924, 3 vol., vol. I, p. 46.
15. 'Whereas the freeholders of the corporation of Woodbridge have according to their charter made choice of Samuel Dennis [et al.] . . . as fit and capable to serve and bear the offices of justice of the peace, for the said corporation, and have presented the same to the Deputy Governor . . . *Now know ye*, that we have approved of their said choice, and . . . name . . . them . . . justices of the peace of the said

Westchester had a minor town court prior to its borough charter.[16]

It will also be remembered that in the English boroughs these local 'courts' operating in an administrative capacity often had the authority to enact numerous by-laws and to impose local rates. The possibly more logical but somewhat corrosive doctrine of separation of powers had not yet reached the municipalities ; and judicial, executive, and legislative functions alike were performed by the local courts and county or borough justices. The variation in these powers was so great and their possession by towns as well as boroughs so frequent that this — the nearest to actual *municipal* functioning of the day that we have — is for all practical purposes of doubtful value as a juristic criterion, however interesting it may be historically and sociologically.[17]

The power of separate representation in the colonial legislative bodies is a useful criterion. There is considerable evidence that in North Carolina, perhaps in early New Jersey, and certainly in early Virginia the terms 'borough' or 'city' were used primarily when referring to this particular aspect ;[18] and in North Carolina[19] and New Jersey,[20] the term 'town' ordinarily applied to the same community in its other aspects. A similar use of

corporation, to do . . . such . . . acts, and to hold courts and keep the King's peace . . . within the limits . . . according to the powers . . . in their said charter.' (Governor's Commission, 1683, in Leaming, A., and Spicer, J., *Grants, Concessions, etc., of New Jersey*, Philadelphia, 1752 [Reprint, Somerville, 1881], p. 255.)

16. Minutes, Town Board, July 12, 1681.
17. Cf. p. 22ff.
18. Cf. p. 94.
19. *State Records of N. C.*, vol. VI, p. 400, etc.
20. *Pennsylvania Journal*, Oct. 3, 1745 ; *New Jersey Archives*, 1st ser., vol. II, p. 405f., vol. XI, pp. 529ff. ; cf, also p. 181.

terms was characteristic of Westchester.[21] However, even such use was not consistently followed, and the composite 'borough town' is equally frequent. Of course, this particular power was by no means universal in England. It also breaks down as an absolute criterion when in New England, New Jersey, and Savannah we find the towns likewise with such representation, while boroughs in Pennsylvania were not receiving it. Yet it was one of the grants frequently, perhaps normally, associated with the royal prerogative of incorporation, and consequently deserves inclusion in our discussion. It was this power for which the Board of Trade and the governor held out as the final prerogative of the Crown in the dispute regarding the power of the North Carolina assembly to incorporate boroughs, after they had yielded all the others.[22]

The various powers associated with trade monopolies fall into another more or less clear category. The privilege of markets and fairs was particularly valued ; and, in the more highly urbanized communities, the monopolies of merchant guilds and craftsmanship were prized. Here also there was clear evidence of the normal association of these privileges with the chartering prerogative of the proprietor or the Crown ; but exceptions in the form of assembly action occurred, and for the most part remained unchallenged. These were most frequent in the numerous Maryland and Virginia 'towns' created by their respective legislatures. It apparently was customary also in many colonies to endow 'shire towns' with this privilege

21. DeLancey, E. F., *Origin and History of Manors in New York and Westchester,* New York, 1886, p. 87.
22. *State Records of N. C.,* vol. V, p. 405f. ; Labaree, L. W., *Royal Instructions to British Colonial Governors,* vol. I, pp. 103f., 108ff.

of markets and fairs.[23] The boroughs almost always, perhaps always, enjoyed this particular privilege.

Government was more chary of granting the superior rights of a 'port,' and such rights were normally determined not by the possession of a charter, but by the government's desire for revenue and the practicabilities of the situation.

Finally, the terminology of the day furnishes some guidance in delimiting the present study. Yet Gloucester (N. J.) is spoken of as a 'city'[24] and the term 'town' is almost generic. The terms 'port' and 'metropolis' ordinarily have a special significance, but not always. The latter seems to have been used to indicate the seat of the assembly and provincial courts. Usually, but not always, the term 'township' indicates a jurisdiction inferior to that of a 'town' ; but Schenectady after incorporation is called a 'township.'[25] By 1774 the terms 'town-corporate' and 'borough' were used interchangeably in New Jersey laws, while 'township' was used as the next lower category and 'city' the next higher. Only cities, counties, and 'towns-corporate' or boroughs had their own justices of the peace.[26] Usage of all these terms varied from colony to colony and from period to period without any set rule.

Although nothing permanent resulted therefrom, one notes with interest that the colonies of Raleigh and Georgia were themselves constituted municipal corpora-

23. Cf. p. 87.
24. Mickle, I., Reminiscences of Old Gloucester, Philadelphia, 1845, p. 18.
25. O'Callaghan, Documents Relative to the Colonial History of New York, vol. VIII, p. 443f. The incorporation had probably lapsed apart from the separate representation in the assembly.
26. Cf. particularly Acts of New Jersey (Samuel Allinson, Comp.), Burlington, 1776, Chap. DLXXXIX, Mar. 11, 1774 ; Chap. DXC. A 'precinct' was the lowest unit.

tions.[27] This form may have been adopted in preference
to the full colonial type because the municipal or corporate form more readily permitted a delimiting of the
scope or function of the governing body, whereas it was
more difficult to limit an assembly or parliament. It will
be remembered that the 'corporation' in the England of
the day represented not a territorial expression, but a
set of rights and privileges. The incorporators of Raleigh
(1587) were those associated with Sir Walter Raleigh in
its inception and forwarding ; and one of the privileges
granted them was 'free libertie to carrie with them into
the late discouered barbarous lande . . . called . . . Virginia such and so many of her Majesties Subjects as shall
willingly accompany them . . .' The incorporators of the
'Citie of Raleigh' were termed the 'Governour and Assistants.'

Clearer in its intent, because more permanent, was the
charter of Georgia (1732). In this instance the 'common
council' represented a committee of the corporation,
named in the charter. Though remaining in England,
none the less this common council exercised its powers
by setting up in Savannah (1733) an embryo administration. It laid out the town in wards and tithings, appointed
three bailiffs and a recorder — constituting the town court
— and also a register, constables, tithing men, and conservators of the peace. In 1739 we find a 'pindar' also. In
1735, it appointed a similar set of essentially municipal
officials for Frederica in the southern part of the colony.
Further changes (1741, 1743) set up modifications in the
direction of the county type, without entirely abolishing
the earlier arrangements. These changes were all by authority of the common council in England. The corpora-

27. Of a similar genus were the four great corporations of early Vir-
    ginia. Cf. pp. 92-7. Barbadoes was similarly organized in 1663.

tion survived many difficulties, but eventually gave up its charter in 1752 and Georgia became a royal province.

(C)

Before attempting a systematic treatment of the bona-fide borough incorporations, some attention should be directed to certain classes of incipient or quasi-incorporations.

The 'towns' comprised the most numerous group, but here certain distinctions must be drawn. The New England town system, for example, seems to have projected itself into certain incorporations in Long Island and New Jersey and there to have evolved in a somewhat altered form. In part, the variants were the outgrowth of their original formation in Dutch territory.[28] In the instances of Newark and Woodbridge they apparently represented very liberal incorporations granted (in accord with Jersey precedent) by the assembly to townsfolk who had migrated there and who wished to retain the spirit of the New England forms with which they had become familiar. In the instance of Woodbridge we have noted how this resulted, judicially speaking, in the enjoyment of powers greater than in New England.[29] Similar powers were extended to Newark in 1668.[30]

Delaware towns were a curious hodge-podge, reveal-

28. Mespeth (1642), Hempstead (1644), Flushing (1645), Gravesend (1645), etc. The structure was largely English ; the terminology, Dutch. After the English took over control, New England precedents were largely followed. (Stiles, H. R. (Edit.), *Illustrated History of Kings County*, Brooklyn, 1884, vol. I, pp. 164, etc. ; cf. Wood, Silas, *Settlement of the Towns on Long Island*, First Edit., Brooklyn, 1824 [Reprint, Furman Club, 1865].)
29. Cf. p. 79.
30. Barber, J. W., and Howe, H., *Historical Collections of the State of New Jersey*, 1844, p. 177.

ing elements of two Dutch occupations, the English government from New York, inclusion in Pennsylvania, separate government of the 'three counties,' and possibly even Swedish influence. No other colony experienced such governmental vicissitudes. Elsinburgh for a while was governed by a special commission of six, appointed by Governor Andros — but with appeal to the court at Newcastle.[31] In 1758 Newark (Del.) received royal 'letters patent' granting fairs and markets privileges, as did Dover in 1763 — in the latter instance repeating or confirming an earlier grant. Representation in the assembly was by counties, not even Wilmington having the normal privilege of separate representation. The little community on the Whorekill, originally a group of Mennonites, had been granted a liberal charter from the City of Amsterdam, including locally nominated magistrates and voting locally by ballot on all laws.[32] It was seized and more or less despoiled by the English, but on reoccupation by the Dutch in 1673 was made the seat of a judicatory.[33] The court was continued by the English, the place now being called Lewes.[34] By 1742 it had been endowed by act of the assembly with a market, and apparently belonged in the category of a 'shire town.'[35]

The many town incorporations of Maryland, Virginia, North Carolina and, in isolated instances, of South Caro-

31. In New Jersey, but for a while under the Delaware jurisdiction (quoting Penn's Breviat, in Hazard, S., *Annals of Pennsylvania,* Philadelphia, 1850, p. 458).
32. O'Callaghan, E. B., *History of New Netherland,* New York, 1846-48, 2 vol., vol. II, pp. 466ff.
33. Smith, S., *History of the Colony of Nova Caesaria* (Reprint, 1877), p. 110.
34. Conrad, H. C., *History of the State of Delaware,* vol. II, p. 716.
35. Powell, W. A., *History of Delaware,* Boston, 1928, p. 108. Cf. p. 240 below for Newcastle and Wilmington.

lina were in more or less the same category. Whether by
general or blanket act or by separate treatment, for the
most part they were successful examples of their assemblies' right to incorporate such minor forms. Ordinarily
the acts creating them named commissioners who were
to lay out the towns (if this had not previously been
done) in accordance with boundaries specified in the
acts. In the enabling act — or later, if the growth of the
town warranted it — these commissioners were usually
given the power to make by-laws. The commissioners
themselves were usually under the direction of the county
justices and were often in personnel virtually a sub-committee or panel of these justices.[36] As size warranted,
further powers were extended perhaps for a port or to
hold a market ; and the power to elect the commissioners
might be vested in the freeholders or inhabitants. In
towns such as Annapolis, Norfolk, and Wilmington
(N. C.), full borough incorporation followed in due
course. In other instances, such was the nature of the
original town incorporation and of the privileges subsequently granted, that it became exceedingly difficult
in practice to distinguish towns from incorporated
boroughs.[37] For example, by 1750, Charlestown (Md.)
elected its commissioners, had power to fix wharfage rates,
to compel labour on highways, to erect public buildings,
to control its common land, to 'publish' a fair — powers
considerably greater than those of many 'boroughs.'[38] In
certain instances, for example the incorporation of Mar-
cus Hook as Chichester,[39] the town incorporation was by

36. e. g. Mereness, N. D., *Maryland as a Proprietary Province*, p. 415f.
37. Cf. pp. 52-8 for the fostering of these towns.
38. Mereness, op. cit., p. 417f. ; Andrews, M. P., *History of Maryland*, p. 270.
39. 1701, cf. Ashmead, H. G., *History of Delaware County*, Philadelphia, 1884, p. 458, for copy.

royal or proprietor's charter rather than by act of assembly.

Apparently, in Pennsylvania, New Jersey, and possibly Delaware, the 'shire town' represented a special category, midway between the 'town' and the 'borough.' It was made the seat of the county justices, was itself a quasi-corporation, and customarily was singled out for bestowal of the right to markets and fairs, one of the usual corporate prerogatives of boroughs.[40] The English parallel is obvious.

Another group of towns, often duplicating the foregoing categories, inasmuch as the designation was as much a function as a classification, were those known as 'port towns.' As discussed more fully elsewhere,[41] this category involved certain monopolies or privileges in connection with exports and imports. The designation of a certain locality as a port town usually, though not always, implied the existence or creation of a town or city corporation to act as local agent for administrative purposes. Beaufort (S. C.), 1711, Salem (N. J.), between 1682 and 169 ?, and Oxford or Williamstadt (Md.), 1694, will serve as examples of towns primarily and deliberately incorporated for this purpose.[42]

40. e. g. Reading, Pa., 1764 (Montgomery, M. L., *History of Berks County*, p. 657f.) ; Bristol, Pa., 1697 (Bache, William, *Bristol Borough*, Bristol, 1853, pp. 13ff.) ; Cohanzie, N. J., 1695 (Elmer, L. Q. C., *History of Cumberland County*, Bridgeton, 1869, p. 71), 1697 (Barber, J. W., and Howe, H., *Histor. Collec. of N. J.*, p. 143) ; Gloucester, N. J., 1773 (Heston, A. M. (Edit.), *South Jersey*, vol. I, p. 355) ; Trenton, N. J. (Walker, E. R., *et al.*, *History of Trenton*, Princeton, 1929, 2 vol., vol. I, pp. 349ff.) ; and Lewestown and Dover, Del., *supra*, p. 85. This privilege was also widely extended by the South Carolina assembly in 1722 and 1723 (Trott, N., *Laws of the Province of South Carolina*, Charles-Town, 1736, var.).
41. Cf. pp. 155ff.
42. *Andrews' Almanack*, 1765, lists three ports in South Carolina — Charleston, Beaufort, and Georgetown.

The Dutch incorporations represent a group so important and so peculiar as to deserve special treatment.[43] At this point it need only be mentioned that such incorporations account for anomalies not otherwise explicable in the status of Bergen (N. J.), Kingston (N. Y.), Newcastle (Del.), and of New York City and Albany in their early periods.

A small group of towns or 'cities' probably represent the attainment of borough privileges by a kind of 'accretion,' consisting of successive legislative acts or separate privileges extended by a succession of governors. In this classification belong Perth Amboy, Albany, and (probably) Burlington in their early stages,[44] and Jamestown or James City.

James City, never having received a formal charter as far as its residents were concerned, will serve as an example. It was originally 'chartered' in England as one of the groups of early Virginia incorporations entitled to representation in the house of burgesses.[45] In 1624 (reenacted in 1632 and several years thereafter) we find it as the sole port of entry except by the governor's permission.[46] In 1627 the 'corporation' conducted an expedition against the Indians.[47] In 1634 it gave its name to one of the 'shires,' and as far as representation was concerned it seems to have continued for many years as a county only.[48] In 1639 it was made the 'chief town' and residence

43. Chapter IX.
44. Cf. pp. 426f., 431f., for their detailed consideration.
45. Cf. pp. 91-7.
46. Hening, *Statutes of Virginia,* vol. I, pp. 126, 163, etc.
47. 'Virginia Council and General Court Minutes,' in *Va. Mag. of Hist.,* vol. XIX, p. 122.
48. Hening, op. cit., vol. I, p. 283. There is some doubt as to whether the City and the County were actually conterminous in this period.

of the governor, and may have been given authority to make by-laws.[49] An act of 1646 dealing with the licensing of liquor sale 'within the corporation of James City or the island' left the enforcement to the county courts.[50] In 1649 it was given the privilege of a weekly market, although the clerk of the market was to be appointed by the governor.[51] In 1645 it was allowed one of the representatives from James City County,[52] and in the 1660-61 session, 'being the metropolis of the county (they) shall have the privilege to elect a Burgesse for themselves.'[53] In 1676 (disallowed the next year, but possibly kept in practice none the less) the householders and freeholders were given the right to make such by-laws as did not infringe upon James City County privileges.[54] We note also a change in phraseology in 1664 and certainly in 1682 whereby the City seems to be distinguished from the County in that persons from outside its limits were exempt from arrest during quarter courts and assemblies — so that they might be free to bring petitions, prosecute, etc.[55] The 1680 General Act of incorporation included James City ; and many earlier attempts, often reflected in laws, indicated the seriousness of the efforts to make it a worthy 'metropolis.'[56] Yet in 1673 the gov-

49. Blodgett, J. H., 'Free Burghs in the United States,' in *Amer. Hist. Assoc. Ann. Rpt.* for 1895, pp. 299-317, esp. p. 307. The author has been unable to trace Blodgett's authority for this conjecture.
50. Hening, op. cit., vol. I, p. 319. (Act 19, 21st Chas. I.)
51. Ibid. p. 362.
52. Ibid. p. 299f.
53. Ibid. p. 20.
54. Hening, op. cit., vol. II, p. 362.
55. Ibid. pp. 213, 503.
56. e.g., in 1662. Hening, op. cit., vol. II, p. 172. During the reign of Charles II, a serious attempt was made to make it the seat of a bishop (*Virginia Hist. Mag.,* vol. 36, pp. 45-53). Cf. also Tyler, *Cradle of the Republic,* pp. 50, 54ff., 63, etc.

ernor and council set aside the common, and Tyler was probably right in his conjecture that there was no town government, but that it was largely run by the colonial authorities.[57] It was burned soon after by Bacon, but in 1679 the privy council ordered its rebuilding as the 'metropolis.'[58] In 1682 the inhabitants petitioned for authority to make by-laws on account of the poor health conditions that had from the beginning been associated with the place. They also asked that their bounds be fixed, as by no 'public Act or Instrument had they been ascertained ; but by report of ancient inhabitants.'[59] No records have been found as to whether such a petition was granted. In 1699, after a fire, the seat of government was moved to Williamsburg — where a new and more successful 'metropolis' was fostered. James City's privilege of independent representation lingered on till the Revolution, and it is possible that the town was also benefited by general enactments vesting towns and boroughs with powers. In 1722 it was described as 'an abundance of rubbish with three or four inhabited houses.'[60] Yet here was a 'Citty' known as such, which for years exercised many of the usual prerogatives of boroughs, even though it was apparently without any formal instrument of incorporation and without records extant to indicate by what agency or group (for example) the separate burgesses in the Virginia house were chosen in the later years. By 1750 the Ambler and Travis families seem to have owned virtually the entire island, and it is possible that they did not even go through the form of election,

57. Ibid. p. 66.
58. Cf. Labaree, L. W., *Royal Instructions to British Colonial Governors,* vol. II, p. 545.
59. Quoted in Tyler, op. cit., p. 74.
60. Ibid. p. 83.

but decided quite informally whether an Ambler or a Travis should be the burgess.[61]

(D)

For the most part the various actual or alleged borough incorporations, together with a discussion of any special problems presented by each, are best treated in an appendix.[62] An exception will be made of the early Virginia boroughs of Bermuda City, James City, Henrico, and certain other Virginia 'plantations.'[63] As the first municipal incorporations in America they deserve special treatment.

It is probable that these 'cities' can be best understood in the light of parallel incorporations in Ulster about the same period, concerning which rather more information is available. These Ulster corporations were given the opportunity of a considerably longer period of evolution. Such a period was denied the Virginia towns through the forfeiting of the charter of the Virginia Company and the supersession of the proprietary government by that of a royal province. In the king's scheme for the Ulster plantations (about 1607), there were to be numerous 'corporate towns, or Borrowes erected . . . with Markets and Fairs and other reasonable Liberties, and

---

61. Burgesses : Philip Ludwell, 1742-1749 ; Edward Travis, 1752-1759, 1761-1765 ; John Ambler, 1759-1760, 1765-1766 ; Edward Ambler, 1766-1768 ; Champion Travis, Jr., 1769-1776. (Stanard, W. J. and M. N., Compilers, *Colonial Virginia Register*, Albany, 1902.) Cf. Tyler, op. cit., pp. 86ff.

62. Cf. Appendix A.

63. Cf. Brown, A., *First Republic in America* ; Osgood, H. L., *American Colonies in the Seventeenth Century*, New York, 1904-7, 3 vol. ; Stanard, M. N., *The Story of Virginia's First Century*, Philadelphia, 1928 ; Bruce, P. A., *Institutional History of Virginia in the Seventeenth Century*, New York, 1910, 2 vol.

with Power to send Burgesses to Parliament.'[64] Artisans and tradesmen from England were to be levied to people them, and extensive land was attached to each town. The City of London appeared among the patentees. For the 1613 (Irish) Parliament, James created thirty-nine new boroughs (nineteen in Ulster). The significance for our purpose does not lie in the Irish aspect, or in its subsequent development ;[65] rather are we concerned with the fact that the municipal corporation was a recognized device to be used in settlement and in developing trade ; that, as such, it was favoured by the sovereign ; that plans (and even incorporations) might pre-date actual settlement of the locality or area ; that incorporation came from the sovereign ; that representation in Parliament accompanied it more or less normally.

So also in the Virginia incorporations, the charters were apparently made by the Virginia Court (in England) in the nature of land grants or patents to specified incorporators, many of whom may actually have remained in England. As incorporators, they sought to develop the territory for which they had been granted the

---

64. Harris, W. (Edit.), *Hibernica*, pp. 55, etc. The first volume, printed in Dublin in 1747, contains a collection of documents concerning the Ulster Plantations. It has been used extensively in the present study, and particular weight has been given to documents such as Pynnar's *Survey of Ulster 1618-19* therein contained. No account hitherto given of these early Virginia incorporations seemed to the author to have been satisfactory or to have grasped their real nature. Hence he was led to a study of the parallel developments in the 'plantations' of Ulster, with the references herein included — which he believes to be valid. The meaning of the expression 'plantation' at this period was 'colony' or 'settlement' of a group of people removed from one area and settled in another.

65. Progress was relatively slow, and many boroughs never materialized in contemplated form. (Harris, op. cit., pp. 73ff., 118, 119 ; Bagwell, R., *Ireland Under the Stuarts*, London, 1909-16, 3 vol., *passim*. esp. vol. I, p. 186.)

patent. Thus in 1613 or 1614 a group of settlers was incorporated to Bermuda City (or Towne) for three years
of service, after which period they were to be free. Theoretically they were themselves stockholders in the company, albeit indentured and under a martial law of
great severity. We read that they, being freed, 'with
humble thanks to God, fell cheerfully to their own particular labors.'[66] The land granted this group was adjacent to, but not actually in the area which had been ear-
marked for the construction of the 'City,' and was known
as Bermuda Hundred. It seems to have been the hope of
the incorporators — being themselves mostly Londoners — that these and other settlers would form the nucleus
of that artisan population which was considered a necessary part of the population of any true 'city.' Accordingly,
when this group, after freedom, declined to co-operate
with the scheme and gave their time presumably to farming, the governor wrote back to England : 'The citizens
of Bermuda hundred claim ye privilege granted them
which I can't refuse, and therefore I can't force the artificers there to follow their arts, to the great prejudice of
the Colony. None hereafter to be made free of ye Colony
till bound to follow their trades . . .'[67] He had previously replied to Rolfe (the 'recorder') and nine of these
citizens who had apparently asked (1617) for their rights,
'I will not infringe your rights being a member of that
city (i.e. corporation of Bermuda City) myself but I beg
that ye Colony servants may stay there this year.'[68] Similarly in 1619, Governor Argall, declaring the bounds of
Jamestown, said further, 'I hereby give leave and license

66. Cf. Brown, A., *First Republic in America,* vol. I, p. 240.
67. Quoted in Brown, A., *First Republic in America,* vol. I, p. 260.
68. Ibid. p. 258.

for the inhabitants of Jamestown to plant as members of the corporation and parish of the same.'[69]

As in Ulster, so in Virginia it was desired and expected that towns would grow up, and patents were issued for this purpose. In both lands, building construction had yet to take place and the towns had to be laid out *subsequent to their incorporation*. In any event, it was customary to include in the incorporation a large amount of surrounding land, part to be reserved for commons, part for the corporation, part to be parcelled out among the inhabitants. 'Borough towns' in both instances were allowed 'burgesses' in a representative assembly. In Virginia, usually the commander of the plantation was the first burgess. Actual local self-government was preceded by a stage of military rule with marshals, etc., for which the boroughs (and hundreds) served as convenient units under the direction of the original proprietors. The further stage of *corporate* local self-government by the actual inhabitants of a borough was reached in Ulster in certain instances : but apparently not in Virginia, though we read that in 1620 'The rigour of Martial Law, wherewith before they were governed, is reduced within the limits prescribed by his Majesty ; and the laudable forme of Justice and Government used in this Realme established and followed as near as may be.'[70] However, these Virginia boroughs were genuine incorporations, with charter grants or patents authorized by a competent body. They exercised one, at least, of the perquisites of incorporation, the right to elect burgesses. Furthermore, these boroughs were intended eventually to be urban centres of trade and craftsmanship, and the urban-minded Virginia court never did reconcile

69. Ibid. p. 287.
70. Force, P., *Tracts and other papers relating to . . . the Colonies*, Washington, 1836-46, 4 vol., vol. III, Orders and Constitutions.

itself to the impracticability of such ideas. Dale, the active deputy governor (1611-1616), certainly did all he could to realize these ideas in practice.

It is to English parallels that one is also driven to account for a grouping of these units or boroughs into four great municipal corporations with numerous sub-corporations. This grouping was formally decreed in 1619, but the boundaries may possibly have been surveyed earlier in a preliminary fashion.[71] Probably negotiation for this quadruple division of territory took place among the various 'incorporators' through the agency of the Virginia Court, members of which many of them were. A paper plan seems thereby to have been evolved by which eventually sub-corporations (represented by existing boroughs, hundreds, and plantations) would be set up (with corporate privileges), but under the nominal chartering by the four major municipal corporations of Henricus, Charles City (formerly Bermuda City), James City, and Kiccowtan (later Elizabeth City), then presumably in existence and legally functioning *in England.*[72]

71. Cf. Green, W., *Genesis of Certain Counties in Virginia,* p. 120 (in Slaughter, P., *Life of William Green,* Richmond, 1883) ; also 'Instructions to Governor Yeardley, 1618,' reprinted in *Va. Hist. Mag.,* vol. II, pp. 154ff.

72. To the extent that this represents conjecture on the part of the author, he would welcome information concerning sources that would shed light upon this obscure aspect. The records of the Company prior to 1619 have been lost or destroyed (cf. Osgood, H. L., *American Colonies in the Seventeenth Century,* vol. I, p. 60). Some indications point to Bermuda City being the only one formally chartered by the court of the company. For example, in the instructions to Governor Yeardley in 1618 (Reprint in *Va. Hist. Mag.,* vol. II, p. 156), the words are used : 'our intent is to establish our equal Plantations . . . be reduced into four cities or Boroughs.' This may mean also that many of the patents had hitherto been issued to individuals directly, and not through the (possibly four) intermediary corporations, and that these patents were to be brought under the latter. In the same instructions, the phrase is used, 'companies Lands belonging to those cities and Burroughs.' (Ibid. p. 158.)

For the moment the only privilege of the sub-corporation was to be that of electing a burgess. This in fact was apparently their only actual justification as yet for being classed as a 'borough' at all. Indeed, many of them bore the humbler but parallel titles of 'hundred' and 'plantation.' Such a hierarchy of corporations was recognized as legally practicable, and was paralleled in English experience.[73] The spirit of this elaborate scheme was conceived *a priori* ; the several units chosen were determined by the conditions of actual settlement. Thus we read : 'In order to establish one equal and uniform kind of government over all Virginia, such as may be to the greatest benefit and comfort of the people, each town, hundred, and plantation was to be incorporated into one body corporate (a borough), under like laws and orders with the rest ; and in order to give the planters a hand in the governing of themselves each borough had the right to elect two burgesses to the General Assembly.'[74] These plantations, etc., were grouped into the four great borough corporations mentioned, and courts were then held in each of the four. Provision was made for city common land and for benefits to the settlers.[75]

Much of the foregoing analysis of these early Virginia settlements is necessarily conjectural, both because the records were lost, and indeed because the precise form of government had not yet been finally determined — for in 1620 Sir Edwin Sandys proposed and the Virginia Court named a committee to perfect a 'particular government by way of incorporation for every city and

73. Webb, B. and S., *The Manor and the Borough*, vol. I, p. 381.
74. Brown, A., *First Republic in Virginia*, vol. I, p. 313f. ; also 'Instructions to Governor Yeardley,' op. cit.
75. Ibid. p. 324.

borough.'[76] Soon after this, King James, believing Virginia à 'Seminary of Sedition,' annulled the rights of the colony, and these incipient boroughs after a period of rule by commissioners took their place in the ordinary scheme of county government — not as boroughs, but as shires.[77]

Patronage of the minister and parishes of the 'Fower Ancyent Buroughes' had been reserved to the Company.[78]

It is worth while to quote in conclusion Hamor's description of Bermuda City, the first municipal incorporation in the Thirteen Colonies : 'Bermuda Citty, a businesse of greatest hope ever begunne in our Territories' — where each new comer might have a house of four rooms ('or more, if he have a family') rent free ; permission to plant a garden, and twelve month's provision. 'But it must bee his care to provide for himselfe and family ever after. To this end he was promised tools, poultry, and swine, and, if he deserve it, a Goate or two and perhaps a cow.'[79]

(E)

In all, the total number of municipal incorporations in the Colonies lay somewhere between twenty and forty-five according to the criteria chosen. The colonies from North Carolina through New York contained the overwhelming majority of these incorporations. Except for those of the North Carolina boroughs, most bona-fide

76. See p. 192.
77. Earle, S., et al., The Chesapeake Bay Country, Baltimore, 1923, p. 26. This period of transition needs further study.
78. 'Virginia Council and General Court Minutes,' in Va. Mag. of Hist., vol. XIX, p. 386.
79. Hamor, R., A True Discourse of the Present Estate of Virginia, p. 181.

charters were granted between 1680 and 1740. As the description unfolds of the powers and internal organization of these communities, the impression of wide variations and minute gradations will come to dominate our thinking. We shall be less concerned with a search for exactness in categories, and more concerned with a realistic picture of what was by no means the least interesting institution of colonial days.

V

THE PRIVILEGES, JURISDICTION, AND POWERS OF INCORPORATED BOROUGHS

THAT the colonial incorporations were essentially English has more than once been emphasized. While there were differences between the two countries in the relative importance of the various classes of municipal powers, there were virtually no differences in kind. That these powers were at times both wide and ample may be judged from the reference to them in the petition for the New York City (1730) charter as 'Rights, Liberties, Privileges, Franchises, free Customs, Preheminencies, Advantages, Jurisdictions, Emoluments, Immunities, Lands, Tenemants, Public Buildings and Heriditaments.'[1]

What these powers really involved has been indicated already in the discussion of the reasons for incorporations. The more significant types were also noted in the attempt to discover criteria which would allow one to determine whether or not a particular municipality might be deemed to have been incorporated. Thus the groundwork has already been laid for a fuller understanding. Inasmuch as special chapters will be devoted to powers and activities in connection with the control of trade, to the 'functions' of a municipality in a modern sense, and to the secondary or derivative function of finance, these three categories will receive only such incidental mention in the present chapter as will serve to place them in their proper perspective. This will leave for emphasis in the present chapter most of the activities of the boroughs as corporations and as 'courts.'

1. Petition of Aug. 3, 1730, in *Coll., N. Y. Hist. Soc., 1885*, p. 479.

In many respects these boroughs did not differ materially or legally from private corporations. They could sue and be sued ; they had the right of perpetual succession ; they could own property. Where the specific listing of these powers happened to be omitted from the charter, the powers were implied ; and no legal difficulties presented themselves in practice to their exercise. The right to a seal perhaps more clearly indicated the superior prestige of government, and much ingenuity was exercised to devise a suitable one by those boroughs to which this dignity was granted.[2]

It was the ownership of property which proved the most significant of corporate powers in the narrow sense of the term. We have already noted the extent to which this ownership influenced the evolution of British municipalities. While parallel developments in the Colonies were not so marked, such ownership may well have been a factor in the increasing gulf between the 'close' corporation of Philadelphia and the citizens generally.[3] One writer conjectures that it was the absence of property — or rather of property vested in the corporation — which was responsible for the ephemeral nature of Schenectady's attempt at municipal organization.[4] Certainly, corporations like New York City or Albany or even tiny Bristol seem to have flourished and revealed constant activity, in part because of the extent of the property which was theirs

2. Governor Lovelace indicated his good will to the recently acquired City of New York by presenting the city fathers with a seal, mace, and gowns (Peterson, A. E., and Edwards, G. W., *New York as an Eighteenth Century Municipality*, p. 6f.). The seal of Williamsburg was ' "City of Williamsburg" surrounding Minerva in her double capacity of war and wisdom' ('Seal of Williamsburg,' in *William and Mary Quarterly*, vol. XXV, pp. 157-160).
3. Cf. p. 215.
4. Pearson, J., *et al.*, *History of the Schenectady Patent*, p. 431.

to manage. One of the reasons alleged by Albany in 1686 for the grant of more formal incorporation was that 'the inhabitants of the said town have erected, built and appropriated at their own proper cost and charges, several public buildings . . . as also certain pieces . . . of ground . . . that is to say the town-hall or stadt house . . . the church . . . the burial place . . . the watch house.' The charter proceeded to grant the city all waste and vacant land and the right to purchase land from the Indians. In St. Mary's, 1676, we read that by authority of the proprietor the corporation received a legacy for the maintenance of a minister in St. George's and Poplar Hill hundreds — as the only corporation in the province capable of receiving and administering such a legacy.[5] In the incorporation of Westchester the 'Trustees of the Freeholders and Commonalty of the Town of Westchester' were apparently created by charter as a body separate from the mayor, aldermen, and assistants who formed the 'court.' These 'Trustees' incidentally were empowered to hold the common property 'according to the manner of East Greenwich in the county of Kent, within our realm of England.' One of the main reasons why New York City sought and paid well for its charter of 1730 was to secure title to its water front farther out and the sole power over ferries and docks.[6] Power of eminent domain in laying out streets was occasionally granted — for example, by the Delaware legislature to Wilmington in 1772.[7] This was made use of in the following year. Great care was taken

5. Sparks, F. E., *Causes of the Maryland Revolution of 1689*, p. 63.
6. Peterson, A. E., and Edwards, G. W., *New York as an Eighteenth Century Municipality*, pp. 218ff.
7. *Laws of Delaware*, 1700-1797, New Castle, 1797 (G. Read, Compil.), vol. I, p. 481 (June 13, 1772, Chap. CCVIa). Whether this was usual, I have been unable to discover.

in assessing the gains and damages therefrom, the devices used being committees of non-residents and a jury.[8]

The power to admit freemen was of vital importance. This was not merely because freemen often participated in the municipal electoral processes or voted for representatives in the assembly. Equally important was the freeman's right to trade or pursue his craft even in a number of important towns which restricted the electoral privileges.[9] Such a restriction might have assumed a sinister aspect if and when the power of admitting freemen rested in the hands of a close corporation such as Philadelphia. Even in the more democratically chosen corporations in England it will be remembered that such a power tended away from democracy, inasmuch as freemen possessing such privileges tended to be reluctant to increase the numbers of those enjoying them.[10] Only occasional evidence of any such tendencies appeared in the Colonies prior to the virtual collapse of such restrictions through their unenforceability.[11]

(B)

It was in the corporation's powers as a court that the greatest variation occurred. The value placed on such powers has been indicated more than once. In a few towns the duties as 'magistrates' completely overshadowed those per-

---

8. The Minutes of the Burgesses and Assistants (MS. in Hall of Records, Dover) are filled with references to these transactions, chiefly between Feb. 13, 1773 and Feb. 27, 1773. At least ten such meetings were held, including the meetings of the jury.

9. Cf. pp. 192ff., 204f.

10. Cf. p. 23.

11. Cf. p. 138f. Incorporated towns also frequently exercised this same right — Bergen and Woodbridge, for example, controlling the admission of inhabitants ; and such a practice prevailed in New England. In the latter, it was the fear of increasing the pauper class as much as the desire to safeguard local trade that was the motivating force. (Cf. Sly, J. F., *Town Government in Massachusetts.*)

formed in the capacity of a 'common council.'[12] This is
the more understandable when one considers that the
administrative powers themselves were largely derivatives of the judicial, and at first were scarcely appreciated
as different in kind. In cities such as New York, Annapolis, or Norfolk, the mayor's courts were not unworthy imi-
tators of the powerful mayor's courts of London and
other English boroughs.[13] Moreover, it was a convenience
as well as a dignity and privilege for a town to obtain
exemption from the jurisdiction of the county courts —
even though the cases involved were but minor.[14] Naturally once an endowment of this kind had been obtained
by a corporation, its enlargement was eagerly sought.[15]

12. Notoriously true in the latter years of Philadelphia, where 'municipal activities had come to be the province primarily of boards and
commissions. A large part of the activity of the common council
by 1770 consisted in acting upon petitions for remission of fines imposed in city court. (*Minutes of Philadelphia City Council*, partic.
1760-1775.) An examination of the Annapolis records indicates a
parallel development. Probably such magisterial duty made up almost all of the corporation activity in Perth Amboy, Burlington,
Chester.

13. Cf. Morris, R. B. (Edit.), *Select Cases of the New York City Mayor's
Court*, Washington, 1935, Introduction, pp. 1-62, for an excellent
treatise on this court as a type.

14. In 1704 'sundry poor inhabitants' of Philadelphia presented a petition to the governor alleging that the fees in connection with the
new mayor's court were so excessive that many could not pay these
fees and their creditors both, and had been put in gaol for their
debts. (Petition, MS. in Library of Historical Society of Pennsylvania.)

15. In the Minutes of the Lancaster borough council for Feb. 18, 1772,
the corporation wished to draft a bill to this effect : 'And as the
Inhabitants of this Borough seem desirous that the Magistrates
elected by themselves should have the same Powers and Authorities
with the Justices of the Peace of the County in determining of controversies and other matters within the said Burough which merely
affect its Inhabitants . . . Power [should be given] to the Burgesses
. . . to act in Matters relative to the Borough and its Inhabitants as
fully and effectually as Justices of the Peace for the county . . .'
(MSS. in city clerk's office, Lancaster.)

The only borough incorporations which seemingly did not carry with them at least some separate jurisdiction, however minor, in civil and criminal cases were those of North Carolina prior to 1763[16] and Lancaster, Chester, and possibly Bristol[17] in Pennsylvania. It is possible that even in these boroughs more complete information would indicate the existence of such separate judicial powers. In these small Pennsylvania boroughs the charter did at least grant the burgesses the powers of justices of the peace within the borough limits, which meant that for certain matters they could hold their own court. Thus, apart from the North Carolina incorporations, which were little more than towns with commissioners enfranchised for purposes of representation, all boroughs and cities and many towns thus enjoyed to some extent their own tribunals.[18] In some the powers were extremely limited ; in others the powers were merely such as appertained to any justice acting singly. Newcastle, where bailiff and assistants (1672) were allowed to try cases without appeal up to ten pounds for debt or damage,[19] is an example of an intermediate type.

For the most part, however, the grants of jurisdiction

16. With reference to Wilmington (N. C.) : 'on the 5th of March (1763), a charter was granted to the town of Wilmington, its precincts and liberties, constituting a borough, with a mayor and aldermen's court, having a limited jurisdiction of suits between the inhabitants and transient persons, not residing in the province, with other privileges.' (Martin, F. X., *History of North Carolina*, vol. II, p. 174.)

17. Even the Salem (N. J.) Minutes of 1697 show its burgess exercising judicial powers (MS., Rutgers Univ. Library).

18. As previously noted, the incipient boroughs of early Virginia and of Savannah and Frederica had courts appointed by the parent corporation. [Gamble, T., Jr., *History of Savannah*, p. 28 (*City of Savannah Annual Report for 1900*) ; Jones, C. C., Jr., *Dead Towns of Georgia*, pp. 96, 124 ; Brown, A., *First Republic in America*, vol. I, p. 324.]

19. Scharf, J. T., *History of Delaware*, vol. II, p. 862.

were ample and generous. In New Jersey, all royal charters gave the mayor, recorder, and aldermen the full jurisdiction of county justices, including the coveted quarter sessions, and (except for Burlington) that of the court of common pleas. In the East Jersey 'Fundamental Constitution,' it was specifically provided that boroughs should have the power to choose their own magistrates.[20] Apparently such a privilege was also extended to certain of the towns, for Woodbridge, and evidently Newark also, enjoyed it.[21] In West Jersey a more limited jurisdiction was conferred upon the burgess of Salem when that town was incorporated in 1695. He might hear causes only up to forty pounds, but was empowered to grant and revoke tavern licences and punish offenders.[22]

Once a court was granted, extension and amplification of its powers might be sought if the original jurisdiction had been limited. There is evidence of this in Williamsburg and Norfolk. Curiously — although the possession of a court was one of the basic charter powers — extension in these cities came through an act of the house of burgesses rather than through the Crown. Inasmuch as all such acts were theoretically reviewable by the Privy Council or one of its committees, it might be argued that the royal prerogative was safeguarded, even though the house of burgesses took the initiative. In 1728 the powers of the Williamsburg hustings court were enlarged to include regulation of ordinaries (taverns) as in counties.[23] In 1736, a further extension of powers gave the court ju-

20. Clause IX.
21. Leaming, A., and Spicer, J., *Grants, Concessions, etc., of New Jersey* (Reprint 1881), p. 255 ; Barber, J. W., and Howe, H., *Hist. Coll. of State of New Jersey*, p. 177 ; Van Winkle, D., *History of the Municipalities of Hudson County*, vol. I, p. 46.
22. Barber and Howe, op. cit., p. 435.
23. Hening's *Virginia Statutes*, vol. IV, pp. 138ff.

risdiction over all cases triable in a county court.[24] This particular provision was a great convenience, inasmuch as hitherto it had been necessary to prove, for example, that an actual transaction resulting in a debt had taken place within the city limits. Eventually, so effective and speedy was the court that it came to be favoured for such actions over and above the ordinary county courts.[25] In 1742 the court was given exclusive jurisdiction over licences to ordinaries.[26] In 1774 the corporation was empowered to build a prison.[27] In 1752 these privileges were extended to Norfolk, copying the Williamsburg Act word for word.[28] Further enlargement took place in 1765, in part because the county court was being clogged.[29] However, the very efficiency of the Williamsburg court was in a measure responsible for its undoing in 1770, when the Virginia legislature by a close vote repealed the portion of the 1736 Act permitting the trial of cases originating outside the city borders. Probably resentment on the part of debtors at the unusually speedy action of the court was responsible. Elsewhere in Virginia such cases would be tied up for many years.[30]

Naturally such variations in jurisdiction brought variation and at times confusion in the judicial and administrative relations between the boroughs and their counties.

24. Ibid. p. 542.
25. Letter of John Tazewell to John Norton, Esq., London, July 12, 1770 (Copy from Department of Research and Record, Colonial Williamsburg, Inc.).
26. Hening, op. cit., vol. V, p. 207.
27. Ibid. p. 263.
28. Ibid. vol. VI, pp. 261ff.
29. Ibid. vol. VIII, p. 153f.
30. Letters of John Tazewell to John Norton, July 12, 1770 ; May 20, 1771 ; June 4, 1771 ; Aug. 27, 1772 (Copies from Department of Research and Record, Colonial Williamsburg, Inc.).

It must be remembered that, except for New England, the county was a major governmental unit — perhaps the most characteristic and all-pervading unit of local government. Characteristically, its chief officers were its commissioners or justices of the peace. These were ordinarily appointed by the governor and were always commissioned by him.[31] This custom of personal selection gave way about 1700 in New York and Pennsylvania to election by the people. In Virginia, on the other hand, the county courts became 'close' bodies, and were recruited by cooption. While these county justices sitting together constituted the chief court, the quarter sessions, individually or in pairs or in small panels, they tried the less important cases in petty sessions. Nor were their duties by any means limited to judicial matters. Gradually in England, and hence by custom in the Colonies, the county justices acquired a large number of administrative duties as well. Chiefly these duties were concerned with roads, licensing, land titles, supervision of poor relief, collection of taxes, enforcement of law and order. In this connection also, the justices served collectively for the county, and individually or in pairs for minor divisions.[32] This somewhat intricate jurisdiction was bound to raise questions when other agencies, such as city incorporations, were 'carved out' of their territory and endowed with similar powers.

Pennsylvania — the only colony apparently making a reasonably clear distinction between 'borough' and 'city' — placed its boroughs under their county courts of 'quar-

---

31. For instructions to governors concerning the issuance of such commissions, cf. Labaree, L. W., *Royal Instructions to British Colonial Governors*, vol. I, pp. 366ff.
32. Cf. Dodd, W. E., *The Old South : Struggles for Democracy*, New York, 1937, pp. 97ff. ; Ferguson, Isabel, 'County Court in Virginia, 1700-1830,' in *North Carolina Hist. Rev.*, Jan. 1931, pp. 14-40.

ter sessions, Oyer and Terminer, and Gaol Delivery' ;
while in the city of Philadelphia the city magistrates
themselves constituted these courts for their area. Even in
Pennsylvania the boroughs reveal variations in their relations to the county courts. In Chester, the chief burgess
was *ex officio* a justice of these higher courts, but not so
in Bristol and Lancaster.[33] However, in all three boroughs
the burgesses had the power of justices of the peace 'to
arrest, imprison, and punish rioters and breakers of the
peace, and to bind them . . . and return or bring the
recognizencies by them to be taken to the Court of Quarter Sessions.'[34] They were distinguishable from the other
county justices only by the area electing them. In Germantown, 'the Bailiffe and two oldest Burgesses . . .
shall be Justices of the Peace . . . and that they . . .
shall . . . hold . . . before the Bailiffe and three of the
oldest Burgesses . . . and the Recorder . . . One Court
of Record to be held every Six Weeks in the Yeare . . .
for . . . all civill causes.'[35] We read also : 'Having a
court of their own, the citizens thought that they ought
to be independent of the court of Philadelphia County.
They lived to themselves, settled their own quarrels, their
court ordered the overseers of ways to make roads, and
the county was not regarded as essential to their happiness or welfare.' Yet such an assumption of independence
did not go unchallenged ; for in 1706/7 the Queen's Attorney appeared to lay before the Court the fact (among
others) that it did 'Bind over to the peace and not to
Philadelphia Courts.'[36] In this and other respects he chal-

33. Green, D., *History of Bristol*, Camden, 1911, p. 60, claims that origi-
    nally the burgesses of Bristol had this power, but lost it by act of
    the assembly.
34. Cf. the various charters.
35. Charter of Germantown. Cf. Appendix B.
36. Bolles, A. S., *Pennsylvania, Province and State*, vol. II, p. 267f.

lenged their authority, with the following result as recorded in the minutes of the court : 'The said Attorney General promising them to procure the Government's power to qualify them himself, the which nevertheless he did not, though often required and well paid, and therefore from thence no more Courts were kept at Germantown ; and the above charged points being partly false and the others sufficiently answered, convinced the said Attorney General as by his own handwriting, hereunto affixed may appear.'[37]

Interlocking personnel among the magistracy of all units of government was customary. An extreme example was furnished in the court of assize held at New York City under Governor Andros. There were present, in addition to the governor and his council, the mayor and aldermen of New York, two commissioners of Albany, one justice of Esopus, two of New Jersey, two of Pemaquid, eight from the various 'ridings,' the high sheriff of Yorkshire, and the chief justice of Nantucket.[38]

It was similarly customary, chiefly among the smaller boroughs, to provide for a certain amount of duplication of personnel between county and borough magistrates. This undoubtedly eased many complicated questions which might otherwise have resulted.[39] In Burlington, the county officers exercised specially assigned city functions, and (as was the chief burgess of Chester) the mayor, recorder, and aldermen of the city were made 'Justices of the County Commission of Oyer and Terminer

37. Germantown *Rathbuch*, final entry (translation and MS. in Library of Pennsylvania Historical Society).
38. Wood, Silas, *Settlement of the Towns On Long Island*, p. 149.
39. e. g. in Norfolk. An examination of the minute books of the Norfolk County Court, 1744-1746, shows almost half of the county justices in attendance also as aldermen of the borough of Norfolk. (MSS., Norfolk County Court House, Portsmouth, Virginia.)

and Gaol Delivery.'[40] Inasmuch as these 'magistrates' were usually drawn from the upper classes in city and county, they were quite accustomed to associate and co-operate with each other.[41] In Albany the position of city and county was reversed and the city court served for the county as well.[42] An attempt by these Albany magistrates to claim the even wider prerogatives of sitting on the supreme court and the court of oyer and terminer met with a sharp rebuff. These courts replied to the Albany request as follows : 'We cannot conceive that your City Charter can be so construed as to render this honorable Court a Mob, instead of a Bench of Judges with full consideration of their dignity and responsibility.' An appeal by Albany to the colonial authorities brought no satisfaction.[43]

Yet, following a verdict not to his liking, Governor Evans challenged the apparently clear provisions of the Philadelphia charter, arguing the 'concurrent' jurisdiction of the county justices. However, this challenge was probably part of a larger dispute involving the city's attitude toward the proprietor, as well as but one aspect of a personal grudge on the part of the governor himself for having been caught in a disreputable resort, the verdict against which he had set aside.[44]

Occasionally there also arose questions involving the separation of the borough and county militia, the validity

40. By charter.
41. For Williamsburg, cf. Gulick, L., and Pollard, J. G., *Modern Government in a Colonial Town*, p. 34.
42. Cf. Pearson, J., *et al.*, *History of the Schenectady Patent*, pp. 427ff.
43. Howell, G. R., and Tenney, J. (Edit.), *History of the County of Albany*, New York, 1886, p. 467.
44. Cf. p. 370 ; also *Colonial Records of Pennsylvania*, Harrisburg, 1851-53 (S. Hazard, Edit.), 16 vol., vol. II, p. 165 (Minutes of the Provincial Council) ; Shepherd, W. R., *Proprietary Government in Pennsylvania*, p. 299.

of county by-laws within city borders, and exemption from militia duty.[45]

After the incorporation of Annapolis (1708) the county officers still continued their jurisdiction over the port, and county courts might still sit within the city. Cases involving persons not actually inhabitants of the city also remained outside the scope of the mayor's court. However, the charter grant to the city of independent jurisdiction was none the less quite broad. After declaring that the mayor, recorder, and aldermen were to be justices of the peace, with power to make constables, the charter goes on to say : 'Noe other justices of the peace or quorum within our said county or province, doe at any time hereafter, take upon them . . . to execute the office of a justice of the peace within the said Citty . . . ; notwithstanding any commission at large, authorising them thereunto, saving the authority and jurisdiction of her majesties' justices of oyer and terminer and gaole deliver, now or hereafter to be assigned during the time of their holdeing their several respective Courts in the said Citty.'

The high-water mark of freedom from county jurisdiction was found in those municipal corporations which by charter were vested with the privileges of being 'counties of themselves.' They and they alone could appoint their own sheriffs. New York City and Albany had such a right from Dutch days, perhaps because it was almost inevitable to recognize the 'schout' as the counterpart of the sheriff.[46] The Annapolis charter granted a similar right at the expiration of six years from the date of chartering. In Perth Amboy and New Brunswick the sheriff was to

45. e.g., Norfolk, 1738, *Hening's Statutes*, vol. V, p. 81 ; Albany, Howell and Tenney, op. cit., p. 461f.
46. Quoting petition of Nov. 9, 1683, in *N. Y. Hist. Soc. Coll.*, 1888, p. 43f. ; for Albany, cf. Howell and Tenney, op. cit., p. 461f.

be apart from the county.[47] In St. Mary's, the county sheriff needed the corporation's permission to enter its limits. This permission was granted only upon conditions : 'that the sheriff . . . of St. Maryes County shall and may Execute all writts and process within this City upon any pson . . . against whom such precept shall issue : The said Sheriff . . . first giving notice thereof to any the Magistrates, or to the Clarke of this City that the same may be Entred ; for which Entry the sd. Clarke shall have and receive of the P[ll] in such case the summe of 12d or twelve lbs. of Tobacco as ffee for the same.'[48]

Apart from these few instances, there do not appear to have been any other full 'county boroughs' created in colonial times. Certainly not Philadelphia, where the county sheriff was specifically to serve for the city ;[49] and probably not elsewhere.[50]

Appeals to these higher jurisdictions were consequently quite normal, and in this connection the abortive 'General Act' of Virginia of 1680 may be instanced as perhaps reflecting the prevailing attitude and practice better than any one charter. These 'burghs' were each to have a hustings or court with jurisdiction over civil suits and criminal cases involving fines not over £30. Appeals were to the county court. The local court was to be a court of record and to have a common seal.[51]

If the foregoing account of court jurisdiction and of the interrelations of boroughs and counties appears to be

47. By charter. Cf. Appendix B.
48. *Maryland Archives*, vol. XVII, p. 420 (Proceedings of Council, Oct. 13, 1685).
49. Charter provisions. Cf. Appendix B.
50. Possibly the ill-fated 'charter' of Charleston (1722) may have granted such powers, inasmuch as it was modelled after that of New York City.
51. Cf. Berkley, H. J., 'Extinct River Towns of Chesapeake Bay,' in *Md. Hist. Mag.*, vol. XIX, p. 127f.

confused, it is because the various charters themselves revealed no underlying unity in this matter. Rather did
they show a minute gradation from no court at all up
through the full power of a city that was a 'county in itself.' This variation once again betrayed unmistakably
the English nature, origin, and spirit of the colonial city.

(C)

The present age would regard the *administrative* rather
than the judicial functions of these courts as the real
'municipal government.' The origin of these non-judicial
duties must be sought in the early and somewhat obscure
days in England when these borough corporations were
emerging. By the seventeenth century, such administration had long since become recognized practice, though
its precise forms had undergone and were to undergo significant changes. Furthermore, the practice had already
been instituted of utilizing these English county justices
as administrative agents of the central government ; and,
in so far as the colonial municipalities were also regarded
as counties, they likewise experienced a similar but somewhat more limited accession of powers. Thus in the Wilmington (Del.) charter of 1739 this administrative aspect was more specifically recognized than perhaps was
usual in current statements. The burgesses were empowered 'to be conservators of the peace within the said
borough, with power . . . to remove all nuisances and
incroachments on the streets and highways . . . and also
to arrest, imprison and punish rioters and other breakers
of the peace, and to bind them and all other offenders
. . . to the Court of General Quarter Sessions . . . of
the said County of New-Castle . . . and to do and perform all and singular other matters and things within the

said borough, as fully and effectively to all intents and purposes as Justices of the Peace in their respective counties could or might lawfully do.'[52] These powers appertained to the borough magistrates endowed as justices of the peace, not to the borough court in its capacity of successor to the court leet or court baron of the manor.[53]

However, the original sources of administrative powers were the English manorial 'court barons' and 'court leets.' The latter in particular could still be recognized in the power of the borough courts to command the compulsory services of the freeholders and inhabitants to repair and make streets and to take their turns in the 'night watch.' As the Webbs expressed it, this method rested originally upon 'the enforcement by a jury of presentment of the householder's obligation to do all that the common good requires, and to refrain from doing anything that is injurious to the King's subjects.'[54] Particularly in Annapolis and Charleston (S. C.), this practice of unpaid householder service seemed to have retained much of its earlier vigour even at the close of the period.[55] But in the Colonies, as in England, the reliance upon communal service was yielding to 'government' by paid officials, though the functions performed by the latter traced their legal origin in part to the former practice. In part also these administrative functions were derived from the 'management' of common property by the 'association of producers,' which constituted one aspect of the English 'court baron.'

By 1700 and increasingly thereafter, the function of these 'courts,' even in the mind of the populace, was be-

52. Cf. *Laws of Delaware*, 1772, Chap. CCVIa.
53. Cf. p. 25.
54. Webb, B. and S., *The Manor and the Borough*, vol. I, p. 229.
55. Cf. p. 267.

ginning to be regarded as primarily *governmental*.[56] The charters and acts of the assemblies soon reflected this altered attitude.

The power to license taverns and ordinaries lay on the border line between the judicial and the administrative functions of the 'court' of the borough. When within the competence of the incorporation, this power was normally vested in the mayor and aldermen (as justices) rather than in the entire council, in towns where the latter body included councillors as well as aldermen.[57] The policing of these places also occupied much of the time and attention of the local magistrates. This power of licensing was by no means universal ; and, even where granted, was often shared with the county justices or the governor.[58] It was an even more important power in those days than now ; and offered not dissimilar problems of favouritism, disorder, sales at forbidden times, etc. Fees for licensing were customarily charged, and augmented the revenue of the corporation.

Control over other types of trade lay similarly on this ill-defined borderline between the judicial and the administrative. Such control was customarily exercised by implication, if not by specific grant. Among municipal functions generally, it played a role so important that it will be reserved for special consideration.[59]

The by-laws, ordinances, and 'laws' passed in great profusion by the more amply endowed of these corporations represent the very basis and expression of 'functions of government' as we would understand them to-day. The

56. Cf. p. 276.
57. Cf. p. 170.
58. e. g. Philadelphia (Shepherd, W. R., *Proprietary Government in Pennsylvania*, p. 80f.). For policing functions, cf. pp. 271ff.
59. Chap. VI.

colonial period stands astride the transition between the
time when the corporation was regarded as an 'administrative court' and that more modern view of it as a legislative, and perhaps a representative body as well. The extent to which this power to make local laws was granted
varied as did the other powers ; but whatever the power
may have been in the original charter, assemblies did not
hesitate to add further specific authorizations as the need
arose in the more active and vigorous communities. The
fields covered varied widely, in part with local variations
in the powers of the vestries, commissions, and other governmental agencies operating in the same area.[60] In some
the charter contained a 'blanket' clause or clauses. In Germantown (1691) the 'blanket' authorizing clauses read
as follows : 'to act and doe in all those matters and things
whatsoever, soe as they shall judge necessary and expedient for the well governing and government of the said
Corporacon . . . and . . . to doe and act any other
matter or thing whatsoever for the good government of
the said Corporacon and the Members thereof, and for
the managing and ordering of the Estate, Stocke, and af-
faires of the said Corporacon.' This grant was in addition
to the usual specified grants concerning courts, admission
of freemen, markets, etc. Under this grant the laws drawn
up by the town's 'General Court' included land boundaries, allocation of land, eminent domain for mill sites,
keeping the streets clean, protection of the trees on the
common, building of cross streets, fences, roaming of cattle and pigs, bounty for killing of wolves, care of poor, fire
menaces, branding of products, sale of drink to the Indians, etc.

The 'blanket' clause in the Philadelphia charter of

60. Cf. Chap. X.

1691 allowed any ordinances and laws save only those repugnant to the statutes of England and the province. We read that in New York City in 1683 the mayor and aldermen 'did make such peculiar laws and orders as they Judged Convenient for Ye Well Governing ye Inhabitants of said Corporation.'[61] The 1686 charter sanctioned the making of laws not contrary to those of England and the province — but, unless re-enacted, they were not to be valid longer than three months. Under the charter of 1730 the limitation was fixed at one year, save by permission of the governor. Another type of grant attempted to specify in detail the subjects to be covered by the by-laws. Thus in North Carolina there was the most minute prescription of the matters on which the 'borough' commissioners might legislate — the records of each session of the legislature being filled with acts empowering Wilmington to appoint guards and watches, or New Bern to levy a tax for a fire engine, or Bath to prohibit swine from running at large, or Edenton to build a pound. A somewhat similar jealous limitation of boroughs to specified powers may be noted in Virginia. However, there is no reason to suppose that in these states any very serious obstacles were placed in the way of additions to the lists.[62] Yet in spite of fairly ample delegations in the Pennsylvania city and borough charters, the provincial assembly was prone to enact detailed laws for its communities. It is thus interesting to note that even in colonial times a distinction is unconsciously drawn between that kind of 'home rule' which allowed a city to do anything not specifically forbidden and the doctrine of 'specifically delegated powers' which required and was to require

61. Quoted in Peterson, A. E., and Edwards, G. W., *New York as an Eighteenth Century Municipality*, p. 10.
62. Cf. p. 339f.

such an infinite amount of special legislation by the legislatures.

Annapolis (in 1746) codified all its by-laws, by repealing all hitherto enacted and replacing them with fourteen others.[63] Their scope will serve to illustrate the nature and extent of the powers of this type enjoyed by the average incorporation of the period :

1. To prevent nuisances.
2. To ascertain the allowance to juries for verdicts.
3. To oblige officers to attend to their duties.
4. To prevent the damages which may happen by the firing of chimneys.
5. For security of the peace.
6. To prohibit keeping sheep, hogs, etc., within limits except in inclosures.
7. To prevent accidents by fire.
8. Encouragement of tradesmen.
9. To prevent vexatious suits for small debts.
10. To fine any one refusing to take office of sheriff.
11. To prevent accidents in shipbuilding, etc.
12. To prevent entertaining and harbouring of slaves.
13. Sundry irregularities.
14. Repair of streets, etc.
15. Repeal all former laws.

So little, then, did the 'courts' of the time distinguish between their judicial and administrative aspects.

For a larger city, the New York City Codification of 1775[64] will serve to represent the stage of development

---

63. Minutes, Annapolis City Council, 1746 (MS. Hall of Records, Annapolis) ; codification printed in Riley, E. S., *The Ancient City*, Annapolis, 1887, p. 109f.
64. *Minutes, New York City Council*, Jan. 12, 1775, etc., vol. VIII, pp. 72ff.

reached by the dawn of the Revolution. The subjects of its ordinances were :

1. Sunday observance.
2. To prevent strangers from being a charge.
3. To appoint sworn surveyors.
4. Preventing fire.
5. Marking bread.
6. Regulating negroes, etc.
7. Regulating carts and carmen.
8. Regulating gaugers, packers, and cullers.
9. Making freemen.
10. Regulating the lying of vessels in the dock.
11. Preserving the commons.
12. Regulating inviters to funerals.
13. Paving and cleaning the streets and preventing nuisances.
14. Prohibiting hawkers and pedlars.
15. Preventing frauds in firewood.
16. Marking of butter.
17. Regulating public slaughter houses.
18. Regulating fences.
19. Regulating midwives.
20. Regulating the office of chamberlain.
21. Securing against danger of gunpowder.
22. Night watch.
23. Use of the seal.
24. Regulating markets, forestalling, etc.
25. Preventing the sale of unripe fruit and oysters.
26. Additional law regulating the market.
27. Assize of bread.
28. Additional law regulating the market.
29. Prohibiting the gift or sale of liquor to the 'Centinels.'

30. To prevent raffling.
31. Assize of apple barrels and weight of onions.
32. Regulating sale of hay.
33. Size of lumber, etc.

The power to impose a rate was a derivative of these other powers ; but its full consideration must be deferred until later.[65] It is enough at this point to call attention to the fact that the various colonial legislatures for the most part insisted upon specific authorization before the corporations were permitted to impose general taxes.[66]

Finally, it is desirable to examine the question of the *areas* in which these borough courts, judicial or administrative, functioned.

To quote the Webbs again concerning the 'freeholders of the borough : 'We must of course visualize them, not as the owners of freehold houses in a crowded city, but as the owners of scattered strips of arable land in the "borough yards," or common fields, with rights of common pasturage.'[67] Again, they wrote : 'A Municipal Corporation was not primarily a territorial expression as were the parish and the County. It was rather a bundle of jurisdictions relating to persons.'[68] In New Jersey, for example, the city boundaries were approximately conterminous with the original town boundaries, and thus included mostly open country. Indeed, the territory was almost large enough to pass for a county. It did, however, focus in a more or less built-up market town or trading centre.[69] For example in the 1682 'incorporation' of Bur-

65. Cf. p. 305f.
66. Cf. pp. 306ff.
67. Webb, op. cit., vol. I, p. 94.
68. Ibid. p. 288.
69. Scott, Austin, *Early Cities of New Jersey*, p. 169 (*N. J. Hist. Soc. Coll.*, 2nd ser., vol. IX).

lington as a town, the townsfolk were empowered 'to choose among themselves some persons to regulate the affairs of the Town in such matters as relate to fences, cattle, highways and all such things as usually fall within the compass of ourselves in corporation.' Yet this was the place that the assembly had just declared 'shall be the chief city' of the province.[70] It has already been noted that the jurisdiction of the Albany court extended beyond the borough limits,[71] and the two somewhat separated ports of Williamsburg were included in the corporate limits.[72] The court of the bailywick of Newcastle also embraced more than the town limits, including 'all Plantations upon the Delaware River.'[73]

Extensions of area were variously accomplished. When Agamenticus was made Gorgeana and raised to 'city' status, its bounds were considerably enlarged by charter.[74] Governor Nichols included the hitherto independent minor court of New Harlem within the jurisdiction of the City of New York.[75] The extension of area of Norfolk was by act of assembly.[76]

The area of a given incorporation was usually definitely fixed but occasionally varied according to the pur-

70. Woodward, E. M., and Hageman, J. F., *History of Burlington and Mercer Counties*, p. 121 ; Heston, A. M., *South Jersey — a History*, vol. II, p. 638.
71. Cf. p. 110.
72. By charter.
73. Conrad, H. C., *History of the State of Delaware*, vol. II, p. 512. Also in the equally ephemeral charter of 1724, by which the boundaries were extended five miles beyond the earlier town limits (Keith, C. P., *Chronicles of Pennsylvania*, vol. II, p. 681f.).
74. Moody, E. C., *Agamenticus, Gorgeana, York* (*Handbook History of the Town of York*), Augusta, 1914, p. 21.
75. Petition of the city to Governor Dongan, Nov. 9, 1683 (in *N. Y. Hist. Soc. Coll.*, 1885, p. 43).
76. Hening's *Statutes of Virginia*, vol. VII, p. 434.

pose or function involved.[77] Almost without exception, the bounds of a municipality included more acres of rural than of urban territory. Here, also, we must accustom ourselves to think in other than modern terms of these colonial boroughs ; for this wide area was a derivative of the emphasis, which prevailed in the period, on 'common' land and on accurately surveyed and attested land tenure and patents.[78] Only in Philadelphia, Bristol, and perhaps Norfolk did the built-up area become conterminous with the corporation bounds ; and only in Bristol were considerable unbuilt areas, commons, etc., not included at the time of incorporation.[79]

Certain aspects of the power to elect representatives to the legislatures are better discussed in another connection.[80] In St. Mary's, the officers of the corporation selected the representatives ;[81] but this was an exception. Choice usually was granted to all normally franchised freeholders and inhabitants. In James City, for example, this power had been granted and was thus exercised,[82] though apparently the 'metropolis' had no formal corporate body. The abortive General Acts of Maryland (1683) and Virginia (1680), and the Act of North Caro-

---

77. Note, in addition to the example of Albany already cited, that Philadelphia's jurisdiction under the charter of 1701 extended 'into all such creeks, rivers, and places . . . as the said mayor [etc.] with the approbation of the chief officer of the King's customs, shall from time to time think fit to appoint.' On the other hand, the Philadelphia area was much more limited than usual in incorporations, and by 1750 was outgrown.

78. e. g. The early Virginia incorporations issued land patents ; so also 'water rights,' etc., of New York City.

79. Compiled from a study of the early maps of the various incorporations.

80. Cf. pp. 334ff.

81. Steiner, B., 'Royal Province of Maryland in 1692,' p. 142f. in Md. Hist. Mag., vol. XV, pp. 125-168.

82. Hening's Virginia Statutes, vol. II, p. 20.

lina (1715) apparently recognized that a certain size ought to be attained before a 'borough' or 'town' was enfranchised. In Maryland it was the ability of the 'port town' to pay the expenses of the member of the assembly that was to have been the criterion.[83] In Virginia[84] and North Carolina[85] a town must have sixty families, but the latter made exceptions. In Albany, the question was complicated by the right (not, however, exercised) of residents of the 'two Mannors and a Borough' (Schenectady?) within the borders of the county to vote for the two members from the 'City and County' in addition to having separate representation themselves.[86] It was normal to grant a borough representation, and regardless of whether the borough was governed by a 'close' corporation, its freeholders and other eligibles voted for the 'burgess' or representative.[87]

These then were the powers of boroughs, in so far as such powers were set forth in the letter of the law. How they compared with the powers exercised in actual practice, it is difficult to say. Certainly considerable evidence exists that the two were often quite different. Occasionally, such difference consisted in an overstepping of authority, but more usually there had taken place a lapse through disuse or yielding to challenge, or a loss to rival units or forms of government. It is true that in 1693 the townsfolk of Burlington assumed that their officers had

83. *Md. Archives*, vol. VII, p. 618 (Assembly Proceedings).
84. Hening, op. cit., vol. II, p. 471.
85. *State Records of North Carolina*, vol. XXIII, p. 79 (Ch. LII).
86. O'Callaghan, E. B. (Edit.), *Documents Relative to the Colonial History of New York*, vol. VIII, p. 565.
87. The privilege of sending four deputies to the first Maine provincial court was accorded to Agamenticus (1640) (Banks, C. E., *History of York, Maine*, p. 122).

the power of a 'Court of Record' and acted accordingly,[88] and that the assembly passed an act (1695) confirming this power[89] — but this was exceptional. Even Burlington apparently had allowed many of its powers to lapse before its charter of 1733.[90] In Annapolis there was a similar lapse. A move to restore infringed rights was dramatized by Samuel Chase and others by lifting the lid of a coffin (in which he had covertly deposited the charter of the city) in the presence of a large group of citizens assembled in the State House. The charter was then read and created a profound impression, with the result that the lost rights were restored.[91] In 1739 in Philadelphia certain of the tradesmen forced the 'close' corporation to refrain from further exercising the city's supposed right to force removal of slaughterhouses, tan-yards, etc.[92] The actual loss in Philadelphia of power and prestige on the part of the city corporation was much more a loss to the numerous other boards and commissions established for municipal functions.[93] In many instances, notably in the capital cities, the assembly appeared to regard itself as the actual government of the town, solemnly considering details which might more properly have been delegated — and which in fact in some instances had actually been so delegated — to borough 'courts.'

Thus the powers were not different in their trends

88. Township minutes. Cf. also Woodward, E. M., and Hageman, J. F., *History of Burlington and Mercer Counties,* p. 124.

89. Chap. XII, 2nd Session.

90. The township minutes of Jan. 15, 1733/4, speak of 'restoring to ancient rights and privileges.'

91. Cf. account in Riley, E. S., *History of Anne Arundel County,* Annapolis, 1905, p. 74. Prior to this time the city council had come to be more or less moribund, if one is to judge by the infrequency of meetings recorded in the minutes (cf. p. 219 below).

92. Scharf, J. T., and Westcott, T., *History of Philadelphia,* Philadelphia, 1884, 3 vol., vol. I, p. 208f.

93. Cf. p. 255f.

from those of the British cities of the period. In the latter, the rise of the justices of the peace, the vestries, and the special commissions was more marked ; but instances of losses of the same type to these other agencies also occurred in the Colonies. Moreover, in the Colonies, the legislature exercised a much more detailed control than the British Parliament could or wished to exercise. The same ubiquitous nature of action on the part of the administrative courts revealed itself — but this action was increasing its scope in America while for the most part diminishing in England. The same wide variety of jurisdiction, the same decline to virtual extinction of the court leet and court baron, the same complexity and interlocking of relations, jurisdiction, and personnel of borough and county, the same sense of an institution in transition — all these characterized the municipal incorporations of both nations by 1775.

VI

MUNICIPAL CONTROL OF ECONOMIC LIFE

THERE is one function of municipal government of the seventeenth and eighteenth centuries unfamiliar to us of the present day, and yet of such importance to its time that it deserves separate treatment. It is difficult for one to visualize an age in which economic life, relatively speaking, was split into such small manageable units that the municipality could be regarded as an effective agent in economic control. Yet we have already noted how large a part this concept played in the moves to foster city growth and to seek city incorporation : from the government's standpoint, to control trade and yield revenue ; from the inhabitants' standpoint, to secure to themselves special privileges which would allow their several incomes thereby to be enhanced.

We need for its fuller understanding to be able to project ourselves into the ideology of the times. No *laissez-faire* doctrine had arisen to act as a counter-weight to those whose faith in the efficacy and beneficence of governmental action led them, as to-day, to seek social or private ends through such action. Such use of the governmental machinery simply was not questioned ; it was too much a part of the experience and accepted doctrine of the time.

The medieval guilds by 1600 had lost much of their initiative and by 1775 were but the faint shadow of their former selves. Tudor sovereigns had used them as their agents and thereby dealt a fatal blow to their spontaneity. It remained for the later period to reduce them to a position of relative unimportance. Yet this did not mean that the local units were entirely or even largely abandoned as vehicles for economic control. It implied rather that the county justices, and hence the municipal corporations whose chief officials were themselves justices, were looked to by their inhabitants to regulate as a matter of course the price and quality of basic articles. If anything, this was more true of seventeenth century America than of England. In the former, distances between communities and greater difficulties of communication and transportation were such as to render a community and its hinterland 'more self-contained than in England.

One must not make the mistake of supposing that every detail of economic life was thus regulated, or that such regulation extended in its full scope down to the Revolution. Regulation of price and quality of important commodities, of wages, of the time and place of marketing, and above all of who should sell were assumed as necessary municipal functions in the seventeenth century. They still appeared as at least proper and legitimate functions, in the eighteenth century, of all those municipalities which attained an appreciable size. While this more or less held true regardless of the particular manner in which the community was governed, it seems to have reached its fullest development in those incorporations such as New York and Albany, whose government rested upon what was, for the times, a fairly broad popular base. Hence in these colonial boroughs we witness once again that pull and tug of economic forces which have made up so much of the warp and woof of governmental action down through the ages — save only in the very limited period and the very limited territory within which the *laissez-faire* doctrine was in the ascendant. The definition, 'Politics is the battle of interests masquerading as principles,' was every bit as true of colonial towns as it is of the United States as a whole to-day. It may be rather more difficult to discover always what were the forces which were operating in the earlier period, because they were not so frequently challenged. Hence it is necessary constantly to infer rather than to demonstrate, calling attention to the fact that in a more complete study of the personnel of the councils or perhaps in unpublished correspondence or diaries there doubtless lies material for 'an economic interpretation of colonial boroughs' fuller and more accurate than the present study can hope to be.

It must be remembered that even in the Colonies this period almost to its end was socially an era of unchallenged rank and status.[1] In any society in which this is true we may expect to find special privileges also entrenched and unchallenged. In the eyes of the people it was 'right' that the rich and high-born should not only rule but also should entrench themselves with economic privileges of exclusive trading rights, or the other privileges of 'freemen' of the community. This was, relatively speaking, as true of the theological aristocracy of New England as of the New England and New York City and Philadelphia merchants or the tidewater planters of Virginia. Eventually in each case there was revolt, a revolt that played no small part in the events leading up to the Revolution — but it is the municipal and not the national aspects of the results of this social stratification with which we are concerned. The fact which it is difficult for us to realize to-day is not so much that these borough aldermen usually regulated the economic life of their community in accordance with their own privileged status, but that it was accepted as part of the folkways of the day that they should so regulate it.

In so far as incorporation was an effective weapon for

1. Notably so along the coast where the cities were located. In the back country, rank and status were more suspect.

accomplishing such ends, we have seen that it was sought by the inhabitants — a weapon against 'foreigners,' and a means of organizing and entrenching the power and privileges of their group locally. Yet there was another tradition, perhaps almost equally potent in motivating trade regulation, handed down from guild days — the tradition of 'fair price and good quality.' It was not merely that these 'freemen' or 'aldermen' were consumers ; such an explanation was far too simple. It was rather that this finer side was every bit as genuine and just as frequently expressed itself in corporate action as did the aforementioned unquestioned special privilege. Poor quality and extortionate price were felt somehow to be 'wrong,' and a constant struggle was waged against both.

The elaborate and detailed regulations which these incursions into economic control entailed were never fully successful, even in their heyday. By 1750 they gave very definite indications of cracking under the strain of the mobility and stir which had begun to characterize the urban centres of Philadelphia and New York. Boston seems never to have gone quite as far as her sister cities along this path of regulation.

The legal basis for such controls was partly specified in the charters and partly implied from the general grants of power or from the precedents of other communities. In Williamsburg, the common council was specifically given power to make laws governing trade when not in conflict with colonial laws.[2] The Annapolis charter of 1708 specified the power to make by-laws to regulate trade. Yet no real difference can be traced between such communities and those whose charters were not so specific. Equally

2. By charter. Cf. Appendix B.

they undertook such regulation, and this regulation remained for a long time relatively unchallenged on legal grounds. When it finally did give way, it was not because of attacks on its legality, but under pressure of economic and social forces of a new era.

(B)

With a view to orderly discussion it is proposed first to consider the controls from the standpoint of the various classes for whose benefit they were designed — buyers, sellers, consumers, craftsmen — and then to discuss the specific institutions of markets, fairs, and ports.

It was the Dutch in Albany and on the Delaware that seem most to have developed the use of incorporation as a weapon in the interest of the buyers. In Albany, for example, the inhabitants were almost exclusively preoccupied with trade with the Indians. This was true long after the English theoretically took over control. The burghers of Albany possessed from Dutch days at least a nominal monopoly of the fur trade, just as New York City had been granted the staple for wheat export. Albany constantly struggled to enforce its particular monopoly against Schenectady, just as New York found Albany a menace to its own special privileges. In Altena (Wilmington) a town meeting was called in 1657 because 'some people do not hesitate to ruin the trade with the Indians, by running up the price of deer-skins by more than one-third their value to the great and excessive disadvantage of the poor community here' ;[3] and the meeting proceeded to fix prices and penalties

3. Scharf, J. T., *History of Delaware*, vol. II, p. 855.

for violating the same. Such regulation on the part of the Albany corporation was carried much further, and was the most frequent of all subjects of the by-laws, at least down to 1710.[4]

This preoccupation on the part of Albany with Indian trade was turned to interesting account by Governor Fletcher in 1695. We read : 'He ordered two of the principall gates of the Citty where the Indians used to enter, to be shut up, cautiously alledging the danger of keeping open so many gates during the war ; severall poor traders who had built their houses near these gates purposely for the Indian trade would have been ruined if these gates had continued shut, and therefore rais'd a contribution of fifty or sixty of their best furs which they presented to his Excellency and thereby removed his Excellency's apprehensions of the danger those gates exposed the Citty to ; for at the request of the May'r and Aldermen the gates were opened and the Citty as safe as when they were shut.'[5]

Among the most heinous offences, judging from the frequency with which ordinances were passed and trials held concerning it, was that of taking Indians into one's

4. Munsell, J., *Annals of Albany*, Albany, 1850-59, 10 vol., *passim*. For example, under the Dutch, the problem of employment of brokers as agents was the subject of considerable legislation by the court (Van Laer, A. J. F., Edit. and Trans., *Minutes of the Court of Albany, Rensselaerswyck, and Schenectady*, Albany, 1926-32, 2 vol., *passim*). In 1698 the corporation built houses to accommodate the Indians when they came to trade (Howell, G. R., and Tenney, J. (Edit.), *History of the County of Albany*, p. 465). In 1673 the corporation petitioned the new Dutch authorities to give no further privileges to Schenectady, but to continue to confine the latter's residents to agriculture as heretofore, and reserve the trade privileges to Albany (Weise, A. J., *History of the City of Albany*, p. 155).
5. Quoting one of the contributors to the 'present' in O'Callaghan, E. B. (Edit.), *Documents Relative to the Colonial History of New York*, vol. IV, p. 223.

own house for the sake of trade ; thereby presumably breaking the 'buyer's ring' and otherwise obtaining 'unfair' advantage. The attempt to confine the trading to the Indian houses outside the walls was continuous.[6] In 1707, for example, there appear in the city minutes no less than four separate proclamations and ordinances concerning the Indian trade, reasserting or altering trade practices. That the Indian's own interest was not wholly disregarded can be inferred from a similar series of ordinances against selling or giving him liquor, although here also the thought may have been that the more unscrupulous thereby obtained an advantage in the trading.[7] The very frequency of such regulations is its own best comment on the difficulty of their enforcement. After 1715 they fade out of the picture — why, must be the subject more or less of conjecture.

The occasional efforts to ensure advance publication of notices concerning auctions of merchandise also belong to this category of protection of buyers.[8] Of the same sort were the fairly frequent ordinances providing for the licensing of 'vendue masters or auctioneers.'[9]

The situation of Albany was the exception among incorporations. Far more usual, and actually of the same general nature, were the efforts at safeguarding the vested rights of local merchants and tradesmen. Of course, to-day we should regard certain aspects of such trade rings more or less as 'rackets' ; but the early-evidenced phenomenon of opposition to the entry of 'foreigners' or 'outsiders' is still very much with us in our Civic Defense Leagues, our

6. 'Council Minutes' in Munsell, J., *Annals of Albany*, vol. IV, pp. 105-122.
7. Ibid. vol. V, pp. 194, etc.
8. e. g. Philadelphia, petition in 1695 (Scharf, J. T., and Westcott, T., *History of Philadelphia*, vol. I, p. 126).
9. e. g. *Minutes of Common Council*, Philadelphia, Apr. 9, 1731.

anti-chain store agitation, or even in the occasional *municipal* by-laws directed at the 'fly-by-night' merchants.

In New York City, such monopoly of local trade dates from the days of the Dutch when the institution of *'Burgherregt'* was installed as early as 1657. The casual pedlar had been hurting the regular businesses. The burgomasters and schepens, after their earlier attempts to deal with these problems of trade rights had been overruled, had petitioned the director general and council on the basis of the Twelfth Article of the Freedoms. By this Article, the staple for the entire colony was to be on Manhattan. The petition was granted, but the proviso was inserted that burgher right might be purchased, to lapse when the pedlar left. Even this was not effective, for the itinerant traders sold outside the city limits. In consequence in 1659 the city authorities asked for the monopoly for the whole colony, including particularly Fort Orange (Albany), and that a three year residence be required except on payment of 1,000 guilders. This last was not granted but the request for exclusive staple right was.[10] However, the provisions at times were more honoured in the breach than in the observance. Twenty persons were granted the great burgher right and one hundred and twenty-six the small burgher right in the first year. The fee for the former was fifty guilders ; for the latter twenty guilders.[11] Apart from certain political privileges reserved for the former, the privileges were identical, particularly as to trading. The distinction between the two types was abolished not long after the English took control (1668),[12] but the restrictions on trading

10. *N. Y. Hist. Soc. Coll.,* 1885, Documents 3-7 and pp. 27ff.
11. Cf. pp. 230ff.
12. A distinction between the fee for merchants and the fee for artisans established in 1675 was continued as late as 1815 (Seybolt, R. F., *The Colonial Citizen of New York,* Madison, 1918, p. 16f.).

were retained.[13] By 1684 the right to trade was in practice open to any one who cared to qualify by payment of a moderate fee for this 'freedom.'[14] Under these circumstances, acquisition of freedom really amounted to the payment of a reasonable licence fee. Residence at the time of the Dongan Charter automatically constituted freedom, provided the individual registered and paid 9 d.[15] In 1773, if one were born a freeman or apprenticed, the fees were raised to 7/6 for the clerk, 1 d. for the cryer, and 6 s. for the mayor.[16]

In Boston, 1657, the town meeting passed the following ordinance : 'None but admitted inhabitants could keep shop or set up a manufacture within the town except those who were twenty-one years of age and had served seven years apprenticeship.' The penalty was fixed at 10 s. a month.[17]

In the Perth Amboy charter of 1718, 'Trade, art, or mystery' were to be restricted to citizens except during fairs.

---

13. Certain loopholes were left, for we note that in 1676, while the right to trade was declared to be confined to freemen, the mayor and aldermen might issue special licences with the approval of the governor. (*Minutes, Common Council*, Jan. 20, 1676.)
A petition on the part of the burghers of Albany in 1679 to legalize the practice of shipping flour direct instead of through the New York merchants was denied by Governor Andros. (Van Laer, A. J. F. (Edit. and Trans.), *Court minutes, Albany, Rensselaerswyck, and Schenectady*, 1679, var., esp. vol. II, pp. 404-414.)
14. *N. Y. Hist. Soc. Coll.*, 1885, p. 47. A student of municipal 'freedom' is referred to *Burghers of New Amsterdam and Freemen of New York, 1675-1866, N. Y. Hist. Soc. Collections*, New York, 1885. This contains lists of freemen, usually with their occupations, and is an invaluable source of information concerning the population composition of the City.
15. Seybolt, op. cit., p. 19.
16. Ibid. p. 6.
17. Quincy, J., *Municipal History of Boston*, Boston, 1852, p. 5.

Westchester in 1697 went so far as to forbid the erection of any saw mills other than those owned by Caleb Heathcote, then mayor.[18]

By 1725, interest in enforcing such monopolies had begun to wane ; and by 1750 in the larger cities the door either was thrown open for a moderate fee, as in New York, or was largely disregarded, as in Philadelphia, through the growth of numerous unlawful shops of one sort or another.[19] In Charleston (S. C.) the merchants formed an association to enforce the laws against unlicensed hawkers and pedlars.[20] In Albany in 1711 action was taken by the corporation against those who retailed without being freemen ;[21] but this is the last of such entries that I have been able to discover in their minutes. Sporadic efforts to enforce restrictions still appeared occasionally in New York City. In 1731 the price of freedom was increased for non-residents,[22] and in 1750 a petition of merchants and shopkeepers indicated that enforcement of the provincial law against pedlars had largely lapsed, to the detriment of those who 'pay rents and contribute to the public taxes and watch of the City.'[23] The ritual was retained in the New York City charter of 1730 ; and, in a few of the smaller cities where the stakes involved were not so high, this exclusive right may have lingered on fairly effectively down to the Revo-

18. Book of Records of the Trustees, July 26, 1697. Cf. also a similar instance on May 13, 1702.
19. Scharf, J. T., and Westcott, T., *History of Philadelphia*, vol. I, p. 211.
20. Leiding, H. K., *Charleston, Historic and Romantic*, Philadelphia, 1931, p. 99.
21. 'Minutes of Common Council,' in Munsell, J., *Annals of Albany*, vol. VI, p. 258.
22. *Minutes of Common Council*, vol. IV, p. 96f.
23. Petition, MS. in Original Records of Common Council, 1750.

lution. Evidence of such ordinances is lacking in many of these smaller towns.[24]

Once in a while an entry occurs which indicates that such monopolies were also exercised in the direction of preservation of standards of quality on the part of the tradesmen, etc., at least for purposes of export : 'Noe Flower was to be bolted or packed or biskett made for exportation butt in the Citty of New York being for the encouragement of trade and keepeing up the Reputacon of New York flower which is in greater request in the West Indies.' However, the same document goes on to say that this export is 'the only support and maintennance of the Inhabitants of this Citty and if not confirmed to them will ruine and depopulate the same.'[25] But such standards, where imposed by the corporation, seem to have been more frequently opposed than supported by those regulated.

Of a similar nature, and in fact normally bracketed with the monopoly of trade, was the monopoly frequently

24. An ordinance recorded in the Lancaster Minutes, Sept. 13, 1742, is worth quoting for its illuminating phraseology : 'It being moved that the Liberty taken by Chapmen licensed to travel with goods for supplying the Country in setting up stalls within this Corporation, particularly at the time of Elections and Court . . . is an infringement of the Rights and Privileges of shopkeepers . . . and a great discouragement of tradeing people settling within the same . . . and as travelling chapmen are conceived to be licensed to supply people in the country who are at a distance from Stores and Shops, and not intended to enter Corporations or Markett Towns, not having any legal settlement there to sell their Goods in prejudice of the Freemen and Inhabitants settled and trading in the same way — It is ordered that no persons except Freemen and Inhabitants within this Corporation shall presume to sett up stalls within the same for the sale of their goods or otherwise expose any Goods to sale, save at the Times of Fairs, under pennalty of Five Pounds . . .' Yet this is very different from the elaborate guild monopolies of earlier centuries, and did not point to a privileged group *within* the city.
25. Petition to Governor Dongan for a new charter, Nov. 9, 1683 (*N. Y. Hist. Soc. Coll.*, 1885, pp. 43-47).

granted to the various crafts and professions. It followed a somewhat similar course, though the attempt at effective regulation seems possibly to have lingered a bit longer.[26]

There is a striking quotation from the previously cited petition of New York City for a new charter, which called attention to this particular one of the existing rights :

'None were to be esteemed Freemen of the Citty but who were admitted by the Magistrates aforesaid, and none before such admission to sell by Retayle or Exercise any handicraft trade or occupacon and every merchant or shopkeeper was to pay for the publique use of the Citty three pounds, twelve shillings. Every handycrafts man one pound foure shillings on being made free.'

The carters and porters seem to have been the 'stormy petrels' among occupations. In 1667 in New York eight 'carmen' petitioned the mayor's court that they be recognized as a guild and that all newcomers be forbidden to cart within the city. The request was granted 'until more carters are required.' There followed in the ensuing years a number of regulations, including the imposition of penalties if they 'manny times use ill and bad language to the Burghers.' Their charges were regulated and they were given a 'superviser.' Such regulation was evidently not always to their liking, for in 1684 they went on a strike against the ordinances of that year. The city retaliated by taking away their privileged status and advertising for others. Only a few of the original group were reinstated and they had to pay a fine. In these early days, however, the city fathers required or attempted to require certain services in return for the monopoly thus granted the carters. They were (1667) bound to help extinguish

26. McKee, S., Jr., *Labor in Colonial New York,* New York, 1935, pp. 32ff., 53f., contains an excellent summary of these efforts in New York City.

fires. In 1670, they agreed to fill up the holes in the streets
and cart off the dirt from the paved streets. By 1693, however, we find them paid a small fee by the load for this
service.[27]

Other occupations presented perhaps less of a problem
by way of regulation, but were customarily extended
monopoly privileges in at least these larger boroughs.
The earlier attitude towards occupational rights — an attitude strikingly similar to present-day jurisdictional disputes of organized labour — is reflected in a court order
in New York City in 1674.

'Upon the Petition of the Corne Porters and Wyne
Porters, shewing their agrievance by Brewers, Bakers,
and others setting day Laborers on worke to carry up
their corne and other things, which of right apper-
teynes to them — The court thereupon orders that the
Brewers shall have the wyne porters to carry out their
Beere as formerly was accustomed, and the Bakers are
not to hyre or permit any corne to bee carryed up or
brought down in their houses or garretts by any other
persons than their owne servants or the corne porters.'[28]

Similarly it was ordered (1676) that there shall be two
tanners (duly named) and two only, and but one 'cur-

27. Cf. Peterson, A. E., and Edwards, G. W., *New York as an Eighteenth
Century Municipality*, pp. 63ff.
   In Albany the carters were 'sworn in' as freemen in 1686 and licensed.
   In 1729 they were given a new and detailed code with elaborate
   specifications of charges. Ordinances of this sort continued down to
   the Revolution (*Minutes of Council*, in Munsell, J., *Annals of Albany, passim*, esp. 1751, 1752 [vol. X, pp. 130-151] ; 1700 [vol. IV,
   pp.105-122] ; 1729 [vol. IX, p. 44f.]) ; also in Munsell, J., *Collections on the History of Albany*, Albany, 1865-71, 4 vol., vol. I, *passim*.
   In Philadelphia also they were continually 'regulated' : e. g. a revision
   of the permissible charges was granted on their petition, June 19,
   1719. (*Minutes of Common Council.*)
28. Minutes, Mayor's Court, Dec. 1, 1674. (MSS. in Hall of Records, New
   York City.)

rier.' Butchers were not to be curriers, shoemakers, or tanners ; nor were tanners to be curriers, shoemakers, or butchers.[29] Most picturesque to modern eyes in this connection was the licensing in New York City of 'inviters to funerals.'[30] In the creation of these occupational monopolies, the problems were difficult. Attempts at enforcement were apparently sporadic, as the 'evil' of newcomers became exaggerated or the groups in question bestirred themselves. Thus, in 1718, in Philadelphia, the tailors and cordwainers complained that their trading rights were being infringed by non-freemen and asked that regulations be drawn up to remedy this evil. 'The recorder was (accordingly) requested to inspect the books and report a proper method of incorporating particular bodies within this corporation.'[31] We read that in 1717 there had been a considerable admission from these and other groups to the freedom of the city, so that it is not unreasonable to conjecture that this renewed interest in rights followed this influx of new blood. Evidence indicates that in certain instances 'companies' or guilds were subsequently formed.[32] In the typical smaller city of New Brunswick there was periodic activity on the part of the city council to confine the practice of any manual occupation to those who had taken out their freedom.[33]

Where the occupation in question was connected with some privilege or activity conducted or supervised by the

29. *Minutes, Common Council*, Aug. 25, 1676.
30. Cf. Petition of John Van Hoernen, July 27, 1715 (MS. in the Original Records of Common Council), in which this forerunner of the modern mortician advanced as his argument that he had been performing these services at cut rates.
31. Scharf, J. T., and Westcott, T., *History of Philadelphia*, vol. I, p. 199.
32. A total of 424 were admitted in one month. Ibid. pp. 194, 232.
33. *New Brunswick City Council Minutes*, Dec. 24, 1735, etc.

city, such as the market or streets, restriction by licensing or otherwise could be fairly effective ; but those licensed usually objected to any augmenting of their number. So in 1765 there was vigorous protest in New York City against adding to the number of the 'meeters' (i.e., measurers).[34] In similar fashion, the lessee of the city slaughter house protested against the 'illegal' slaughter elsewhere which deprived him of his fees.[35]

That the competition of slave labour was felt by the artisan group would appear to be a fair inference from an Act of the South Carolina assembly in 1764 concerning Charleston, which provided that 'it shall not be lawful for the master or owner of any negro or other slave . . . to permit . . . such . . . to carry on any mechanic or handicraft trade of themselves, nor . . . to put a negro . . . to learn any . . . trade of another slave . . . provided always, that nothing herein contained shall extend . . . to hinder any mechanic or handicraft tradesman . . . from teaching their own negroes or other slaves the trades which they respectively exercise, so that they have and constantly employ, one white apprentice or journeyman for every two negroes.'[36]

Supervision of the indentures and training of apprentices was occasionally undertaken,[37] and the witnessing of the indentures by the magistrates was usual. Contracts

34. Petition, Apr. 21, 1765 of the Measurers of Grain, Coal, etc. MS. in Original Records of Common Council.
35. Petition, *circa* 1730, of John Kelly. MS. in Original Records of Common Council.
36. Quoted in *South Carolina Gazette*, August 25, 1764.
37. e. g. New York City, 1695. Cf. *N. Y. Hist. Soc. Coll.*, 1885, p. 52. For a series of illustrative cases, cf. Morris, R. B. (Edit.), *Select Cases — New York City Mayor's Court*, pp. 182-188. For an excellent account of the apprenticeship system in eighteenth century New York, cf. McKee, S., Jr., *Labor in Colonial New York*, Chap. II. McKee noted (pp. 62f., 88) some decline in the system prior to 1776.

(by the laws of England) had to be registered before the town authorities as a matter of course, but the New York City council reaffirmed this in 1694, confining apprenticeships to the sons of the freeborn. As brief a period as four years of apprenticeship was allowed until 1711, when the customary English term of seven years was imposed. The four years had been found insufficient time in which to master a trade. However, the practice remained anything but uniform, whatever the laws on the subject. None the less it is important for our purposes to note that at the expiration of their indentures the young men were made 'free of the city' if they had 'well and truly served.'[38]

By 1750 there was unmistakable evidence that such restrictions on occupational mobility, and such enforced monopoly were breaking down. Few records of admissions occur in the Philadelphia *Minutes*. Even as early as 1727 there was reluctance to continue special privileges for freemen, as it was voted that the renewal and consideration of these should be at present suspended.[39] In 1747 the craftsmen of New York appealed to the governor for redress ; but he referred their petitions back to the mayor and the regular channels under the charter.[40] The *New York Gazette*, March 17, 1755, carried an illuminating bit of news from New Brunswick (date of March 14) : 'On Tuesday last came on the annual Election for chusing the Aldermen and Common Council men of this Corporation, when Alderman Wetherill, with a Body of People, it seems, had formed a Design to put in two or three new Aldermen in the Country : for which and for asserting among other Things of the like Tendency, that

38. Seybolt, R. F., *The Colonial Citizen of New York City*, pp. 10ff.
39. *Minutes of the Common Council*, June 26, 1727.
40. *N. Y. Hist. Soc. Coll.*, 1885, p. 510. Cf. also McKee, op. cit., p. 53f.

no one of any Trade was obliged to take up his Freedom, as by the Charter is directed . . . has the Mortification to be voted out from being an Alderman . . . but being loth to part with so valuable a Post, demanded a Scrutiny, the Result of which must be waited for.'[41]

It will be remembered that the obscure bond taken out by the Schenectady aldermen and assistants in 1766 in connection with a prospective new charter suggested that the new charter would or should include a number of more democratic provisions. Among these were that 'none of the Inhabitants of said Burrough shall be obliged to take out a License for there Wagons but to use them at there will and Pleasure And that the Children of the Freeholders and free men give a Certain Sum Not Exceeding Six Shillings for their freedome.'[42]

On the basis of these few instances, it is probably presumptuous to conjecture much in the way of general restlessness at craft monopolies. However, like the analogous efforts at establishing or enforcing monopolies in trade, there is decreasing evidence of activity in the larger towns after 1725, and only the most occasional mention of the subject at any time in the smaller ones. Artificial restrictions of this sort were exceedingly difficult to implement — given large communities and a mobile population. They were scarcely worth while in the smaller ones. Repeated regulations, followed by a period of silence about a particular subject, meant either adequate and satisfactory enforcement or tacit abandoning of the field by the governmental agency concerned. In the regulation of these monopolistic practices, evidence points unmistakably to the latter situation. Even in certain notori-

41. Cf. p. 203f., for the implications of this as regards the right to vote.
42. Reprint from one of the Vrooman Papers, in Munsell, J., *Annals of Albany*, vol. I, p. 368.

ously monopolistic professions, disintegration had set in. In Philadelphia, unlicensed vendue masters were practising at will in the Northern Liberties in 1752, and it was from the assembly, not the corporation, that redress was sought.[43] In New York in 1746, it was the assembly that — apparently riding rough shod over charter rights — opened the right to practise law in the mayor's court to qualified lawyers from all over the province.[44] A new age was even then dawning in which municipal control of economic life was to yield almost its last prerogatives to the larger units of state and nation.

One should not leave discussion of these rights of freemen without one final tribute to its finer side, involving duties as well as privileges, in the form of the quotation in full of the freeman's oath in New York City:

> Ye shall Swear, That ye shall be good and true to our Sovereign Lady Queen Anne, and to the Heirs of our said Sovereign Lady the Queen. Obeysont and Obedient shall ye be to the Mayor and Ministers of this City, the Franchise and Customs thereof. Ye shall maintain, and this City keep harmless in that which is in you is. Ye shall be contributing to all manner of charges within this City as Summons, Watches, Contributions, Taxes, Tallages, Lot and Scott, and all other Charges, bearing your part as a Freeman ought to do. Ye shall know no Forreigner to buy or sell any Merchandise with any other Forreigners within this City or Franchise thereof, but ye shall warn the Mayor thereof, or some Minister of the Mayors, Ye shall implead or sue no Free-man out of this City, whilst ye may have Right

43. Scharf, J. T., and Westcott, T., *History of Philadelphia*, vol. I, p. 245.
44. Peterson, A. E., and Edwards, G. W., *New York as an Eighteenth Century Municipality*, p. 233.

and Law within the same. Ye shall take no Apprentice, but if he be free-born (that is to say) no Bond-man's son, nor the Son of an Alien, and for no less term than for four years, without fraud or deceit ; and within the first year ye shall cause him to be enrolled, or else pay such Fine as shall be reasonably imposed upon you for omitting the same ; and after his term ends, within convenient time, being required, ye shall make him free of this City, if he have well and truly served you. Ye shall also keep the Queens Peace in your own Person. Ye shall know of no Gatherings, Conventicles or Conspiracies made against the Queen's Peace, but you shall warn the Mayor thereof, or let it to your power. All these Points and Articles ye shall well and truly keep, according to the Laws and Customs of this City. So help you God.[45]

(C)

Regulation for the benefit of the consumer was equally widespread, but showed equal difficulties. The underlying struggle was between the ideal of a fair price and good quality, and the constant tendency of human nature then as now to 'chisel.' Certainly the present age does not suffer by comparison. Then as now the effectiveness of such regulation depended upon the efforts of the more stable element among the tradesmen themselves towards their own protection, fully as much as upon any agitation on the part of consumers. Bread, meat, and firewood were the three commodities most frequently — and perhaps one might say normally — singled out for regulation ; and

---

45. This oath was an adaptation of the oath taken by freemen of the City of London. It was shortened somewhat in 1731. (Reprint in Seybolt, R. F., *The Colonial Citizen of New York City,* p. 22.)

the 'assize of bread'[46] appears to have continued unabated from the earliest period of corporate existence down to the Revolution in large and (where necessary) small communities alike.[47] By 1770 the Lancaster corporation adopted the mild procedure of calling in the bakers and butchers to give them a hearing, before proclaiming the assize and market regulations.[48] A resolution of the Albany corporation (Dec. 11, 1688) will serve by way of further illustration : 'Whereas divers complaints have been made concerning ye bakers who sell there wheat bread at such dear rates notwithstanding ye cheapness of ye corn, Ordered yt ye bakers and whatever persons who expose bread to sale in this city doe take no more than one penny, half-penny or five stuyvers reward for a loaf of fine wheat bread, which must weigh one pound English weight and ye same finenesse as hitherto they have made, which order to continue for ye space of one whole year after ye date hereof or further order.'[49] It must have been a move popular at least with the consumers when, in 1696, the Albany council took steps to force merchants to sell wheat in Albany to the people at a fixed price which was but one half of what they had been obtaining through shipping it to New York.[50] In 1773 the New York City bakers complained to the council that its law governing the assize of bread was twenty-five years old ; and meanwhile their costs had gone up so much that they no

46. The 'assize' was an ordinance fixing the price, weight, and quality of the commodity.
47. Regulation in South Carolina began in 1750 and was undertaken by the assembly for the entire province. Cf. *South Carolina Gazette*, Apr. 2-9, 1750, which published the elaborate Act in its entirety.
48. Minutes, Lancaster Council, Sept. 29, 1770, Oct. 3, 1771.
49. *Minutes of the Council*, in Munsell, J., *Annals of Albany*, vol. II, p. 103.
50. Howell, G. R., and Tenney, J. (Edit.), *History of the County of Albany*, p. 464.

longer made any money.[51] Such regulation was frequent in the smaller borough towns as well. For example, as late as 1773 the commissioners of New Bern were empowered to regulate the assize of bread.[52] Perhaps we may infer from the petition of the Philadelphia bakers in 1752 to be relieved of this assize, that such price regulation was tolerably effective.[53] Yet in 1750 in Norfolk, when it was decided to fix the price of meat, butter, eggs, bread, and meal, the drafting of a law was referred to a committee, and, so far as the minutes reveal, was never heard of again.[54] The regulation of the quality of the flour consumed in New York City was in the hands of the corporation, and it was alleged that this was much more effective than was the regulation of that for export by the provincial authorities.[55] Certainly there was strong local support for maintaining standards, although the standards were often more nominal than real.[56]

It is recorded that one of the early judgments of the newly chartered corporation of Lancaster was to fine a butcher £5 for 'blowing up' (i.e., inflating his meat by air sealed with tallow).[57] In Annapolis and elsewhere

51. Petition of March 8, 1773/4. MS. in Original Records of the Common Council.
52. *State Records of North Carolina*, vol. XXIII, pp. 916ff. (Chap. XIX.)
53. Scharf, J. T., and Westcott, T., *History of Philadelphia*, vol. I, p. 245.
54. Council Orders, Norfolk Borough, 1736-1798 (MSS. in city clerk's office, Norfolk). June 24, 1756, an ordinance fixing the price of bread was carried.
55. Peterson, A. E., and Edwards, G. W., *New York as an Eighteenth Century Municipality*, p. 266f.
56. Cf. Petition of Merchants to City Council ; *Minutes of Common Council, N. Y. C.*, January, 1733/4 (vol. IV, p. 169f.). 'Many Great Frauds & Abuses for divers years have been and still dailey are practiced and Committed . . .' which, if continued, will ruin the reputation of the flour merchants of the City. It was signed by many of the most influential merchants.
57. Riddle, W., *The Story of Lancaster*, pp. 38ff.

similar punishments for this offence are recorded.[58] Penalties were dealt out for short measures in bread and cordwood, and 'measurers' came frequently to be included in the growing roster of municipal officials. A particularly illuminating incident occurred in New York in 1763 — one of the type which revealed the underlying economic forces at work. The butchers and the country folk had combined to raise the price of meat ; and the city council had stepped in to check the rise with fairly successful regulation.[59] However, this not only stirred up a certain amount of defiance in the city, but brought retaliation in the legislature.[60] Thus early appeared the cleavage between farm and city, of which other evidences were to occur down through American municipal history.[61]

The quality of other articles was regulated from time to time in one or more communities. In Wilmington (N. C.) in 1765, an ordinance concerning milk was introduced with the preamble, 'Whereas great abuses are daily committed by mixing milk with water and other such mixtures and afterwards exposing such milk for sale in the said borough.'[62] A by-law in Annapolis dealing with frauds in the sale of butter was short-lived.[63] In New York City, 1737, the quality of bricks was specified.[64] Incidental regulation of charges for night's lodging occa-

---

58. Annapolis Mayor's Court Records, Jan. 31, 1758. Cf. Appendix B.
59. Cf. petition of inhabitants, Aug. 15, 1763, asking for revision downward of the assize of meat on account of the plenty following the end of the French and Indian War (MS. in Original Records of Common Council).
60. Peterson and Edwards, op. cit., p. 280f.
61. Cf. p. 343f.
62. Waddell, A. M., *History of New Hanover County*, p. 197.
63. Records, Annapolis City Corporation, Feb. 29, 1759 ; *Maryland Gazette*, June 19, 1766.
64. McBain, H. L., 'Legal Status of the American Colonial City,' in the *Polit. Sci. Quart.*, vol. XL, p. 198f.

sionally accompanied licensing of taverns.[65] Tobacco was
frequently made the subject of regulation, but more in
connection with its export from port towns. In Charleston (S. C.) in 1764, the grand jury presented 'as a Grievance, the want of a proper officer whose sole business shall
be, to see, that the Firewood sold in Charlestown be duly
measured, and to prevent forestalling the same to the
great detriment of the poor.'[66] A letter published in the
South Carolina Gazette the following February emphasized the evil, and called upon the fellow citizens to 'rouze
them' and 'instruct our Representatives ; petition the
General Assembly for a proper law ; apply for an Act to
Incorporate the Town, or do any Thing else that becomes
us, to extirpate this Evil of the Blackest Dye.'[67]

Towards the end of the period efforts in the direction
of protecting the consumer took the form more and more
of efforts towards honest weights and measures, foreshad-
owing the later standardization of such practice.[68] The
Wilmington (Del.) code drafted in town meeting, July
24, 1741, was one of the most comprehensive. After fixing
an elaborate assize of bread, it proceeded to order the
purchase at borough expense of a set of standard weights
and measures. The clerk of the market, the high constable, and such others as the burgesses might direct were
to conduct at least semi-annual inspections, and 'no person shall presume to Buy or sell by any weights or measures than such as have been first tryed by the standard
and duly marked . . .' The clerk is to be paid fees for all

65. e. g. Annapolis Records, Jan. 27, 1767.
66. *South Carolina Gazette,* Nov. 5-12, 1764.
67. Ibid. Jan. 26-Feb. 2, 1765.
68. e. g. Norfolk, June 24, 1762 (Council Orders — Norfolk Borough,
    1736-1798). 'Yet the petition (Feb. 11, 1772) for sworn measures was
    rejected as outside the Council's jurisdiction.' Cf. also Philadelphia,
    as early as Aug. 14, 1713 (*Minutes of the Common Council*).

measures 'made just' by him. Surprise inspections of weight of butter were ordered. Other items were beer, ale, milk, cordwood.[69] New York City (1775) required an oath of its licensed measurers that they will report instantly to the proper authorities any inferior quality of grain or seed.[70]

Perhaps the extent of inspection can best be indicated by listing the various officers in one or two communities whose task it was to carry out these local ordinances. In Baltimore, the assembly in 1771 authorized the town commissioners to appoint inspectors for flour, staves, grain, salt, flax, hay, and cordwood.[71] In New Haven, 1762, the following officers (among others) were chosen : eight branders, a gauger and packer, a sealer of leather, a sealer of weights, a sealer of measures, an excise master.[72] In Newburyport, 1764, the newly incorporated town chose the following (among others) : three cullers of staves and hoops, eight surveyors of lumber, two cullers of fish, five clerks of the market, two sealers of leather, one hayward, one sealer of weights and measures. Subsequently, two measurers of salt and sea coal were added.[73] Actually there appear to have been more offices to be filled than residents eligible to fill them.

It was, however, chiefly in connection with the markets and fairs that such regulation was most in evidence.[74] The right to hold these institutions was highly valued and the grant of a charter ordinarily carried such a right

69. Wilmington Minutes. This was but part of a more comprehensive market code, re forestalling, hucksters, etc.
70. Ordinance, Feb. 9, 1775, Minutes of Common Council.
71. Griffith, T. W., Annals of Baltimore, p. 47.
72. Gipson, L. H., Jared Ingersoll, New Haven, 1920, p. 24.
73. Currier, J. J., History of Newburyport, Newburyport, 1906-09, p. 26f.
74. Cf. Sellers, Leila, Charleston Business on the Eve of the Revolution, Chapel Hill, 1934, pp. 21-23, for an excellent description of a market of colonial days.

with it.[75] It has also been noted that in certain colonies, some of the towns — usually shire towns — were granted a similar privilege. From the standpoint of the corporation, the fees and rents normally forthcoming were a major source of revenue ; from the standpoint of the inhabitants generally, particularly those who sold in the market, the grant of such a privilege meant enhancement of profits through the attraction the markets — and even more the fairs — held for people from miles around. If the number of stalls was limited, competition was keen to possess them, whether open bids or sub-letting were the practice.[76] It was occasionally a matter of some dispute whether or not the markets were an advantage to the consumers, though generally they were welcomed. In Boston, it was feared that their establishment would encourage forestalling (i.e., the buying up or cornering of goods in advance in order to fix higher prices) ; and it was only after several very close votes at town meeting that three markets were established in 1734. In 1737 the meeting voted that two of the markets should be put to other uses, and a mob tore down the third one. However, in 1740, by a close vote of 367 to 360, the offer of Peter Faneuil to build and present a market was accepted on condition that 'the market people should be at liberty to carry their marketing wheresoever they pleased about

75. It was a dispute relative to opening an additional market place that played a large part in the events leading up to the Wilmington (Del.) charter of 1739. There was rivalry between the poorer people associated with Willing in the lower part of the town and Shipley and his group in the upper part, even resulting in disorders. The charter vested the power to select market sites in the borough meeting, which forthwith (Dec. 10, 1739) voted for both sites. (Wilmington Minute Book.)

76. e. g. Philadelphia, where additional stalls were ordered when it was discovered that sub-letting was taking place at several times the rent charged by the city (*Minutes of the Common Council*, Nov. 24, Dec. 29, 1718).

town.' Between 1746 and 1753, it was alternately voted opened and closed ; but was finally opened in the latter year and remained open.[77] In Savannah, on the other hand, the colony appointed commissioners to establish a market, because 'great˚Extortions, Impositions, and Ir-regularities have been Committed by Forestallers, In-grossers, . . . etc. . . . for want of a Market.'[78] Thus sales outside the market were frequently forbidden. An ordinance of Annapolis, 1717, is worth quoting : 'none of the inhabitants . . . shall buy any flesh or fish, living or dead, eggs, butter, or cheese (oysters excepted) at their own houses, but shall repair to and buy the same at the flagstaffe on the state house hill, until such a time as there shall be a market house built — on penalty of 16/8 . . . And that the market shall be opened at 8 or 9 o'clock . . . and that the drum beats half quarter of an hour to give notice thereof, and that no person presumes to buy anything until the drum be done beating, and that the market days be on Wednesday and Saturday.'[79] As late as 1754 the same city passed a by-law fining any one 20s. who 'shall presume to buy or cause to be bought from anybody bringing Victuals into the city, except at the specified hours and days at the Market House.'[80]

In the Lancaster charter of 1742 the office of the clerk of the market was specifically connected with the assize. In New York City the corporation simplified its problem

77. Quincy, J., *Municipal History of Boston*, p. 11f.
78. *Colonial Records of Georgia*, Atlanta, 1904-06 (A. D. Candler, Edit.), 26 vol., vol. XVIII (Colonial Acts), pp. 8off.
79. Ridgely, D., *Annals of Annapolis*, Baltimore, 1841, p. 122.
80. *Maryland Gazette*, Feb. 5, 1754. Cf. also ordinance (undated) of New Brunswick forbidding the sale of any food except on market day at the market (Scott, A., *Charter and Early Ordinances of New Bruns-wick*, New Brunswick, 1913 ; cf. also the ordinance of Norfolk, Dec. 20, 1736, establishing the market, fixing fees, and prohibiting sales elsewhere (Council Orders — Norfolk Borough, 1736-1798).

of collections in 1741 by letting the whole market by auction to the highest bidder, who then sublet the concessions.[81] In general, the 'market house' was one of the principal public buildings and the opening of a new house always was an event in the simple colonial days.[82]

Here, also, the action of a city reveals the impact of economic interest.[83] Thus in Philadelphia (1773) a great controversy arose over an additional market house, people tearing down at night what was built in the day time. The initial decision to build had apparently been forced by the strength of the rural legislators in the assembly ; whereas the local opposition was probably monopolistic and selfish in nature — although its slogans included 'swallowing up the people's liberties' and other stereotypes with which to this day vested interests deck out their case. In any event the corporation abandoned its attempt, and enlarged the existing markets.[84]

Even more than the market, the annual or semi-annual fair had become, not merely a place for trade, but a social institution. Restrictions of conduct as well as trade were quite commonly ignored, and the carnival spirit ruled. Of course, disputes were bound to arise in connection with its commerce ; and for the settlement of these, the ancient 'court of piepowder' held at the fairgrounds or-

81. Peterson, A. E., and Edwards, G. W., *New York as an Eighteenth Century Municipality*, p. 277.
82. e. g. Norfolk, which in 1757 as a growing city obtained permission to hold markets as often as it wished instead of three days a week, and to build a new market house. (Hening's *Virginia Statutes*, vol. VII, p. 137.)
83. Cf. also the petition of the New York City butchers, August 26, 1735, alleging discrimination in use of the market house, in favour of 'the country people who have acted as if they only had a right to use these Markets.' The result of the petition was a decision to let the stalls to the highest bidder and to do away with certain fees to the clerk of the market. (*Minutes, Common Council*, Sept. 16, 1735.)
84. Scharf, J. T., and Westcott, T., *History of Philadelphia*, vol. I, p. 266.

dinarily sufficed. In the absence of alternative amusements and distractions, these fairs were the great occasions of the year at which people spent their meagre savings in purchase — and, it must be feared, in debauchery as well. Ordinarily a fair lasted two or more days. 'They were attended by all classes, some to make purchases, others for a frolic ; horse-racing, drinking, gambling, and stealing were the prevailing amusements and customs. On the last day of the fair, masters permitted their slaves to attend, and the latter regarded the day as a grand jubilee.'[85]

As to the more strictly commercial aspect, the advertisement of the city of Burlington as it appeared in the *Pennsylvania Gazette* of October 18, 1764, is worth quoting as typical :

City of Burlington, Oct. 5, 1764.

The public is hereby advertised, that in order to promote the bringing of Horses, Cattle, Sheep, and Swine to the Fairs held in the City of Burlington, . . . for Sale, that Corporation has provided . . . Lots . . . free of Charge, for the reception of such Beasts as may be brought for that purpose. The Corporation also invite all Persons to bring to the said Fairs all kinds of Linen and Woolen Manufactures, of this and the neighbouring Colonies ; and for the Encouragement of those who shall furnish such Manufactures, four convenient Stalls will be assigned them Gratis for those Commodities only. The Fairs are held twice in every Year, viz. on the 12th and 13th Days of November ; and on the 21st and 22nd Days of May.

By order of the Corporation,
Samuel Allinson, Clerk.

85. Bolles, A. S., *Pennsylvania, Province and State,* vol. II, p. 269 (concerning Bristol fair).

Sometimes the sales were (as in Lancaster)[86] restricted to freemen; but more commonly all and sundry were invited, and the appropriate fees collected.[87] Occasionally the inhabitants were exempt from such fees.[88]

By the eve of the Revolution, either because of a quickened conscience or because of the veritable nuisance which the fairs had become, a number of New Jersey and Pennsylvania towns took steps to bring them to an end. In Bristol, for example, 'the carousing and worldliness troubled the worthy leaders of the borough, and consequently, in 1773, they resolved that the fair was no longer needed because stores were so numerous; and that the debauchery, idleness, and drunkenness consequent on the meeting of the lowest class of people were real evils, and called for redress. They had no authority to abolish them, as they were granted by charter and though urging the Legislature to do this for them, that body did not comply until 1796.'[89] A similar petition on the part of the Philadelphia city council in 1775 had more success, and the assembly abolished them for ever.[90] Abolitions in New Jersey began with Trenton's surrender of charter in 1750. This was followed by Salem in 1764 and Greenwich, 1765; and by Burlington, Princeton, and Windsor in

86. Klein, H. M. J. (Edit.), *Lancaster County — A History*, New York, 1924, 4 vol., vol. I, p. 322.
87. e. g. New Jersey. Cf. Scott, Austin, *Early Cities of New Jersey*, in *N. J. Hist. Soc. Coll.*, 2nd ser., vol. IX, p. 158.
88. e. g. Wilmington (Del.), by town meeting resolution, Oct. 20, 1740. (Wilmington Minute Book.)
89. Bolles, A. S., *Pennsylvania, Province and State*, vol. II, p. 269f.
90. This was rather more than the corporation had wanted, and it protested to the governor against being deprived of possible future rights therein (*Minutes of Common Council*, Apr. 3, 1775). Cf. also Scharf, J. T., and Westcott, T., *History of Philadelphia*, vol. I, p. 294.

1772.[91] The fair as an institution had had a long and eventful history, adding much to the glamour of the somewhat drab life of the period ; but in the old form its days were numbered.

Perhaps enough has already been written to indicate the peculiar position in the regulated economy of the period occupied by the 'port-town.'[92] The legal definition of a port was summarized about 1700 by the attorney general and solicitor general in reply to an enquiry by the Board of Trade in connection with the rival claims of Perth Amboy and New York :

We are humbly of opinion that a Port in our Law is understood to be a place appointed for the lading and unlading of Goods and Merchandise, for the better Collecting his Majesties Customes and other Duties And that such Ports (by an Act made the 25th Car. IInd. Chap. 7th For better Securing ye Plantac'on Trade) are to be appointed in the plantac'ons by the Commissioners of the Customes in England by and under the authority and directions of the Lord Treasurer or Com'issioners of the Treasury, in the respective plantations, for the Collecting such Customes as are due to his Majestie in those plantac'ons.[93]

In proprietary colonies, the proprietor naturally re-

91. *N. J. Archives,* 1st. ser., vol. XXIV, p. 332 ; Whitehead, W. A., *Early History of Perth Amboy,* New York, 1856, p. 306. Wilmington (Del.) also passed an ordinance restricting the sale of liquor at fair time to the usual taverns (Minutes of Burgesses and Assistants, Sept. 26, Oct. 8, 1774).
92. Cf. pp. 55ff.
93. *N. J. Archives,* 1st ser., vol. III, p. 177f. It must be borne in mind, however, that the power to establish such ports was normally granted to proprietors, and eventually it was held that it had been so granted by implication to the Duke of York and then [specifically] by him to the Jersey proprietors. Cf. below, pp. 358ff.

served or attempted to reserve their determination to himself ; but in the royal provinces the last word belonged to the officials in the mother country as part of the regulation of customs. All through the seventeenth century, there was a constant rivalry among the colonial communities for the coveted privilege of being designated as a 'port' — for the growth and prosperity it would mean to the community. Perth Amboy and New York waged a continuous struggle in asserting their 'rights' and otherwise seeking to deflect shipping, until the ensuing century witnessed the passing of most of these attempts to enforce monopoly of clearances.[94] Maryland and Virginia tried the contrasting experiments of creating 'sole ports' and of incorporating them in large numbers. Neither attempt was really successful.[95] North Carolina abandoned the attempt at this type of control when it was discovered that the net result was to divert trade to Virginia.[96] So much was its 'staple right' considered in the nature of a vested right by New York City that it even asked for financial compensation when the territories of New Jersey and Delaware were detached in 1685 ; though no apparent action was taken with regard to the protest.[97] In April, 1697, the common council memorialized the sovereign in no uncertain terms, asking him to annul the Act of the assembly repealing the Bolting Act. They mentioned the interruption of the growing and flourishing state of the city ; the implied opposition to the royal prerogative that had granted that New York City be

94. Cf. pp. 358ff. Order of Lords of Trade to Governor Dongan, Aug. 14, 1687 ; Order of Proprietors to Mr. Laurie, Sept. 21, 1683 ; Representations of Proprietors to the King, June, 1687, etc.
95. Cf. pp. 55, 57.
96. Instituted 1741 ; repealed 1745 (*State Records of North Carolina*, vol. XXIII, p. 219).
97. *New Jersey Archives*, 1st. ser., vol. I, p. 491f.

'the only granary of all your majesties plantations in America'; that it had served well in this capacity, whereas now 'The cry in the streets is the want of bread, tho' it be after one of the plentifullest harvests.'[98] Instructions to the governors continually stressed the policy of reserving the Hudson River and the Indian Trade to New York.[99] Of the larger towns, New York City seems to have put up the longest struggle, and probably its position at the mouth of the Hudson made a measure of success possible. It finally lost the last of such exclusive privileges in 1771.[100] Elsewhere the coast line was too long and the harbours too numerous to channel trade so rigidly at a time when smuggling was an honourable profession. Thus in the eighteenth century such restrictions came to be fewer in number. In any event they had been largely provincial or even English in their enforcement, rather than municipal. Apart from enhanced trade, the interest of the municipality had been primarily in the wharf and dock revenues.

Regulation or intervention of other types did occur, but was not usual. The Albany council in 1751 offered a bounty to any one discovering minerals within the city limits.[101] The Chamber of Commerce of New York City dates from 1768, and its opinions immediately became influential with the city fathers.[102] Among its avowed pur-

98. April, 1697, MS. in Original Records of Common Council.
99. Labaree, L. W., *Royal Instructions to British Governors*, vol. II, p. 661.
100. Inspecting and packing of flour were made legal in the four other counties. (Peterson, A. E., and Edwards, G. W., *New York as an Eighteenth Century Municipality*, p. 267.)
101. 'Minutes of Albany Council,' Aug. 15, 1751, in Munsell, J., *Annals of Albany*, vol. X, p. 143.
102. For example, it recommended certain by-laws or acts dealing with fair business practice. These were usually passed by the city council or the assembly. (Stevens, J. A., Jr., *Colonial Records of the N. Y. Chamber of Commerce, 1768-1784*, New York, 1867, pp. 59, 71, etc. *Minutes, Common Council*, June 7, Mar. 21, 1770.)

poses was to procure 'such laws and regulations as may be found necessary for the benefit of trade in general.' Early Virginia incorporations (also Annapolis) granted liberal subsidies to attract artisans.[103] Germantown in its early days regulated the branding of horses and the location of mill sites.[104] New York City licensed the masters of vessels.[105] But these were exceptional, and were ordinarily accounted for by some peculiar local problem or event.

(D)

How far did this regulation of commerce and trade reflect itself in the governmental structure of the corporations ? As far as the crafts or the guilds were concerned, for all practical purposes not at all. No American city wove into its structure of municipal government the guild hall, or common hall, or the various 'liveries' as did London and a number of other British cities. After all, even in England the life had gone out of the guilds so far as their playing a part in promoting incorporations was concerned ; and the American incorporations of the seventeenth century took place before the particular communities were large enough to have developed a guild organization. By the eighteenth century these guild institutions in their capacity of regulators were dying. Such regulation as remained was in the hands of the borough court — or more probably had passed to the assembly. The nearest that American towns came to such incorporation in their actual structure was in the aforemen-

---

103. Cf. p. 93. For Annapolis, 1718, cf. Riley, E. S., *The Ancient City*, p. 96f.
104. Pennypacker, S. W., 'Settlement of Germantown,' in *Proc., Penn.-German Soc.*, vol. IX, pp. 326, 333.
105. McBain, H. L., 'Legal Status of the American Colonial City,' in *Pol. Sci. Quart.*, vol. XL, p. 198f.

tioned abortive attempts of Virginia in 1680 and 1705 to create town organizations. These were to have merchant guilds, and the governing board was to be known as 'benchers of the guild hall,' all of whom must be members of the merchant guild.[106] But these acts were disallowed, and nothing came of the grandiose plans. Merchant and craft guilds were indeed formed from time to time in colonial towns, but left no trace upon the governmental structure, in spite of the influence they wielded in affecting governmental policy. It is possible that an exception should be made of the 'cape company' of Williamsburg merchants formed in 1750, in view of the fact that it apparently regulated exchanges, meeting twice a year for this purpose.[107]

The system of detailed regulation did leave a trail of various officials behind it, some of whom were retained after their functions were largely obsolete — but this was all.[108]

One exception, and an important one, may be granted. Apprenticeship was at least in the larger communities still a normal path to 'freedom' of the city ; and, in so far as freedom involved the right to vote for officials, may be said to have incorporated the craft structure into the town government of places like New York. Yet freedom was ordinarily so easily acquired, and voting so frequently associated with freeholding that the implication of such an acquisition of freedom by apprenticeship was by no means as great as in the average British city recognizing the practice. Notice of the extent to which

106. Berkley, H. J., 'Extinct River Towns of Chesapeake Bay,' in *Md. Hist. Mag.*, vol. XIX, pp. 127ff.
107. Tyler, L. G., *Williamsburg, The Old Colonial Capital,* Richmond. 1907, p. 20.
108. Cf. pp. 184ff.

the various trades influenced the elections must be left till later.[109]

(E)

One major interpretation runs through the economic activities of these municipalities. It is the old, old story — the utilization of the weapon of governmental action in economic warfare. The ordinances may be clothed in emotional symbols ; they may include considerations of health and morals ; but by and large these ordinances represented economic stress and strain in an age in which the struggle was hard. The precise location of the franchise influenced the nature of the ordinances, resulting perhaps in New York City and Lancaster paying more attention to protecting craftsmen and shopkeeping than did Philadelphia and Norfolk ; whereas almost without exception all groups were ready to unite against the foreigner or the itinerant huckster.

All in all, the impact of these municipal corporations upon the economic life of their day forms a striking and interesting episode in American municipal development. These were indeed 'free cities' as those of our present era never can be. No longer can the course of trade or the development of craftsmanship be confined or regulated by any unit so narrow as the city. Even the state no longer seems adequate.

By 1775 this all-inclusive concept of the municipality had yielded to the force of circumstance ; and only the hollow shell of limited trade regulation remained. The local monopolies were largely passing ; the fairs were losing ground ; markets were no longer exclusive ; the regulation of price and quality alone gave signs of real vi-

109. Cf. pp. 364ff.

tality, even though confining itself to obviously glaring abuses ; its detailed and intimate quality had been relegated to the limbo of a former age. Exclusive port cities and staple rights had gone for ever from American experience. The province was taking up the control of trade where the city had left off — and at this stage came the American Revolution.

VII

THE INTERNAL CONSTITUTION OF COLONIAL BOROUGHS

THUS far this study has been confined largely to the powers of the boroughs and the reasons for their incorporation. In their study of the English borough, the Webbs pointed out that it was this bundle of rights and privileges which was the primary and all-important fact in an incorporation. Maitland in writing of an earlier period stated : 'During the Middle Ages, the function of the Royal Charter was not that of "erecting a corporation" or of regulating a corporation that already existed, but that of bestowing liberties and franchises upon a body, which, within large limits, was free to give itself a constitution from time to time.'[1] As the Webbs discovered, in the seventeenth and eighteenth centuries changes even as radical as the establishing of a 'close' body were introduced by a mere by-law or standing order ; and the type of structure set up in a charter formed no real guide as to the type in actual operation. They found it necessary to examine local usage for the necessary information. The set of powers and privileges was primary ; the constitution secondary.[2]

Because of their more recent establishment and relatively short term of functioning, no statement so drastic as this can be made concerning the colonial incorporations ; and the structure set up in the charter furnishes a much more reliable guide than in England. The most striking and perhaps the only example of a democratic corporation becoming 'close' through usage was Annap-

1. Cf. also Maitland, F. W., *Township and Borough*, pp. 85, 98 ; Webb, B. and S., *The Manor and the Borough*, p. 271.
2. Webb, B. and S., *The Manor and the Borough*, pp. 271-275.

olis. The minutes are largely lost, but by 1720 the existing members of the corporation were co-opting to fill such vacancies as occurred.³ When the restoration of popular rights took place, I have been unable to discover ; but when the minutes are again extant (1757), elections for vacancies were by the freeholders, etc., as provided in the original charter.⁴

A shorter span of existence also meant that there was relatively less variety than in England, where vestiges and customs of former ages were preserved intact long after the reasons for them were forgotten. Not that there was any lack of variety in American charters, as we have noted on occasion ; but, inasmuch as these charters for the most part were actually drawn up in America, it is probable that memories were blurred a bit. Thus a simplification of outline took place by comparison with those English charters which, as a part of the remembered experience of at least some of the draftsmen, were used as patterns. That such a simplification did take place — particularly when a document was drafted for what it was hoped would be a city, rather than to meet the practical needs of what already existed — can be noted in the plan drawn up by that theoretician, Locke, for the potential boroughs of the Carolina Palatinate : 'All towns incorporate shall be governed by a mayor, twelve aldermen, and twenty-four of the common council. The

3. Minutes in Proceedings of the Mayor's Court, Sept. 29, 1720 and Sept. 6, 1721.
4. City Records, Feb. 9, 1760. One other fairly drastic alteration by usage may have taken place in Perth Amboy, where there is some evidence that the four aldermen prescribed in the first charter were reduced to two, one for each ward. An Act of N. J. Assembly (ch. DXLIX, 1771) speaks of *either* of the aldermen. The 1753 charter is apparently missing, and the post-Revolutionary 1784 charter specified 'Aldermen not exceeding three.' The Minutes of Germantown, Dec. 2, 1706, show three burgesses instead of the four customarily chosen.

said common council shall be chosen by the present householders of the said town ; the aldermen shall be chosen out of the common council ; and the mayor out of the aldermen, by the Palatine's court.'[5] It would not have been easy to find in all England any municipality possessing such a rhythmic charter.

A second major factor in this tendency to simplification has been noted already in another connection. This was the almost total absence of guild organization in any American municipality at the time its charter was framed.[6] Then, too, there were not the onslaughts upon the charters by sovereigns interested in controlling Parliament, or the subsequent period of uncertainty which resulted in curious combinations of the old and the new. Yet variety there undoubtedly was, springing in part from the somewhat blurred difference felt (but never clearly expressed) between town, borough, and city ; in part from the numerous incorporating 'persons' of thirteen separate colonies ; in part from other and local factors — time, place, experience, need.

(B)

In any attempt at analysis is no basis of classification of framework is wholly satisfactory, but perhaps the most useful is found in grouping the incorporations into three main groups — the 'towns,' the 'minor' boroughs, and the more elaborately organized boroughs and cities. The distinction between the latter two groups is by no means clear. Size had something to do with it, but the distinction was really primarily subjective, and its best criterion lay in whether or not the incorporation was vested with

5. Cf. p. 35.
6. Cf. p. 158f.

a full-fledged set of officers — mayor, recorder, aldermen, councillors or assistants ; or confined to a smaller group — perhaps a burgess or two and assistants. Even here the distinction broke down in certain instances, and the gradations which separated the various categories were always more or less minute. A fourth type should possibly be added — that which was evolved from certain Dutch incorporations, when taken over by the English.

It is unnecessary and largely outside the sphere of this study to do much more than mention the incorporated towns. New England for the most part was organized around the town meeting, with its selectmen or deputies or council assuming the necessary administrative responsibility between times. Rhode Island, in 1733, excluded the justices of the peace from sitting on the town councils because 'several of the inhabitants within the respective towns . . . are dissatisfied . . . that . . . there are more justices than town councilmen, whereby the towns are defeated of the privilege of having their prudential affairs carried on by persons of their own choosing.'[7] Thus Rhode Island, where there had hitherto been the greatest deviation from type, brought its town government more or less in line with the rest of New England. Towns elsewhere were for the most part governed by trustees or commissioners, usually appointed by the colonial assemblies (with power to co-opt) from the county justices.[8] To these latter they were frequently responsible. Later (or even initially, if the town grew) the commissioners might come to be locally elected. In a highly developed corporate town, like Gloucester

7. Quoting the preamble of the Act, in Stokes, H. K., *Finances and Administration of Providence,* Baltimore, 1903, p. 70f.
8. In Annapolis, 1696, they were largely chosen from colonial office-holders (Mereness, N. D., *Maryland as a Proprietary Province,* p. 417).

(N. J.), its overseers of the poor and of highways might be distinct from those of the separately incorporated township.[9] The North Carolina 'boroughs' often evolved by way of the 'commissioner' stages, and the majority of them never outgrew it. Under the 1739 incorporation of Wilmington (N. C.), the town commissioners were named in the act and given power to co-opt their successors. In 1740, the inhabitants were given the right to nominate five, from whom the governor was to select three ; but this was exceptional, and in 1745 in Wilmington all were made popularly elective.[10]

The towns or borough towns of Burlington and Salem (N. J.) and Chester may be thought of as transitional in their organization from the town with commissioners to the simpler type of distinctively municipal organization. In Burlington (1694) and Salem (1695) a 'burgess' appeared, who was the head of the town and who was vested with judicial powers. Both towns had recorders. Salem had a bailiff ; Burlington two councillors, a treasurer, and a town clerk. By charter Chester was to have four burgesses and a high constable and such other officers as the town meeting directed. These three communities represent the very simplest form which, in spirit and terminology, might be deemed to constitute a 'borough.' All three retained the town meeting, and in Chester the 'borough' part of the organization seemingly soon dwindled to the election annually of the chief burgess only.[11]

The second type of municipal organization, the 'minor' borough, was characterized by a 'head,' known as a bur-

9. Heston, A. M. (Edit.), *South Jersey — A History,* vol. I, p. 355, quoting Mickle, I., *Reminiscences of Old Gloucester.*
10. *State Records of North Carolina,* vol. XXIII, pp. 133, 146ff., 234f.
11. Cf. p. 434.

gess or bailiff (bailey), and a relatively smaller number of assistants or councillors.[12] Lancaster and Bristol had two burgesses, but one seems to have been designated as 'chief.' To this type belong Newcastle (1672), Bristol, Lancaster, Wilmington (Del.). The one or two burgesses were usually the only ones vested with judicial power.[13] Bristol apparently had four burgesses at its inception, but by 1732 its minutes show that it was functioning with two burgesses and six common councilmen.[14] This was a rare instance in which by charter the borough might largely determine its internal structure by local action without authorization from a higher authority.[15] Newcastle (1672) had a bailey (bailiff) and six assistants. Ordinarily these variously designated officials were ultimately to be chosen by the people, but in the first instance were usually named in the charter. Collectively in each instance they constituted the administrative court to draft the necessary by-laws, a power frequently shared

12. 'Assistants' in Newcastle, Lancaster ; 'assistant burgesses' in Wilmington (Del.) ; 'councillors' in Bristol.

13. It is worth re-quoting the functions of the Wilmington burgesses as outlined in the letters patent setting up the corporation. They were empowered 'to be conservators of the peace within the said borough, with power . . . to remove all nuisances and incroachments on the streets and highways . . . and also to arrest, imprison and punish rioters and other breakers of the peace, and to bind them and all other offenders . . . to the court of General Quarter Sessions of the Peace of the said county of New Castle . . . and to do and perform all and singular other matters and things within the said borough, as fully and effectually to all intents and purposes, as Justices of the Peace in their respective counties could or might lawfully do.' Cf. p. 19.

14. Increased to nine, Sept. 9, 1748, probably by town meeting ; reduced to seven, Sept. 21, 1761, by a (probably illegal) vote of the council itself — unless ratified subsequently by town meeting (Bristol, Minute Book, 1730-1825, MS. in office of city clerk).

15. The Bristol charter provided for burgesses, named two, and 'all such other Officers . . . for serving and assisting the Burgesses in managing the affairs of the said Borough in keeping of the peace . . . from time to time as the said Electors or the majority of them shall seem requisite and necessary.'

with the town meeting ;[16] and they (or the borough town meeting) were vested with authority to choose the usual minor officials. In all this group (except Newcastle), a 'high constable' appeared who was the executive arm of the 'court' (judicially speaking), and who had charge of the enforcement of by-laws, etc. In Bristol he served also as clerk of the market.[17] In certain instances he appears to have been at least a regular attendant upon, and possibly a voting member of the governing body.[18]

It will be noted that this group of minor boroughs — and also Burlington and Salem — lie entirely in the adjacent colonies of New Jersey, Pennsylvania, and Delaware ; and it is not unfair to conjecture that this fact may have had some influence on the similarity of type and terminology. Certainly, in Pennsylvania 'boroughs' the similarity was apparently deliberate and did represent a conscious differentiation from the 'city' of Philadelphia. It seems to have provided — characteristically in conjunction with the town or borough meeting — a simple and satisfactory government for small communities.

The earlier incorporation of the borough of Germantown and the royal charter organizations (1760 and after) of Wilmington (N. C.), Edenton, New Bern, and Halifax, probably belong to the third or full-fledged type of corporation ; but they may be considered intermediate between types two and three in certain particulars.[19] Germantown was headed by a bailiff, but for the administrative court (known as the general court) there were

16. In Bristol, ordinance power rested with the town meeting, but by 1732 the meeting of the common council was called 'town meeting' in the minutes.
17. By charter.
18. e. g. Bristol, for which see its Minutes of the Council.
19. Bristol may be deemed to have evolved into this 'intermediate' type by usage, rather than by charter (cf. p. 181).

added four burgesses and six 'committee.' Only the bailiff and the oldest three burgesses (with the recorder) made up the formal 'court of record,' and only the bailiff and the oldest two burgesses were given the powers of justices of the peace. Were the records of this short-lived borough more complete, it would be interesting to trace whether or not these distinctions were observed in practice.[20] In Wilmington (N. C.) the charter specified a mayor, recorder, and eleven aldermen ; the mayor to be selected annually by the freeholders. In 1765, we read of the 'Mayor, Aldermen and Freeholders convened in Common Council.'[21] This probably indicates that the eligible voters were so few that administrative business was customarily transacted in borough meeting. However, the records are scanty, and one cannot be certain. From an examination of the North Carolina records it seems that incorporations were also issued in 1760 for Halifax, Edenton, and New Bern. In the instance of New Bern, the minute reads : 'Upon a petition of the inhabitants of the Town of New Bern Praying that the said Town be Incorporated in the like manner as the Towns of Halifax and Edenton Except that the number of Common Council men be eight instead of twelve which was accordingly granted.'[22] These charters apparently never went into operation and the towns remained under their commissioners.

All other incorporations appear to belong in class three, the most highly developed municipal type. This included a mayor, recorder, aldermen, and common council (or assistants). All but the common councillors had judicial

20. Apparently not, for 'cases' and 'ordinances' follow each other indiscriminately in the *Rathbuch*.
21. Quoted in Waddell, A. M., *History of New Hanover County*, p. 197.
22. *State Records of North Carolina*, vol. VI, p. 333f.

powers and the entire group sat as members of the 'common hall' or 'corporation' or 'council' or administrative court, to manage the city property, decide upon its by-laws, and (where such power was included) levy a rate.[23] The differentiation as to service as county justices or on the city court (of whatever rank) ordinarily seems to have been the only differentiation in powers between the aldermen and the common council or assistants ; but, in so far as the functions of such justices were numerous, the difference may be deemed important.[24] For the usual municipal business they sat together and their votes counted equally. In Albany the 'mayor's court' seems ordinarily to have met on the same day, just prior to the council meetings. In Annapolis there was greater differentiation. The mayor's court maintained the tradition of 'quarter sessions,' while the city corporation — nominally meeting at stated intervals — actually seems to have met only when business warranted.[25] At one period the

23. In Trenton these were known as chief burgess, burgesses, and councilmen (also a recorder) ; in the ill-fated Virginia General Act of 1708, eight 'benchers of the guild hall,' including one director, and fifteen 'brethren assistants' for the 'common council.'

24. In Gorgeana, only two aldermen and the mayor served as justices. In Westchester, the assistants also had judicial powers. A differentiation appearing, so far as I can discover, only in Westchester and (possibly) Schenectady was the vesting of the control of the property of the corporation, not in the mayor, aldermen, etc., but in 'trustees' who were separate juridically, although in practice there was probably an over-lapping of personnel, at least in Westchester. For Schenectady (trustees of Arent Bradt), cf. Pearson, J., et al., History of the Schenectady Patent, p. 431. For a century these lands were the subject of litigation between the community and the trustees.
A similar separation occurred in Annapolis in its second charter, in so far as it was provided that 'the Town Common shall remain with the proper owners.' This type of provision, very frequent in the New England towns, apparently marked an unwillingness to extend into the economic sphere the measure of democracy accorded in the political.

25. Based upon examination of city records 1757-1766, and the scattering records surviving before and after that date.

records of meetings of the entire corporation which survive would apparently indicate that this body concerned itself only with the races held in connection with the annual fair ; and with the (illegal) election of their own successors. The court (i.e., mayor, recorder, aldermen) had in practice usurped a certain amount of authority belonging to the entire body ; but municipal functions were attenuated.[26]

The number of aldermen varied from four to twelve ; the councillors or assistants, from six to twenty-four. The latter number, appearing in the elaborate Gorgeana charter as the 'four and twenty,' may possibly not have been meant literally. This expression, 'four and twenty,' appeared in numerous English incorporations of the day as one of the corporate institutions, and was used with little regard for the actual number included in its membership. It also occurred in the Fundamental Constitutions for the Province of East New Jersey as given by the twenty-four proprietors : 'Foreasmuch as there are not at present so many towns built . . . at present *Four and Twenty* shall be chosen for the eight towns that are at present in being.'[27] It is significant that in the 'Constitutions' the word 'boroughs' is used interchangeably with 'towns.' I have been unable to find any trace of these provisions having been put into operation ; but it is possible that they did operate. In this event they may account for certain obscurities in the early history of Perth Amboy.[28]

The extant charters to be included in this classification of fully developed municipal organisms are : Agamenticus and Gorgeana ; St. Mary's ; Philadelphia, 1691

26. Mayor's Court Proceedings, 1720-1726.
27. Thorpe, F. N., *American Charters, Constitutions, and Organic Laws,*
    vol. V, pp. 2574-82.
28. Cf. p. 431f.

and 1701 ; Albany ; Westchester ; New York, 1686 and
1730 ; Annapolis, 1708 (both charters) ; Williamsburg ;
Norfolk ; Perth Amboy ; Burlington ; New Brunswick ;
Elizabeth ; Trenton ; Schenectady — a considerable majority of the colonial incorporations.

In at least the New Jersey communities, the town or
ward meetings retained or assumed a considerable measure of activity.[29]

Traces of Dutch incorporations in the charters issued
or confirmed by the English will be considered in connection with the former.[30]

It is difficult to find any two methods of selecting officials which were identical. This same characterization
also applies for the most part to tenure and qualifications
for office. In New York, Albany, and Schenectady, mayors
and recorders were appointed by the governor, often
from among the aldermen.[31] The same practice was followed in Perth Amboy, Burlington, and New Brunswick,
but not in Elizabeth and Trenton. Elsewhere it was
more usual to have the head of the city and its recorder
chosen by the aldermen or the entire council. In Westchester and Wilmington (N. C.) the mayor was chosen
by the freeholders ; and this practice appears to have
been frequent among the borough heads of the intermediate category of charters, perhaps indicating that Wilmington itself should have been classed as belonging to
this more simple category.

The aldermen most usually were chosen by the entire
council and normally from the councillors or assistants.

29. Minutes of Burlington township ; Elizabeth Town Book, MS. in
    Princeton University Library ; Charters of New Brunswick (1763)
    and Perth Amboy (1753) ; *Statutes of New Jersey, passim.* Cf. pp.
    233ff.
30. Cf. pp. 233f., 236f., 239f.
31. Cf. p. 375, for popular election of the mayor in New York City in 1689.

However, several instances occur of their popular election — for example, Westchester, New Brunswick, Burlington, and Elizabeth. In Annapolis they were chosen by the mayor, recorder, and aldermen from the councillors.[32]

The councillors or assistants were chosen either by co-option or by a more or less popular vote. This particular distinction served to separate the municipalities into the two groups of 'close' and 'open' corporations, which distinction was noted also in England as being of very considerable significance. The details of this as well as of other aspects of popular participation will be reserved for later discussion.[33]

The tenure of office of the mayor was ordinarily one year, but it was quite common to reappoint or re-elect him. The recorder seemed to have been much more permanent. The aldermen and councillors either retained office 'during good behaviour,' or came up for election annually.[34] In a few cities, the aldermen were semi-permanent, the councillors or assistants elected annually. In the close corporations, permanence of tenure was naturally customary. Few provisions involving removal appear in the charters, and I have not discovered any instance of such removal in colonial times except of Mayor Fishbourne of Philadelphia.[35] Under the Philadelphia charter of 1701, the mayor or another member might be removed by vote of the remainder of the council.

In Schenectady, the 1765 charter provided that the aldermen and assistants should hold office during good

32. Charter and minutes. Cf. Appendix B.
33. Cf. pp. 192-207.
34. Elizabeth, triennially.
35. Cf. p. 391f.

behaviour, but there is some evidence that such dissatisfaction arose from this and certain other provisions, that the corporation voluntarily surrendered its charter almost immediately, and petitioned for a new one which should provide for annual or triennial elections.[36]

Where qualifications for office-holding were specified in the charter, they usually provided that the respective officers should be freeholders, or 'from the freemen,' and should have been residents for a year or two. Philadelphia (1701) included the clause : 'have an estate of inheritance or freehold therein, or are worth fifty pounds in money or other stock, and have been resident in the said city for the space of two years, or shall purchase their freedom of the mayor and Commonalty.'[37] In New Bern the commissioners were made popularly elective in 1756, but were required to have a house 16' x 24' with a brick chimney, together with a visible estate of £100, to be eligible for election.[38] In Williamsburg, in 1742, it was provided that they need not be freeholders, but must be residents at least one year.[39] The actual effect of such provisions where they occurred was more or less negligible, inasmuch as the council was normally chosen from the gentry or merchant class in any event.[40] However, it appears that the democratizing tendencies of the years just prior to the Revolution may have affected Annapolis as well as, for example, New York City. In the minutes of the Annapolis mayor's court for January 29, 1765, the court thought it necessary to give a declaratory judgment as to qualifications in the following terms :

36. Cf. p. 427f. ; also *Cadwallader Colden Papers*, vol. VII, pp. 13ff. (*Coll.*, *N. Y. Hist. Soc.*, 1923) ; Munsell, J., *Annals of Albany*, vol. I, p. 368.
37. This applied to 'freedom' as well as to office holding.
38. *State Records of North Carolina*, vol. XXIII, pp. 451ff.
39. Hening's *Virginia Statutes*, vol. V, pp. 204ff.
40. Cf. pp. 381ff.

That in the original appointment of the Common
Council, it was directed by the Charter that ten of the
most sufficient of the inhabitants should be of the Common Council and it can't be reasonably supposed such
care was taken in the first appointment . . . and so
little care taken of the succession that the most insufficient of the inhabitants might qualify themselves to be
of the Common Council when the making of Bye
Laws, and Ordinances would probably become a more
important duty.

Because every Member of the Corporation is as such,
intitled by the Charter to vote in the Election of Burgesses ; but every Freeholder is not, and it would therefore be unreasonable that ; when a Freehold is required in both instances an Inferior Freehold should
be admitted in the first : for then the result would be
this, vizt. — He who hath a Freehold in a Foot or Inch
of soil is qualified in respect of his Freehold to be of
the Common Council, and as a Member of the Common Council hath Incidentally a right to vote in the
Elections of Burgesses ; but yet no other persons are
Instructed with the priviledge of voting in the Elections of Burgesses, in respect of Freehold, than the
owners of whole lots, etc. — which would be absurd.

Most of these offices, and many of the minor ones, were
ordinarily unpaid ; and several cities retained the English custom of fining those who were unwilling to serve.
This seems to have been usual in the New England towns
also. It was a tradition handed down from an age when
duties were more a corollary of rights than in modern
times. Inasmuch as the claims on a man's time were frequently onerous and the dignity, especially in some of the

smaller boroughs, rather doubtful, there was occasional difficulty in securing suitable men, particularly for the mayoralty. Germantown passed a by-law, 1696, that 'Each and all who are chosen by the general court for any kind of commission or service shall be compelled to enter on such duties and fulfill them faithfully under penalty of three pounds fine.' Exemptions might be granted on the grounds of conscience, youth, age, or a previous year's service.[41] By 1707, however, it apparently proved impracticable to find enough willing to serve even on the court itself, and the borough forfeited its charter. Philadelphia intermittently had difficulty in securing mayors, many choosing to pay the £20-£30 fine rather than serve. In part, this was because of the great expense to which an incumbent was customarily put by way of entertainment. In the decade 1740-1750, Mayor Hamilton started what became more or less of a precedent for a half dozen years by substituting a gift of £150 towards some public building for the usual banquet on retirement.[42] In 1747 the corporation voted its mayor a salary of £100, but even then it was difficult to find willing candidates.[43] The following year this grant was repealed, because 'the business of the mayoralty had grown more profitable,' presumably from the legitimate fees of the office.[44] It is related that in 1747 Alderman Morris went into hiding so that he could not be served with the notice of his elec-

41. Pennypacker, S. W., 'Settlement of Germantown,' in *Penn.-German Soc. Proc.*, vol. IX, p. 331.
42. *Minutes of the Common Council*, Feb. 2, 1753 ; Oct. 4, 1748 ; May 21, 1751 ; etc.
43. Mayor Willing returned the £100 to the city as a gift (*Minutes*, Oct. 3, 1749). The salary was restored in 1760, the 'profits having fallen short of expense' (*Minutes*, Oct. 7, 1760).
44. *Minutes*, Oct. 3, 1749.

tion as mayor, and his wife refused to receive the notice. Hence William Atwood was chosen.[45] By 1760, mayors frequently refused to serve, and the fines became a source of real corporate revenue.[46] Elsewhere, there did not appear to be quite this difficulty, though occasional refusals are noted, with fines usually imposed, but less usually collected.[47]

(C)

Evidence concerning the functioning of these councils, once they were chosen, requires a close study of the minutes — many of which have been lost. It does not appear that the standing committee system gained any very permanent foothold as an administrative device. On the other hand, *ad hoc* or special committees were appointed as the occasion arose. Between 1757 and 1766, the following special committees were recorded in the minutes of the Annapolis city corporation : to employ a surveyor to try the angles of the streets ; to inspect the town fence ; to collect the by-laws ; to superintend the overseer in the repair of the streets ; to inquire into condition of the tobacco inspection house, to collect such sums as were due, and to decide upon a site for a new warehouse. A possible exception to the failure to use the device of standing committees was New York City, which by 1750 appears to have had a certain number of such committees, includ-

45. Biddle, H. D., 'Colonial Mayors of Philadelphia,' in *Penn. Mag. of Hist.,* vol. XIX, p. 65f.
46. Scharf and Westcott, *History of Philadelphia,* op. cit., p. 257. The *Minutes* would point to the statement of Scharf that it had become 'fashionable' not to serve as a bit extreme.
47. Annapolis, in 1746, provided fines also for a sheriff refusing to serve (Minutes of Common Council, 1746). Occasional declinations are revealed in examination of the minutes of Annapolis, Wilmington, Norfolk, Bristol, etc.

ing ones dealing with audit, leases, public improvements, construction of water works.[48]

Everywhere the special committee was used as the accepted device for the transaction of business. To it were entrusted matters as diverse as the drafting of an ordinance, supervision of construction of a market house, inspection of streets, clearing the gutters, audit of accounts, preparation of a petition, 'agreeing with a carpenter' for repairs, preparing of assessment lists. Reports were frequently dilatory, and occasionally substitute committees were named by way of censure. Sometimes the 'unfinished business' was, perhaps conveniently, buried in committee.[49]

By-laws or standing orders governing the conduct of business, where they existed at all, were relatively simple. New York City apparently insisted upon all requests or proposals being made in writing. Philadelphia evolved a set order of business, fairly rigidly followed. Norfolk referred virtually all new business to a special committee, perhaps to gain time for mature consideration by delaying action until the next meeting. As early as 1701, the mayor's court of New York adopted a fairly elaborate procedural code of twenty-one articles.[50]

The meetings were held at the town hall, the county court house, or perhaps in the more genial atmosphere of one of the taverns. For years the minutes of Wilmington (Del.) usually read : 'The burgesses met at the Widow Allison's.' The meetings of the Annapolis corporation and court were in the latter years held regularly at the

48. Peterson, A. E., and Edwards, G. W., *New York as an Eighteenth Century Municipality*, p. 231.
49. Cf. p. 403f. for financial aspects ; p. 296f. for administrative aspects.
50. *Minutes of Mayor's Court*, Apr. 8, 1701.

home (tavern ?) of William Reynolds. The 'Common Hall' and hustings court of Williamsburg, which had long used the county court house of James City County on sufferance, in 1745 acquired the historic Williamsburg playhouse for their meetings. This served till 1770, when with the county court they moved into the new court house.[51]

Only in New York, Perth Amboy, and New Brunswick does there appear to have been any very considerable development of the ward system which was later to play such a part in American municipal affairs. Such a division was specifically requested and granted in the New York charter of 1686, to the effect that 'the Freemen in each ward doe once every yeare elect their own officers' that is to say Aldermen, Common Councilmen, Constable, Overseers of the poore, Assessors, Scavengers, Questmen, or other officers usefull and necessary for the said Corporation and Ward.'[52] By 1688 the aldermen were even allowed to spend for poor relief on their own authority instead of by vote of the council ;[53] but, this not proving satisfactory, numerous experiments were tried. In 1695, overseers were made separate officials, and one from each ward chosen by the council.[54] About 1700, the aldermen and assistants of each ward were made responsible for the lighting of their ward ;[55] and for a while they were in charge of voting.[56] This latter proving unsatisfactory (as well it might), it was finally altered in 1771.[57]

51. Shurtleff, H. R. (Edit.), 'The Williamsburg Playhouse,' typed MS. in possession of The Williamsburg Restoration, Mar. 26, 1935.
52. Petition, Nov. 9, 1683 in N. Y. Hist. Soc. Coll., 1885, pp. 43-47.
53. Peterson, A. E., and Edwards, G. W., New York as an Eighteenth Century Municipality, pp. 183ff.
54. Ibid. pp. 185, 186, 297.
55. Ibid. p. 104f.
56. Ibid. p. 249f.
57. Ibid. p. 251.

The number of wards was increased by charter from six to seven in 1730.

Perth Amboy in 1753 and New Brunswick in 1763 revised their charters partly with division into wards in view. In these two New Jersey communities the area was large, and in Perth Amboy the river formed a natural division. The ward in these two cities seems to have been akin to a 'town' organization, in that ward meetings were held ; it occasionally was the unit for taxation for special public works ; it was an electoral unit for choice of city officers, and also a unit for poor relief.[58] However, nowhere, other than in these three towns, does the ward appear to have been a genuine administrative unit, and in the majority of the boroughs it did not even exist.

Elsewhere occasional division into wards did occur for minor purposes. From the beginning the ward served as an electoral unit in Albany.[59] The assessors and constables as well as the aldermen and assistants were thus chosen. In Annapolis, the inhabitants were divided into three 'districts' for purposes of operating the fire engine.[60] Norfolk (1765) divided itself into eight wards, for purposes of the night watch.[61] This device represented a mere ephemeral convenience, and had little significance otherwise.

The town or borough meetings in those communities which retained them were of genuine significance. Such meetings were integral parts of the government of a num-

58. In both cities the records are scanty, but cf. Allinson, S. (Compiler), *Acts of New Jersey*, Chap. CCCCXXXVII, June 28, 1766 ; Chap. DLXXXIX, Mar. 11, 1774 ; Chap. DCV, Mar. 11, 1774. Cf. also the charters of the two cities.
59. Charter and minutes in Munsell, J., *Annals of Albany*, vol. II, var.
60. Minutes, 1757 (undated meeting). Likewise Albany, for which cf. Munsell, J., *Annals of Albany*, vol. X, p. 96, etc.
61. Minutes of the Council, Apr. 5, 1765.

ber of boroughs. In Bristol, Chester, and Lancaster ordinances appear to have required some such sanction for their validity — at least at first.[62] Bristol evaded the requirement by calling its council meeting a 'town meeting,' with at least the justification of having added a number of democratically chosen common councillors to the officers specifically mentioned in the charter.[63] Elizabeth, New Brunswick, Burlington, and perhaps Perth Amboy and Trenton, continued their town organization parallel to that of the borough after the latter was chartered. The New Brunswick town organization had been irregular, the community legally having been a part of the town of Piscataway.[64] At times it would appear that the town government remained the reality in Elizabeth and Burlington, even after city incorporation, including still in its functions land surveys, poor relief, tax levies.[65] The system of making the town in part responsible to the county justices, which was characteristic of the vestry-county relationship in England, prevailed to a limited extent in New Jersey in poor relief and certain minor functions.[66] In New Brunswick, the functions of

62. By charter. Cf. Appendix B.
63. Minutes, 1732, etc. The minutes before this year are missing, so that the device by which the transition was effected is not definitely known.
64. Scott, A., 'Charter and Early Ordinances of New Brunswick,' in *New Brunswick Hist. Club Public.*, 1913, p. 97.
65. Town Book, Elizabeth ; Township Book, Burlington. It may be conjectured that in these two cities the 'Magistrates' court' (i. e., the mayor and aldermen) ran the markets and fairs, and probably passed and enforced ordinances. For example, the latter no longer appear in the Township Book entries of Burlington. Fragments only survive of the Elizabeth records, but a MS. in the city clerk's office (July 5, 1762) contains an ordinance regulating the public landings, passed by the city council.
66. Act of Apr. 4, 1709 : Overseers with one or more of the justices may bind out orphans. Act of Mar. 11, 1774 : justices to hear appeals concerning legal settlement. (Also others.)

the city administration appeared to be more those of the normal incorporation. Perhaps the same was actually true of the other Jersey boroughs also, but their minutes are lost. It is interesting to note that the 1733 charter of Burlington was largely drafted in a town meeting.[67]

In Wilmington (Del.) a situation similar to that of the Pennsylvania boroughs ruled, whereby assent of the inhabitants to most (possibly all) of the by-laws was secured in borough meeting. Only occasionally do the minutes record a by-law passed at an ordinary council meeting, although such meetings were held with considerable frequency.[68] Sometimes the inhabitants also gathered at 'the Widow Allison's' ; sometimes elsewhere, for we read that in 1773 'those who were for opening and laying out said streets should range themselves along Market Street in the intersection of High Street, and those who were against the same should range themselves opposite the northward in High Street between the gutters . . . they (the tellers) did severally declare that . . . the majority . . . were for laying out . . .'[69] As for the other cities, only in Wilmington (N. C.), Westchester, and possibly in Annapolis, do there appear to be traces of such borough meetings as an integral part of the municipal government.[70]

The mayor (chief burgess, bailey) everywhere was a prominent figure ceremonially, and frequently administratively as well. In many communities he held *ex officio* a number of other offices, such as coroner,[71] clerk

67. Burlington Township Minute Book, Jan. 15, 1733/4.
68. Minute Book of Burgesses and Assistants (after 1771).
69. Wilmington Minute Book, undated town meeting, 1773 ; recorded in Minute Book of Burgesses as Feb. 13.
70. For Wilmington (N. C.), cf. p. 213f. The Annapolis meetings seem to have been spontaneous or emergency gatherings.
71. Albany, Westchester, New York (1730).

of the market,[72] or water bailiff.[73] In New York (1730) he was allowed to select a deputy. In Philadelphia, soon after the charter came into operation, he was made city treasurer and was frequently assigned administrative duties.[74] In port cities he often claimed jurisdiction over the harbour. For example, a fragment has survived indicating that the Mayor of Gorgeana (1641) once sent his 'serjant of the white rod' to demand the presence of the captain of a ship forced into the harbour.[75]

The mayor, the recorder, and the aldermen were made excise commissioners in New York City in 1753, but this practice was discontinued the following year.[76] Apart from these New York towns and Philadelphia, the mayor's administrative responsibility does not appear to have been sharply differentiated from the other members of the governing body — such variations as there were in this respect running true to the diversity in English precedent.[77]

The recorder was the chief legal adviser of the court. He attended to matters such as the drafting of by-laws ;

72. Albany, Westchester, New York (1730), Perth Amboy.
73. Norfolk, New York (1730). Peterson and Edwards, op. cit., p. 32, stated that he held all these offices prior to 1730. In Norfolk, the Norfolk Borough Register (MS. city clerk's office) indicates that the mayor was continually occupied certifying bills of lading, etc.
74. e. g. Dec. 1, 1704, he was directed to go the rounds of the bakers once a month to inspect the weight of bread (*Minutes of the Common Council*, Dec. 1, 1704). It is perhaps not entirely correct to view this type of duty as peculiarly the mayor's, for other of the magistrates from time to time were assigned special commissions. The *Minutes* indicate that later a separate treasurer was chosen to take over the mayor's duties in this capacity.
75. Trelawney Papers, 279 (Cited in Banks, C. E., *History of York, Maine*, p. 130).
76. Peterson and Edwards, op. cit., p. 269.
77. It is true that the Elizabeth charter used the expression : 'Mayors . . . shall have the charge,' but this was probably in practice titular only.

and as he himself was a member and versed in law, he was frequently a dominant force when the court met in its judicial capacity. In New York City, where he was appointed by the governor, he seems to have acted in a liaison capacity between the latter and the council.[78] The office was one of great dignity.

There is little to add to the description of the bailiff as given for the English cities.[79] He was either the 'head' of the corporation,[80] or an officer usually concerned with serving writs, and other papers — a kind of miniature sheriff. Few cities had sheriffs of their own.[81] However, this officer was of great importance in the county. The water bailiff (in port cities) was in charge of quarantine and (occasionally) of customs, the entry and clearance of ships, etc.

The minor administrative officers were legion.[82] Where the town meeting tradition survived (e.g. New Jersey towns, in part) these petty officials were customarily chosen by the inhabitants. Elsewhere it was normal for the corporation to select them. Election by wards, as in New York City, New Brunswick, and Perth Amboy, was exceptional and even then extended to but a few officers. An exception must also be made of the assessors who were usually chosen by popular vote. Account should

78. Peterson and Edwards, op. cit., p. 226f.
79. Cf. p. 27f.
80. Newcastle, 1672 ; Germantown, 1691.
81. Cf. p. 111f.
82. The officers chosen at the town meeting of Portsmouth (N. H.) in 1766 in addition to the moderator and selectmen were as follows : three overseers of the poor, three agents for the town, three auditors, one sealer of weights, one clerk of the market, nine firewards, eleven surveyors of highways, two attorneys, three constables, one collector for the Church of England, three searchers and sealers of leather, three cullers, searchers, and packers, one pound keeper, six tything men, five hog reaves, five measurers of wood. (*New Hampshire Gazette*, Apr. 25, 1766.)

be taken of the fact that units other than the corporation, such as the vestry, the county, various commissions, often exercised functions in the same territory, so that it becomes still more difficult to generalize. Any critique of these various local officers from the standpoint of the science of administration will be deferred until later,[83] as will also a more detailed treatise on their functions.[84] At present all that will be attempted is an analysis of their origin and a rough attempt at their classification.

A few officials were ceremonial. Gorgeana, for example, had enjoyed 'serjants of the white rod.' Even the tiny communities of Westchester and Schenectady were given sergeants of the mace. Beadles and cryers occasionally appeared in the lists. Just how much dignity was actually attached to these offices is doubtful, for in Philadelphia (1713) it is recorded that 'William Hill, the Beedle of this City, having lately in a heat broke his Bell, and given out that he would Continue no longer at the Place, but now Expresses a great Deal of Sorrow for his so doing, and humbly desires to be Continued therein During his Good Behaviour, And the Premises being Considered And the Vote put whether he should Continue the Place any Longer, It past in ye affirmative.'[85]

Others were connected with the enforcement of the decrees of the court. Constables existed in almost every community ; and occasionally marshals, and undersheriffs. The viewers and searchers of chimneys of New York City, occasionally the beadle, and the town whipper of Albany belong in this general classification. Of the latter, it is recorded that he, Rick Van Toper, was voted a bonus of 5/6 in addition to regular fees 'for the due and

83. Chap. XV.
84. Chap. XI.
85. Quoted in Scharf, J. T., and Westcott, T., op. cit., vol. I, p. 193.

wholesome manner in which he laid the lash upon the back of Tiberius Haines, who had been convicted of beating his wife in a most cruel and heartless manner.'[86] The watchmen seem to have been differentiated from the constables, in so far as they patrolled regularly, whereas the latter usually carried out specified tasks — as in Wilmington (N. C.) when they were commissioned by act of the colonial assembly to walk the streets during divine service to prevent disturbance.[87] Probably the town clerk, in charge of the records but often assuming other duties, belonged in this category also. In the larger cities he was an influential figure, albeit behind the scenes.

In connection with municipal activity in control of trade, a clerk of the market and numerous 'inspectors' were obviously called for — or perhaps a 'corder of wood.' The highways required 'overseers' or 'roadmasters' and 'surveyors' — the latter term often used also in connection with laying out or determining the boundaries of land. As the town grew, 'scavengers' appeared, and 'pound keepers.' Albany had a city porter, who was paid 28 'pieces of eight' a year to open and close its gates. The term 'overseer' was an ubiquitous one — applying at times to poor relief, to road building and mending, or to public works.

Assessors, a treasurer or chamberlain, and collectors were sufficient financial officers — these communities not having reached the dignity of a director of the budget or a controller.

These numerous offices by no means always implied an

equal number of incumbents. The prize, however, appears to belong to one Bernard Devonish who, in 1694, in Burlington, served as 'Sergiant, Clerk of the Market, Cryer of the Town, and officer to view the Assise of Bread and Liquor and to supervise and examine weights and measures.'[88]

Such, in general, was the internal structure of the boroughs in so far as a study of the charters and the rather scanty records reveal it. To this period we owe the terminology of most of our cities — mayor, aldermen, common council — and the custom of some differentiation at least of the functions of the mayor. The union of the judicial and administrative functions is quite unfamiliar to our modern concepts, and we recognize at least the beginning of change in the towns that gave their common council no share in judicial business, but restricted them to the more purely administrative duties. The minor officials were the outgrowth, not so much of the traditional English background, as of the functions to be performed. As such, they bore only a faint resemblance to the municipal officers of to-day.

88. Burlington Township Minutes, 1694. Such a grouping of minor offices and duties was not unusual in the smaller boroughs. In general, these boroughs appear to have had one or two handy men to whom they assigned numerous duties and titles.

VIII

POPULAR PARTICIPATION –
ITS EXTENT AND LIMITATIONS

IT will be remembered that in only a minority of the English boroughs of the day did even approximately democratic forms rule. While the majority were 'close' corporations, this rather distinguished minority — notably the City of London — were known to many of the colonists. Hence it was not unnatural that fairly liberal municipal institutions should evolve among these colonists, especially when there were also examples of political liberalism at hand in the New England towns. However, it must also be remembered that the 'close' corporation was also natural, perhaps more so. Hence, after all, it is perhaps more necessary to account for the *open* corporation among colonial boroughs as the real deviation, rather than the 'close' type.

In any general discussion of 'popular participation,' one must first determine the meaning of the concept itself. What actually is involved ? The percentage legally eligible to vote is important, but it may well be quite different from the percentage actually exercising the franchise. Furthermore, even the number exercising the franchise may have but minor significance if bribery or pressure or intimidation are at all prevalent. Then, too, citizens may well have channels other than the ballot box for interesting themselves in municipal affairs. These and other problems all enter the picture.

From one point of view, then, popular participation involves consideration of the extent to which such participation was legal ; that is to say, to what extent it was incorporated in governmental forms. How many people

188

were permitted to vote ; who were they ; for what officers and on what questions ?[1]

But over and above these fairly obvious questions, we have already suggested that there are other questions which transcend the forms and letter of the law. These concern, not the legality of popular participation, but its vitality and effectiveness. In any attempt to answer such questions, governmental forms play a distinctly secondary role, and one finds himself largely in the sphere of attitude and custom. How many individuals were really interested in their borough governments ? What were the issues that concerned them ? How far was it customary or feasible to express this interest ?

Among the imponderables, the prevailing deference must rank as a major influence. While certain aspects of the early experience of the colonists generally may have somewhat weakened, they could not destroy the acceptance of a stratified society as the normal state of affairs. Reference has been made earlier to the acquiescence in special privilege as a corollary to this. Where the prevailing creed was Anglican, as it was in most municipalities in the colonies (at least from Maryland south), such social stratification was even incorporated into the church architecture of the day. Special pews were normally set aside for the gentry, elevated somewhat above those allocated to the common people.

By way of pointing out some of the effects of these class distinctions, in some instances it is possible to compare the personnel of the city council with the assessment roll. One may thus obtain some idea of the social strata from

1. When one considers actual popular participation in government in the Colonial Era, one need take little account of the women ; nor need one include the free negroes, although theoretically this latter class could vote, if it had the necessary property and other qualifications, in all but South Carolina and Georgia.

which council members were drawn. Taken in conjunction with available occupational data, the picture presented is unmistakable. It was normally the group of wealthy, of leading citizens, that made up the membership of the council.[2]

Every now and then one happens upon an incident which was particularly illuminating in its implications. Thus, when it is discovered that by law in the planning of the town of Annapolis a certain area was to be reserved for the homes of the 'gentry,' one learns much as to accepted attitudes.[3] It implies the strong probability of a society in which it is also the accepted thing for these same gentry to govern. Nor was criticism encouraged on the part of the rank and file who were 'fortunate' enough to be so governed. Neither the equalitarian doctrines of the French Revolution nor the levelling tendencies of the frontier had as yet affected the tide-water district of these Southern colonies. When the first democratic rum-

2. In Bristol, a Quaker borough of perhaps 1,000 inhabitants, in 1746, five out of the ten wealthiest men were members of the common council, and made up a majority of its nine members. Only one member fell below the upper 40 per cent. When the number of the council was increased to eleven in 1748, six of the wealthiest nine were elected to membership. It would be illuminating to make a similar study of other communities. Internal evidence indicates that the result would not have been materially different. (Bristol Minute Book, 1730-1825, Oct. 25, 1746, July 4, 1748.)

For New York City, where the merchant class ruled, cf. Peterson, A. E., and Edwards, J. W., *New York as an Eighteenth Century Municipality*, p. 259. Cf. also the reply of the Annapolis corporation to Samuel Chase and the grand jury in the *Maryland Gazette*, June 19, 1766 : 'how licentiosly they asperse the Character of their Betters, not only in Rank, but in every species of *real* Merit (as will readily appeaɪ upon a comparative view of their *Names* . . .).' For Albany, cf. Tax Lists for 1766, etc. (MSS. in New York Public Library) and Munsell, J., *Collections of Albany*, vol. I, for lists of council. Ordinarily it seems that nine or ten of the twelve aldermen and councillors were chosen from the top 10-15% of the assessment roll.

3. Norris, W. B., *Annapolis : Its Colonial and Naval Story*, p. 31.

blings came in 1765, and, when Jeffersonian and Jack-
sonian democracy finally entered to undermine the *status
quo*, it is small wonder that those whose accepted position had been to govern thought that the end of all
things had come.

Quite apart from these social factors, it must be remembered that the only experience which these people had
had with county government — which was the all-pervading local institution of its day in England — was with
a government by appointed justices who virtually always
were members of the landed aristocracy. It bespoke crea-
tiveness of thought beyond the ken or the experience of
the times to visualize alternatives. Such county government by 'magistrates' was soon set up in practically all
the colonies from New York south — and also in Rhode
Island. While this practice was subsequently modified
(notably in New Jersey and Pennsylvania), the inhabitants of all these regions were more or less familiar with
the institution. Consequently, the cities also were often
thought of as having not so much a 'government' as
'magistrates.' A city like Williamsburg tacitly accepted
this parallel to the county in its attitudes and internal
organization. The functioning of democracy on a broad
basis may be better measured in practice by the 'specific
gravity' of deference than by the size of the vote. Where
deference is the accepted attitude socially, it behooves
one to discover whether it is not so also politically. In
such a situation there is little genuine popular participation. This participation must await the advent of a self-
reliant frontier, the stimulus of a radical lawyer, or the
influx of the audacious Irish, to be real.

(B)

The law on the subject was fairly clear. Broadly speaking, all charters divided themselves into the two types — close and democratic.

The close corporation was by definition the type which perpetuated itself by co-option. Its original members (usually mayor, aldermen, councillors, recorder) were named in the charter and by charter were vested with the power of choosing their own successors in the event of vacancies. Among the full-fledged colonial incorporations, Germantown, Philadelphia (both of its charters), Annapolis (the first charter and at one time by usage under the second charter), Williamsburg, and Norfolk certainly belong in this category. In addition, a few of the North Carolina borough towns, at least initially, must be included, inasmuch as their commissioners were also self-perpetuating.

Of the missing charters, Bermuda City and the other early Virginia corporations, St. Mary's, Charleston, and Newcastle (1724) probably belong in the same classification, though one cannot be certain. The early Virginia incorporations were obviously initially oligarchic. However, there is considerable evidence — in connection, for example, with the admiration felt by Sir Edwin Sandys for the City of London — that the Virginia company, had it continued in control, eventually would have democratized its municipal institutions. As to St. Mary's, one is left almost totally without evidence. Its charter was issued by Lord Baltimore at a time when he was attempting to develop manorial, aristocratic institutions, and also at a time when virtually all the charters issued in England were of the close type. Newcastle, in 1724, was incorporated as a city, rather than as a borough. Its incorporation was granted by the same man who was governor of Pennsylvania and hence familiar with the close corporation of Philadelphia. The Newcastle charter was not well received locally. An added dignity, such as a city charter implied, would probably have been welcomed, had it not been at the expense of something else — such as popular participation in government — which was even more valued.[4] On this basis, it is fair to say that this charter was almost certainly of the close type. The 1722 Act incorporating Charleston, also lost, in all probability belonged in the same category. Wallace, apparently from documentary material in the South Carolina records, stated that the councillors were elected for life and had power to co-opt to fill vacancies.[5]

4. Cf. Keith, C. P., *Chronicles of Pennsylvania*, vol. II, p. 681f.

5. Wallace, D. D., *History of South Carolina*, 1934, vol. I, p. 286f., citing Public Records of South Carolina, MSS., X, 74, 82-86, 92, 94-95, 104, 113, 115, 159.

A petition of 123 inhabitants begged that the Act be disallowed — among other reasons, because of the burdensome requirement of fourteen courts a year. Some discrimination against the Huguenots was also alleged, which accounts for the presence of a number of the wealthy of this group among the petitioners. The defence by the provincial agent was to the effect that the assembly, in 1721, had instructed the agents to obtain permission to incorporate Charleston on the New York City model, and a law was passed accordingly. The inhabitants were under the impression that the mayor and council of Philadelphia, New York, and most of the New England cities (actually there were none) held their posts for life. The legal council of the Lords of Trade advised that the charter provided 'the completest oligarchy that was ever seen,' and it was disallowed after operating fifteen months.

McCrady gives the account of this episode as follows :

'The passage of the act was bitterly resented, and appeals were at once made both at home and in England for its repeal. A petition was addressed to the Hon. James Moore, Speaker, and the rest of the commons house of assembly by persons claiming to be the major part of the inhabitants of the town against it, and praying its repeal. In the signatures to this petition which have been preserved there are one hundred and twenty names, more than half of which are French . . . There are a few names of prominent English colonists . . . but besides these there are none of the names which we should expect to see to a petition of such consequence if the measure was an unpopular one. And this, Gov. Nicholson was quick to point out. His excellency was incensed at the opposition, and flew into one of the passions for which he had been noted in his younger days. He sent a message to

The wording of the Newcastle charter of 1672 is obscure. This charter (if charter it be)[6] may also possibly be classed as a close corporation. Nominations for the six 'assistants' therein provided were first to be made by the governor ; and at the expiration of their terms, 'four of the six [were] to go out and four others to be chosen in their places.' This may have meant nomination or it may have meant popular election. If this Newcastle charter had provided the ordinary type of close corporation, it would have been unusual to specify definite terms of office. Perhaps the Dutch custom of rotation in office was implied.

Omitting the early Virginia corporations and the borough towns of North Carolina, there were probably eight close corporations[7] and sixteen more or less democratic among the twenty-four municipal incorporations of colonial times.[8] Is it possible, then, to discover why these particular sixteen corporations were of this latter type ?

It is only remotely possible that the dates at which these charters were granted may have been something of a factor. Most new charters in England were issued

the Assembly, contemptuously alluding to the signers of the petition as strangers, sailors, convicts, and keepers of punchhouses. He pointed out that the opposition came from the country and not from the townspeople.'

This, according to McCrady, was only in part true, for to some extent the townspeople had been surprised into the law. (McCrady, E., *History of South Carolina, 1719-1776,* pp. 40ff.)

The account of the hearings may be found in Great Britain : *Journal of the Comnrs. for Trade and Plantations,* Dec. 4, 1722 ; May 14, 29, 30, 1723.

6. Cf. pp. 239, 435, for discussion of its origin.
7. Germantown, Philadelphia, Williamsburg, Norfolk, St. Mary's, Charleston, Annapolis, Newcastle.
8. Gorgeana, Albany, New York, Schenectady, Westchester, Perth Amboy, Elizabeth, New Brunswick, Burlington, Trenton, Wilmington (Del.), Wilmington (N. C.), Annapolis, Bristol, Lancaster, Chester.

prior to the beginning of Queen Anne's reign (1702). Except for a few democratic charters between 1660-1664 and again between 1689-1695, the charters during the reigns of Charles II, James II, and William and Mary were of the close type.[9] During the reign of Anne and the first two Georges, very few charters were actually granted in England, but those that were granted were of the close type. Occasional democratic charters appeared under George III. Thus during the period of issuance of the close charter in the Colonies, 1667-1736, English precedent was almost uniformly on its side ; for even in the two brief periods mentioned as marking the issuance of some democratic charters, there were an equal number of close charters issued.[10]

The key to any deviation from the English type must accordingly be found in the particular colonial situation. The afore-mentioned precedents and early appearance of a stratified society in the cities would lead one to expect a close corporation. Moreover, it cannot be repeated too often that the corporate and juridical tradition of the borough was in this earlier period much more clearly defined in people's minds than the governmental. Traditionally, the judiciary was appointed rather than elected ; and the management of corporate property not unnaturally was considered the function of those who themselves possessed it. This normally was the kind of person named in the charter. The amount such persons possessed might be small in comparison with modern standards or even with those of England, but the sense

9. Wisbech, 1669, was an exception, but its democratic character can be accounted for by special circumstances. Cf. Webb, B. and S., *The Manor and the Borough*, vol. I, p. 143.

10. The foregoing summary is based upon a detailed study of the *First Report of the Commission on Municipal Corporations* (H. C. 116, 1835).

of property has always been relative to the amount possessed by others rather than according to an absolute norm.

In accounting for the deviations from the close type, the particular situations which produced the charters themselves for the most part contained the clue. Moreover, apart from one or two isolated instances, the desire on the part of the Crown to control elections to the legislature was lacking;[11] and it was this desire which had been tremendously powerful in dictating the epidemic of close charters under the Tudors and Stuarts. Yet this was not all.

The Gorgeana charter was issued in 1642, when the intention of the Stuarts to control Parliament by forfeiting and reissuing charters had become obvious. Why the democratic form was adopted must remain largely conjectural; but Sir Ferdinando Gorges was for his time enlightened and altruistic; and the neighbouring New England colonies had the most democratic of institutions.

At least two other factors appear to have operated in New York City and Albany in 1686. In the first place, these towns were still predominantly Dutch, and the Dutch municipal institutions were essentially in advance of their times in the matter of popular elections. This was conspicuously true of Amsterdam, and the Dutch of New Amsterdam had a tradition back of them of a battle with their governors for similar institutions in their new country.[12] It is true that the people never actually participated in the choice of the aldermen under the 1665 charter of confirmation in New York City,[13] inasmuch as the governor appointed to vacancies from double the

11. Cf. p. 18.
12. Cf. Chap. IX.
13. Cf. p. 233f.

number presented by the existing magistrates.[14] None
the less, Dutch influence, if not experience, was on the
side of popular participation when the time came for a
bona-fide royal charter. This factor was aided by Governor Dongan, who had come with specific instructions
from his sovereign, James II, to favour liberal institutions.[15] It is said that the latter had been influenced by the
advice of William Penn, who had suggested that self-
government meant more revenue and less trouble.[16]
Subsequent charters in New York (Westchester, 1696,
New York City, 1730, and Schenectady, 1765) naturally
followed this precedent.

The democratic boroughs of West Jersey, Burlington,
and Salem, and the equally democratic towns of East
Jersey were actually incorporations of their own legislatures, under the far-reaching grant of self-government by
the proprietors. They were democratic in their origin,
and retained the town meeting, of which they had had
experience, as an integral part of their constitution.
Hence these Jersey boroughs were naturally and inevitably of the open type.

The later boroughs of Pennsylvania — Chester, Bristol, Lancaster — require more explanation of their democratic character than it is possible to give with the meagre
records available, particularly in the instance of Chester.
The move on the part of Bristol came from the inhabitants themselves ; and by the time the charter of Lancaster was issued, the county government of Pennsylvania
had been democratized. The borough meeting appears to
have been retained, at least in Chester and Lancaster. By

14. *Minutes of Mayor's Court,* 1665-1684, var.
15. Cf. Andrews, C. M., *Colonial Period of American History,* New Haven,
    1937, vol. III, p. 121, for a favourable opinion of Dongan's own char-
    acter.
16. Fiske, J., *Dutch and Quaker Colonies in America,* vol. II, p. 170.

1739, Wilmington (Del.) could be depended upon to follow the precedent of its neighbouring boroughs, and in any event its chartering was largely motivated by an effort to solve a troublesome local situation as democratically as was feasible.[17] The episode has already been noted in which the original close corporation charter of Annapolis was changed to a more democratic form by the instantaneous unfavourable reception accorded it by the inhabitants and the assembly.

Annapolis had had democratic institutions as a town, and the Puritan element in its population was strong. Hostility to the governor added to the strength of this popular reaction.[18] Wilmington (N. C.) merely replaced democratically elected commissioners with a correspondingly democratic borough government. It will be recalled that virtually all these later incorporations, unlike the earlier fostered ones, were at the request of the inhabitants themselves.[19] In other words, they were distinctly colonial, not English, in their genesis, though in their general form they drew heavily on English types.

Were there moves in the direction of democratizing the existing close corporations ? In Philadelphia the problem of an oligarchy, in so far as there was a problem, was solved otherwise. This was through the transfer of the municipal activity of the corporation to popularly elected boards.[20] In Annapolis an eventual restlessness was sufficient to alter what had become by usage a close corporation. In Norfolk the rejection of a petition on the part of the inhabitants to elect the common council is recorded in the minutes of February 14, 1774, but by a

17. Cf. p. 150.
18. Cf. p. 41f. Also Mereness, N. D., *Maryland as a Proprietary Province*, p. 421f.
19. Cf. pp. 64ff.
20. Cf. pp. 252ff.

resolution at the January 31, 1774, meeting the people were allowed to sit in the gallery during council meetings.[21] Thus it is fair to say that in these citadels of local oligarchy, democracy was making progress. Even had the Revolution not intervened, it would have been but a question of time before popular election came to be universal.

(C)

A general discussion of the franchise in the Colonies as a whole will not be attempted. Those interested are referred to McKinley's study.[22] Nor, except for occasional illustrative purposes, need consideration be given to the status of the franchise in the New England towns, where religious as well as property qualifications were frequent. The interest at this point lies in the suffrage qualifications of the several boroughs. Naturally the borough practice was coloured by, and often identical with, the franchise for the colonial assembly. It was frequently more liberal than the franchise for the county.

It will be remembered that practice varied in the North Carolina borough towns, and in the towns of Maryland and Virginia. Initially, commissioners and trustees were customarily named in the act. Either they were given power to co-opt in vacancies, or provision was made (as in Salisbury, N. C.) for county justices to fill vacancies. In growing towns, such as Wilmington (N. C.), New Bern (N. C.), or Charlestown (Md.), the choice of commissioners seems customarily to have been

21. Williamsburg records are so lacking that no positive statement can be made concerning this city.
22. McKinley, A. E., *Suffrage Franchise in the Thirteen English Colonies*, Philadelphia, 1905. This work contains some excellent material dealing with the boroughs. For Pennsylvania boroughs, cf. pp. 296-298.

democratized with increase of population. Those eligible to vote came to possess much the same qualifications as in the ordinary boroughs.

It has already been mentioned that in the democratically constituted cities voting always took place for the councillors or assistants, frequently for the aldermen, rarely for the mayor,[23] frequently for the assessors, at least occasionally for other officers. The request (1730) on the part of New York City to be allowed to choose locally those officers (mayor, recorder, etc.) then appointed by the governor was not granted, but there would have been both colonial and British precedents for such direct election.

In studying the actual terms on which the franchise was forthcoming in these various boroughs, one finds two ideas interwoven — the idea of residence and property, and the idea of formal admission as a 'freeman.' The two were by no means identical, and neither was universal. At times they were in the nature of alternatives. More usually the 'admission' was the formal act registering the fact of residence and property.

Residence qualifications were not as frequently specified as property. This was doubtless because ownership of the latter in practice so usually implied residence that it was unnecessary to specify such residence. Also, absentee property owners (and freemen) customarily voted in such English boroughs as still allowed voting by persons not among the members of the corporate governing body. By way of example of a residence qualification, in New York City the provision read : 'If any Freeman should be absent out of the Citty the space of Twelve moneths and

23. Cf. p. 172f.

not keepe fire and candle and pay scott and lott should loose his Freedom.'[24]

As regards property qualifications, there is little to be gained by a minute catalogue of all the minor variations, particularly as these were probably not rigidly adhered to in practice. Where the borough was still predominantly rural, as Gorgeana, New Bern, Salem (N. J.), the simple term 'freeholder' met the needs of the occasion.[25] Where the urban element had begun to creep in, and houses were often rented, or where freeholding of a certain amount was specified and it was desired perhaps to include certain professional classes, the alternative of the ownership of a certain amount of personal property was occasionally offered. Williamsburg (in voting for the burgess) gave the alternative of a visible estate of £50 ;[26] New Jersey (according to the Queen's Instructions of 1705) for its assembly required £50 of personal property of those who did not own 100 acres of land.[27] Likewise, the South Carolina Act of 1721, in addition to requiring residence of one year, stipulated a freehold of fifty acres or a tax of 20s.[28] These requirements applied to elections for the assembly, but it seems probable in view of the apparently small number voting that in effect they applied also to the elections for the St. Philip's Vestry officials who were primarily responsible

24. Quoting petition of Nov. 9, 1683, in *N. Y. Hist. Soc. Coll.*, 1885, pp. 43-47. Cf. also Seybolt, R. F., *The Colonial Citizen of New York City*, p. 33.
25. Gorgeana, by charter ; New Bern, 1756 (*State Records of North Carolina*, vol. XXIII, pp. 450ff.) ; Salem, Barber, J. W., and Howe, H., *Historical Collections of New Jersey*, p. 435.
26. Hening's *Virginia Statutes*, vol. V, pp. 204ff.
27. Smith, S., *History of the Colony of Nova-Caesaria*, p. 236.
28. Trott, N., *Laws of the Province of South Carolina*, pp. 373ff. (Act No. 463).

for the local government of Charleston.[29] Details concerned with the extent of property ownership or occupancy were also quite frequent. Typical provisions are as follows : New York City, freeholders over £40 ;[30] Wilmington (N. C.), 1739 (in voting for the burgess), tenant or owner of a house 16′ x 20′ if frame, or 16′ x 30′ if brick ;[31] Wilmington (Del.), freeholders or tenants of £5 yearly.[32] Alternative qualifications might also be allowed.

In addition to or as an alternative to these property qualifications, the expression 'by the freemen' was constantly reiterated. The freedom of the city (or colony)[33] might be an automatic affair for those enjoying the ownership of a certain amount of property or the occupancy of a certain office or position (clergy, military, etc.). On the other hand, it might be accompanied by all the formalities of admission before the appropriate magistrates. In the latter instance alternatives to property-owning qualifications appeared more often. Most usual was qualification by apprenticeship or by purchase. Apart from these two channels, the number of voters in a truly urban incorporation such as New York City would have been very small indeed. It is difficult to form any accurate picture as to the number of towns that legally or in practice admitted apprentices to freedom at the close of their apprenticeship and thereafter allowed them the vote. Wherever the expression 'freemen' or 'traders'

29. Cf. pp. 246, 248.
30. Peterson, A. E., and Edwards, G. W., *New York as an Eighteenth Century Municipality*, p. 243.
31. *State Records of North Carolina*, vol. XXIII, p. 133.
32. Scharf, J. T., *History of Delaware*, vol. II, p. 637.
33. e. g. Under Clause VI of the Berkeley-Cartaret Concessions in Jersey, freedom was to be provincial, not local (Leaming, A., and Spicer, J., *Grants, Concessions, etc., of New Jersey*, p. 17).

occurred, it is probable that such admission existed, and
it was considered unnecessary to specify it more particularly.[34] This is a really important question, inasmuch
as the presence or absence of this avenue to freedom had
perhaps more to do than any other one factor in the
larger boroughs with whether or not they approached
representative democracy in the modern sense. This has
been well pointed out by the Webbs in their study of the
English boroughs.[35] They found that only in places so
enfranchising by the channel of apprenticeship did the
total number of freemen exceed 10 per cent of the adult
males. Instances in the Colonies include New York City,[36]
Albany,[37] Schenectady,[38] Annapolis,[39] (probably) the
New Jersey boroughs,[40] and possibly others. For the representative of the borough in the assembly, freemen (including those by apprenticeship) were allowed to vote
in Philadelphia,[41] Williamsburg,[42] and Norfolk[43] — corporations which, domestically speaking, were close. In
New Brunswick, even this relatively democratic franchise was evidently not enough for the liking of some
people, for we read in the *New York Gazette* of Mar. 17,
1755, that Alderman Wetherill and a 'body of People'
asserted 'that no one of any Trade was obliged to take

34. On the other hand, the practice of Westchester was to exclude free-
    men. Cf. p. 204.
35. Webb, B. and S., *The Manor and the Borough*, vol. I, p. 302.
36. Cf. p. 211f.
37. By charter.
38. By charter.
39. Cf. p. 212.
40. e. g. New Brunswick, certainly (*N. J. Archives*, 1st. ser., vol. XXVII,
    pp. 187f., 218 ; XIX, p. 473f.). The Perth Amboy charter, 1718, speaks
    of 'freeholders and freemen' as entitled to vote.
41. By charter.
42. Hening's *Virginia Statutes*, vol. V, pp. 204ff.
43. Blodgett, J. H., *Free Burghs in the United States*, in *Ann. Rpt., Amer.
    Hist. Assoc. for 1895*, p. 319.

up his Freedom, as by the Charter is directed, and that
Freeholders in general (tho not Freemen in whom the
Charter only and expressly vests the Rights of chusing)
have a Right to vote.'[44] It is possible, of course, that the
corporation of New Brunswick had revealed the tendency of so many English boroughs towards setting undue
barriers of a financial nature or otherwise upon the purchase or acquisition of 'freedom.'

The converse appears to have been true of Westchester, at least in the years immediately prior to the
Revolution. In 1768 in a close election for borough member, the returning officer denied the vote to freemen,
while extending it to freeholders. This denial was based
not only upon 'usage' of the borough, but also upon a
provincial law confining the suffrage to freeholders of
£40, 'except in the corporation of New York and
Albany, where freemen by the same act are entitled
to vote.'[45]

It is worth quoting the provision of the Philadelphia
charter of 1701, even though the acquisition of freedom
in that city did not include the right to vote for the city
council. Freemen should 'have an estate of inheritance or
freehold therein, or [be] worth fifty pounds in money or
other stock, and have been resident in the said city for
the space of two years, or shall purchase their freedom of
the Mayor and Commonalty.' Formal admission was
originally customary here as well as in New York City.
Its privileges were far more valued for their vocational
implications than for their incidental enfranchisement.
When enforcement of monopolies grew lax (as in Phila-

44. N. J. Archives, 1st ser., vol. XIX, p. 473.
45. Correspondence, etc., in New York Gazette and Weekly Mercury,
Feb. 29, Mar. 7, 1768. The vote was exceedingly close, with Lewis
Morris and John deLancey as the two contestants.

delphia), so also the formal admissions to freedom diminished or were allowed to lapse.[46]

New York City was among the most generous in admitting to freedom. An ordinance of 1702 (later repealed) authorized that those who 'are poor and not able to purchase their freedoms be made Freemen of this Citty Gratis.' This was not, however, the permanent policy ; and may have been designed for only a few special cases.[47] The fee, itself, was ultimately quite low. The grant at the time of the charter had also been extremely comprehensive : 'all inhabitants of this Citty ; their Apprentices and Children that were here att the time the Charter was granted be allowed and Deemed Freemen of this Citty,' subject only to the requirement of registering and paying 9d.[48] It is worthy of note that the Earl of Bellomont alleged that Governor Fletcher had secured an assembly favourable to himself in part by making a number of sailors freemen.[49] Of a different nature was the honorary freedom of a city conferred as a mark of honour or gratitude. Distinguished guests or others who deserved well of the community were frequently so honoured.[50] The custom survives to this day in many of our incorporations.

The Virginia house of burgesses was normally quite

---

46. After about 1720 the records of admissions to freedom in the *Minutes of the Philadelphia Common Council* grow less and less, and finally disappear altogether. It is, however, possible that the form may have been altered or records kept elsewhere.
47. Seybolt, R. F., *The Colonial Citizen of New York City*, p. 18.
48. Cf. ibid. p. 19.
49. Report to the Board of Trade, in O'Callaghan, E. B. (Edit.), *Documents Relative to the Colonial History of New York*, vol. IV, p. 223.
50. Usually the colonial governors ; but others were occasionally honoured. Capt. Peter Solgard, for having captured a pirate ship, was awarded this distinction by New York City (*Amer. Weekly*, Sept. 19-26, 1723).

liberal in its ideas as to franchise. In its general Act of 1680, property owners might vote in the towns,[51] and, in the 1705 general Act, this was extended to read 'freeholders and inhabitants.'[52] In the latter year it also authorized the incorporation of Williamsburg, to the intent that all should be freemen who had 'interest, freehold or habitation' in the community.[53] In 1676 (in Bacon's rebellion laws — subsequently disallowed) James City 'householders and freeholders' were given power to make by-laws.[54]

That in New York State, at least, this privilege of non-property-owning freemen to vote and hold office was valued, may be indicated by the specific reference in the Constitution of 1777 to these rights in New York City and Albany.

Some boroughs were even more generous, and in the extent of voting permitted represent probably the greatest extension of democratic control in all the colonies. In this respect they exceeded the New England towns, which had by this time introduced a property franchise. The microscopic borough of Westchester, in 1695, granted the right of suffrage to 'freeholders and inhabitants.'[55] A similar provision was apparently included or implied in the 1693 incorporation of Burlington.[56] Schenectady enfranchised by charter all those of 'lawful age as have been born therein.' Campbelton (N. C.) reached the high (or low) point in suffrage by allowing all those

51. Cf. p. 159.
52. Hening's *Virginia Statutes,* vol. III, p. 404.
53. McBain, H. L., 'Legal Status of the American Colonial City' in *Pol. Sci. Quart.,* vol. XL, p. 189.
54. Hening, op. cit., vol. II, p. 362.
55. By charter. This must have been curtailed subsequently, for cf. p. 204.
56. Woodward, E. M., and Hageman, G. F., *History of Burlington and Mercer Counties,* p. 123.

to vote for their borough representative who happened
to be within two miles of town on the day of election.
This was too much even for the relatively democratic
and politically-minded folk of North Carolina. In 1772
this charter was voluntarily surrendered, and a petition
filed for a new charter that would not allow 'persons altogether destitute of Property or any permanent Residence in the said Town or Liberties and even not intitled
to the denomination of House-keepers' to vote.[57] These
three or four communities were very small (except for
Schenectady) and consequently were perhaps not fair
examples. On the whole, however, the franchise of
boroughs was definitely liberal. Where the road to freedom in these cities was open by way of apprenticeship
and purchase, the percentage receiving such freedom
ordinarily exceeded the percentage eligible to vote in
their respective colonies, and in some instances the percentage in the New England towns.

(D)

In turning to consideration of the extent to which the
inhabitants actually participated in or influenced the
government of their local units we come to a still more
difficult problem.

The background of attitudes of the New England town
need deter us only incidentally, inasmuch as it has had
adequate treatment elsewhere. Its tradition of Congrega-
tionalism made for genuine popular interest in things
temporal as well as spiritual. This held true even if, in
practice, it meant at times that such interest was to be con-

---

57. *State Records of North Carolina,* vol. IX, pp. 79, 270f. Campbelton
    was settled largely by Highlanders, friendly to the governor ; and
    hostility to the latter may have motivated the assembly's part in the
    change.

fined to God's elect. When one considers the practices of this period — perhaps of any period — it would be difficult to exaggerate the vitality of the town meeting. Perhaps as the town grew, the meeting tended to be controlled by a caucus, but at least the opportunity and occasionally the spirit of a vigorous opposition were present. This in itself was one of the earmarks of genuine popular government. In municipal boroughs, were there any comparable institutions and attitudes ? or were these New England Yankees right when they clung to their old devices rather than risk anything as doubtful or as potentially oligarchic as the incorporated city ?

The problem was complicated by the fact that the balloting was often in open meeting or non-secret. Under such circumstances opportunities were present for social and economic pressures in an age in which such pressures were the accepted state of affairs.[58] In 1769 a public meeting gathered in New York City at the Liberty Pole, and voted with but ten dissentients to promote a bill to provide the secret ballot.[59] Yet a counter-petition soon appeared, alleging that such a ballot 'would be an implicit surrender of one of the most invaluable Privileges which we Enjoy as Englishmen, to wit, that of declaring our sentiments openly on all occasions.'[60]

It is worthy of a modern note that the grand jury in 1771 in South Carolina included in its presentments 'that the Inhabitants of Charlestown, and the Province in General do not attend at Church on Easter Monday for the election of Parish Officers ; by which Neglect, Persons

58. Cf. Bishop, C. F., *History of Elections in the American Colonies,* New York, 1893. This was a pioneer study, which is now superseded in many of its aspects. It is still useful for its account of the procedures for managing elections. The material on municipal elections is scanty.
59. *New York Gazette and Weekly Mercury,* Jan. 8, 1770.
60. Ibid. Jan. 29, 1770.

interested in serving those offices, although often ignorant of the Duties incumbent on them, find means to
get themselves elected to the great Prejudice of the
Public.'[61]

Towards the end of the period, bribery was fairly
prevalent in New York and Philadelphia, and this invali-
dated still further the size of a vote as an indicator of
popular interest.[62] In addition, perhaps a majority of
local elections were not contested, and hence under such
conditions the number turning out to vote would not be
large in any event. Until the last decade or two prior to
the Revolution, it had been more or less the accepted
thing to return to office those councillors who desired it.

Occasionally an incident is recorded that illumines
the subject of how informal an affair the voting actually
was. In Philadelphia in 1705 the 'country party' protested that the election of representatives to the assembly
took the whole day and the sheriff was then elected by
show of hands. After they (the country party) had gone
home, the 'town party' demanded a ballot and elected
their candidate — probably also by allowing unauthor-
ized persons to vote.[63] In New York City, for years, the
voting was *viva voce* by wards, with the alderman of the
ward presiding.[64] In 1770 there was such agitation for
reform and the secret ballot that the procedure was reorganized the following year, and repeating and false
registration checked. Repeating, it is true, had been

61. *South Carolina Gazette,* Feb. 7, 1771.
62. Note also the wholesale fraudulent voting in Lancaster County (Pa.)
    in 1749, when stuffed ballots were alleged to exceed the total number
    actually voting (Eshleman, H. F., *Political History of Lancaster
    County's First Twenty Years,* in *Lancs. Co. Hist. Soc. Papers,* Lan-
    caster, 1896/7 — , vol. XX, p. 67f.).
63. Scharf, J. T., and Westcott, T., *History of Philadelphia,* vol. I, p. 246.
64. Peterson and Edwards, op. cit., p. 249.

legitimate hitherto, if property were owned in more than one place. The secret ballot was not granted.[65] Generally, voting was by a 'majority of voices' ; but particularly in Pennsylvania (and occasionally elsewhere, if requested) by 1775 the written ballot or 'ticket in writing' had been introduced.[66]

Under circumstances such as these, effective, genuine democracy was scarcely possible. As to the pressures of an economic or social nature to which reference has already been made, a broadside issued in New York City in 1770 calling for the secret ballot will serve to express the situation in the language of the day : 'It will prevent Men of Property, Power and Tyrannical Dispositions, from prostituting their Wealth and Influence, in giving Weight to their threats, and thereby intimidating the Electors from a free disposal of their Votes, according to their Understanding and Consciences . . . And effectually Screen all honest Burgers and Tradesmen, who may incline to Vote contrary to the Sentiments of their Employers or Landlords, from their Resentment.'[67]

(E)

In the light of these difficulties, are there then any even approximately accurate measures of popular interest available ? It is still possible to use the total vote cast as a rough indicator of the legality and actuality of participation in the few vigorously contested elections of which the records survive. In Boston in 1733 the maximum vote cast on the hotly disputed question of establishing a public market was 805 out of a total population of 16,000 — a total of about 5 per cent, or perhaps 20

65. Ibid. p. 251.
66. e. g. Lancaster, 1774 (Chap. 1687, *Laws of Pennsylvania*).
67. Quoted in Peterson and Edwards, op. cit., p. 250.

per cent of the adult males.[68] In general, for its representatives to the general court the vote in Boston was but 3
to 4 per cent of the population, although 16 per cent
were probably eligible.[69] In Wilmington (Del.) in 1739,
96 voted at the first borough election out of a (probably
somewhat over-estimated) population of 600. This was
16 per cent, or over one-half of the adult males — a far
higher percentage than in supposedly democratic Boston,
obviously indicating either the much more liberal nature
of the borough franchise, or a higher percentage of eligibles who voted.[70] Even the average poll in Wilmington
probably reached 7 per cent, which was higher than the
Boston maximum. This impression is confirmed also by
New Haven, where in 1766 only 275 'voters' attended a
very important meeting — about 4 per cent of the inhabitants — or only 16 per cent (approximately) of the adult
males.[71] In New York City in 1699 there were 632 votes
cast at an election for the city's representatives in the
assembly. The population was probably 8,500 at this
time, indicating 7½ per cent of the inhabitants or 30 per
cent of the adult males participating.[72] This particular
election was vigorously contested, involving the after-

68. Quincy, J., *Municipal History of Boston*, p. 11.
69. McKinley, A. E., *Suffrage Franchise in the Thirteen English Colo-
    nies,* p. 356f.
70. The Minute Book of Wilmington preserves a record of all the votes
    of the successful candidates from 1739. Probably the one who ob-
    tained the maximum vote in most instances was elected virtually
    unanimously, so that his total gives a rough indication of the num-
    ber voting. The high and low figures for the decades follow : 1740-
    1749, high 103, low 48 ; 1750-1759, high 129, low 25 ; 1760-1769, high
    73, low 28 ; 1770-1775, high 144, low 44. The population probably
    grew from about 600 to 1229. Sharply contested elections brought out
    the vote ; uncontested re-elections were by nominal polls.
71. Gipson, L. H., *Jared Ingersoll*, p. 19.
72. O'Callaghan, E. B. (Edit.), *Documents Relative to the Colonial His-
    tory of the State of New York,* vol. IV, p. 508.

math of the Leisler troubles and the dethronement of James II.[73] About the same time (1701) a hotly contested municipal election brought out about four hundred voters in the three wards in which the records survive. After deducting the illegal voters, this would indicate fully as great an interest in municipal as in provincial affairs, or at least in the personnel of the aldermen.[74] The percentage of inhabitants voting in New York City in an average year began to increase about 1730, and by 1760 was about 9 per cent.[75] During this period enforcement of voting qualifications was exceedingly lax.[76] In 1769, however, only 1515 voted — 506 as freeholders, 602 as freemen, and 407 as both.[77] This analysis of distribution is interesting as indicating the very substantial percentage that must have been disfranchised in other towns and boroughs which held to an exclusively property qualification. In Annapolis, in 1759, 120 voted in a contested election to the common council[78] and in 1764 approximately 140-150 voted for the representatives to the general assembly.[79] This represented perhaps 7 per cent of the white inhabitants, or 28 per cent of the adult white males — not far from the percentage in New York City, which also enfranchised on apprenticeship. Even

73. Cf. pp. 374ff.
74. *Minutes of Common Council,* Sept. 29, 1701.
75. Peterson, A. E., and Edwards, G. W., *New York as an Eighteenth Century Municipality,* p. 245f.
76. Ibid. p. 249. Cf. also in the *Minutes of the Common Council,* Sept. 29, 1701, an instance in which an actual scrutiny revealed at least 15 per cent of the voters as not being properly qualified according to the letter of the law. Evidence is lacking, but it is probable that in other cities also an informal disregard of qualifications prevailed for the small minority of the poorer group who really took the trouble to vote.
77. Peterson and Edwards, op. cit., p. 243.
78. *Maryland Gazette,* Jan. 11, 1759.
79. Ibid. Nov. 29, 1764.

in New York City, then, where the avenue for acquisition of freedom was unusually easy, there were evidently a large number of freemen who did not trouble to vote and a large number of non-freemen who did not bother to take out their freedom — amounting in all to the majority of the adult males. Furthermore, there is always a question as to whether a high percentage voting in a heterogeneous city, such as New York, indicated much more than emotional loyalty to one's own group and prejudice against groups other than one's own.[80]

Apart from the number voting, were there any other indications of the importance to be attached to the factor of popular interest and of the extent to which it was generated ? Mention has been made, in other connections, of the number of boroughs that retained or incorporated the 'town meeting' idea in some form or other in their charters.[81] The election of officers, the passing of by-laws, the voting of rates were the usual occasions for such meetings.[82] New York City by 1769 used public mass meetings to nominate candidates.[83] In an account of one of these meetings at Wilmington (N. C.), the minutes record that 'The Mayor, Aldermen, and Freeholders of Wilmington convened in common council at the court house. At this meeting the following resolution was adopted : "That the following rule be observed by the Mayor, Recorder, Aldermen, and Freeholders in all debates : That the

80. In 1772, 189 votes were cast in Westchester in a contest for the mayoralty. This probably represents a very high percentage of the inhabitants, although population estimates are not available. (Records — Town of Westchester, May 4, 1772.)

81. Cf. pp. 180ff.

82. Waddell, A. M., *History of New Hanover County*, p. 196, quotes a resolution of a Wilmington (N. C.) town meeting : 'William Robinson and a majority of the inhabitants having agreed to a tax. . . .'

83. Becker, C. L., *History of Political Parties in the Province of New York, 1760-1776*, Madison, 1909, p. 18.

party speaking should not leave the subject in debate to fall upon the person of any member of the common council or other person." [84] Apart from these more or less formalized meetings, others occurred from time to time when the occasion warranted. In Burlington in 1733 the proposed borough charter was worked out in such a meeting.[85] Even in the close corporation of Germantown, the people were called together once a year to have the laws read to them.[86] The sole evidence of municipal democracy in early Savannah (governed then as a municipal corporation from England) occurred when the pindar called together the inhabitants to propose voluntary regulations concerning cattle.[87] Bristol, Wilmington (Del.), Burlington, Elizabeth, and New Brunswick seem to have made most use of borough meetings. These meetings were to play a large part in the events leading up to the Revolution, but that story belongs elsewhere.[88]

The device of petition was very frequently used — directed either to the assembly or to the borough corporation — and its exercise was at least some indication of popular interest. In Annapolis in 1708 the 'greater parts of the inhabitants' are recorded as signing a petition to change the close corporation to one more democratically elected, and for other changes.[89] In Charleston a petition was directed against the charter.[90] In Philadelphia, 1695,

---

84. Waddell, op. cit., p. 197. Jan. 29, 1765.
85. Cf. Scott, Austin, *Early Cities of New Jersey*, in *N. J. Hist. Soc. Coll.*, 22nd ser., vol. IX, p. 168.
86. Scharf, J. T., and Westcott, T., *History of Philadelphia*, vol. I, p. 117, quoting Löher.
87. McCain, J. R., *Georgia as a Proprietary Province*, Boston, 1917, p. 189.
88. Cf. p. 376f.
89. Cf. p. 41f. ; also Mereness, N. D., *Maryland as a Proprietary Province*, p. 421f.
90. Cf. p. 193.

it was directed to the deputy-governor, beseeching him (among other items) for better men in office.[91] The close corporation of Philadelphia received frequent petitions, and certainly was subject to considerable popular pressure (for example, from the grand jury), even if not directly responsible to the electorate. Craftsmen would petition concerning infringed rights, and agitations against removal of slaughter-houses would prove effective.[92] By 1750, however, we find these Philadelphia petitions customarily directed not to the corporation, but to the assembly — possibly in a small way a barometer of the loss of touch with the general public on the part of the corporation.[93] The Albany corporation seems to have been particularly sensitive to public opinion. Germantown, though a close corporation, rescinded the exemption of its general court from compulsory service 'after repeated and final solicitation of the Community.'[94] Akin to the device of the petition was the pressure occasionally brought to bear upon a city government in the columns of the newspaper — sometimes by correspondence and sometimes by the manner in which the news was written.[95] The rivalry of the *New York Gazette* and the *New York Journal* in the conservative-liberal cleavage of New York from 1733 on was the best known and the most dramatic instance. This rivalry was particularly keen during the days in which Zenger controlled the *Journal,* and

91. Scharf and Westcott, op. cit., vol. I, p. 126.
92. Ibid. pp. 199, 208f., etc.
93. Ibid. p. 245.
94. *Pennsylvania Colonial Records, Minutes of the Provincial Council,* vol. I, p. 326.
95. An example of the latter was the campaign waged in the *Virginia Gazette,* looking toward the establishment of a watch in Williamsburg. (Cf. p. 274.)

levelled his shafts against the 'court party' in city and province.[96]

In general, the petition was the vehicle of communication used by any group wishing to effect a change in municipal policy. Seldom did such agitation for a change reach the point of the present day tactics of running opposition candidates, although frequently it might result in a broadside. It was the petition which was used for revision of assizes, against hucksters, for democratizing a close corporation, for a new market, against a new market, for the alteration of methods of disposal of water lots, for or against a new bridge or street. Furthermore, the petition was also the customary procedure adopted by an individual who wanted a special favour or the carrying out of an agreement — a water lot, remission of a fine, a little patch of land for charity's sake, an exemption from a building code, a minor municipal job, the enforcing of a grant of an exclusive privilege (e.g. a slaughter house or concession, abatement of rent, a piece of land). The minutes of all the councils are full of records of both group and individual petitions, which collectively furnish much of what little we really know about the issues agitating these municipalities and their ways of conducting business.

No account of popular participation in colonial municipal government is complete without recognition of the potential and actual role of the grand jury. This venerable institution, whose most striking function was doubtless in connection with the county and provincial courts, operated also in conjunction with certain of the mayor's

96. Cf. Edwards, G. W., 'New York City Politics before the Revolution,' in *Pol. Sci. Quart.*, vol. XXXVI, pp. 586ff. Cf. p. 219 for the use made of the columns of the *Maryland Gazette*.

courts. If, as in Charleston (S. C.), there was no municipal corporation, the grand jury in its presentments for the district often turned its attention to matters that were not well with the community.

For the most part, such presentments were routine — on the basis of information forthcoming from the prosecutor or from certain members of the jury itself. Yet at other times the jury would apparently conduct a miniature crusade against a particular offence, perhaps thereby reflecting at least a momentary reform wave. Thus, in the mayor's court of Annapolis in 1759, it brought in a dozen or more presentments for driving carts with a tread of less than five inches to the detriment of the condition of the streets.[97] Included in those 'presented' were the mayor and one of the aldermen ! In the same court a few years later about thirty persons and a total of over two hundred separate presentments were made for various liquor violations — chiefly for selling liquor to servants.[98] Instances such as these were likewise significant as revelations of previous laxity of enforcement and of prevailing custom.

More important as evidence of the grand jury's role in popular participation were its 'grievances' and 'remonstrances,' whereby it would call attention to abuses or neglect in administration, to the need for additional by-laws, or even to desirable reforms in the charters or statutes themselves. In Philadelphia, where the city corporation had become a moribund oligarchy, the jury took an active part in moves for better paving and lighting of streets.[99] Some action followed, although as yet the

97. Annapolis Mayor's Court Minutes, Jan. 30, 1759.
98. Ibid. Jan. 29, 1765.
99. Scharf, J. T., and Westcott, T., *History of Philadelphia,* vol. I, pp. 208, 218.

individual householder was still in part at least held responsible. The grand jury of the provincial court at Charleston (S. C.) was continually active during the last decade or so before the Revolution.[100] They presented as grievances : 'the want of a proper officer whose sole business shall be, to see, that the Firewood . . . be duly measured,' (Oct. 17, 1764) ; the quality of the Constables 'being in the execution of Persons of a mean low Character, whose poverty and ignorance subject them to take Bribes,' (Jan. 24, 1772) ; the disorderly behaviour of the town watch (ibid.) ; 'the want of a proper House of Correction in Charlestown, the work-House now used for that purpose being insufficient, whereby notorious bawds, strumpets, vagrants, drunkards and idle persons, who might be there committed, reign and infest the said town with impunity' (Oct. 17, 1764) ; the failure of magistrates and constables to carry out the Sabbath observance laws (Mar. 20, 1765) ; the rioting of negroes at night and the selling of spirits to sailors and negroes and 'that too little attention has been paid to grand jury presentments' (Oct. 16, 1765) ; 'the want of a law to prevent the storing of hemp in the heart of the town' ; the need for increasing the watch, better lighting, and a fire company (Oct. 19, 1767) ; 'that the laws for regulating the Markets are not properly attended to by the Commissioners, but left principally to the Management of their Clerk' (Jan. 21, 1771) ; 'that the Inhabitants of Charlestown . . . do not attend . . . on Easter Monday for the election of Parish officers ; by which Neglect, Persons interested in serving those offices, although often ignorant of the Duties incumbent on them, find means to get themselves

100. The references that follow are from the *South Carolina Gazette*.

elected to the great Prejudice of the Public,' (Jan. 21, 1771.) In other words, in this thriving community, where only the parish organization apparently served as a vehicle for democratic action, the institution of the grand jury succeeded in furnishing a channel for agitating municipal reform not without its success in inducing provincial and local action in the city's behalf.

At least as early as 1760 the Annapolis grand jury was making 'remonstrances' about the condition of the streets and docks and the unsatisfactory uncertainty concerning the by-laws, with but modest results. While it does not seem possible to claim that the action of the Annapolis grand jury of 1766 was wholly disinterested or devoid of factional significance, none the less it is noteworthy that it apparently formed the vehicle for crystallization of protest against the moribund state into which the nominally democratic city council had fallen.[101] The latter had met less and less frequently ; some of its members, including the recorder, never attended (they were elected for life) ; the accounting for the proceeds of a lottery had been at least somewhat questionable ; the docks, streets, and landings were neglected. All these grievances and others were included in a 'remonstrance' ; and, while the city corporation struck back in vehement defence and denial (in part sheer casuistry), it began to meet more frequently, held elections to fill vacancies, decided to fine its members for non-attendance, and otherwise stirred itself.[102] Incidentally, the corporation's defence brought out the fact that on two or three occasions the grand jury had made specific remonstrances, which had been fol-

101. Minutes, Annapolis City Council, 1760-1766, and *Maryland Gazette,* Mar. 13, 20, 27, May 1, June 19, 1766.
102. Minutes, Annapolis Mayor's Court, Jan. 29, 1765, etc.

lowed by by-laws — one concerning frauds in the sale of butter,[103] and another dealing with 'Bog Houses' that proved nuisances.[104] In 1758 the grand jury had proposed a lottery of £435 to raise money for a dock, and the corporation named a committee to manage it.[105]

Evidently in the foregoing instances (and probably many others) the grand jury played an important part in the general pattern of political behaviour.

As evidencing popular interest of quite another nature, mention should be made of the amount of unpaid service rendered by the inhabitants on roads or as night watch. This service was largely confined to the seventeenth century, but lingered on in some of the smaller communities till much later.[106] Perhaps inevitably it faded out of the picture as towns grew in size ; but must be included in any account of popular activity.

(F)

Thus popular participation varied greatly from place to place. New England towns as a group probably led the way, though by no means as decisively as usually supposed. At their town meetings these New Englanders voted instructions to their representatives, chose their officers and held them closely responsible, and debated the various questions of the hour — local, colonial, and 'national.' If the numbers participating, particularly in the eighteenth century, seem small to us, one must place this in perspective over against the age — realizing that the actual participation involved on the part of the single

103. Repealed soon afterwards ? Cf. *Maryland Gazette,* June 19, 1766 ;
    Minutes, Annapolis City Council, Nov. 11, 1758 ; Feb. 29, 1759.
104. *Maryland Gazette,* June 19, 1766.
105. Minutes, Feb. 3, 1758.
106. Cf. p. 259f.

individual was much greater than to-day, when voting, perhaps at the behest of a party, is almost the only act of citizenship performed by perhaps the minority of adults who do even this.

Outside of New England, participation on the part of the 'urban' electorate rested frequently on a broader suffrage base than in the rural districts, although the close corporation of Philadelphia was an exception. Even here, if the various local governing bodies of the Philadelphia area were included, the picture might be altered to conform with that of the other boroughs.[107] In general, the boroughs of the Middle Colonies furnished a real challenge to the alleged superior democratic functioning of the New England town. Certainly the numbers participating in the voting were proportionately much greater, and it is by no means certain that actual interest may not also have been more intense and widespread. This is particularly true when the borough meetings, formal and informal, and the growing cosmopolitanism are taken into account. New York State cities and boroughs were usually liberal in their franchise ; and in New York City particularly there was considerable genuine popular interest. In New Jersey, also, the traditional interest of the town meeting survived ; and, with liberal suffrage provisions, popular interest may even have exceeded that of the majority of the New England towns. Wilmington (Del.) seems to rank first among the larger boroughs in its broad suffrage base and ranks high in actual popular interest. In Virginia, popular participation in the government of the towns and boroughs was sporadic, and very much thwarted by the prevalence of the close corporation. It is doubtful, however, whether

107. Cf. p. 256.

the situation would have been much altered, even had the councils been regularly elected in Williamsburg and Norfolk — which alone were chartered. In North Carolina, the towns, small though they were, according to Raper, 'became much more important as centers of political activity than they did of commercial, industrial or social life. They were centers of local government and often of political conflicts.'[108] This opinion is borne out by their relatively democratic franchise and the epidemic of incorporations itself. However, much of this interest found expression through the medium of the assembly, which passed legislation of infinite detail concerning the individual towns. In South Carolina and Georgia the assembly was even more the medium for government of the localities. In all these Southern colonies, suffrage was about the average as to property qualifications.

All in all, the impression one gains of the colonial period is that genuine interest in borough government for the most part was confined to the property owners, with here and there a sprinkling of artisans — whose participation may have added more colour but not necessarily greater integrity to the electorate. In a society which, though starting simply, had in its urban and later manifestations outgrown this simplicity and developed fairly rigid stratification, the presence of an inarticulate mass of humanity making up the majority of the urban population and neither knowing nor caring about borough government was to be expected. Nor was it deemed incongruous that this mass should not have the vote.

108. Cf. Raper, C. L., *North Carolina, A Study in English Colonial Government*, New York, 1904, *passim*. The quotation is from a conversation with the author.

IX

THE DUTCH INCORPORATIONS

THE local institutions established by the Dutch in their settlements along the Hudson and the Delaware were distinctly apart from the main current of colonial municipal history. By the beginning of the eighteenth century all trace of their influence, structurally speaking, appears to have vanished. Yet they represent an interesting and illuminating episode, and, as such, merit separate treatment.[1]

The early and middle decades of the seventeenth century saw Holland in the vanguard of civilization and enjoying her 'golden age.' Measured by the extent of popular education and the democratic nature of her institutions, she was almost two centuries ahead of her time on the continent and well in the lead of England. From the standpoint of military and naval power she at least owned no superior ; and she finally lost New Netherland to England, not through conquest, but through a re-shuffling of territory after a long continued but indecisive struggle. Fiske rightly called attention to the influence of Holland on William Penn, in all of whose political ideas there was 'the broad and liberal temper that characterized the Netherlands before and beyond any other country in Europe.'[2]

New Netherland was entirely economic in its origin. The Dutch West India Company, to whom the concession was granted, was interested in the profits of the fur trade. The overwhelming majority of the numerous na-

1. Cf. O'Callaghan, E. B., *History of New Netherland* ; Jameson, J. F. (Edit.), *Narratives of New Netherland,* New York, 1909 ; also various histories of New York State.
2. Fiske, J., *Dutch and Quaker Colonies in America,* vol. II, p. 355.

224 AMERICAN CITY GOVERNMENT

tionalities who made up the settlers came also from an economic motive. Neither the altruistic strain which entered into the development of so many of the English proprietary colonies, nor the religious motives which were so strong in the settlement of New England and Pennsylvania were present as motivating factors in the exploration, government, and settlement of New Netherland, as long as it was under the Company's directors. Except as the tolerance of New Amsterdam, and subsequently New York, attracted a few of the persecuted from Europe, the migrant religious groups largely passed by the Hudson Valley.[3] Only when the Delaware area was transferred from the Company to the City of Amsterdam was this element particularly welcomed. The principal instance occurred in the southern section, where the City of Amsterdam granted the Mennonites a liberal charter for their settlement on the Hoarkill. There were also along the Hudson a few grants of land to patroons. These grants were designed to be manorial in their nature, and the resultant system did produce a feeble agricultural development. Their evolution lies outside the sphere of municipal institutions — except that it was in order to challenge the manor of Rensselaerswyck that Governor Stuyvesant extended municipal privileges to Beverwyck (Albany), its principal community.[4]

As the colony developed, there developed among its inhabitants a restlessness at the autocratic nature of the institutions set up by the Company, and the last decade or two of the colony's existence witnessed a more and more intense struggle for a grudgingly granted local self-

3. A fairly large colony of Huguenots settled in the valley of the Wallkill, and there were a few other smaller groups.
4. Van Laer, A. J. F. (Edit. and Trans.), *Minutes of the Court of Fort Orange and Beverwyck*, Albany, 1920-23, 2 vol., vol. I, p. 7.

government. To the credit of the States General and also
the City of Amsterdam Corporation, these two bodies
were apparently on the side of the inhabitants in the
effort towards more liberal institutions ; but the Company was on the spot, and the strong, autocratic, able per-
sonality of Governor Stuyvesant was generally decisive in
the direction of negativing these moves. Only in the territory directly under the control of the City of Amsterdam was genuine progress made.

Under these circumstances, for a long time the colony
did not grow with anything like the rapidity of its New
England neighbours ; and so little did its administration
commend itself to the actual residents that it yielded to
the English and soon accepted the latter's institutions and
government with scarcely a sign of local resistance. This
occurred in 1664 ; and from that date on, with only the
brief episode of Dutch reoccupation in 1673-4, the
remnants of local government that were peculiarly
Dutch rapidly faded and ultimately vanished altogether.

The intervention of the City of Amsterdam furnished
almost the only bright spot in the picture. 1656 saw the
Dutch West India Company hard pressed financially, and
accordingly it sold the southern section of what is now
Delaware to the City. Subsequently, in 1663, the remaining part of the Delaware area was likewise sold. This enlightened and wealthy corporation set up a board of
commissioners in their city to manage their unique colonizing venture ; and the liberal charters of New Amstel
and Hoarkill were the result. This project, with those
of the Company, passed into English control too soon
thereafter for much municipal history to result.

(B)

Just as the incorporations in the English colonies are not

understandable apart from a knowledge of English boroughs, so these Dutch towns require at least an elementary knowledge of the institutions of Holland to be appreciated. Here as in England there was considerable
variation, but the prevailing type of the larger town
seems to have made something of a distinction between
administrative and judicial duties. The latter were customarily in the hands of schepens who held courts similar
to the courts of the mayor and aldermen in the British
boroughs. Assisting them was an officer of great prestige
and influence known as a schout, who served as sheriff and
prosecutor. The administrative functions largely fell to
the lot of the 'burgomasters' who attended to police,
finance, etc. In smaller communities, there might be no
burgomasters, in which case there might be a 'tribunal
of well-born men,' or the schepens might assume
simple administrative duties. Even in the larger towns
the schepens often performed certain legislative functions.

In old Amsterdam, which naturally was the chief inspiration for these newer communities overseas, the burgomasters were the chief rulers : 'the principal churchwardens ; the guardians of the poor, of widows and
orphans ; and without their consent, no woman or minor
could execute any legal instrument. They held in trust
all city property and managed the same. They also
formed the city excise, and assisted in the enactment of
the city laws. No distress could be levied on a citizen's
property unless one of them were present ; their consent
was necessary before sentence of death could be pro-
nounced on a burgher, and in their presence only could
such a sentence be executed . . . In their capacity as
guardians of the public peace, they had certain authority
over the military and power to quell riots. They were

keepers of the city seal, and in their names were all public instruments drawn.'[5]

Popular participation varied. In Amsterdam, freedom or *'Burgherregt'* was of the guilds. Municipal officers, as mentioned, might be elected directly by the burghers or chosen by a 'tribunal of well born men,' usually nine, who were themselves elected. The schout and schepens might be named by the local lord from two or three times the number nominated by the burghers or the tribunal. This 'double nomination' was one of the favoured devices in New Netherland and lingered on after other institutions vanished. Close or self-perpetuating corporations also were found ; as were, also, on the other hand, 'common councils,' popularly elected.   Whichever the type, it was a Dutch tradition to favour a certain amount of rotation in office.[6]

The principal town in New Netherland was New Amsterdam. Almost from the outset it was intended that it should have the 'staple right' for the entire colony, and its struggles to maintain this have already been related.[7] In spite of such favours, its population did not reach 1,000 until 1656, or thirty years after the purchase of the land by Peter Minuit. Its efforts to secure municipal self-gov-

5. O'Callaghan, E. B., *History of New Netherland,* vol. II, p. 211f.
6. Cf. the Ordinance of the Director General and Council setting up the Court at Wildwyck, May 16, 1661 : 'Whereas it is customary in our Fatherland and other well regulated governments, that some change be made annually in the Magistracy so that some new ones come in [and] a few continue in order to inform the new ; the Schepens now appointed shall pay due attention to the conversation, demeanor, and fitness of honest and decent persons . . . in order to be able, about the time of changing or election, to furnish the Director General and Council with correct information as to who may be found fit, so that some may then be elected by the Director General and Council.' (Oppenheim, S. [Trans.], *Dutch Records of Kingston 1658-1684,* New York, 1912, 2 vol., vol. I, p. xii.)
7. Cf. p. 156.

ernment reveal a picture of similar arrested growth. It was evident that in the early stages the Company was not strongly averse to municipal institutions, for in its proposals in 1640 to the patroons the establishment of such institutions was clearly contemplated.[8] The terms of the charter of that date for the colony were most liberal, and it was stipulated that municipal governments must be conferred upon any communities large enough for them.[9] In 1642, however, when a board of twelve men, chosen to advise on a murder case, also petitioned for sundry privileges and self-government, it was dissolved 'as the same tends to a dangerous consequence, and to the great injury both of the country and of our authority.'[10]

In 1647, however, a body of 'Nine Men' was set up, from eighteen chosen popularly by Manhattan, Breuckelen, Amersfoort, and Pavonia. This group, true to custom, was itself to nominate eighteen candidates, from which again nine were to be chosen to succeed the original nine. In 1649 this group took up directly with the States General the case for a charter for New Amsterdam and for wider self-government generally, in their memorial calling attention to New England where 'neither patroons, nor lords, nor princes are known, but only the people.'[11] This request was at least nominally effective, for the States General the following year issued a provisional order directing the establishment of such municipal government. This was on advice of a committee set up by that body to investigate these complaints.[12] The

8. O'Callaghan, E. B. (Edit.), *Documents Relative to the Colonial History of New York*, vol. I, pp. 120, etc.
9. Ibid. p. 120.
10. Ibid. p. 203.
11. Quoted in Fiske, J., *Dutch and Quaker Colonies in America*, vol. I, p. 218.
12. O'Callaghan, E. B., *History of New Netherland*, vol. II, p. 136.

Company finally complied in 1652 by conferring a charter, democratic as regards the letter of its provisions — the first charter of what is now New York City. There was to be a schout, named by the governor as representing the Company, and burgomasters and schepens elected by the people.[13] This latter provision was immediately disregarded by Governor Stuyvesant, who proceeded to name the entire slate. Nor, in spite of requests and protests, did he, until 1658, concede to this corporation named by himself the customary right to nominate double the number from whom he should choose its successors — and even then hedged the concession about with numerous conditions. Nor was this all. Though the corporation represented his own appointees, he habitually ignored it or reversed its decisions, if they were not agreeable to himself. The schout was the Company's fiscall, who 'imprisons and releases citizens without the court's knowledge, and executes the court's judgments with contempt.'[14] The governor also claimed that he himself still had the right to make ordinances and publish interdicts.[15] When criticized and his attention called to the fact that the charter provided for popular election, the doughty Stuyvesant replied : 'The magistrates of New Amsterdam are proposed to the commonalty in front of the City Hall, by their names and surnames, each in his quality, before they are admitted or sworn into office. The question is then put, Does anybody object ?'[16] Apparently nobody ever did — and in the light of the choleric nature of the governor, this was not surprising. The following year, all

13. O'Callaghan, E. B., *History of New Netherland*, vol. II, p. 212f.
14. Ibid. p. 256.
15. Fiske, J., op. cit., vol. I, p. 228.
16. Lincoln, C. Z., *Constitutional History of New York*, Rochester, 1906, 5 vol., vol. I, p. 420.

but two were renamed. The group was also now to be paid for its services.[17]

Under such circumstances, it is not surprising that these officers were not particularly effective or respected. In 1658 the schout complained that in execution of the burgomaster's orders against thatched roofs and plastered chimneys, he 'notified them to remove them and that they made fun at him.' Consequently he asked for penalties for disobedience.[18] Yet the city was growing, and there is evidence that the burgomasters took their responsibilities seriously. Beginning in 1657, they held separate meetings once a week on account of 'divers matters' which concerned 'only the Burgomasters ; such as the repairs and construction of necessary works ; finances, how to find means ; and order, that everything should proceed in order ; also should anyone have to request or propose anything relating to the City, to direct it for the public good.'[19]

One of the main questions agitating the community was the exercise of its promised privilege of staple right. As early as 1648 the director general and his council had, at the request of the local merchants, forbidden casual traders the right to carry on their transactions. In 1654 the company rescinded this, reprimanding the council for it.[20] The twelfth article of the Freedoms had specifically promised that the stapleright for the entire colony should be on Manhattan ; and this, together with the renewed trouble from casual traders, caused the city corporation in 1657 to petition for the institution of

17. O'Callaghan, E. B., *History of New Netherland,* vol. II, p. 257.
18. Peterson, A. E., and Edwards, G. W., *New York as an Eighteenth Century Municipality,* p. 172.
19. Stokes, I. N. P., *Iconography of Manhattan Island,* New York, 1915-28, 6 vol., vol. I, p. 65.
20. Documents in *N. Y. Hist. Soc. Coll.,* 1885, pp. 1ff.

'*Burgherregt*' or burgher right. This time the petition was granted, but on condition that it could be purchased by non-residents, to expire when the non-resident pedlar completed his trading and left the city.[21] Under this arrangement several residents of Beverwyck (Albany) took out such burgher right.[22] Even this was not sufficient protection, for these regulations were not rigidly observed or enforced.[23]

This burgher right was important because it was by definition the 'freedom' of the city ; and, thus retained under the English, constituted the primary basis for the relatively liberal franchise of New York City. A distinction was made at first between the great and small burgher right, a distinction which was finally abolished in 1668.[24] Great burgher right carried the additional privileges of office-holding, exemption from watches and expeditions for a period, and freedom from arrest.[25] Those receiving it comprised :

1. those who have been, and at present are, in the High or Supreme Government of the Country, them and their descendents in the male line ;

2. all former and actual Burgomasters and Schepens of this City, their descendants in the male line ;

3. the Ministers of the Gospel formerly and at present in office, them and their descendents in the male line ;

21. Ibid. Docs. 3-7.
22. Weise, A. J., *History of Albany,* p. 109.
23. Cf. the numerous subsequent edicts and petitions. Cf. also *supra* p. 133f.
24. Fiske, J., *Dutch and Quaker Colonies in America,* vol. II, p. 18. However, in 1675 a distinction between merchants and little burghers as to the cost of 'freedom' was introduced. (Seybolt, R. F., *The Colonial Citizen of New York City,* p. 16.)
25. *N. Y. Hist. Soc. Coll.,* 1885, p. 10f. Cf. also p. 133 *supra.*

4. the commissioned officers . . .
Further, all others who desire and are inclined, or hereafter may be desirous and inclined, to be enrolled . . . shall . . . apply for the same to the Burgomasters, and receive it on paying therefor the sum of Fifty Guilders . . .

The following were entitled to the small burgher right :

1. all those who have resided and kept fire and light within the City one year and six weeks ;
2. all born within this City ;
3. all who have married, or may hereafter marry, native born daughters of Burghers, provided that all Burgher Right be not lost or forfeited by absence . . .
Further, all others who either now or hereafter will keep any shop, however it may be called, and carry on business within this City or the jurisdiction thereof shall be bound to apply to the Burgomasters for the small Burgher Right, and pay Twenty guilders.[26]

The money from these was to be spent by the burgomasters primarily in strengthening the city.

With difficulty, but none the less surely, the corporation continued to assert their rights over against Stuyvesant. In 1656, he granted them the privilege of nominating their successors, but on condition that acting magistrates normally should be retained, that nominees should always be favourable to the director general and council, and that the latter should have the right to appoint one of its number to assist in the nomination. However, a

26. Ibid. pp. 14ff., being a Proclamation by the Director General and Council. Feb. 2, 1657.

pretext was found to suspend the operation of this until 1658, when it finally was given effect.[27] Thus, with limitations, New Amsterdam finally came to be a fully established 'close corporation,' self-perpetuating, but with the Dutch customs of double nominations and fairly frequent rotation. Thus the city carried on, increasingly asserting its powers and exercising its functions. In 1660, the city was granted a separate schout.[28] Provision was also made in this same year for the annual renewal and publication of ordinances, so that people might not violate them through ignorance.[29] In 1664, the first general assessment for city expenses was made. In 1664, the city fell into the hands of the English in spite of the brave efforts of Stuyvesant to rally to resistance a population which had grown tired of his autocracy. Stuyvesant himself lived on for many years a respected resident of the city he had served so long and honestly, albeit arbitrarily.

For a while the Dutch corporation continued to exercise its functions in the old way, its charter rights confirmed by the articles of capitulation. On June 12, 1665, Governor Nichols appointed and proclaimed altered forms in the English style — but retained the small board of five 'aldermen' (formerly schepens) and made the mayor the chairman. The schout reappeared as the sheriff. I have been unable to discover what happened to the burgomasters. Presumably, in the confusion, they had lessened their functioning ; and, as officials, their position being unfamiliar to the new governor, they were ignored and omitted. Just how vacancies, if any, among the aldermen would have been filled in the normal course of events prior to 1668, I have been unable to dis-

27. O'Callaghan, E. B., *History of New Netherland*, vol. II, pp. 311f., 360.
28. Ibid. vol. II, p. 371.
29. Stokes, I. N. P., *Iconography of Manhattan Island*, vol. I, p. 78.

cover;[30] but in that year Governor Lovelace agreed to return to the Dutch custom of choosing magistrates from double the number presented by those in office.[31] In 1673, the Dutch again took control, named the city New Orange, ousted the English among the magistrates, and restored the government by schout, burgomasters, and schepens. The schout was to preside except when he acted as prosecutor. The burgomasters were to rotate in rank, and were given the usual duties. Inferior officers were to be named by the court as a whole. The new officers had to be threatened with removal to persuade them to act, inasmuch as they said that 'they did not intend to do anything.'[32] However, the following year the English again resumed control, the minutes began to appear in English (they had hitherto been in Dutch) and presumably the Dutch modification of the close corporation resumed its functioning — to be permanently superseded by the entirely English charter of 1686.

Apart from New Amsterdam, a number of other communities received local courts of schout and schepens by proclamation. These in every instance appear to have been named by the director general; but in certain instances, perhaps in all instances, were allowed to nomi-

30. In the Court Records of June 11, 1667, it was noted that the governor had commissioned the existing mayor, aldermen, and sheriff for an additional period till July 24. There is no record of a meeting on this latter date, but the minutes of July 30, 1667, reveal some change of personnel and also the swearing in of Alderman DePeyster, 'he being absent at the election.'

31. Cf. Morris, Richard B. (Edit.), *Select Cases — New York City Mayor's Court*, p. 45.

32. For account of local government under the Dutch restoration, cf. Brodhead, J. R., *History of the State of New York*, New York, 1853-71, 2 vol., vol. II, pp. 218, 219, 224-230, 242 ; O'Callaghan, E. B. (Edit.), *Documents Relative to the Colonial History of New York*, vol. II, pp. 678ff.

nate their successors, by the double nomination process
mentioned before.[33] They were apparently not in receipt
of formal charters, nor did they have burgomasters ; but
these courts did exercise (subject to review) certain administrative functions. A rough indication of their rank
might be found in the number of schepens assigned.
Breucklen, 1654, Swaenenburg (Kingston), 1673, and
Williamstadt (Albany), 1673, were given four schepens.
The Albany charter of 1686 speaks of this as a 'schepenen,' whereas the earlier grant to it in 1652 as Beverwyck (which stipulated four or more 'commissarissen,'
with two 'extraordinary' ones often added) was called a
'town.' Its chief was called a 'commies' and later the vice-
director. This Beverwyck court, however, was for the
entire area, rather than for the village alone. Yet a number of the incidental ordinances applied largely, if not
entirely, to the village. The preamble to such ordinances
(1659) read 'the vice-director and magistrates of Fort
Orange, village of Beverwyck, and the dependencies
thereof.'[34] Whether this is or is not to be regarded as sig-
nifying a higher status is uncertain. In addition to Beverwyck, Mitwout in 1654, Bergen in 1661, and Wildwyck
(Kingston) in 1661, and possibly one or two others were
given three schepens. The numerous remainder had two
only. Frequently one schout served for several of these
villages. The Wildwyck grant (charter ?) is worth quoting in part : 'considering the increased population of

33. Van Laer, A. J. F. (Edit. and Trans.), *Court Minutes of Fort Orange
and Beverwyck,* vol. I, p. 9. He asserts that these successors were
chosen from double the number 'chosen by the inhabitants.' The
minutes, at least of Beverwyck and Wildwyck, would indicate that
the double nomination was made by the existing justices, i. e., a
'close corporation.' I do not know upon what Van Laer bases his
generalization — possibly upon certain Long Island towns.
34. Ibid. p. 8.

said village, [we] resolve to favor its inhabitants with a subaltern court of justice, and to organize it as far as possible, and the situation of the country will permit in conformity with the customs of the city of Amsterdam in Holland, but so that from all judgments an appeal may be made to the Director-general and Council in New Netherland . . . Should the situation of affairs be such that the Schout and Schepens deem it advisable for the security and peace of the inhabitants, during the absence of the Director-general and Council . . . to issue in said district any order, respecting public roads, enclosure of lands, gardens or orchards, and further, what might concern the country and agriculture ; so, too, relative to the building of churches, schools, and other similar public works ; as well as the means from which, and in what manner, these shall be regulated, they are authorized to bring their considerations . . . in writing, support these by argument, and deliver them to the Director General and Council, to be, if deemed useful and necessary, confirmed. . . .'[35] Formal ordinance power was extended in 1664.[36] The Beverwyck court likewise passed ordinances, attended to the church repairs, tried cases, watched over estates, planned the defence against the Indians, appointed the rattle watch, all in their capacity as magistrates. Together with the former magistrates in extraordinary session, they even concluded treaties with the Indians.[37]

With the coming of the English, various dispositions were made of these village governments. For the most part, in the chief ones (e.g. Brooklyn, Albany), the rights

35. O'Callaghan, E. B., *History of New Netherland*, vol. II, pp. 432ff.
36. Oppenheim, S. (Trans.), *Dutch Records of Kingston*, vol. I, p. xii.
37. Van Laer, A. J. F., (Edit. and Trans.), *Court Minutes, Fort Orange and Beverwyck*, var., esp. vol. II, pp. 208-219, 226.

and privileges were confirmed, the schepens re-chris-
tened commissioners or commissaries,[38] and the schout
continued in office. In 1665 the jurisdiction of the Albany court was widened to include Rensselaerswyck, and
the schout of the latter was appointed for the combined
court.[39] Apparently the justices of this particular court
were chosen half from the Albany area and half from
Rensselaer until 1671, when one more was added from
Albany.[40] These gradually came to resemble the ordinary
county justices of the peace. Fordham and New Harlem
in 1669 were added to the jurisdiction of the New York
City court.[41] In 1671, the chairman of the Albany board
was addressed as 'mayor' by Governor Lovelace.[42] In
1669, Kingston was given a village government of a new
type, in the form of eight overseers, chosen by the people.[43] It is not our purpose to say whether these towns
should be included in any list of Dutch municipal corporations, because the Dutch custom in these matters
was other than the English ; but rather to picture them
as they were — appointed boards, usually self-perpetuating, governing the villages and often a wide area there-
abouts. By 1700, all trace of the Dutch influence upon
their structure appears to have passed.

In 1655, the New Netherland authorities forced the

38. The title 'commissarissen,' in Dutch, was used for the Beverwyck
magistrates.
39. Van Laer, *Court Minutes, Albany, etc.*, op. cit., p. 7. Van Laer also
claims that the burghers elected his successor in 1670. The wording
of the minutes (p. 196), Nov. 1, 1670, would seem to justify this,
but it is just possible that the term 'burghers' may have applied
to the magistrates only.
40. *Minutes of the Executive Council of the Province of New York*, vol.
II, pp. 432ff.
41. Peterson, A. E., and Edwards, G. W., *New York as an Eighteenth Century Municipality*, p. 149.
42. Quoted in Munsell, J., *Annals of Albany*, vol. IV, p. 21.
43. Schoonmaker, M., *History of Kingston*, New York, 1888, p. 61.

surrender to their authority of New Sweden on the Delaware.[44] In the part retained under the control of the Dutch West India Company, there is nothing of significance municipally to record except the setting up of village courts (Dutch style) for the Swedes on Tinicum Island (1658), for Altena, and for Upland.[45] In the part purchased by the City of Amsterdam, a definite attempt was made to establish municipal institutions at 'New Amstel' — later Newcastle. The future colonists were promised that such institutions would be regulated 'in matters of police and justice in the same manner as here in Holland,' one schout or officer as the head of justice appointed by the West India Company (which until 1663 [?] apparently retained some jurisdiction), three burgomasters appointed by the common burghers, five to seven schepens chosen by the director general and council from a list of double that number elected by the burghers. On reaching two hundred families, a common council of twenty-one was to be set up to meet with the burgomasters and schepens and resolve together on all matters relating to the city government. Appeals would only be granted in major cases. Vacancies apparently were to be filled by the corporation itself.[46]

After the conquest of the Swedes by the Dutch, the territory was placed under a temporary, semi-military tribunal. This was allowed to continue for a while by Vice-Director Alrichs 'until the arrival of the Ship *de*

44. O'Callaghan, E. B. (Edit.), *Documents Relative to the Colonial History of New York,* vol. XII (B. Fernow, Trans. and Compil.) is basic to an understanding of the story of the settlements on the Delaware.
45. Cf. de Valinger, L., Jr., *Development of Local Government in Delaware,* var. (unpublished thesis, U. of Delaware).
46. Cf. the draft of the agreement in O'Callaghan, E. B. (Edit.), *Documents Relative to the Colonial History of New York,* vol. I, pp. 619-24 ; also de Valinger, op. cit., p. 31f., who states that the common council was never set up.

Waeg, when seven Common Councilmen and from them three new schepens were chosen ; also another Secretary and Schout, Two Elders and Two Deacons.'[47]

In 1658, the settlement's population numbered about 600 more or less poor, half-starved people ; and the agents of Amsterdam actually had to assume much of the responsibility belonging to the newly established municipality. However, in 1661, the jurisdiction of the court was substantially increased, and appeals in criminal cases were no longer granted to New Amsterdam. Furthermore, it was exempted from the staple right of the latter, and the military garrison was to be removed.[48] The right to have three burgomasters was reaffirmed in 1662 together with the power of their election by the common burghers. Apparently this provision must actually have come into operation, for when the English occupied the area in 1664, it was with the burgomasters that Sir Robert Carr concluded the agreement for the area. He continued them provisionally for six months.[49] No further records are available to indicate what happened until 1668, when we read that Deputy Governor Carr formed a temporary council of himself, the 'schout,' and five others.[50] In 1672 the bailywick of Newcastle was set up, which incidentally retained the Dutch custom of double nomination.[51] In 1673, when the Dutch reoccupied the area, they set up three courts — at New Amstel, Upland, and Hoarkill.[52]

47. Letter from Alrichs to Burgomaster de Graef of Amsterdam, in O'Callaghan, op. cit., vol. II, p. 68.
48. O'Callaghan, E. B., *History of New Netherland,* vol. II, p. 462f.
49. *Duke of Yorke's Book of Laws : Charter and Laws of Pennsylvania,* 1879, p. 446.
50. *Records of the Court at Upland* (*Memoirs of Hist. Soc. of Pa.,* Philadelphia, 1826-95, 14 vol., vol. VII, p. 24).
51. Cf. p. 435.
52. Smith, Samuel, *History of the Colony of Nova-Caesaria,* p. 110 ; Conrad, H. C., *History of the State of Delaware,* vol. II, pp. 512, 716.

These were then apparently continued by the English and gradually transformed to the English type.

One other Delaware charter was issued by the City of Amsterdam. This was given to a group of Mennonites who settled on the Hoarkill in 1662.[53] This charter was also of the liberal type, allowing the double nomination privilege — the City of Amsterdam then to select one half. It granted local popular voting by ballot on all laws, with a two-thirds majority needed for their enactment — subject to approval of the City in each instance.[54] After being despoiled by the English, this settlement apparently revived enough again to be granted a court by the Dutch in 1673, which was continued by the English under the name of Lewes. It subsequently became a 'shire town.'[55]

(C)

What permanent contribution did the Dutch make to American municipal government ?[56] Structurally, none whatsoever, although some writers profess to find Dutch influence in the organization of New York State villages. Institutionally, claims have been made that the written ballot was of Dutch origin and that liberal suffrage owes much to Dutch example. This first claim is doubtful, inasmuch as the written ballot appears to have been fairly common in England also at this period. The latter, in certain instances, is a somewhat more defensible claim, at least as far as the early years of New York City and Albany are concerned. Yet other and more powerful influ-

53. Cf. p. 85.
54. O'Callaghan, E. B., *History of New Netherland,* vol. II, pp. 466ff.
55. Cf. p. 85.
56. Dutch settlers from Albany in New Brunswick may have led this latter community to seek incorporation (as the charter puts it) as being at the 'head of a navigable river.' Cf. *supra,* p. 57.

ences swept eastward from the Piedmont and frontier. These were accelerated by democratic theories of other origins, and doubtless did more to bring about an eventual wholly democratic suffrage than did the examples of the Dutch.

The question of the contribution of ideals remains, and does not properly belong here. Certainly New York City's cosmopolitan tradition dates from Dutch times. Such influences are indefinable at best, and become inextricably fused with the main stream of national life and culture.

We may close with one of Fiske's striking generalizations :

> The two great middle colonies present a most interesting subject of comparative study because both have been profoundly influenced by Holland, but in the one case the Dutch ideas have been worked through the crucible of an individual genius (William Penn), while in the other case they have flowered with random luxuriance. In the cosmopolitanism which showed itself so early in New Amsterdam and has ever since been fully maintained, there was added to American national life the variety, the flexibility, the generous breadth of view, the spirit of compromise and conciliation needed to save the nation from rigid provincialism. Among the circumstances which prepared the way for a rich and varied American nation, the preliminary settlement of the geographical center by Dutchmen was certainly one of the most fortunate.[57]

57. Fiske, J., *Dutch and Quaker Colonies in America,* vol. II, p. 355f.

X

VESTRIES, BOARDS, AND COMMISSIONS

IN the complete picture of the structure of government of colonial municipalities there is room for at least a brief description of certain other special bodies that exercised various governmental functions in the urban or semi-urban areas. The counties have already been mentioned, and the role of the colonial assembly will be reserved for later discussion.[1] There remain the vestries of the parishes and wards and certain *ad hoc* bodies set up to administer specific functions. In practice, these latter bodies were important only in the two larger cities of Philadelphia and Charleston, and the smaller but important community of Savannah.

It will be recalled that in the illogical but spontaneous development of urban governmental institutions in England such special boards came to be a characteristic feature of the eighteenth century. This was especially true of areas administered by close corporations. Police, lighting, and street paving and cleaning were the functions most frequently singled out for such treatment. Usually, but not always, members of the city corporation would be *ex officio* members of the new board, and occasionally were themselves empowered to name remaining members. In addition, the Elizabethan Poor Law had seized upon the parish vestries as the local unit most suitable to administer relief. Certain other functions of local government (including some responsibility for highways and occasionally appointment of constables and inspectors of tobacco[2]) had also been conferred upon or assumed by

1. Chap. XIII.
2. Cf. Rainbow Papers, Black Book, vol. VIII, pt. 1, Church Vestry Papers. MSS. in Hall of Records, Annapolis.

these vestries. For the most part, in rural areas these vestries were strictly supervised by the county justices ; but a wide variety of custom existed in their relations with the municipal corporations. In a few instances, the municipal corporations had themselves absorbed the functions of the vestries or rather were constituted the vestry for their area ; in others the corporations appointed the vestry ; in others, supervised them — particularly when the city was a 'county of itself' ; in perhaps the larger number the jurisdictions of the two bodies were separate legally, but identical or overlapping territorially.[3]

The number of urban communities in the Colonies was scarcely large enough to duplicate the variety of English precedent ; and the systems of town meeting, town commissioners, and borough charters between them accounted for local government in most communities, and ordinarily proved sufficient — at least for administering functions other than poor relief.

A few incidental and exceptional arrangements may be mentioned in passing. The New York assembly in 1754 named a board of two excise commissioners for New York City — a power normally under the city corporation or the county justices.[4] The Maryland assembly in 1718, at the petition of the Annapolis corporation, appointed commissioners to lay out a new section.[5] The

3. Disputes as regards 'settlement' were frequent between these smaller units which had charge of the poor. In the upper part of the county of Philadelphia it was reported in 1753 that a poor blind man 'about whose maintenance there was a dispute between two townships' hanged himself. (*Maryland Gazette,* May 17, 1753.)

4. Peterson, A. E., and Edwards, G. W., *New York as an Eighteenth Century Municipality,* p. 269.

5. Riley, E. S., *The Ancient City,* p. 96f. This was an instance of the custom of a number of the assemblies of appointing commissioners for various tasks.

little community of Bath (N. C.) in 1715 received a gift
of some books, and eleven sections of an act of the legislature of that year were devoted to detailed instructions
to a board of 'Commissioners and Trustees for the due
Inspection and Preservation of the Library.' The members of the board (named in the Act) included the governor and council of the province, certain judges, and
several others.[6] This was interesting also as a commentary
upon the value placed upon books in colonial times. Instances of the incorporation of the mayor, aldermen, etc.,
in a special capacity for a specific purpose — perhaps with
others besides these officials added — occur in Elizabeth,
1754, for building and managing the poor house ;[7] and
in New York City, 1771, for the 'Society of the Hospital
of the City of New York in America.'[8] The 'Trustees of
New Castle Common,' incorporated in 1764, function to
this day, from time to time voting the profits of the land
rents for some worthy object in the town. Members are
elected by the people for life.[9] There were in all probability other arrangements of the foregoing character
when occasion arose.[10]

The role played by the parish, its wardens and its
vestry, varied from colony to colony. In general, govern-
mentally speaking, the chief function of the vestry was
relief of the poor, but in certain instances it absorbed
other functions. It reached its highest development in

6. *State Records of North Carolina,* vol. XXIII, pp. 73ff.
7. McBain, H. L., 'Legal Status of the Colonial City,' in *Pol. Sci. Quart.,*
   vol. XL, p. 196.
8. Lincoln, C. Z., *Constitutional History of New York,* vol. I, p. 743.
9. Cf. *Title Papers of the New Castle Common,* 1893. The original land
   had probably been so allocated from Stuyvesant's time, but rested
   primarily upon a grant by Penn in 1701.
10. e. g. the 'Trustees' of Westchester, who continued to handle trans-
    actions involving land, even though this microscopic town was pro-
    vided with a complete borough corporate organization. Cf. p. 172.

Charleston,[11] but in Williamsburg and elsewhere assumed a few other minor duties.[12] In Annapolis, for instance it named the 'Inspectors' for Annapolis and Indian
Landing.[13] North of Maryland the parish was either non-
existent or of less importance. New York City experimented with various agencies, public and private, in the
care of its poor, and in 1745 adopted the policy of electing two vestrymen in each ward and entrusting them with
poor relief and maintenance of the minister. The mayor's
court retained a certain amount of supervision.[14]

Originally these vestries in Virginia may have been
chosen in parish meeting, but sooner or later they usually
developed into the close or self-perpetuating type.[15] Normally they were the civil aspect or expression of the
Anglican parish and church. The county justices assumed some responsibility for supervising their activities in the function of assessment, etc.[16] In Charleston
they were popularly elected down to the Revolution.[17]

To carry out certain of their duties they commonly
chose two of their number to serve as churchwardens.
These wardens also frequently performed the function
of presentment to county court of various offenders
against the moral code.

(B)

A sharp distinction should be drawn between the spe-

11. Cf. p. 249.
12. Gulick, L., and Pollard, J. G., *Modern Government in a Colonial
City*, p. 32.
13. St. Anne's Parish Records, Vestry Minutes, 1760, etc., MSS. in custody of the church.
14. McBain, op. cit., p. 196 ; Peterson and Edwards, op. cit., p. 298.
15. e. g. St. Anne's, Annapolis, judging from the Minutes.
16. e. g. St. Anne's Parish Records, Vestry Minutes, Nov. 4, 1760. etc.
17. St. Philip's Parish Records, Vestry Minutes, MSS. in custody of the
church.

cial commissioners, etc., set up in Philadelphia, Charleston, and Savannah, and the previously discussed various trustees and commissioners set up for the 'towns.'[18] These latter were designed for incipient or small municipalities, primarily during the stage of land surveys and sale, and normally assumed all appropriate governmental functions ; the former were the outgrowth of genuine urban problems and were designed for special functions. In these three communities, they were so interwoven with other governmental agencies that it seems desirable to consider each separately and to avoid much attempt at generalization.

In any consideration of Charleston, the initial warning must be given that a number of the acts of the South Carolina assembly have apparently been lost (surviving in title only), and it is frequently necessary to piece together bits of information from other sources. Furthermore, the early journals of the vestry of St. Philip's parish were all burned by the wife of the deceased clerk, who was unwilling to surrender them to his successor.[19] The vestry records from 1755-1761 are also missing. Even during the period of extant records there are many years in which one cannot be certain what agencies were exercising particular governmental functions. The assembly met in Charleston, and throughout the period appears to have been in intimate touch with its problems and responsive to its needs. In general, the governmental functions of the town at any one time were shared by two or three boards and the vestry and wardens and other officers of St. Philip's parish and church.

For a while the assembly itself attempted to govern the

18. Cf. p. 165.
19. Authority of incumbent clergyman, St. Philip's Church, Rev. M. F. Williams.

town without creating administrative agencies to carry out instructions.[20] In 1696, it provided for the appointment of commissioners for the care and education of the poor, and in 1698 these commissioners were given power to levy a rate.[21] Whether it was these same commissioners or whether, as is more probable, there had been another board set up for the town after the usual fashion from Maryland south, records exist in 1698 of commissioners vested with authority over nuisances, the pulling down of houses in the event of fire, overseeing the repair of sidewalks, etc. Vacancies were to be filled by appointment of the governor.[22] In 1701 the town watch was placed under the control of three commissioners named in the act, and assessors also were named to levy the appropriate rate. Here again the governor was empowered to fill vacancies, but the assembly reserved the right of removal of the assessors. This particular commission was disbanded in 1704, but re-instituted in 1708.[23] Under the 1701 Act the officers and eight of the watch were to attend the governor twice on Sunday at church. These various measures concerned with the watch were in large part accounted for by the state of war between England and France and Spain.[24]

In 1704, a new commission was created to deal with fire prevention, the providing of buckets, enforcing the law against chimneys, etc. This commission was vested also with certain quasi-judicial powers in hearing com-

20. Except possibly the county courts. Cf. p. 107.
21. Pringle-Smith, J. J., *Government of the City of Charleston,* in *Charleston Year Book for 1881,* p. 332.
22. McCord, D. J. (Edit.), *Statutes at Large of South Carolina,* vol. VII, pp. 7ff.
23. Ibid. pp. 40, 49ff., 57 (Stat. 207, 232, 276, 282) ; Pringle-Smith, op. cit., pp. 22ff.
24. Pringle-Smith, op. cit., pp. 22ff.

plaints and levying fines for infractions. A further act (1713) had to be passed to name new commissioners — the first act having failed to provide against vacancies, and there being but one of the original group left. The governor and council were empowered to fill vacancies.[25] It was the assembly, however, that in 1754 resolved to send for a fire engine for the town.[26]

In 1711, commissioners were appointed to build a new parish church.[27]

In 1712, poor relief was made the function of the parish vestries, who were given the power to nominate overseers of the poor to serve with the church wardens. If needed, a rate might be levied.

The abortive attempt to incorporate Charleston as a city has been mentioned elsewhere.[28]

In 1704, Charleston had been made into St. Philip's parish ; and while a second parish, St. Michael's, was established in 1751, the care of the poor and certain incidental police functions for the entire town,[29] acquired in the intervening time, remained with St. Philip's. The acts vesting the parish of St. Philip's with these additional powers I have been unable to locate. However, in the Vestry Journal of 1742 there appear for the first time records of numerous officers elected at the annual parish meeting. It is recorded that there were elected 'by Inhabitants and Freeholders' five firemasters, five commissioners of workhouses and markets, six packers, six wood measurers, five commissioners of highways. These were in addition to the seven vestrymen and two church ward-

25. McCord, op. cit., pp. 41ff., 58ff. (Stat. 234, 235).
26. *Maryland Gazette,* July 18, 1754.
27. McCord, op. cit., p. 56f. (Stat. 296).
28. Cf. p. 193.
29. McCord, op. cit., p. 83 (Stat. 795) ; Pringle-Smith, op. cit., p. 332f.

ens who were recorded as regularly elected in previous years.[30] It is accordingly fair to assume that about this time the South Carolina assembly set up for the town a government of a democratic type for most of its functions. This was in the form of a government of a 'parish,' which, while it was the approximate equivalent of a 'town' or 'township,' was none the less a term usually restricted elsewhere to ecclesiastical matters. That such was the case is indicated by an entry in the Vestry Journal of April 23, 1764, which introduces the account of the election of the several minor officers by the phrase 'pursuant to the several Acts of the General Assembly.'[31] There is no evidence from the minutes that the vestry as such performed civil functions other than poor relief.

It appears that from time to time special commissioners were appointed by the assembly to lay out particular streets or sections ;[32] and in an Act of 1764 street commissioners were named with the more general duties of keeping streets and wharves clean, planting trees, regulating cartage, supervising foundations of houses, etc., as well.[33] Nine in all were so named, and they were given power to co-opt, in case of vacancies.[34] Customarily they were recorded in the minutes of the vestry of St. Philip's as 'appearing' at the annual Easter Monday parish meeting at which the other officers were chosen.[35] Apparently there was also in existence about this time a commission to build an exchange ; for, in 1768, this commission was also given the duty of building the poor house and the

30. Journal, Vestry of St. Philip's, Book I, Apr. 1742.
31. Ibid. Book II.
32. e. g. 1734, Stat. 579.
33. Pringle-Smith, op. cit., p. 339f. Cf. also *supra*, p. 247.
34. Act of April 10, 1764, printed in *South Carolina Gazette,* Aug. 25, 1764.
35. Journal, Vestry of St. Philip's, *passim.*

hospital.[36] In 1768 an act of the assembly substituted five coal and wood measurers for the three wood measurers hitherto chosen, retaining, however, their election at the parish polls.[37] This may have followed a grand jury presentment of 1764 concerning forestalling and false measuring of wood.[38]

By way of summary, the government of Charleston under the intimate care of the assembly had evolved by 1775 so that its functions were distributed as follows among six main agencies :[39] the judicial duties rested largely with the county and district justices — with quasi-judicial functions exercised by other agencies ; the laying out, paving, and care of streets were in the hands of street commissioners ; the watch was under another commission ; fire-prevention under still another ; the workhouse and markets under still another ; and poor relief and miscellaneous functions were administered by the vestry. In a sense, some of these bodies were obviously responsible more to the assembly than to the inhabitants of Charleston, in so far as only a minority of their members were democratically elected. Only the abortive attempt at a charter in 1722 gave any indication of a desire for formal municipal incorporation.

The government of Savannah followed a somewhat similar evolution, under the fostering care of the Georgia legislature, which met there as the capital city. When the town was laid out in 1733 it had, it is true, been divided

36. McCord, op. cit., p. 90f. (Stat. 966).
37. Journal, op. cit., Book II, 1768.
38. Cf. p. 218f.
39. An excellent and fairly detailed picture of the Charleston of this period is given in Sellers, Leila, *Charleston Business on the Eve of the Revolution*, pp. 16-24. Cf. particularly pp. 21-23 for a description of the markets.

into wards and tithings ; but this division seems to have been followed by no actual local government apart from the paternalistic measures of the colonial authorities.[40] In 1755, a beginning was made by naming commissioners for the market established that year.[41] In 1757, a watch was established with the superintendents named in the act ;[42] but in 1759 this was modified to constitute the resident justices, together with the church wardens and vestry, the superintendents *ex officio*.[43] In 1759, these same church wardens of Christ Church parish were placed in charge of the fire engine and the purchase and inspection of buckets — with the necessary assessing power.[44] In 1760, commissioners were named to clear the streets of rubbish and prevent encroachments,[45] but in 1766 this function was also transferred to the church wardens.[46] About 1764, two Acts were passed appointing commissioners respectively to rebuild the court house and to repair Christ Church.[47] In 1768 (by general act) the wardens, with the justices, were vested with power to prevent entry of those afflicted by smallpox.[48] At this stage it might be surmised that Savannah had evolved a fairly simple government under the control of its vestry of church wardens — a government more or less unique among colonial municipalities ; but this simplicity was not to remain for long. In 1770, a commission was set up (named in the Act) with power to assess for and con-

40. *South Carolina Gazette,* Aug. 18-25, 1733.
41. *Colonial Records of Georgia,* vol. XVIII, pp. 8off.
42. Ibid. pp. 212ff.
43. Ibid. pp. 290ff.
44. Ibid. pp. 308ff.
45. Ibid. pp. 455ff.
46. Ibid. pp. 753ff.
47. *South Carolina Gazette,* Mar. 10-17, 1764.
48. *Colonial Records of Georgia,* vol. XIX, Pt. I, p. 24.

trol the town watch.[49] The Act was eventually disallowed, and presumably the justices and wardens resumed control. The final commission, named in 1774, was for the purpose of licensing porters and regulating slave labour.[50] Thus, during the whole period after 1752, the day-to-day administration was largely concentrated in the wardens, with occasional special commissions. The responsibility for policy appears to have remained throughout with the assembly.

The story of Philadelphia is the story of a close corporation which, at least in part because of its undemocratic character, declined in prestige and function in its later years ; while many of the functions normally belonging to a municipal corporation were shared with *ad hoc* commissions. As such, it furnishes perhaps the nearest parallel in America to the close corporations and governments of certain larger English boroughs.

Perhaps the first major sign of lack of confidence in the corporation was revealed in the action of the assembly in 1740, in curtailing the power to levy taxes — this power being vested, in spite of the corporation's protest, exclusively in assessors and commissioners.[51] Hitherto, it had (1712) been vested in the elected assessors and the corporation acting jointly for city charges and public works.[52]

For several years prior to 1750 there had been considerable agitation for a paid and more efficient watch. This was finally climaxed in a grand jury presentment ; and in 1750 an act was passed setting up a board of six ward-

49. Ibid. pp. 147ff. ; Flippen, P. S., 'Royal Government in Georgia,' in *Ga. Hist. Quart.*, vol. VIII, p. 283.
50. De Kenne, op. cit., pp. 416ff.
51. Scharf, J. T., and Westcott, T., *History of Philadelphia*, vol. I, p. 209.
52. Keith, C. P., *Chronicles of Pennsylvania*, vol. II, p. 505.

ens — named in the Act, but subsequently to be elected by the freeholders — with power to erect and maintain street lamps and appoint watchmen. However, the actual regulation of the watch was to rest with the mayor, recorder, and four aldermen.[53] In 1756, another special board of six wardens was set up to assume responsibility for both lighting and watching ; but this time the mayor, recorder, and four of the aldermen were also to be included on the board. After the terms of those named in the Act expired, successors were to be elected annually — two each year for three year terms. The wardens and assessors were to choose a treasurer. The wardens were also empowered to dig wells and fix pumps.[54] This Act was to continue for seven years. Re-enactment came in 1771, but with six men named in the Act empowered to appoint the wardens, and the latter thereafter to be elected. The wardens (in conjunction with the assessors) were given taxing power.[55] In 1761-2, a second major board of commissioners was set up, this time to assume responsibility for paving and cleaning the streets.[56] In 1763, having found their powers quite inadequate, they complained to the assembly. Their complaints led to a series of acts concerning nuisances, size of wheels, encroachments, responsibility of owners of abutting property, etc.[57] This board also was interlocked with the city corporation, in that its powers were nominally exercised in conjunction with the mayor, recorder, and four alder-

53. Scharf and Westcott, op. cit., vol. I, p. 218 ; McBain, H. L., 'Legal Status of the American Colonial City,' in *Pol. Sci. Quart.*, vol. XL, p. 195f. ; *Wharton School Studies : City Government of Philadelphia*, p. 152.
54. *Pennsylvania : Charters and Acts of Assembly* (1762 Edit.), vol. II, p. 228.
55. Scharf and Westcott, op. cit., vol. I, p. 264.
56. Cf. McBain, op. cit., p. 196.
57. McBain, op. cit., p. 258.

men. Its own members were directly elected, two a year for three year terms.[58] The minute book of the commissioners (1762-1768) has survived and furnishes an interesting and graphic insight into their activity.[59] Here was obviously the real centre of Philadelphia urban management. The commissioners met very frequently, usually twice a week. An entry of December 31, 1763, will indicate the scope of their activity : 'The Commissioners considered their own Services for the year past and for attendance at two stated meetings in every week, for divers days spent in adjusting the Tax, laying out the lines of Dock Street and the Walls of the Water course of the Dock, for attendance several whole Days and peices of Days at making regulations and fixing the Depth of privies, for continual attendance and Oversight of Paviours, Labourers, and Carters and for a Variety of other Burdensome Duty and agreed to charge only for two Days Service in each Week.'

On important occasions, perhaps once or twice a year, when the contract for street cleaning was to be let, or a decision was to be made concerning the paving of a new street, the presence of the mayor, recorder, and aldermen appears to have been necessary. The part played by the latter group was fairly perfunctory ; and one year, when they did not turn up at all, the commissioners let the cleaning contract in their absence.

Furthermore, the commissioners wielded a number of quasi-judicial powers, fining carters for narrow treads, for failure to paint their initials on their carts, etc.[60] When

58. Scharf and Westcott, op. cit., vol. I, p. 261.
59. MS. in possession of the Library Company of Philadelphia.
60. Cf. also the entry of May 16, 1767 : 'The Commissioners spent this Evening in signing notices to the several Inhabitants whose footway want either paving or Repair.'

a tax was to be levied, they met with the assessors, and jointly with them sat as a board of tax appeals. Characteristically, they also sponsored lotteries to raise additional funds. The advent of this and of the other boards was evidence of renewed municipal vigour, in which no small part was played by Benjamin Franklin.

Poor relief never was directly a function of the Philadelphia city corporation, but had been under the control of boards of overseers named by the county justices.[61] In 1749, the overseers were incorporated and given the power to levy rates. They were required to render a yearly account to the corporation.[62] In 1770 their area was altered to coincide with the township, but the power to appoint the overseers remained as before.[63] In 1766 the control of the almshouse had passed to a board named by the private contributors.[64]

A board of wardens for the port was set up in 1766.[65]

Thus the precise responsibility for the municipal government of Philadelphia was very much scattered by the eve of the Revolution. The corporation itself appears to have had sole responsibility only for the judicial process, markets and fairs (the latter abolished in 1775), the management of property, and the granting of 'freedom of the city.' All other major functions it had been forced to share with other groups : with two principal boards, the commissioners for light and watch and the commissioners for street cleaning and paving ; with as-

61. Davis, J. S., *Essays in the Earlier History of American Corporations*, vol. I, p. 72f.
62. *Pennsylvania : Charters and Acts of Assembly* (1762 Edit.), vol. II, p. 228.
63. Bolles, A. S., *Pennsylvania, Province and State,* vol. II, p. 266f.
64. *Wharton Studies,* op. cit., p. 38.
65. *Report on the Public Archives of the City and County of Philadelphia,* in vol. II of the *Annual Report of the Amer. Hist. Assoc.,* 1901, p. 289.

sessors for the levying of rates ; with the overseers for poor relief ; with the Pennsylvania assembly for an indeterminate and undefined supervision and intervention.[66] The two special boards and the assessors rested their authority upon the fact of their popular election ; and, even though members of the city corporation were *ex officio* members of the boards, this one fact of direct election would appear to place these popularly elected members in the position of greater prestige. As far as the meetings of the street commissioners were concerned, the *ex officio* members from the corporation seldom attended. However, the picture given by certain writers of a corporation divorced completely from all share in municipal functions is not borne out by the evidence.

One further fact in connection with Philadelphia is worthy of note. It was in this area that for the first time the problems of a metropolitan area showed themselves in an American city. Built-up areas began to appear outside the rather narrow city limits and created problems of government peculiar to this type of situation. In 1769, there were 553 houses in the built-up area of Northern Liberties and 603 in Southwark.[67] The solution chosen was the setting up of special commissions, surveyors, assessors, supervisors of streets and highways, in a kind of township organization. No uniform pattern was followed. In Southwark (1762), three surveyors, three assessors, and three supervisors of highways were provided — all to be elected by the inhabitants. The county justices were

66. e. g. 1721, Act for regulating Party-walls, Buildings, and Partition Fences, noted in the *American Weekly*, Sept. 7-14, 1721. Detailed acts were numerous and were by no means consistent as to functions dealt with.

67. Scharf, J. T., and Westcott, T., *History of Philadelphia*, vol. I, p. 261. At this time there were 3,318 houses in Philadelphia alone.

empowered to audit the accounts.[68] In Northern Liberties, 1771, surveyors only were provided, and these were
to be appointed by the county commissioners and confirmed by quarter sessions.[69] The preambles of the acts
set out in detail the situation and the difficulties arising
therefrom — difficulties of laying out streets, titles to the
same as public property, nuisances, need of gutters, wells,
etc. Further developments of this problem of metropolitan administration belong to a later period.

(C)

These various arrangements for Philadelphia, Charleston, and Savannah add still further to the picture of
extreme variety already presented in our earlier consideration of the internal structure of the municipal corporations. In the light of these facts, it cannot then be said
that the Colonies by 1775 had evolved any specific type
of municipal government. Of the seven largest communities, three (Boston, Newport, New Haven) were governed by town meeting ; one (Charleston) by a parish
vestry and several boards ; one (Philadelphia) by a close
corporation and several boards more or less interrelated ;
one (Norfolk) by a close corporation ; only one (New
York City) was under the control of a democratically
elected, comprehensive city government. In the policies
of all, the colonial assemblies played a more or less important part.

68. Laws of Pennsylvania (1803 Edit.), vol. I, pp. 382-8 (Chap. 481).
69. Ibid. pp. 509-13 (Chap. 624).

XI

THE FUNCTIONS OF AN EMERGING URBANISM

In the consideration of the judicial powers of colonial municipalities, and in examining the important and interesting use of their 'courts' in connection with the control of economic life, there have already been passed in review two of the major groupings in municipal functions.

As in the scrutiny of these economic functions, so also with those now to be considered, it is essential that in some measure at least one should try to relive the experiences and attitudes of another age. In the baffling complexities of present-day urban life it is of great value to understand something at least of the elemental forces that made the city government what it is to-day — to discover, as it were, a kind of rationale for its many functions — to see in their historical perspective how the two forces of growth in size and growth in technical knowledge have made the city what it is. At no stage in their development, and least of all in the early and formative stage, is there more than a minor place in a historical study for a mere catalogue of functions. Rather should one endeavour to unravel the underlying forces and circumstances leading to the adoption of particular functions ; and then reweave them into a connected and consistent unfolding pattern. This we shall attempt to do, leaving till later a critique of administrative standards.

Whether as town or microscopic borough, each American community passed through what might be called the 'intimate' stage of its governmental development. The vehicle chosen to govern might be a town meeting ; it might be nominated commissioners ; it might be a corporation,' or a combination of 'borough meeting' and

corporation.' Whatever its precise form, in this intimate
stage the government was that of a unit sufficiently small
so that the persons involved were known to each other,
and something really approaching common agreement
was possible. Social pressure as well as (or instead of)
legal pressure could ordinarily be counted upon to assure
the necessary degree of co-operation in community projects. These people went to church together ; they delib-
erated both in and out of town meeting the hiring of a
teacher for their children ; they arrived at working agreements concerning the use to be made of their common
land. In this situation the obligations of members of the
community to do their stint of service in road building
and repair ; to take their turn in the watch against fire,
or against the French or the Indians ; to provide a fire
bucket or two ; to hang a lantern at night by their door —
all could command that measure of common co-operation
which made these methods not too great a strain on human nature to be practicable and economical. Thus in
1627, the 'corporation' of James City could undertake, as
quite the natural thing, an expedition against the Indians. The arbitration of a local court would be accepted
as to land titles. Conventions, written into by-laws, concerning Sunday observance would be generally accepted.
The Germantown ordinance of 1696 may be quoted by
way of illustration :

> The roadmaster, as often as common service is
> needed to be done, shall the day before call upon as
> many persons as he considers necessary for the present
> work, and those persons are bound to be upon hand
> and to work. Whoever does not come himself or send
> some capable person in his stead, shall have to pay six
> shillings fine for each day, but if he is so sick that he

cannot do his own work, or if he has a wife in child bed in his house, in this case he is not compelled to serve. The aforesaid road master must always keep just and accurate reckoning with all of those who remain in arrears, and give over the same annually in the last court of record in the same year.[1]

By way of illustrating the concept of a rotating unpaid watch, the act of the Georgia assembly setting up such a watch for Savannah will serve : 'Whereas the safety of this Town of Savannah, next to the divine Protection, chiefly depends on the Care and Vigilance of the Inhabitants thereof,' every male, age 16 to 60, who has lived in the town two months shall be liable. The superintendents were named in the act.[2]

It was this period in which the by-laws of a 'city' were distinctly rural in their flavour. There was the ordinance of Burlington, for example, designed to 'regulate the affairs of the town, in such matters as relate to fences, cattle, highways, and all such things, as usually fall within the compass of ourselves in corporations in England.'[3] The borough of Edenton insisted that 'only inhabitants are to keep . . . horses in town limits . . . [They are] limited to six sheep, one cow, and one horse to run at large within bounds.'[4] Witness also that 'in a certain street called the Broadway,' in New York City, Thomas Bains stole William Butler's milch cow ; and was duly punished.[5] In Annapolis there was so little municipal

1. Quoted also in Pennypacker, S. W., 'Settlement of Germantown,' in *Penn.-German Soc. Proc.*, vol. IX, p. 337.
2. De Kenne, G. W. (Compil.), *Colonial Acts of Georgia*, pp. 139ff.
3. Burlington, 1682 (Leaming, A., and Spicer, J., *Grants, Concessions, etc., of New Jersey* (Reprint 1881), p. 454).
4. Edenton, 1745 (*State Records of North Carolina*, vol. XXIII, p. 232f.).
5. Quoted in Peterson, A. E., and Edwards, G. W., *New York as an Eighteenth Century Municipality*, p. 23.

business in the early years that the corporation as such seems at times to have done little save to concern itself with the annual fair.[6]

However, if the community grew at all, there soon came a kind of transition stage in which these old intimate arrangements began to break down. The strain to which they were subjected was dual. On the one hand, any community, however small, was bound to have among its inhabitants a certain number of ultra-individualists who resented any attempt at coercion. If the attempt happened to be of a nature that affected their income, particularly in an age and situation in which income was exceedingly difficult to attain, there was likely to arise a kind of bristling cantankerousness, a defiance of one's neighbours — over against which, just because they were neighbours, these latter found it difficult psychologically to undertake other than social sanctions. On the other hand, once the community began to grow, these arrangements were subject to shock from another and ultimately fatal quarter. The element of heterogeneity entered — religious, economic, or social ; and no longer could general acceptance of community co-operation be counted upon through the sanction of social disapproval. When we read that in 1756, in Wilmington, N. C., the constables were directed to walk the streets during divine service to prevent disturbance, we sense the picture of an unregenerate group outside the pale and the conventions of the majority — and hence the kind that had begun to require the imposition of the arm of the law.

One of the chief evidences of the difficulties presented by the individualist can be found in the numerous by-laws dealing with hogs and other animals at large in the

6. Minutes, etc., Annapolis Mayor's Court, 1720-26.

streets. It was obviously to the economic advantage of the individual that his hogs should root around in the streets and enjoy to their full the mud and garbage there found. 'To ring or not to ring' was the burning question in many a community, and the alternation of such regulations by their very frequency revealed the essential difficulty of *enforcement* of any rule in what was still predominantly a neighbourhood. Some of these regulations are worth quoting :

> It is Ordered that Swine wch are nott shutt up and that keepe about the Towne or wth in two miles of the Towne, All such swine shal be well and Sufficiently Rung by the Owners thereof or at their Cost and charge . . . And if any swine above three months old shalbe found after the 25th day of March yearly without such Swine shall pay three pence a peace . . .[7]

In Germantown, 1691, the by-laws allowed chickens freedom to run about, but 'Ducks, however, it is hereby strictly prohibited to keep, together with other injurious things.'[8]

Albany, April 13, 1706, passed an ordinance prohibiting the running of hogs ; on November 11 this was repealed, and their ringing was required. On May 6, 1707, the following illuminating ordinance appears :

> An whereas notice has been given for ye Ringing ye hogs of this Citty to prevent their Rooting up ye grasse notwithstanding wh Diverse have neglected or Refused to Ring ym by wh great Dammage doth Insue, it is

---

7. Quoting minutes of Springfield (Mass.) town meeting, 1664, in Burt, H. M., *First Century of History of Springfield*, Springfield, 1898-99, 2 vol., vol. II, p. 61.
8. *Pennsylvania Colonial Records — Minutes of Provincial Council*, vol. I, pp. 322ff.

therefore hereby ordered, by ye mayor aldermen and
Commonality aforesaid, yt henceforth it shall and may
be Lawful for any Person or Persons to Seize upon Such
hogs not Ring'd for his or thir use, benefit and behooffe
as a forfeiter for their master's neglect.[9]

This indicates clearly the transitional stage mentioned
above. The town was not yet ready to accept the consequences of urbanization and hire special law-enforcers
for this kind of infraction ; it had found that common
agreement was no longer effective or social pressure adequate as a sanction. It is not surprising to learn that this
Albany ordinance had to be repassed in 1708, 1712, and
1713.[10] Thus an intermediate device of appealing to the
self-interest of other members of the community to secure
enforcement — a fighting of fire with fire — was tried. It
was a characteristic ear-mark of this stage in many communities that the authorities frequently used the device
of rewarding an informer by allowing him one-half the
proceeds of fines for disobeying particular ordinances.[11]
The intimate stage was obviously passing, but its methods were not wholly left behind ; the organized discipline
necessary for the urban stage had not yet been accepted.

A further mark of this transitional stage was the increasing difficulty in enforcing the obligation of indi-

9. Munsell, J., *Annals of Albany*, vol. V, p. 153f.
10. Munsell, op. cit., var. Similarly, the South Carolina assembly in 1692
    passed an act for Charleston to prevent swine running at large. The
    enforcement was left to citizens in general who were allowed to seize
    them or kill them — but must first 'cry them . . . in four several and
    usual places' to give the owner a chance to redeem them for 5s.
    (McCord, D. J. (Edit.), *Statutes at Large of South Carolina*, vol. VII,
    p. 5f.)
11. e. g. Annapolis (1754) included such a provision about informers in
    its ordinance prohibiting sales of victuals except on market days and
    at the market house. (Minutes of Annapolis City Council.)

vidual service for the watch or for work on the streets. Even at the outset of the imposition of such services, frequently the individual would be allowed to commute for a money payment sufficient to hire a substitute or was allowed exemption under certain circumstances. Actually only in a truly intimate community, where social sanction would reinforce the legal, could this old medieval method of 'common obligation' function effectively. In theory it was altogether admirable ; in practice it crumbled under the strain. In matters concerning the streets, the original method was usually to hold each individual responsible for repairing or paving (and cleaning) the part in front of his own house ; and then to supplement this by work under a 'roadmaster' for a certain number of days a year.

In 1666, in Rhode Island, it was provided that 'housekeepers' must work three days a year with a fine of 2/6 per day for refusal unless they 'can excuse themselves justly either by sickness or their oxen cannot be found.' Inasmuch as one result was that nearly every one became sick or lost his oxen, the excuse clause was repealed.[12]

The Philadelphia corporation, having adopted the usual compulsory service with commutation allowed, by 1718 found it necessary in many cases to do the paving itself and then assess the cost against the 'defaulting' householders.[13]

The approaching disintegration of the co-operative watch was evidenced at an even earlier stage. Whether or not this indicated that the desire for sleep was more powerful than the desire to enhance one's income by working at one's own must be left to the imagination of the indi-

12. Stokes, H. K., *Finances and Administration of Providence*, p. 84.
13. *Wharton School Studies : City Government of Philadelphia*, p. 130.

vidual reader. Of course, the zeal for keeping the watch naturally fluctuated with the imminence of the need. In time of war or threat of Indian attack or immediately after a conflagration, it would be kept fairly consistently. As the days — or the nights — wore on and nothing happened, the inevitable slackness would appear. Yet over and above this, once the intimate stage was passed, a volunteer watch was necessarily unreliable. Thus, in the Albany minutes of October 29, 1689, the entry occurs :

Ye watch of this citty is so irregularly kept that few or none of ye inhabitants of this citty doe appear upon ye guard when it is there turn.

The description by Franklin of the Philadelphia night watch about 1745 is worth quoting also. 'It was managed by the constables of the respective wards, in turn ; the constable warned a number of housekeepers to attend him for the night. Those who chose never to attend paid him six shillings to be excused which was supposed to be for hiring substitutes, but was in reality much more than was necessary for that purpose, and made the constable-ship a place of profit ; and the constable, for a little drink, often got such ragamuffins about him as a watch that respectable householders did not choose to mix with. Walking the rounds, too, was often neglected, and most of the nights spent in tippling.'[14]

As Morse pointed out, 'An abuse, nourished by copious rum, strikes its roots deep.'[15] It took years before the various vested interests involved yielded to reform.

In another connection, the transition from the intimate stage in Annapolis revealed itself in connection

14. Bigelow, J. (Compil. and Edit.), *Autobiography of Benjamin Franklin*, New York, 1932, p. 214.
15. Morse, J. T., Jr., *Benjamin Franklin*, Boston, 1889, p. 37f.

with the collection towards the expense of a prize at the races. In the minutes of the corporation, August 12, 1720, the following entry occurs :

> And whereas the plate that is to be Runn for is raised by Voluntary Subscription in which most of those that kept booths at the fair are concerned, yet some of them who are supposed to reap the most advantage by such Publick Occasion have refused so to do, having dependence on the generosity of others to support their interest —
>
> Thereupon Ordered that No Person keep a booth in the City of Annapolis on the said fair day unless by lycence from three of the Magistrates of the Mayor's Court . . . and that no such person be Lycensed unless they either have subscribed to the present plate or shall subscribe as much to the next plate as others in their Rank have done to this and likewise as much to the others also . . .

By the next year the fiction of a subscription list had been dropped and a regular assessment decreed.[16]

(B)

The increase of urbanization brought two consequences of cardinal significance in the growth of municipal functions and the substitution of paid for voluntary service.

The first of these, the factor of social heterogeneity with its consequent steady weakening of the effective orbit of social pressures, has already been mentioned. It continued in an ever increasing degree to aid in the disintegration of the unpaid co-operative efforts upon which the community in its early stages relied.

16. May 1, 1721.

The second factor was decisive. With concentration and increase of population there arose as a consequence certain imperatives which demanded an answer. The streets were subjected to increasing and needful uses ; and, if not paved, became virtually impassable. The removal of accumulations, beyond a certain point, of filth and garbage, while not yet associated primarily with disease, none the less was an 'imperative' even to the not too sensitive nostrils or aesthetic sense of the age. Similarly the need for lighting the dark corners on account of the condition of the sidewalks might also be classed among these imperatives, even if person and property were still relatively safe from attack. Fire protection was an absolute necessity in communities whose houses were built of wood and close together. 'Nuisances' of one sort or another demanded remedy. Finally, when a city grew still further, reliance upon wells and pumps for water supply for drinking, washing, and fire-fighting was no longer practicable, and waterworks became technologically imperative.

Paid service, with its consequent growth of a staff of municipal employees, was the only possible answer to the combination of these two factors. For example, in Philadelphia, in 1738, the condition of certain streets was made the subject of a grand jury presentment, preliminary to compulsory paving.[17] In 1670 New York City took advantage of the occasion of granting a monopoly to the carmen's guild to contract with them for repairs to the streets.[18] Wilmington (Del.) in 1749 repealed its compulsory street labour ordinance as ineffectual and provided that the streets 'be hereafter repaired and kept

17. Scharf, J. T., and Westcott, T., *History of Philadelphia*, vol. I, p. 208.
18. Peterson, A. E., and Edwards, G. W., *New York as an Eighteenth Century Municipality*, p. 64.

good at the publick costs.'[19] By 1756, even a town as small as New Bern for a time gave up compulsory labour on its streets and wharves and levied a tax.[20] The Act of 1764, setting up the street commission of Charleston, deserves fairly complete quotation in order to illuminate the extent to which 'urbanization' had proceeded. The powers included :[21]

> to contract and agree with any person or persons, to be scavenger or scavengers, to keep the streets, lanes and alleys, and other parts of the said town, clean and in good order and repair ; to remove all filth and rubbish, to such proper place or places, in or near the said town, as they shall determine . . .
>
> to cause all bridges and causeys to be amended, and all holes in any of the streets . . . to be filled up, and posts to be fixed in any of the said principal streets, and footways levelled and paved . . .; and likewise to sink drains or sewers, and wells . . .
>
> [the expense of the drains, sewers, and paving, etc. to be] paid and borne by the inhabitants [of the parishes of St. Philip and St. Michael, if common and by] the owners and proprietors of the lands and houses lying on the streets . . . that shall be benefitted thereby, rateably and proportionally to the value of the lands and houses.

The commissioners were given power to make the assessment and to issue warrants of distress if not paid. Owners of lands fronting the streets were required to obtain the consent of the commissioners before planting

19. Wilmington Borough Minutes, Apr. 22, 1749.
20. *State Records of North Carolina,* vol. XXIII, pp. 451ff.
21. The Act (of April 10, 1764) is printed in full in the *South Carolina Gazette* of Aug. 25, 1764.

trees. Powers were included to prevent encroachments, the dumping of rubbish, damage by heavy carriages, the licensing of carters and the regulation of their rates and services, prohibition of speeding of horseback riders and drivers. At least once a month they were to meet at the state house.

Furthermore :

> the Commissioners . . . shall be allowed a sum, not exceeding £1400 current money, yearly, to be raised in the general tax, on the estates real and personal . . . for paying a scavenger or scavengers, and defraying the several other charges which shall arise or become due in the execution of this act ; excepting the expense of making and sinking common drains, or sewers and wells, making pavements or posts, which shall be raised and paid in manner hereinbefore directed.

Private open drains were prohibited and permission was required to dig the foundation of new buildings. No one was allowed to keep more than two slaves for hire, and their rates and licensing were prescribed.

The necessities of fair streets brought a whole collection of by-laws aimed at their preservation. Chiefly these dealt with the prohibition of fast driving. The unruly 'carmen' in many towns were forbidden to ride their carts and required to walk alongside them for this reason. Albany (1700), probably with this (as well as safety) in mind, prohibited 'unruly driving of slees [sleighs].'[22] Annapolis (and other towns) laid considerable stress on the damage to streets from driving carts with too narrow treads, and sporadically enforced its by-law against the practice. On one occasion its mayor's court went so far as

22. Munsell, J., *Annals of Albany,* vol. IV, p. 122.

to fine its own mayor and one of the aldermen 40s. each for this offence — and the fines were paid.[23] The street commissioners of Philadelphia even purchased a stock of wide tread wheels for resale prior to the date of enforcing such an ordinance, so as to take away any excuse that the cartmen might offer of inability to comply.[24]

The efforts for reasonably clean streets followed much the same evolution. In 1658, the residents of New Amsterdam were directed to bring their refuse to definite places.[25] In 1695, the city was impelled to hire a scavenger at £30 a year.[26] From 1731-75, the city made (for the time) remarkable gains in sanitation, almost entirely by paid corporate effort.[27] In 1763 the situation was such at Philadelphia that the street commissioners laid a whole group of complaints before the assembly and asked for adequate power to deal with them — accumulation of rubbish, narrow tread wagons, encroachments, filth. This led to the passage of acts dealing with the several problems.[28] By 1765, the city had arranged for the regular disposal of its garbage and dirt by contract.[29] In 1759, the smaller town of Williamsburg was given the power to levy a poll tax for repair of its streets which had fallen into shocking disrepair.[30]

23. Minutes, Annapolis City Council, Jan. 30, 1759; Apr. 24, 1760; Ledger of City Clerk.
24. Minutes, Street Commissioners of Philadelphia, July 2, 1763. The carters, in desperation at the prospect of having to obey a law which cost them something, petitioned the assembly for relief, but eventually complied (ibid. Jan. 17, 1764; Mar. 10, 1764).
25. Goodwin, M. W., *Dutch and English on the Hudson*, New Haven, 1919, p. 105.
26. Peterson and Edwards, op. cit., p. 101.
27. Ibid. p. 369.
28. Scharf and Westcott, op. cit., vol. I, p. 258.
29. Ibid. p. 260. Cf. also Minutes of Street Commissioners, Feb. 19, 23, Apr. 6, 1765; Apr. 14, 1766; etc.
30. Gulick, L., and Pollard, J. G., *Modern Government in a Colonial City*, p. 30.

Another group of municipal functions was that centring around the watch, fire protection, the provision of wells and pumps, and street lighting. Time and again these were linked in legislation and administration. Early provisions for fire-fighting in the 'intimate' stage included items such as the provision of two leather buckets hung conveniently outside each house and the provision of ladders and safe chimneys or a hogshead of water. Salem (Mass.), 1644, is credited with what was possibly the first fire prevention ordinance.[31] A whole series of by-laws dealing with chimneys and other fire-risks marked the fears of the community,[32] but their reiteration and difficulty of enforcement bear witness to the transition from the 'intimate' to the urban stage. When the residents of New Amsterdam laughed at the burgomaster who ordered the removal of thatched roofs and plastered chimneys,[33] and when Albany in 1688 had to provide penalties for 'resistance or insult to the firemaster,'[34] the transition stage had been reached — but the 'imperatives' were also dawning. Regular and paid inspection of chimneys was a logical next step.[35] Charleston suffered from several conflagrations, and the legislation of South Carolina reflected this. In 1704, commissioners were named, and directed to provide buckets, to blow up houses when necessary, to enforce the chimney law and the law against boiling pitch, and to license stills.[36] The

31. Fairlie, J. A., *Municipal Administration*, New York, 1901, p. 151. He also places Boston second ; and gives Boston credit for the first fire engine in 1702.
32. e. g. against smoking in the streets ; carrying uncovered fire ; type of building ; wooden chimneys ; type of blacksmith's forge ; etc.
33. Peterson and Edwards, op. cit., p. 172.
34. Munsell, J., *Annals of Albany*, vol. II, pp. 88ff.
35. Cf. Peterson and Edwards, op. cit., p. 178, for New York City, 1686.
36. McCord, D. J. (Compil.), *Statutes at Large of South Carolina*, vol. VII, pp. 41ff. (Stat. No. 234).

initial enthusiasm waned, several commissioners died or moved away ; so that in 1713 new commissioners had to be appointed and a constructive program directed. The individual items of this program bore silent witness to the growth of the town. An engine was to be bought, wells dug, the type of buildings regulated, and fines imposed — one half to go to the informant.[37] Fire engines had already made their appearance in Boston, and other cities soon followed suit. Following a big fire in Philadelphia, 'several have at this time (for People would not be mov'd at another time) to make a collection of money for a better Engine than what we now have, and for good Buckets.'[38] Yet Annapolis allowed its fire engine to fall into disrepair with disastrous consequences.[39] A kind of throw-back to the days of voluntary service occurred in the actual fire-fighting, in the appearance of those volunteer fire companies that were to play such a dramatic part in the social and political community life of the first half of the next century.

The night watch was originally designed not so much for law enforcement or preservation of the peace, as for protection against fire or attacks by the Indians. Police duty — arrests, dealing with riots, etc. — was the function primarily of the marshals and constables who operated under the direction of the justices or the mayor and aldermen in their capacity of justices. The duty of these constables, etc., was defined in the New York City charter of 1686 thus : [to] 'make a presentment of all such persons as shall neglect or refuse to clean the streets, and of

37. Ibid. pp. 58ff. (Stat. No. 335).
38. *American Weekly Merchant,* Apr. 23-30, 1730.
39. *Maryland Gazette,* July 19, 1753. Subsequently, more vigorous efforts were made in this direction (Minutes, Annapolis City Council, 1757 [undated] ; Feb. 3, 1760 ; etc.).

all such as in any way break the Holy Sabbath, or commit other misdeeds.' The earliest example of a paid watch which I have been able to discover occurred in Beverwyck (Albany) in 1659, when Lambert Van Valckenborgh and Pieter Winnen were 'appointed at the request of the burghers to relieve them of night-watch duty' as 'rattle-watch.'[40] It will be remembered that it was the threat of war that led Charleston in 1701 to institute a paid watch and to direct the necessary levies. This was disbanded in 1704 as no longer necessary ; but renewed with the re-approach of danger in 1708 and thereafter intermittently.[41] These paid provisions so early were abnormal ; for the genuine imposition of a paid watch forced by the circumstances of urbanization, one must go to a later period. Norfolk, 1738, experimented with a paid watch of six or eight men, at £40 a year to be divided among them ; but the borough soon abandoned the project on

40. Court Minutes, Beverwyck, Sept. 3, 1659 ; action of July 6, 1659 (p. 209 of vol. II as edit. in trans. by A. J. F. Van Laer). Their instructions are worth quoting : 'First, the said rattle watch shall be held to appear at the burgher's guard house . . . and together at ten o'clock shall begin making their rounds, giving notice of their presence in all the streets . . . by sounding their rattle and calling . . . until 4 o'clock in the morning.

'Secondly, they shall pay especial attention to fire and upon the first sign of smoke, extraordinary light or otherwise warn the people by knocking at their houses. And if they see any likelihood of fire, they shall give warning by rattling and calling, and run to the church, of which they are to have a key, and ring the bell.

'Thirdly, in case they find any thieves . . . they shall . . . arrest the thieves . . . And in case they are not strong enough to do so, they are to call the burghers of the vicinity to their aid . . .

'Fourthly, in case of opposition, they are hereby authorized to offer resistance, the . . . magistrates declaring that they release them from all liability . . .' (Court Minutes, vol. I, p. 209f.)

Their salary was to be fixed at 1100 guilders in seawan and 100 guilders in beavers.

41. Pringle-Smith, J. J., *Government of the City of Charleston* in *Charleston Year Book*, 1881, var. (Stats. No. 207, 232, 276, 282, etc.)

account of cost.[42] New York City's paid force was authorized in 1741, and in 1742 the City was compelled to augment it on account of the growing disorder[43] — but by
this time the City had begun to deal with another element, the presence of unassimilated groups, and not
merely with fire-risk. After agitation lasting from 1743
to 1750, including a grand jury presentment, Philadelphia was finally allowed to follow suit.[44] A few other
communities were added to the list of those with paid
forces before 1775. Of this group it is interesting to note
that the Williamsburg corporation, which finally engaged such a watch in 1772, did so in part at least because
of the steady campaign of argument and sarcasm waged
by the *Virginia Gazette*. The newspaper seems to have
lost no opportunity to point the moral in the matter of
robberies, etc.[45]

In this interrelated group of functions must be placed
the provision of lights, pumps, and wells — which items
also served other purposes, but the provision of which by
the community was rendered imperative by the fire-risk.
It is worth citing in this connection the report of the
wardens in Philadelphia who had charge of watch and
other items arising out of the need for fire prevention.
In their request of 1765 to levy higher taxes, they mentioned that they had put up 320 street lamps, had 120
public pumps under their care, and employed eighteen
watchmen — but more pumps and lamps were needed.[46]

42. Council Orders, Norfolk Borough, Oct. 14, 1738; Oct. 15, 1739;
    July 7, 1741; Aug. 15, 1744, when the paid watch was superseded by
    citizens chosen by lot.
43. Lincoln, C. Z., *Constitutional History of New York*, vol. I, p. 302.
44. *Wharton School Studies: City Government of Philadelphia*, Phila-
    delphia, 1893, p. 152.
45. *Virginia Gazette*, Apr. 5, 1770; Apr. 25, 1771; May 2, 1771; July 16,
    1772; Nov. 19, 1772.
46. Scharf, J. T., and Westcott, T., *History of Philadelphia*, vol. I, p. 260.

It is recorded that in 1750, in Philadelphia, those who were supposed to put a lamp outside their door met and agreed to pay a man 3/9 a month for the job.[47] In New York City the system of holding the alderman and assistant of each ward responsible to see that every seventh house had a light worked fairly well for over fifty years, but ultimately gave way to a more efficient plan.[48]

Towards the end of the period, construction of something approaching the modern waterworks was forced upon several of the communities. Albany, 1760, was an example among the smaller towns.[49] New York City, 1774, was forced to issue paper money to aid in continuing construction, only to have it interrupted by the Revolution.[50] This new municipal function had, however, barely commenced when the War put a temporary end to its spread.

Finally, in the category of urban 'imperatives' must be placed the suppression of various 'nuisances' not otherwise included. A modern note was struck by Lancaster, when its corporation forbade the playing of ball around the court house,[51] and by Beverwyck (Albany) when it forbade the playing of golf in the streets.[52] In Albany it

47. Ibid. p. 218.
48. Peterson and Edwards, op. cit., p. 104f.
49. Howell, G. R., and Tenney, J. (Edit.), *History of the County of Albany*, p. 465.
50. This reservoir and distribution project of New York City was the largest among the public works undertaken by colonial municipalities. It was proposed by Christopher Colles, and the contract let to him. In all, about £7,700 of city notes appear to have been printed and spent before construction was suspended. (Minutes, Common Council, July 21, 1774 ; Aug. 25, 1774 ; Aug. 2, 1775 ; Jan. 5, 1776 ; Mar. 5, 1776.)
51. Riddle, W., *The Story of Lancaster*, p. 40.
52. *Court Minutes, Fort Orange and Beverwyck*, Nov. 10, 1659 (A. J. F. Van Laer (Edit. and Trans.), vol. II, p. 235).

was forbidden (1686) to rinse clothes near the wells.[53] In Charleston (1704) the killing of beasts within the entrenchments was prohibited.[54] The number of such by-laws was legion, but these will serve as examples. Rarely only did evidences of any connection of 'nuisances' with health appear — in the quarantine laws against smallpox; in the request of James City for power to make by-laws in 1682 ;[55] in Wilmington (N. C.), in 1756, when its commissioners were granted power to issue orders to protect streams from houses draining into them.[56] Of course, the ubiquitous water bailiff always included quarantine in his duties.

Thus a large part, perhaps the greater part of the functions of the colonial city on the eve of the Revolution are understandable only in the light of the transition from the intimate stage to that phase in a city's development in which the imperatives of decency and safety join with the impracticability of compulsory service to dictate a paid staff as the solution. This development in colonial days was a function of size far more than of the date of the action ; for inventions and sharings of the *knowledge* of amenities which play so large a part in the unfolding and increase of municipal activities to-day were few and far between. The fact that the unpaid watch or the compulsory road service had broken down and paid service substituted in New York and Philadelphia was no reason why these earlier devices should not continue — as they did, for the most part, continue — in the smaller towns and boroughs.[57]

53. Munsell, J., op. cit., vol. II, pp. 88ff.
54. Pringle-Smith, J. J., *Government of the City of Charleston*, in *Charleston Year Book*, 1881, p. 38.
55. Tyler, L. G., *Cradle of the Republic*, p. 74.
56. *State Records of North Carolina*, vol. XXIII, pp. 456ff.
57. e. g. Wilmington (N. C.), New Brunswick, etc.

(C)

Another group of functions or spheres for communal action rested upon elements in the social background of the age. Its customs, its taboos, its social institutions were bound to reflect themselves in municipal action ; and their impact upon the cities forms an interesting chapter. In the first place, this was an age of government by legalized conscience, particularly in the early stages when cosmopolitanism was unknown. The little colony of New Haven opened its history by a declaration that the 'laws of this colony shall be the laws of God' — perhaps, as someone has suggested, until they had time to devise better ones.[58] Whether the sentence imposed by the Germantown court on a man who laid a wager 'to smoke above one hundred pipes in one day' was an expression of the current attitude towards smoking or betting is uncertain, but in any event the combination was more than gentle consciences would allow.[59] It was Sunday observance, however, that seemingly was first in importance. St. Mary's, 1685, regulated the sale of liquor and gaming on the Sabbath ;[60] Germantown saw fit to prohibit shooting ;[61] Wilmington (N. C.) prohibited the sale of liquor during service hours and drunkenness at any time during the day ;[62] Boston, 1662, appointed persons to prevent disorders of its youth and in the meeting house.[63] It was

58. Levermore, C. H., 'Municipal History of New Haven,' in Atwater, E. E., *History of New Haven*, New York, 1887, p. 422f.
59. Pennypacker, S. W., 'Settlement of Germantown,' in *Penn.-German Soc. Proc.*, vol. IX, p. 309.
60. *Maryland Archives*, vol. XVII, p. 420 : Proceedings of Council, Oct. 13, 1685.
61. *Pennsylvania Colonial Records*, Minutes of Provincial Council, vol. I, p. 333.
62. In 1745. *State Records of North Carolina*, vol. XXIII, pp. 234ff.
63. Quincy, J., *Municipal History of Boston*, p. 6.

customary in many towns to patrol the streets during the
hours of service. The relative importance attached to this
particular one of the Ten Commandments may be judged
also from incidental items such as the fact that in 1742
the newly chartered borough of Lancaster made this the
subject of its first by-law ;[64] and also the fact that the 1686
Charter of New York City specifically directed attention
to those who 'in any way break the Sabbath.' In 1765, the
failure of the magistrates and constables to enforce the
Sabbath observance laws was made the subject of a grand
jury presentment in Charleston.[65]

If the seventeenth and eighteenth centuries were strict
in their attitude towards Sunday observance, they were
(according to modern standards) lax enough in their
drinking. Further mention will be made later as to its
extent and effects ;[66] but even this unmechanized age of
virtually universal and heavy drinkers could not altogether escape the problems thereby created for urban
communities. Licensing itself was normally, though not
universally, a prerogative of the mayor and aldermen.[67]
In a period marked by the tendency of the New York City
corporation to lease its ferries, markets, etc., it also
farmed out its excise ; but with the result of too free an
extension of retail privileges to low grog shops on the
part of the excise master. This caused the resumption of
control by the city in 1753.[68] Provisions against selling to
the Indians were frequent, and as frequently disobeyed.

64. Minutes of Borough of Lancaster, May 1, 1742.
65. *South Carolina Gazette,* June 1-8, 1765.
66. Cf. p. 395f.
67. In Philadelphia, licensing was by the governor on recommendation
    of the mayor's court (Shepherd, W. R., *Proprietary Government in
    Pennsylvania,* p. 80f.). In a few of the smaller boroughs, it remained
    under the county justices.
68. Peterson and Edwards, op. cit., p. 269.

Even in Dutch days, 1657, regulations were instituted forbidding liquor dealers from acting also as pawnbrokers, on the ground that many tavern keepers 'detained persons as for their own sake and advantage would better attend to their occupations and protect their families honorably with God's help, but cannot make up their minds to it, because of the pleasures they find in drinking and jovial company by which they not only spend their daily earnings but also when out of money pawn the goods serving to the necessities of their families and thereby obtain the means of continuing their usual drinking bouts. Their wives and children suffer in consequence and become a burden to the Deaconry of thie City.' This by-law was also constantly violated[69] — as have been all liquor laws throughout the history of American city governments. Germantown seems to have had the strictest code : no one to be sold more than a gill of rum or a quart of beer every half day, nor any but travellers to drink in inns after 9 p. m.[70] Bath (N. C.), 1715, evidently favoured home industry, for liquors made in the district might be retailed there for ten years without a licence.[71] A somewhat different note was struck in Nantucket, which chose 'a number of men to walk the Town in the night season . . . to put a stop to masters and mistresses of Houses entertaining Minors at unreasonable hours of the Night in Drinking, carousing and frolicking Contrary to the Mind of their Parents or Masters.'[72] In Annapolis, in 1765, at least thirty tavern keepers were 'presented' on over two hundred counts for selling liquor illegally or 'entertaining' servants.[73] All in all, the prob-

69. Ibid. p. 50f., quoting *Rec. New Amsterdam*, vol. I, p. 33f.
70. Pennypacker, op. cit., pp. 335, etc.
71. *State Records of North Carolina*, vol. XXIII, pp. 73ff.
72. Starbuck, A., *History of Nantucket*, Boston, 1924, p. 109.
73. Minutes, Mayor's Court, Jan. 29, 1765.

lems arising from liquor had only begun to be appreciated, not to mention the failure to discover any adequate solution thereof during the Colonial Period — such was the strength of custom of the age.[74]

Here and there, by-laws are discovered indicating that the institution of slavery also presented difficulties for these early communities. Naturally these inferior beings must not be allowed the liquor habits of their masters ; and towns like Norfolk endeavoured to prohibit its sale to them.[75] Burlington (1734) passed a by-law to prohibit profaneness and immorality of slaves.[76] In Charleston, in 1765, the rioting and drunkenness of the negroes were sufficient to be included in the grievances of grand jury presentment.[77] The harbouring or entertaining of slaves was prohibited where it became a problem.[78] Occasionally a curfew law for negroes appeared, perhaps under the heading of fire prevention.[79] On the whole, though, they seem to have been a docile group ; and only these occasional indications appear of their presence as a disturbing and unassimilated factor.

Ever since the 'Jews would have no dealing with the Samaritans,' the stranger or foreigner has been the sub-

74. Cf. also the action of the grand jury in Charleston (S. C.), which in 1767 presented as a grievance the failure to limit the number of licences for selling spirits (*South Carolina Gazette*, Nov. 2-9, 1767).

75. Twice a sub-committee was ordered to draft such a law, but I have been unable to find that the law was ever actually enacted. The minutes for 1743 seem incomplete. (Council Orders, Norfolk Borough, July 7, 1741 ; June 24, 1742).

76. Scott, A., *Early Cities of New Jersey*, in *N. J. Hist. Soc. Coll.*, 2nd ser., vol. IX, p. 168f.

77. *South Carolina Gazette*, June 2, 1766.

78. e. g. Annapolis (Riley, E. S., *The Ancient City*, p. 109f.).

79. e. g. New Brunswick, 1737, where the constables were ordered to arrest negroes found out of their masters' services on Saturday and Sunday nights at 9. They were directed to visit places where 'negroes frolick together.' *New Brunswick City Minutes*, Oct. 18, 1737.

ject for suspicion. Thanks to the light shed upon the subject by the social psychologist, we understand more to-day about the reasons for the hostility. Their 'ways' are different from ours and consequently constitute a threat to our entrenched manner of living. This was particularly true, in these early days, in connection with religious differences ; and such differences were felt then with an intensity to-day ordinarily reserved for suspected advocates of changes in the economic order. This hostility was reflected in colonial days in religious tests for 'freedom' or office holding, or even permission to reside ; but, though the severity of the bigotry and suspicion wore away under the growing cosmopolitanism, its vestiges were none the less evidenced in occasional by-laws. Boston at one time fined its residents for 'entertaining foreigners.'[80] These laws must not be confused with those prohibiting the harbouring of deserting seamen ; those designed to prevent newcomers from becoming a public charge ; or those designed in time of an epidemic to minimize the danger from smallpox.

It may have been something akin to this that was in part responsible for the decay in the original impetus for the provision of schools, a decay that seemed to set in when the community — be it New England town, Dutch village, or in Anglican Virginia — ceased to belong to one church and to be of one 'kind.'

The famous Massachusetts law of 1647 had been the model for certain other parts of New England in the seventeenth century. Each town of fifty householders was required to 'appoint one within their town to teach all such children as shall resort to him to write and read.' The wages were to be paid by the parents or as the town

80. Quincy, J., *Municipal History of Boston*, p. 6.

directed. Towns of one hundred householders were expected to set up a grammar school to fit for the university. Yet enforcement was difficult.[81] While quite often public provision was made for the education of the poor, in general it seems to have been held that those who could afford it should pay.[82] In 1700, Connecticut made a town school tax compulsory, and the practice was commenced somewhat later of setting aside land to assist in financing schools.[83] Connecticut early made a creditable record according to the standard of the age in the matter of publicly provided schools.[84] In New Netherland the efforts were equally advanced.[85] The first public tax in New Amsterdam was in 1638.[86] In 1703, at the request of the City, an act was passed permitting a grammar school, free for all boys of English, Dutch, or French parentage. The salary of the schoolmaster was set at £50.[87] Albany, 1721, offered a house rent free if a schoolmaster would

---

81. Dexter, E. G., *History of Education in the United States,* New York, 1904, p. 34. Connecticut passed a similar law in 1650. Dorchester, 1639, claims to have been the first community to tax for a grammar school (ibid. p. 170).

82. e. g. for Pennsylvania, cf. *Wharton School Studies : City Government of Philadelphia,* p. 48.

83. Walker, Mrs. A. M., *Development of State Support of Education in Connecticut,* Abstract of thesis (Ph.D.), Yale. Hartford, State Board of Education, 1926, p. 7.

84. Cf. Dexter, op. cit., pp. 40, 588. New Haven set up a free school in 1614, and in 1647 the New Haven court ordered all plantations not having a school to start one — the town to bear one-third the cost.

85. Cf. Kilpatrick, W., *Dutch Schools of New Netherland,* Bull., June 1912, U. S. Educ. Off., pp. 11-18. He points out that the relation of the church and municipal authorities had been a problem. The schoolmaster seems to have been engaged by the schout and schepens, with the ministry and consistory participating to a varying degree in the choice.

86. O'Callaghan, E. B., *History of New Netherland,* vol. I, p. 112.

87. Lincoln, C. Z., *Constitutional History of New York,* vol. I, p. 100. Bergen, 1661, was another Dutch community to establish a school with public support (Dexter, op. cit., p. 63).

come.[88] In New Jersey, the town charters between 1682-1702 usually provided for education, at public expense if necessary ; but after 1702 the provision languished.[89] A Maryland Act of 1694 providing for the maintenance of free schools through the proceeds of an export tax was disallowed by the Privy Council in 1696.[90] Instances such as these might be multiplied,[91] but perhaps a few generalizations will suffice. Certain colonies — North Carolina, Delaware — made virtually no public provision of any sort until the eve of the Revolution. In the larger cities — Boston, New York, Philadelphia, Charleston, and in a number of other towns — there was ordinarily some provision made for free education of the poor ; usually in the first instance by private contributions, but often supplemented from taxes.[92] The first half of the eighteenth century seemed to reveal most communities less concerned about schools than they had been earlier, but there were exceptions. Certainly the provision of a school, where it was undertaken at all by a borough — or even in many New England town governments after perhaps 1695 — could by no stretch of the imagination be rated as ranking as a major public function in the minds of the officials or residents of the day. It would have argued a public opinion too far in advance of Hanoverian Eng-

---

88. Munsell, J., *Annals of Albany,* vol. VIII, p. 262.

89. Dexter, op. cit., var.

90. Scharf, J. T., *History of Maryland,* vol. I, p. 351 ; Russell, E. B., *Review of Colonial Legislation by King and Council,* p. 33.

91. Cf. Norfolk, 1762, where it was considered sufficiently a municipal function to form a committee of the council to provide a schoolmaster for the local public school (Norfolk Borough Minutes, June 24, 1762). The minutes contain no record that this committee ever reported.

92. For Charleston, cf. Dalcho, F., *The Protestant Episcopal Church in South Carolina,* Charleston, 1820, pp. 93, etc.

land to have expected more than was actually accomplished. Where and when Calvinist influence was strong — from Holland or Scotland or the Puritan part of England — the devotion to education was carried across the Atlantic, but generally waned with the weakening of religion, the Indian Wars, the coming of heterogeneity, and the lessening of the original drive.[93] Schoolmasters were a mixed lot. In New Netherland they were customarily a kind of assistant to the minister, with religious as well as educational duties.[94] In Maryland the masters were often indentured servants.[95] In other southern colonies perhaps the most usual provision to be made was for the Anglican or Presbyterian clergyman to serve as teacher.[96] In Charleston (1742-1764) and perhaps in a few other places, the church maintained a charity school for negroes.[97] Isolated instances occur of public libraries, but usually by gift. Annapolis and Charleston (S. C.) appear to have appropriated some public money for their support.[98]

Every age and every community has had its numbers of maladjusted ; and rural districts are no exception. None the less, the problem of necessity is likely to be exaggerated in urban areas. The fact of a more complex

93. Those interested in the early history of public schools are referred also to Jernegan, M. W., *Laboring and Dependent Classes in Colonial America,* Chicago, 1931, Chaps. V, VI, VII, VIII (all referring to New England), and to subsequent chapters dealing with the South ; Morison, S. E., *Puritan Pronaos,* New York, 1936, Chap. III.

94. Chitwood, O. P., *History of Colonial America,* p. 555.

95. Ibid. p. 558.

96. Ibid. p. 560 ; Dalcho, F., *The Protestant Episcopal Church in South Carolina,* p. 93.

97. Dalcho, op. cit., p. 192.

98. In Annapolis through the medium of the church rate. The first free municipal library in the Colonies is usually given as that which resulted from the bequest of the Rev. John Sharp to New York City in 1700 (Edwards, E., *Free Town Libraries,* New York, 1869, p. 271).

existence makes greater claims upon individual adjustment ; the compactness of urban life makes for more of friction and trouble to those who are 'normal' as the result of the presence of the atypical. On the other hand, where people are 'known' in the 'intimate' stage of community development, crime, if it exists at all, is at least manageable.

So with the problem of poverty. In rural areas, except in times of great distress, the church or the parish could normally look after its own ; whereas a city, with its flotsam and jetsam and its lack of cohesiveness, must needs engage in organized corporate provision. The workhouse and the almshouse appeared in many a town — where the town was the responsible governmental unit — and taxing for ordinary home relief became increasingly frequent.[99]

It has already been noted that the city corporation was not normally the agency responsible for poor relief,[100] for such provision was usually by the county or vestry. However, in a few places, notably New York City, such poor relief loomed fairly large as a municipal function.[101] Here the old system of private relief broke down, and by 1685 responsibility was assumed by the city.[102] The precise agency and the method of administering relief fluctuated for a number of years,[103] but for a period at least it was to the city magistrates that petitions customarily

99. The vestry of St. Philip's, Charleston, protested to the assembly at the commitment to their workhouse of so many sailors and negroes (Journal, Vestry of St. Philip's, vol. II, 1766).
100. Cf. p. 242f.
101. Substantial expenditures for poor relief appear in the ledger of Annapolis for the first time about 1765 (Ledger, Annapolis, *passim*).
102. Peterson, A. E., and Edwards, G. W., *New York as an Eighteenth Century Municipality*, p. 183f.
103. 1693, overseers and wardens elected by voters ; etc. Cf. *supra*, p. 245.

were directed when relief elsewhere was not forthcoming.[104] The nature of the relief extended at the time may be sensed from a list of some of the items in the accounts of the Philadelphia overseers (1758) : medicines, foods, nursing, removal to other towns, mending spinning wheels, saws, etc., midwives, keeping orphans, wood, 'quart of rum for tailor,' rent, coffins, etc.[105] Boston in 1718 became quite paternalistic, and bought and distributed 10,000 pounds of bread[106] — a fairly typical instance of this kind of action where resources and need justified. Here and there were shown occasional realizations that a factor like drink was operative ; but of efforts towards the prevention or cure of poverty there was virtually no evidence. Community responsibility for relief had begun to be admitted, particularly in the occasional periods of great distress, but social responsibility for the causes of poverty remained for another age to discover.[107]

Mention has already been made incidentally of the growth of crime and lawlessness as factors in the transition from the unpaid to the paid watch. In the earlier period, the indentured servant class occasionally gave trouble. In 1721 the records of the mayor's court of Annapolis contain an account of an apparent convict-servant plot to seize the magazine and the town arms. By 1750, in New York and Philadelphia and to some extent elsewhere, there came to be considerable groups of the outlaw fringe of humanity, unassimilated by the customs and life of the time and in fact, in the matter of

104. Mayor's Court Minutes, New York City, *passim*. The court issued orders for support to the church wardens.
105. *Hist. Soc. of Pa. Coll.*, Philadelphia, 1853, 1 vol., pp. 43-53.
106. *Boston Town Records*, vol. 8, p. 133 (Dec. 29, 1718).
107. The mayor's court had certain responsibilities towards orphans and minors. (Cf. Morris, R. B. (Edit.), *Select Cases — New York City Mayor's Court*, pp. 188-190.)

drink, themselves the unfortunate by-products of some
of these customs. The difficulty of the situation was
further enhanced by the fact that these were also seaport
cities, and the sailor on shore-leave has never contributed
conspicuously to law and order. The grand jury of Philadelphia in 1744 'observed with concern in the course of
the Evidence, that a Neighborhood, in which some of
these disorderly Houses are, is so generally thought to
be vitiated, as to obtain among the common people the
shocking name of Hell Town.'[108] New York City had to
augment its watch in 1742 on account of the numbers of
convicts, deportees, press gangs, and sailors.[109] These
were but faint forerunners of the difficulties that future
generations were to face in their dealings with the maladjusted and the unassimilated and the consequently
lawless that were destined to characterize American cities
perhaps over and above those of any other people. In
1764 the grand jury in Charleston (S. C.) presented as a
grievance 'the want of a proper House of Correction in
Charles-Town ; the Work House now used for that purpose being insufficient, whereby notorious bawds, strumpets, vagrants, drunkards, and idle persons, who might
be there committed, reign and infest the said town with
impunity.'[110]

A curious rough and ready extra-legal 'justice' crops
out occasionally to indicate at one and the same time the
ineffectiveness of the administration of law and the thin-
ness of the veneer of order. For instance, the *Maryland
Gazette* of March 29, 1753 carries an account from Philadelphia of a 'set of regulators — in imitation of those in
Elizabeth town' who 'called a man for horsewhipping

108. *Hist. Soc. of Pa. Coll.*, vol. I, p. 268.
109. Peterson and Edwards, op. cit., p. 315.
110. *South Carolina Gazette,* Nov. 5-12, 1764.

his wife,' secured him and 'flagellated his Posteriors with Birchen Rods,' and warned him about repeating the treatment. The man appealed to justice, 'but what satisfaction he may get, we cannot learn.'

Penalties for crimes were generally severe — death for pickpockets, for example — and often picturesque and ingenious. In Boston, 1753, one Hannah Silkey, convicted of running a bawdy house, was condemned to stand one hour on a five foot stool in front of the court house with a placard of her crime — in addition to a fairly heavy fine.[111] A counterfeiter in Philadelphia was sentenced to stand in the pillory one hour — the tip of his right ear nailed to the pillory — and at the conclusion of the hour, the ear was cut off.[112]

(D)

A complete picture of municipal activity in the colonial period would include a miscellaneous set of functions called out by peculiarities of time or place.[113] Activities of a military or defensive nature have already been noted.[114] Location on a river made a municipally-owned ferry a logical activity, although this would normally be leased. In Bristol, the ferryman would always claim that his rent was too high, and the kind-hearted council would

111. *Maryland Gazette,* June 28, 1753.
112. Ibid. Mar. 29, 1754.
113. Odds and ends of ordinances appeared from time to time, as, for example, Williamsburg's requirement of dog collars for all dogs, together with other limitations to prevent 'fierce dogs . . . running at large' (*Virginia Gazette,* Oct. 1, 1772).
114. Cf. p. 60. Cf. also the erection of a stockade by the corporation of Albany, 1734 (*Cadwallader Colden Papers* in *Coll. N. Y. Hist. Soc.,* vol. II, p. 109) ; also the tax laid in Norfolk, 1772, for the construction of a magazine (Hening's *Virginia Statutes,* vol. VIII, p. 611) ; New York City's defences against the French fleet, 1694 (Peterson and Edwards, op. cit., p. 87), and 1695 (*N. Y. Hist. Soc. Coll.,* 1885, p. 447).

always reduce it by half.[115] To lease or not to lease was the periodic question for the New York City docks ; and the lessee frequently defaulted.[116] Other questions of regulation of wharves, charges, cleaning, repairs, etc., regularly presented themselves to port cities. A few cities had common burying grounds. The building of bridges was normally grouped with the building of roads for administrative purposes. Williamsburg in 1772 seriously considered a project for building a canal between the James and York Rivers, and opened a subscription list for it.[117]

Of public buildings, there were a surprising number in the larger towns. The pound, the market house, the town hall, the gaol, the almshouse, and workhouse were almost universal ; schools, watchhouses, exchange, customs house, hospital, all had made their appearance in one or more cities before 1775. New York's new bridewell, finished in 1775, was the most imposing public building in the city.[118]

(E)

Finally, a word must be added to call attention to those activities which did not appear. Grants of power were customarily ample enough, so hampering by legislatures or the Constitution did not account for such absence. The modern health department and all save a negligible number of its several activities were completely missing.[119] Knowledge had not reached much beyond the quarantine for smallpox. An epidemic of this type was

115. Minutes, Bristol Borough Council, *passim.*
116. *Minutes, Common Council, New York City, passim.*
117. *Virginia Gazette,* Jan. 16, 1772.
118. Peterson and Edwards, op. cit., p. 303.
119. Inoculation for smallpox was occasionally promoted by municipal by-laws, e. g. Annapolis (*Maryland Gazette,* Mar. 14, 1765).

indeed the signal for great activity, and even two or three cases were enough to cause the Williamsburg city fathers to meet every other day.[120] Regulation or licensing of midwives was customary. Community recreation was unthought of. City planning in the modern sense was outside the ken of the age.[121] We have already mentioned the complete absence of the preventive or curative attitude towards poverty and crime. In fact the absence of these 'positives' in all fields, save the monopolistic promotion of trade, is perhaps the most noticeable characteristic of the colonial town. It was of a different age ; its people had a different set of experiences ; its religious and social attitudes were other than those of to-day.

What changes, if any, were there in municipal functions during the period between 1640 and 1775 ? A great many, certainly, but for the most part these were outgrowths of the change from the intimate to the urbanized community rather than changes representing any profound alteration in customs and ideas, or growth in or influence of technical knowledge. Emphasis must once more be laid upon the fact that most of the developments in functions which have been recorded were functions of changing size and not of *changing ideas*.[122] Here and there could be noted the beginnings of a mechanized order, in water works or in such a simple thing as a fire engine. The compact regulation of trade by the individual community was cracking under the strain of an

120. *Virginia Gazette,* Jan. 28, 1768.
121. Charleston (S. C.), Philadelphia, Annapolis, and possibly others were to some extent 'planned' — if checkerboard streets constitute a plan. The street commissioners of Charleston in 1764 were given the power to plant trees (Pringle-Smith, J. J., 'City Government of Charleston,' in *Charleston Year Book,* 1881, p. 339f.).
122. In this connection it is interesting to compare the by-laws of two cities at two different dates. These are set out in Appendix D.

increased mobility. Heterogeneity was taking its toll in a weakening of the social sanctions back of those by-laws which dealt with religion and morals. Yet it was largely urbanization itself that forced the improvements in paving and lighting, in cleaning and police ; as well as urbanization that created the problems of poverty and crime which even this early were baffling to these communities and enlarging the sphere of their corporate effort. Into this dawning complexity of urban government and administration the War of the Revolution was precipitated.

XII

THE FINANCE OF COLONIAL MUNICIPALITIES

To-day the budget of a unit of government is one of the best mirrors of its activities, if not the best. This was far less true of the colonial municipalities. These towns commanded so much in the way of unpaid service in connection with their 'courts' ; so many of their activities (particularly in the 'intimate' stage) were financed by 'service' taxes ; and so many more of their activities (the control of markets and fairs, for instance) were on a self-supporting fee basis — that the tiny 'budgets,' or rather the 'accounts passed,' formed but an imperfect picture of their actual accomplishments.

Generalizations concerning this financial structure are exceedingly difficult. The tendency, particularly in poor relief, was at first to follow the prevailing English precedent of assessment ; but the different conditions of land tenure, the plantation system of the South, individual small holdings in the North, made for other methods, or so modified the English method that eventually the American local revenue system was to develop into something quite different.

Rather less attention need be devoted to the consideration of expenditures than of revenues. Logically, the former should be treated first, inasmuch as a characteristic of colonial finance seemed to be the custom of 'earmarking' — in other words, once an expenditure had been decided upon, an appropriate as well as sufficient revenue would frequently be sought.

The expensive items were apparent in our earlier discussion of functions. When the stage of 'work taxes' and voluntary labour had been passed, the paving and cleaning and repair of the streets and the maintenance of the

watch were the most costly of the usual services. Perhaps
relief of the poor should also be included, although this
was not ordinarily a function of the city corporation
proper. Public buildings, docks, stockades, and other
more or less non-recurring public works were expensive
the year they occurred, and often led to unusual expedients for raising revenue. Minor officials — beadles,
porters, and the like — were paid ; and in the few larger
communities these office-holders were really full time incumbents. Wages in such instances ran from £20 to £50
a year.[1] Schools were a distinctly minor expense, where
they were maintained at all by the towns or boroughs.
Fees from parents, a few grants from the colony, and gifts
met a large part of their cost. A school teacher was usually
paid from £25 to £50 a year. In Charleston (S. C.) £100
(current money, depreciated) was paid to the schoolmaster (in 1712).[2] It will be recalled that the schoolmaster in the South was frequently an indentured servant
or the local minister.[3] Two or three sample annual expenditure lists are cited by way of illustration. The first
is that of the town of Providence in 1725 (population
about 3,000). Poor expenses, $21.00 ; bridges, $2.75 ;

1. e. g. New York City scavenger, 1695, (on contract) £30 (Peterson,
A. E., and Edwards, G. W., *New York as an Eighteenth Century Municipality,* p. 101) ; Norfolk watch, £24-£30 a year (Minutes, Norfolk
Borough, Jan.-Mar. 1770) ; Williamsburg watch, £30 a year (*Virginia
Gazette,* July 16, 1772). Part time salaries in Annapolis (1761) were :
city clerk, £7-10-0 ; constable, £5-0-0 ; gate keeper, £5-0-0 ; day labour
(paid through the surveyor) white, 3s. ; negro, 1s. (MSS. City Accounts). In 1765 the constable was paid £10. Albany paid its porter
in 1697 28 pieces of eight (Howell and Tenney, op. cit., p. 464) ; in
1742, its public whipper was paid £12, and such fees as he might
earn for servicing masters (Munsell, J., *Annals of Albany,* vol. X, p.
98). Of course the value of the currency varied considerably with
the year and the place.

2. Dalcho, F., *Historical Account of the Protestant Episcopal Church in
South Carolina,* p. 95.

3. Cf. p. 284.

highways, $5.30 ; constables, sheriffs, and sergeant's wages, $10.60. In addition to these items there were the substantial 'service taxes' of the 'intimate' stage, together with the usual number of fees for certain officials. The budget of Providence was under $200 a year until 1750.[4]

In 1769, the Tax Act and Estimate for Charleston (S. C.) specified 'Sundries to be paid by the Inhabitants of Charleston' :[5] commissioners of streets, £1,400 ; commissioners of roads, St. Philip's parish, £100 ; several appropriations to specific persons for repairs to public wells, fire buckets, care and repair of fire engine, sinking wells, etc. The total of all the above came to £3,866-17-2, in greatly depreciated currency. (£1-10-00 equalled about $1.00 Spanish.)

In Annapolis, during the year 1763, the following were the accounts allowed : Thomas Hodgkin, clerk, £7-10-0 ; Robert Kenward, for calling meetings, lock and staple, and work on highway, £2-11-5 ; William Reynolds, rental of room for meetings of court and council, £7-15-0 ; Lancelot Jacques, rum furnished labourers, 8/9. In addition, the city sheriff received certain fees.[6] During this decade there were occasional substantial amounts spent for repairs, a gate house, etc. In 1770, the prosecutor was paid £12-0-0 and the clerk of the court, £22-10-0 ; but by this time the currency had depreciated considerably. Expenditures for poor relief had begun to appear in the city accounts.

In New York City, in 1761, accounts were passed total-

---

4. Stokes, H. K., *Finances and Administration of Providence*, p. 121f. The dollars were Spanish silver.

5. The Act, which is printed separately, is in the files of the Charleston Library Society.

6. Not to be confused with the county sheriff, who included among his duties that of custodian of the funds of St. Anne's Parish Church (Minutes of the Vestry, St. Anne's Parish Register, Annapolis).

ling £1,421. It is not possible from the available records to tell just how much of the £832 included under the heading 'John De Peyster' represented balances from the preceding year and carry-overs to the year following in his capacity as custodian of certain funds. Probably a fair amount was of this character. Repairs to bridges, workhouse, etc., totalled £272. Fire buckets and care of the engine came to £26 ; laying and draining a slip, £101 ; taxes on assets of corporation, £52 ; expenses in connection with the watch, £87 — probably but a small fraction of the cost of the whole, of which perhaps the major part was included in De Peyster's account. The remainder was made up of miscellaneous·small items.[7]

Occasionally some extraordinary expenditure would occur which would strain the resources of a corporation. New York City in 1694 found itself in financial straits because of the expenses for defence.[8] On the whole, however, a community would not undertake the building, for example, of a new city hall, unless it knew whence the money was coming. In any event, both the total expenses and the amount raised by taxation appear fantastically small in the light of present-day standards. Even as late as 1730 the total budget of New York City was usually under £600.[9]

The difficulties in accounting, the variations in the value of the currency from place to place and time to time, the amount of voluntary labour, the custom of pay-

7. MSS. Accounts Passed, 1761 — Original Records of the Common Council. By no means were all of these confined to any one calendar year, thus rendering still more difficult any really accurate presentation.
8. Peterson, A. E., and Edwards, G. W., *New York as an Eighteenth Century Municipality*, p. 165. Cf. also Charleston (S. C.), which in 1701 spent £550 for watch, largely on account of fear of the French (Pringle-Smith, J. J., *Government of the City of Charleston*, in *Charleston Year Book*, 1881, p. 22f.).
9. Peterson and Edwards, op. cit., p. 38.

ments in fees, the various persons receiving and paying, the intermittent occurrence of substantial capital expenditures, all combined to make any generalizations as to average of *per capita* expenditures virtually futile.[10]

In amounts so small and in a relatively simple age, it is not surprising that accounting methods were most primitive.[11] Generally speaking, accounts were simply presented to the councils, and 'passed' as they came up.[12] The time of payment depended upon whether funds were in hand. Of controls on amount there were none, apart from the cheese-paring traditions of the day and the consequent pressure of public opinion reflecting the 'property' basis of the franchise. Such extravagance as existed appears to have been quite occasional or accidental. Perhaps, according to modern standards, certain corporations may seem to have spent a rather substantial portion of their total income on 'entertainment,' i.e. banqueting, with liberal refreshment included.[13] This was, however, a custom of the day ; and in many instances the bill would be paid, not from the public funds, but by the mayor personally. The plan used for a while in Philadelphia of paying the overseers of the poor a commission of 9*d.* in the pound of the total spent seems to have been relatively infrequent. It may be used as illustrative of two things. In the first place, the expenditure in question

10. If one were pressed to give an actual estimate it would probably be in the neighbourhood (1760) of 1/6 *per capita* in the larger cities (over 5,000) and 9 *d. per capita* in the smaller ones. This would not include poor relief.
11. Cf. 403f. for a fuller discussion, particularly as regards custody of the receipts.
12. Cf. Wilmington [Account] Book, MS. in Hall of Records, Dover.
13. e. g. account of party at the tavern of Samuel Fraunces, New York City, Aug. 22, 1771. 'Entertainment, supper and constables' came to £15 ; turtle to £4-2-0 ; various drinks to £29-14-4 (Original Records of Common Council).

naturally and perhaps inevitably mounted.[14] In the second place, the plan itself was indicative of an age in which on the whole the voters felt rightly that their officials would be economical ; or no such method would ever have been introduced. Perhaps this assumption was really more significant and illuminating than the consequent extravagance. Another illustration of a somewhat similar unsound practice was that which prevailed for a number of years in New York City, where the City allowed its individual aldermen to spend for poor relief without sanction of the council. Ultimately this had to be altered and collective responsibility restored.[15]

Occasionally in towns such as Philadelphia and New York where the amounts spent were, for the times, really substantial, some rather belated reforms were introduced. New York City in 1710 reorganized the accounting and bookkeeping in its treasurer's office with this in mind.[16] The extravagant overseers of Philadelphia in 1770 were made accountable to the county magistrates acting as auditors, one phase of a general overhauling of poor relief financial methods. In other townships an elected auditor was introduced.[17]

(B)

Mention has already been made of the extent to which expenditures and revenues were interconnected item by item ; and it is worth while examining this fact more closely. In the first place, 'court' officials such as marshals, coroners, or even the ever-present constables were usually

14. Cf. p. 286 for items.
15. Cf. p. 179.
16. Peterson and Edwards, op. cit., p. 29f.
17. Bolles, A. S., *Pennsylvania, Province and State,* vol. II, p. 266f. This general reorganization also included a move to make the township rather than the county the unit responsible for poor relief.

recompensed by fees assessed upon the people served, or by the ear-marking of all or part of the fines imposed. St. Mary's, for example, paid its clerk of the court the fees for recording land conveyance ; as well as other fees.[18] The same custom prevailed at the end of the period. In New York City, in 1773, the fees for being sworn as freemen were allocated : 7/6 to the clerk, 1d. to the cryer, and 6s. to the mayor.[19] Sometimes the detail to which this ear-marking process descended was amusing. In Philadelphia, in 1700, it was provided that the fines imposed for violation of the law against smoking on the streets should be used to buy fire buckets.[20] The excise revenues were also occasionally ear-marked, perhaps with some appropriateness, for the town school. In Charleston (S. C.), 1768, they were used, with still more appropriateness, for the poor house and hospital.[21]

For years in most towns the watch was a combination of voluntary and paid service. Theoretically service was usually voluntary in rotation, but the alternatives of commutation or of hiring a substitute were ordinarily allowed. This practice would result in a steady inflow of money which served to provide a semi-permanent nucleus of personnel.

Officials in connection with the markets, and officials and maintenance charges for the wharves and docks were

18. Proceedings of Council, Oct. 13, 1685, in *Md. Arch.*, vol. XVII, p. 420.
19. Seybolt, R. F., *The Colonial Citizen of New York City*, p. 6.
20. *Report on the Public Archives of Philadelphia*, in *Annl. Rpt. Amer. Hist. Assoc.*, 1901, vol. II, p. 262.
21. McCord, D. J. (Edit.), *Statutes-at-Large of South Carolina*, vol. VII, p. 90f. (Stat. 966). Connecticut in 1766 made excise taxes available locally for school support (Walker, Mrs. A. M., *Development of State Support of Education in Connecticut* [Abstract], p. 21). Cf. also New Bern (1764), which similarly allocated a 1d. a gallon tax on spirits (Dexter, E. G., *History of Education in the United States*, p. 68).

customarily paid by the fees charged. Usually there would be a surplus to add to the general corporate revenue from both these sources. In Annapolis it was customary for the city to impose a semi-compulsory collection upon booth-holders and tavern keepers to provide prizes for the races at the fair.[22]

In New York City for years the question was in dispute as to which fees were personal and which were to belong to the general city revenues. In 1686 the mayor was given separate powers of licensing for sale of drink, and the power to exact the appropriate fees. At the time it was held that these fees belonged to the corporation ; but in 1736 Mayor Richard retained them and also his fees as clerk of the market. The protest at such a practice was immediate and vigorous, and continued intermittently down to 1759. It was then settled by providing that the mayor's perquisite should consist of £125 a year allowance, plus 4s. from each liquor licence.[23] It should be borne in mind that the mayor of New York City was an appointee of the governor, and also that his duties as an administrator had probably expanded beyond those of the mayor of any other town.

(C)

The sources of revenue of a municipality were fairly numerous and perhaps fully as diversified as those of the modern city. By comparison there was proportionately far less reliance upon direct taxation, either on persons or on real estate. Such taxation, till near the end of the period, was regarded as distinctly supplementary, if not 'abnormal.' Except for poor relief, it was not the characteristic method of raising the necessary funds.

22. Minutes, Mayor's Court, var.
23. Peterson and Edwards, op. cit., pp. 27, 223, 224.

Quite frequently, even when expressed in money terms, the various taxes, fees, etc., would be paid in produce or merchandise. The community would then undertake its marketing. In Albany, wheat served for the purpose ;[24] in New York City, at one time, beaver pelts.[25] Annapolis used tobacco as its medium, which the officials then sold.[26] Under these circumstances, and also in a period when the 'service' tax was characteristic, the difficulty of obtaining a true picture of municipal activities from a study of its accounts is the more understandable.

The court revenues — fees, fines, etc. — were undoubtedly considerable ; but these were so frequently directly allocated to officials, that they seldom were entered in the municipal accounts at figures approaching their actual total. In the year 1769, in Annapolis, approximately £200 was received from fines — but this was an exceptionally large amount. In the same year, the licence fees brought in £15-0-0, and sundry revenues £8-0-0. With such large revenues from fines, there was no need that year or most years of a tax for the ordinary expenses of the corporation.[27]

Where, as in New York and Albany, the titles of large areas of land (and water front) were vested in the city at the time of incorporation, it is not surprising that the sale or rent of such properties played a considerable role in the budget. They served New York City in the role of a 'balance wheel' to meet extraordinary expenses. In 1686 the expenses of its new charter were largely met by such land sales ; and in 1699 the new city hall was partly

24. For its rents.
25. Seybolt, op. cit., p. 16. Cf. also Rhode Island (Stokes, H. K., *Finance and Administration of Providence,* p. 99).
26. *Md. Arch.,* vol. XVII, pp. 420, etc. Also Virginia (Hening's *Virginia Statutes,* vol. IV, p. 447f.).
27. MSS. City Accounts.

financed by the sale of water lots.[28] On the other hand, Albany in 1687 voted a tax in preference to selling its land.[29] As New York City grew in commercial importance, this particular source of revenue increased tremendously under the dual impact of increase in land values and increased pressure on the budget to find more revenues. The revenue from lands in 1730 was £28 ; in 1770, £374 ; from water lots, in 1740, £65 ; in 1770, £460.[30]

It had been a custom in Holland to lease or 'farm out' revenues,[31] and this influence and precedent lingered for some time in New York City. Various revenues were put up at auction. For example, excise in 1656 brought 4220 guilders.[32] The 'farming out' continued intermittently under the English at least until 1753.[33] The city market, where the stalls were first leased separately, was in 1741 let as a whole by auction to the highest bidder.[34] In general, the revenues from markets and fairs occupied a substantial place in the receipts of most towns.[35] It was customary also to lease docks and ferries, and this often was quite profitable. The revenues in New York City amounted to £970 from ferries and £690 from docks in

28. Peterson and Edwards, op. cit., pp. 2, 82f.
29. Schwab, J. C., *History of the New York Property Tax*, Baltimore, 1890, p. 30f.
30. Peterson and Edwards, op. cit., p. 397.
31. Schwab, op. cit., p. 32.
32. Ibid.
33. Peterson and Edwards, op. cit., p. 269. Cf. also in Original Records of Common Council, various reports of such awards after public auction — for example, Nov. 10, 1713, to Ebenezer Wilson for £510. By 1730 it averaged £650 or more a year. The city was not always successful in collecting the amount of the contract.
34. Ibid. p. 277.
35. e. g. Lancaster, whose June fair (1759) brought in £63, apparently comprising the larger part of the town's total revenue (Minutes of Borough of Lancaster, Dec. 11, 1759). The total budget in this period seems to have been under rather than over £100.

1770 — the largest two sources of municipal income in that year.[36]

The city corporation of Philadelphia in 1747 secured the bulk of its revenues from ferry rents, and market and vendue stall rents. The former brought in £139, the latter £160, out of a total income exclusive of fines of £308.[37] This was just prior to the civic renaissance which brought taxes for streets, watch, and other items, the spending of which was under the direction of the various commissioners.

Wilmington (Del.) will serve as an example of a smaller town. Its revenues in 1771 were as follows :[38]

Fair stalls	£11- 0-0
Tax	15- 4-0
Fair	3- 0-0
Fines and taxes	1-16-2
Fire Engine	15-0
Fines	1-12-6
Rent of land	1- 0-0
Total (?)	£44- 7-8

There was a certain amount of indirect taxation in most communities, liquor, by quantity or through the licence to sell it, serving as the chief source. Licence fees were also customarily paid by auctioneers, travelling showmen, etc. In New York City these combined sources totalled £524 in 1760 — the second largest source of

36. Peterson and Edwards, op. cit., p. 397.
37. *Minutes of Philadelphia Corporation*, Aug. 3, 1747. It is very difficult, in the absence of any all-inclusive budget, to be certain that these items plus the fines actually made up the entire income.
38. Wilmington (Account) Book, 1769-1801. MS. in Hall of Records, Dover.

revenue ; but fell back to sixth or seventh place in 1770 with a decline to £230.[39] Albany was the only town I have been able to discover that levied 'octroi' or taxes on goods entering the city. Even in Albany, reliance upon this particular source seems to have been confined to the earlier period.[40] The imposition of such taxes required permission from the assembly.

Where the original paving was not the result of compulsory or of commuted labour, but was undertaken by hired labour, it was customary to assess the cost on the abutting property. The sense of 'taxation according to benefit received' was very keen in these early municipalities, arising quite naturally from the 'intimate' stage in which each individual was held responsible for the condition of the road in front of his own home.

There were a number of other miscellaneous expedients for raising revenues, because metallic money as such was scarce in colonial times. New York City in 1774 issued paper money to aid in the construction of its water works.[41] Aid for the schools was occasionally extended from the colony budget. Connecticut, which carried such aid as far as any colony, will serve by way of illustration. Its earlier grants were stabilized in 1750 by payment of 40s. on every £1,000 listed to the towns complying with colonial provisions. In the same year it made its school fund permanent.[42] Attention has already been called to the fact that the 1694 effort of Maryland to aid free schools through the medium of an export tax was dis-

39. Peterson and Edwards, op. cit., p. 397.
40. Lincoln, C. Z., *Constitutional History of New York*, vol. I, p. 19. The market fees for meat fixed by Norfolk in 1736 were of this character, in so far as inhabitants of the borough were granted 50 per cent exemption (Council Orders — Norfolk Borough, Dec. 20, 1736).
41. Cf. p. 275.
42. Dexter, E. G., *History of Education in the United States*, p. 83f.

allowed by the Privy Council.[43] This colony did not, however, wholly stop its aid ; for, after other unsuccessful efforts, it appropriated £1,500 in 1736 for a school at Annapolis.[44] Apart from such occasional aid to schools, the only example I have noted of aid to ordinary local budgets was by Rhode Island (1721-48), which distributed to the towns part of the interest it received on the paper money lent on mortgage security.[45] In 1770, Georgia appropriated £100 to be added to £200 raised locally for the expense of a watch in Savannah, but this was disallowed.[46]

Lotteries as a means of raising corporate revenue were rather late in appearance, but became increasingly frequent after 1750 — almost always as a means of financing capital expenditures. In 1744, Rhode Island used this method to raise £3,000 to build a bridge at Providence.[47] Its next use in this colony was in 1747-48 when a lottery was launched designed to pave the Newport streets.[48] Trenton (1753) used this method to build a school ;[49] Baltimore (1753) to construct a wharf ;[50] Annapolis (1753) for its town clock and to clear the dock.[51] From then on, its use was increasingly frequent. New York City (1756) employed the device to replenish its general funds, which were at low ebb in that year on account of

43. Cf. p. 283.
44. Dexter, op. cit., p. 66 ; Riley, E. S., History of Anne Arundel County, p. 63.
45. Stokes, H. K., Finances and Administration of Providence, p. 121.
46. Flippin, P. S., 'Royal Government in Georgia,' in Ga. Hist. Quart., vol. VIII, p. 283.
47. Stiness, J. H., A Century of Lotteries in Rhode Island, in R. I. Hist. Tracts, 2nd ser., No. 3 (Providence, 1896), p. 2.
48. Ibid. p. 3.
49. History of Trenton, vol. II, p. 707f. (History published 1929, various authors).
50. Griffith, T. W., Annals of Baltimore, p. 34.
51. Maryland Gazette, Mar. 29, 1753.

expenses from the French and Indian Wars.[52] Such opposition as appeared was largely (possibly wholly) confined to private lotteries ; their use for public purposes
was continued and continual.[53]

At least one instance is recorded (in Annapolis) of a
ball and concert being held to raise funds for the repairs
of a near-by road and mill.[54]

(D)

The developments in the field of direct taxation must
receive much more detailed consideration — not because
of their comparative importance financially but because
of their significance in the light of their later evolution.
In almost every instance, the power of direct taxation was
neither granted nor implied by charter ; but required
specific or even annual authorization from the legislature.

However, there were exceptions. For example, the city
of Annapolis evidently had the implied power to levy a
direct tax on horses and cattle, for such a tax was provided in a by-law of July 28, 1757.[55]

A clearer instance of these exceptional powers of direct
taxation was that of Wilmington (Del.), which at the
outset of its existence as a borough levied a rate for the
money subscribed towards the charter and for the town
cage and other expenses. The authority to do this apparently rested upon the clause permitting the making of
the necessary ordinances for the good government of the
town. The town meeting went beyond the endorsing of

52. Peterson and Edwards, op. cit., p. 404.
53. e. g. for Pennsylvania, cf. Scharf, J. T., and Westcott, T., *History of Philadelphia*, vol. I, p. 256.
54. *Maryland Gazette,* June 21, 1753.
55. Minutes of Annapolis Common Council.

the specific rate, and constituted the burgesses and assistant commissioners to act at all future times 'to calculate the publick Debts and Charges . . . and . . . adjust and settle the sums of money which ought of necessity to be raised yearly to pay . . . such publick Debts.'[56] The borough council made frequent use of this taxing power, particularly in the years just prior to the Revolution.[57] Beverwyck (Albany) sought and obtained the specific approval of the director general, when it desired to impose a chimney tax in order to meet the expense of fortifications and repairs to the bridges.[58] The charter of the City of Albany (1686) makes no specific mention of the power to tax ; but, as early as July 21, 1693, there is a record of a direct tax levied by action of the city corporation. Occasional use was made of it from time to time later — for the rattle watch, for repairs of the blockhouse, etc.[59] It is possible that this power was one included in the charter under the general grant of continuance of powers exercised during the previous twenty years — or it may have been considered prescriptive or implied.[60]

The more usual requirement was that of direct authorization by the assembly as a prerequisite to levying a rate. This requirement was partly accounted for by the fact that it was supposed that, for the ordinary town, other revenues would be sufficient ; this requirement prevailed, because the idea was still very strong that a city

56. Minute Book of Wilmington, Dec. 30, 1740.
57. Minutes of Burgesses and Assistants, Oct. 8, 1772 ; Jan. 8, 1774 ; Nov. 19, 1774 ; etc.
58. *Court Minutes, Fort Orange and Beverwyck,* July 25, 1660 (vol. II, p. 287, A. J. F. Van Laer, Edit. and Trans.).
59. Minutes in J. Munsell, *Annals of Albany,* var.
60. Westchester borough trustees levied rates, apparently without specific authorization (Book of Records of the Trustees, Feb. 9, 1702/3).

was a 'court' and a 'corporation' rather than a 'service unit' of government. Numerous examples may be cited. In Williamsburg, 1722, revenues were specifically limited to fines and tolls from markets and fairs. The city was not allowed to levy *octroi* or the ordinary Virginia poll tax on tithables. However, experience was to demonstrate greater need ; and, after an interval during which the two adjacent counties contributed towards the cost of certain of its officials, in 1744 the city was finally allowed to levy a poll tax to meet the expenses of constructing a jail. The power was again extended in 1759 to repair the streets ; and in 1762-64 the city was actually granted general taxing power. However, so radical a policy was reversed in 1764 as 'dangerous to liberties and properties,' and thereafter the grants of the taxing power were specific — for repairing the prison, for hospitals, for the fire engine, etc.[61] These specific authorizations were particularly characteristic of Virginia and also appeared frequently for Norfolk and the various 'towns.'[62]

New York City and Philadelphia similarly were forced to secure specific authorization from their respective assemblies before levying a property tax. So long as the city stayed within what were considered its 'normal' revenues, it was allowed wide latitude in expenditure ; but once the question of a direct tax came up, the assembly jealously guarded what it considered its prerogative. In Dutch days there were instances of levies for general city expenses ;[63] but under English rule for a long time the

61. Gulick, L., and Pollard, J. G., *Modern Government in a Colonial City*, pp. 28, 30, 31.
62. For Norfolk, tax for watch and lighting (1763), cf. Hening's *Virginia Statutes*, vol. VII, p. 654 ; for its magazine, cf. ibid. vol. VIII, p. 611 ; etc.
63. Probably by the director general and council, cf. Schwab, J. C., *History of the New York Property Tax*, p. 23.

particular purpose of the levy had to be specified. As a matter of fact, such direct taxes were not imposed by the city proper (apart from the poor rate) until 1730, when a tax for fire engines was authorized. Authorizations followed in 1737, for debts ; in 1741, for watch ; in 1746, 1753, 1756, and almost annually thereafter for general purposes. It was customary to combine the assessment and collection with the poor rate.[64] Pennsylvania was somewhat more liberal in its extension of powers to Philadelphia, for in 1712 the corporation and the assessors were allowed *annually* to determine the amount necessary for the debts and charges of the city. However, the enabling act fixed maximums, and the power itself was later curtailed.[65]

If even these large corporations were thus restricted as to their taxation, it was to be expected that the 'towns' governed by commissioners and the smaller boroughs would be similarly treated. Thus Bristol (1745) was granted such power, limited however to 3d. in the pound of the 'clear value' and to a poll tax on single men not otherwise rated in the proportion of 3s. to every 1d. of the tax.[66] In Wilmington (N. C.) a tax limit (on 'tithables') of 1/6 was set ; but such a tax required the further authorization of the borough meeting for its imposition.[67] Apparently, by tradition, the New England town meetings found themselves less hampered.

These direct taxes gradually came to serve as the 'balance wheel,' and in a few towns became virtually annual affairs. In the first instance, their imposition had usually

64. Peterson, A. E., and Edwards, G. W., *New York as an Eighteenth Century Municipality*, p. 400f.
65. Cf. p. 252 ; also Keith, C. P., *Chronicles of Pennsylvania*, vol. II, p. 505.
66. *Laws of Pennsylvania, 1700-1802*, 1803, vol. I, pp. 287-292 (Chap. 367).
67. *State Records of North Carolina*, vol. XXIII, p. 234f.

been for poor relief, when gifts and other revenues proved inadequate. For the reasons before specified, their appearance for emergency municipal purposes came later ; and still later was their use to meet ordinary recurring expenditure for streets, watch, etc. Their use for schools was confined largely to the New England towns. Even there such use was normally under the direction and occasionally the duress of general acts of the colony. At least occasionally the imposition of such a tax for the needs of the colony itself preceded its use for local purposes, and furnished the precedent for the latter as to methods of assessment, etc.[68] New York Province in 1683 passed a general Act dealing with assessments for poor relief, which Act later furnished the basis for assessing property for other local purposes.[69] In other instances, for example, Rhode Island, the order was reversed ; and apparently local practice furnished the basis for subsequent colonial enactments.[70]

In Maryland, Virginia, and North Carolina, the poll tax or 'tithable' was the characteristic form of direct tax.[71] It was early discovered that in a slave-owning district the number of persons over sixteen employed or living on a given plantation furnished a rough and ready estimate

68. e. g. Virginia (Channing, E., *History of the United States,* New York. 1905-25, 6 vol., vol. I, p. 522).

69. Cf. p. 317.

70. *Records of Rhode Island* (Bartlett, J. R., Edit.), Providence, 1856-65, 10 vol., vol. II, pp. 111, 301 ; *Records of the Town of Portsmouth* (R. I.) (Perry, A., and Brigham, C. S., Edit.), Providence, 1901, p. 63 ; *Records of the Town of Warwick* (Chapin, H. M., Edit.), Providence, 1926, p. 61 ; etc.

71. In at least Charleston in South Carolina the property tax was occasionally used. In 1701 this was for the watch 'if necessary' [Pringle-Smith, J. J., *Government of the City of Charleston,* in *Charleston Year Book,* 1881, pp. 22ff. (Stat. No. 207)]. In 1761 the bases for the tax for parish funds were the 'estates, slaves, monies at interest, and annuities' (Notice in *South Carolina Gazette,* Jan. 6-10, 1721).

of relative wealth. White women 'not employed in the fields' were customarily not counted ; and the details varied somewhat between the colonies. Under these circumstances, when Williamsburg, Savannah, and Wilmington (N. C.) were pressed for further revenues, a convenient and familiar method was at hand for assessment. New Bern, 1757, wavered somewhat from this basis and provided that only males should be taxed ;[72] but this appears to have been exceptional in the South. How this particular method was regarded, at least in its early stages, may be judged from a letter of the Newcastle court in 1677 : 'The people live distant and their Estates [are] for the most part very Inconsiderable ; that we can find no proper way to discover the vallue of their said estate, and if discovered to bring it in a Valluable shape to Receive. But if your Honor will be pleased to allow of a Levy to be laid by the Pole, as they of Virginia and Maryland doe and have continued it for so many years, not finding out a more easier and better way, then ye Levy can be easier made and Received.'[73]

North of Maryland the poll tax was much less frequently used, nor was it a major source of revenue as in the South. Pennsylvania made some use of it in the period of the Duke's Laws and somewhat later. In 1686, under these Laws, a rate was set of 1d. in the pound on the value of land and 6s. poll tax, with certain exemptions.[74] In the North, property rather than persons was normally the basis of taxation ; and where, as in Bristol (Pa.), a tax was imposed upon single men 'not otherwise rated,' it was by way of imposing an equivalent to the

72. *State Records of North Carolina,* vol. XXV, p. 358f.
73. Quoted in Schwab, J. C., *History of the New York Property Tax,* p. 47.
74. Bolles, A. S., *Pennsylvania, Province and State,* vol. II, p. 262f.

property tax rather than as an independent source of revenue.[75]

It was this property tax that was ultimately to prove by far the most significant contribution of the colonial period to the subsequent course of American fiscal development. The evolution of the tax was never quite the same between state and state; but in general certain broad stages could be detected. In its American genesis it was in the first instance distinctly a New England product. The idea appears to have originated in the intimate period of the town meeting, when it was thought that each man should contribute towards common expenses according to his 'strength.'[76] The situation came to be similar to that which had prevailed in England even as late as the sixteenth century, of which Cannan wrote : 'It is never things but always persons that pay rates and taxes and . . . the metaphor which attributes payment to the thing in respect of which the person is taxed had not taken possession of the ordinary mind as it has now. . . . The total sum to be raised is apportioned directly upon the contributors as the assessors or the inhabitants see fit.'[77] Other and later English ideas and precedents in assessment did come to modify this basis in the Colonies, but in these early days did not really fit the colonial situation.[78]

In the New England towns the contributions were originally voluntary, perhaps scarcely distinguishable

75. Bristol Minute Book, var.
76. Thus the first Newport compact included the clause, 'we do engage ourselves to bear equal charges answerable to our strength and estates in common.' (Stokes, H. K., *Finances and Administration of Providence*, p. 96.)
77. Cannan, E., *History of Local Rates*, London, 1912, p. 22. In certain localities in England this point of view lingered on until after 1800, so English precedent may have influenced the town meetings.
78. Cf. p. 315f.

from contributions for the local church expenses.[79] This
confusion was the more likely in that the latter were
closely associated with the relief of the poor. When this
property tax was first 'imposed,' it often appeared in the
guise of a tax on live-stock, and then gradually was extended to other forms of property. For example, Portsmouth (R. I.) in 1650 levied its rate 'upon cattell.' In
1651, 'upon all Catell from greatest to the least sucking
pigs exsepted wch Catell are to be estimated by the raters
according to the worth of them as they passe amongst us
and such as have litl Catl and great estates the raters shall
rate them according to their estates.' In 1654, the rate was
'according to men's estates' ; in 1661, the ordinance read
'to make the said Rate, upon land and Estats in the
Equallest and Impartiallest way they can.'[80] In Boston,
Nov. 10, 1634, the following entry occurs : they 'shall
make and assess all these rates, vizt. a rate of 30 li to Mr.
Blackston, a rate for the cowes keeping, a rate for the
goates keeping and other charges in rambe goats about
them and for losse in common . . .'[81] Elsewhere, similar
evidences occur of the use of live stock as a basis for a
brief period.[82]

The next phase consisted in an attempt at uniformity
of assessment according to the article taxed. New Hampshire, for example, had specific taxes on polls, slaves,

79. Voluntary contributions for various town projects, for poor relief,
and for schools, were not uncommon throughout the colonial period.
However, Scharf and Westcott were incorrect in assuming that the
subscriptions of the aldermen and councillors of Philadelphia in
1710 for a new market house were in the nature of gifts. They were
to be repaid from the market receipts. (*Minutes of Common Council*,
May 22, 1710.) Cf. Scharf and Westcott, op. cit., vol. I, p. 187.
80. *Records of the Town of Portsmouth* (R. I.), pp. 48, 52, 63, 109.
81. *Report of the Record Commissioners*, Boston, 1876, vol. 2, *Boston
Town Records*, 1634-1661.
82. e. g., Providence (Stokes, op. cit., p. 96).

horses, cattle, land, and orchards ; but wavered a bit in
the direction towards which the property tax was ultimately to move in defining an acre as land 'enough to
produce twenty-five bushels of grain.' The tax rate was
8*d*. an acre.[83] The afore-mentioned town of Portsmouth
(R. I.) had reached this stage by 1680, when the minutes
read : 'for Rule . . . it is ordered that all Lands Rateable
in this Town shall be valued as worth forty shillings the
acre, and all horse Kind and Catell . . . at forty Shillings
a piece . . . and for all other Estate Rateable it is left to
the Ratemakers to do according to their discretion in
the valueing thereof.'[84]

The extreme to which this tendency towards uniformity was carried may be illustrated by the schedule drawn
up for Connecticut : (the value is by the year)

	£	s.	d.
one acre of land	0	10	0
one house	3	0	0
one horse	3	0	0
one ox	3	0	0
one swine	1	0	0
one cow	3	0	0
one two year heifer	2	0	0
one yearling heifer	1	0	0
one poll or male, 16-60	18	0	0
one lawyer for his faculty	20	0	0
one vessel of 100 tons	10	0	0

'Every person annually gives in his list, specifying the
property he possesses, to the selectmen, who send the sum
total of each town to the General Assembly, when a tax

83. Ely, R. T., *Taxation in American States and Cities,* New York, 1888,
p. 7.
84. *Records of the Town of Portsmouth* (R. I.), p. 209.

of 1/ more or less, according to public exigencies is imposed on each pound.'[85]

Outside of New England, this tendency to assess land at a flat rate per acre or per lot was much more marked and lingered longer. It appears in the early New Netherland villages, particularly on Long Island, where New England influence was strong.[86] In fact, under the 'Duke's Laws,' after the English occupation, what had come to be known as the 'New England' practice of assessment, (previously requested),[87] was introduced specifically on Long Island. It is worth quoting the definition of it as the 'true Estimacion of all Psonell and reall Estates.' 'The kinds of property to be taxed are enumerated, the value of cattle is established. Infirm and sick persons are to be exempt from all taxation. Correction of errors in the assessment list is made possible. Payment in kind, imprisonment in case of refusal to pay, and levy by distress are provided for.'[88]

In the Albany area soon after the second British occupation (1676), the governor and council ordered an assessment of 'the capital of all the inhabitants in order to receive thereof the 100th penny.' Assessors were then chosen for the purpose by the Albany magistrates.[89]

In Baltimore, 1750, 1s. was assessed on each lot.[90] Edenton, 1745, was permitted to tax each lot not to

85. Peters, S., *General History of Connecticut,* London, 1781, p. 206f.
86. Schwab, J. C., *History of the New York Property Tax,* pp. 24, 26. In Westchester borough assessments were based 'upon every £25 privilege' (Book of Records of the Trustees, Feb. 9, 1702/3). The New England influence was strong here also.
87. In 1650 in New Amsterdam (Schwab, op. cit., p. 22).
88. Ibid. p. 37.
89. Van Laer, A. J. F. (Edit.), *Court Minutes, Albany, Rensselaerswyck, and Schenectady,* vol. II, p. 161f., Sept. 26, 1676.
90. Hollander, J. H., *Financial History of Baltimore,* Baltimore, 1899, p. 10.

exceed 8*d*.[91] These amounts were relatively trifling, but the humble beginnings were the forerunners of a system which to-day raises billions of dollars every year.

The assessment process itself frequently went through certain stages. Self-assessment was the earliest. This soon gave way to a committee of the town meeting, and later to elected assessors. This last had been an English custom since the fourteenth century, and marked a kind of return to the system of the mother country.[92] Not that all towns went through this precise evolution, even those founded in the seventeenth century. Rather, these stages represented a pattern which, while reproduced perfectly in few localities, yet did on the whole characterize the development of the property tax as far as moveable property was concerned. As late as 1761, the 'enquiries for the parishes of St. Philip and St. Michael' (Charleston, S. C.) gave notice that they would go to the houses of the inhabitants to receive their returns 'upon oath, an account of all their estates, slaves, monies at interest, and annuities.'[93]

But this particular pattern, which came to its climax in Connecticut, whereby each article or each acre was automatically assessed identically with the article or the acre elsewhere, was not the ordinary channel of evolution in the taxation of land and houses. A differentiation between parcels and properties soon set in again, marking a reversion to the original idea of 'ability.' Two ideas of what should constitute the basis struggled for the ascendency, the idea of capital value and the idea of income. Neither was consistently followed even at any one period. On the whole, the idea of assessment according to 'in-

91. *State Records of North Carolina*, vol. XXIII, p. 232f.
92. Schwab, op. cit., p. 30f.
93. *South Carolina Gazette*, Jan. 6-10, 1761.

come' appeared to be prevailing at the outbreak of the Revolution. This indicated a tendency to be strongly influenced by English precedent, which was by this time rapidly crystallizing towards the 'income' basis under the influence of the various poor laws.

It was not always so in the earlier period. For example, in Providence, in 1679, a committee reported 'the suitablest prices which it is meet to be set on ye esteemed rateable estates of ye inhabitants, for to be a help and preparation to ye leviers.'[94] By 1695, on the other hand, the committee appointed was to judge of the yearly profit, 'by rating each person to the value of his estate two pence per pound by the best method they can find . . . That every town shall yearly choose two or three able and honest men, to take the view of each of their inhabitants of their lands and meadows ; and so to judge of the *yearly profit* at their wisdom and discretion ; and so also of merchants and tradesmen, and to make this part of the rate according to the yearly profit, or as they, where they shall have had a more narrow inspection into the lands and meadows, shall see cause to set by the acre.'[95] Later on, however, the colony (Rhode Island) seems to have returned to a property basis, for improved lands and manufacturing plants were to be assessed (1744 Law) at 'ten years rental.' Subsequently this was raised (1762) to 'twelve years rental,' and in 1767 to '15-20 years rental.'[96]

Where a rate 'so much in the pound' was specified, the

94. Quoting records of town meeting of 1679, in Stokes, H. K., *Finances and Administration of Providence*, p. 97.

95. Proceedings of General Assembly, July 2, 1695, in *Records of Rhode Island*, vol. III, p. 300f.

96. Stokes, op. cit., p. 127.

unit was income, not capital value. Bristol (Pa.), 1746,
3d. in the pound on all assets or estates ;[97] Lancaster,
1774, 1s. in the pound maximum for streets ;[98] Connecticut in 1700, 40s. per £1000 for the local school tax[99] —
all refer to 'annual value.' This 40s. was of course
assessed on the 'income' assumed under the elaborate
table cited above.[100] New York (1693), after considerable difficulty in determining the basis, decided to assess
land at its annual yield, and other property at varying
sums.[101]

On the other hand, in one important and to some extent decisive particular, the Colonies broke with English
custom. This was the policy — tentative in many cases,
but growing — of including unimproved land in the
property to be taxed. It may often have been at a lower
rate, but it nevertheless illustrated the persistence of the
idea of *property* or *ownership* ; rather than yield, annual
value, income, or *rent* as the fundamental basis. By this
time in England and English cities, tenure was such that
the tenant rather than the owner of property was customarily assessed — in other words, the *productive* aspect
was the basis for the tax ; and where the owner and
tenant were the same, an assumed or fictitious annual
'rent' was increasingly used.[102] Hence unimproved land

---

97. Bristol Minute Book, Oct. 25, 1746.
98. *Laws of Pennsylvania*, 1774, Chap. 1687.
99. Walker, Mrs. A. M., *Development of State Support of Education in Connecticut* (Abstract), pp. 17, 19 ; Dexter, E. G., *History of Education in the United States*, p. 83f. The tax was reduced to 10s. in 1754 ; increased to 20s. in 1766 ; to 40s. in 1767.
100. p. 313.
101. Schwab, op. cit., p. 56.
102. Lancaster (Pa.) was more or less exceptional, in that there the land was (as in England) customarily leased rather than sold (Rid-dle, W., *The Story of Lancaster*, p. 29f.).

seems to have escaped, and land in general was taxed only in so far as it was productive.[103]

In New York City the contrasting custom dated from Dutch times.[104] Even though the tax was expressed as a flat rate per acre, at least the precedent of taxing unused land was established. In New England, Massachusetts seems to have taken the lead in 1682 in working out the theory as well as practice : 'It appearing a grievance among us that sundry gentlemen, merchants and others, having great tracts of land bounded out to them in propriety, pay not to publicke charges, although they have a considerable profit to themselves by the continuall rise of the estimate of sajd lands, for the easing whereof, it is ordered by this Court, that all lands circumstanced as is above premissed shall, in the levy now to be made by this present Court, for payment of the countrey debts, pay unto the Tresurer of the country two shillings money for every hundred acres, and in like proportion for lesser quantities.'[105] Thus the taxation of the 'unearned increment' entered the theory and practice of American public finance. In Rhode Island the power of the landed proprietors was such that unimproved land was not taxed at all until 1762, when it was taxed at one-third value. In 1767 the valuation was raised to full rate.[106] In Massachusetts, the policy of assessing the unimproved land at one-third rate continued somewhat longer.[107] In 1758, in New York City, a definite move was made to shift the

103. In general, English towns, counties, and parishes assessed the occupier ; but there were still some instances of assessment levied upon the owner. See Cannan, E., *History of Local Rates,* pp. 29ff., 126ff. This is the standard work on the subject.
104. 1658. Cf. Schwab, op. cit., p. 24.
105. *Massachusetts Records,* Oct. 11, 1682.
106. Stokes, op. cit., pp. 99, 127.
107. Felt, J. B., *Annals of Salem,* Salem, 1845-49, 2 vol., vol. II, p. 391.

taxes from the landlord to the leaseholder, on the ground that the former method had been 'found to be Uncertain and Unequal.' 'All Real Estate in the City and County of New York, Shall . . . be Rated or assessed at two-thirds parts of the Rent or Yearly Income of the Same.'[108] This was a definite step in the direction of English practice, but it does not appear to have been imitated elsewhere. For example, the Wilmington (Del.) town meeting of Dec. 30, 1740, included in its rate ordinance the following : 'Whereas, it may sometimes happen that some of the Inhabitants may live in hired Houses . . . and that their Landlords may live out of this Burrough, That in such cases the Tennent shall be charged . . . and the Landlord shall repay him, . . . but where the Landlord shall live in this Burrough, then he shall be . . . Assessed.'[109]

Apart from land, livestock, and houses, all sorts of articles were assessed from time to time under the general heading of the property tax. Ships, merchants' stock, interest of money lent, etc., appear in the lists of one or more localities. In 1676 in New York City, the merchants alone were assessed $1\frac{1}{2}d.$ in the pound for a new dock. Frederick Philipse, the wealthiest, paid £18-5-0 ; the least entry was 6/3.[110]

Yet for the most part these efforts at assessment and taxation of property seldom continued long enough on any one basis to constitute a consistent policy. Collection was difficult at best, for the times were usually hard and the individuals constitutionally averse to taxation. In 1756, it was recorded that the treasury of New York City contained but £1, but that £2,827 was owing it.[111]

108. Peterson, A. E., and Edwards, G. W., *New York as an Eighteenth Century Municipality*, p. 399.
109. Minute Book of Wilmington.
110. Peterson and Edwards, op. cit., p. 109.
111. Ibid. p. 394.

The inevitable pressure from those taxed seems largely to have accounted for the frequent changes in method of assessment. This would appear to account in part for the impression of floundering. To quote one authority : 'the . . . measure of fixing certain values at which different kinds of property were to be assessed was again and again adopted, always to be repealed or to fall into disuse soon afterwards, owing to the severe pressure it brought to bear upon the unfortunate taxpayer. Either the ignorance or the good will of the assessor has always stood in the way of assessing property at its full market value.'[112]

At times, this under-assessment was recognized by law. Thus the New York City Tax Law of 1758 specified that 'all Real Estates . . . shall . . . be Rated or assessed, at two third parts of the Rent or Yearly Income of the Same.'[113]

One further modern note is struck in the tendency towards exaggerated under-assessment on the part of local authorities, when their assessment was made the basis for a state-wide (i.e. colony) tax. In Salem (Mass.) in 1768, for example, the local figure was put at a total of about £60,000 capital value ; while the valuation by the provincial authorities was well over £200,000.[114] In Rhode Island the same difficulty had forced the appointment in 1761 of a colony committee for the purpose of equalization ; but this naturally was not favourably received by all the towns.[115] On the other hand, in New Jersey in 1728, Burlington objected to the 'overruling

112. Schwab, op. cit., p. 60.
113. Quoted in Peterson and Edwards, op. cit., p. 399.
114. Felt, J. B., *Annals of Salem*, vol. II, p. 391.
115. *Records of the State of Rhode Island*, vol. VI, p. 326. Cf. also Stiness, J. H., *A Century of Lotteries in Rhode Island*, Providence, 1896, p. 126.

power of the Country Assessors being nine . . ., against
the Town's assr at the aportioning the Quota's in ye Provincial Taxes.'[116] It may be stated as a general principle
that, wherever apportionment for a larger unit depends
upon local assessors, the strain upon human nature is too
great to allow such a situation without adequate review.

It should be noted that in all the discussion no mention
has been made of a city's borrowing, even for capital
expenditure. Such procedure seems to have been unknown in colonial times, except for relatively short term
loans. These were occasionally negotiated, perhaps by
one of the magistrates himself advancing the money and
later being reimbursed.[117] Extraordinary expenditure
demanded extraordinary methods of raising revenue,
such as the sale of land or a lottery or printing of paper
money. Perhaps the latter might be deemed a method
of borrowing for a short period, and occasionally a float-
ing debt would accumulate. The way of dealing with
such a situation as the latter may be summarized in the
terms of Albany council minutes :

Whereas the Mayor of this Citty doth Inform this Com-

116. Woodward, E. M., and Hageman, J. F., *History of Burlington and
Mercer Counties*, p. 125.
117. Cf. Peterson, A. E., and Edwards, G. W., *New York as an Eighteenth
Century Municipality*, p. 201. In Philadelphia in 1724 the corporation borrowed £300 from the assembly towards the cost of new
market stalls (*Council Minutes*, Oct. 25, 1723 ; Apr. 20, 1724). In
1768 Robert Morris advanced the money to the street commissioners
to enable them to pave a street (Minutes, Street Commissioners of
Philadelphia, July 2, 1768). New York City in 1731 was compelled
to borrow £1,000 it paid to Governor Montgomerie for the new
charter. It paid 8 per cent interest and mortgaged some of its lots
as security (Committee Report, Mar. 31, 1731, in Original Records
of Common Council). Wilmington (Del.) in 1773 borrowed £200
from Dr. McKinly at 6 per cent. It seems to have been largely paid
off by the Revolution. (Minutes of Burgesses and Assistants, Nov.
18, 1773 ; Jan. 9, 1775 ; Jan. 8, 1774 ; Nov. 19, 1774.)

mon Councill that severall Creditors of this Citty for
Daly services done doe almost Every day adresse them-
selfs to him for payment and since there is no Cash in
the Treasurer's hands whereby the said Creditors can
be satisfied doth therefore desyre that ye Common
Councill will Consider and take some method to raise
a fund for to Defray the arrears of the said Citty
Charge. In consideration whereof the Common Councill have Concluded that ye summe of forty pounds be
layd assessed and leveyed.[118]

(E)

It is difficult to survey such a revenue system as prevailed in colonial towns, and still more difficult to attempt to estimate its soundness. Essentially it started out
on the basis of equal sharing of the necessary community
tasks, plus the idea (best expressed in the fee system)
that payments should be in accord with service rendered.
These two canons almost but not quite sufficed for the
service functions of the municipality. One other idea or
canon came in, that of taxation according to ability or
wealth. At first, this appeared the reasonable method in
connection with the raising of funds for poor relief ;
but particularly in New England it was extended to common services. In the other colonies, this canon perhaps
was most frequently applied in the early days in connection with poor relief and defence. Also, it must not be
forgotten that such a taxation base locally in many colonies was but a minor incident compared to its use for the
general expenses of the colony. Precedents established
prior to 1775 in property and poll taxes owe fully as
much to the colony's levies as to those of the towns. Their

118. Munsell, J., *Annals of Albany*, vol. V, p. 123.

weakest aspect was not their theoretical basis of assessment, but their administration and enforcement, as so often is true to-day. Collection was difficult, accurate apportionment even more so. If local assessment was made the basis for provincial taxation, the difficulties were further exaggerated and complicated by competitive under-assessment. Then, too, these assessors were locally elected and known individually to most of the community. It was much easier to shade an assessment favourably or to wink at evasions than to enforce the law impartially.

The property tax as such was still somewhat amorphous. It might quite easily have gone over completely to the ultimate English basis of assessment according to income or rent ; or, if the precedent of taxing unused land were to be the guide, it might evolve (as in fact it did evolve) into something which, while not appreciated at the time, was destined to be profoundly different and far reaching in its effect for good and evil — the American property tax as we know it to-day. The story of the differentiation belongs largely to a later period, but the ground work was laid in colonial times in the system of individual ownership of land on the part of the majority of the whites in the North.

The evolution of the budget from the standpoint of expenditure was primarily a function of size. The larger the city, the more its functions necessarily grew and the sooner the point was arrived at when resort to extraordinary sources of revenue such as taxation or lotteries had to be made. Yet the development of the taxation system was not wholly a function of the growing size of the community. The element of experience also entered, as experiments with various methods were tried, and then discarded for what were hoped would be better ones.

Furthermore, this experience was a shared experience — one city or one colony learning from another, and ushering in one of the first signs of a distinctively American development.

XIII

THE RELATIONS OF THE MUNICIPALITIES
WITH THE GOVERNMENT OF THEIR COLONY

No consideration of the colonial municipality is complete unless it includes a picture of the community in its relationships to the government of the colony. In some ways it was less affected, in some ways more, than is the present day city by the government of its state. Nevertheless, the impact of the larger unit upon the smaller was marked.

Evidence of this has been noted already — proprietors, governors, and assemblies alike fostered the foundation and growth of these cities ; from the governors and occasionally from the assemblies there was sought the sanction of incorporation. Charleston, Savannah, and other communities were described, to all intents and purposes, as actually governed by their assemblies. Incidental mention has been made of the need of central authorization before cities could impose property or poll taxes ; and, for that matter, in many instances before they could do anything other than those things specifically mentioned in their charters. There remains, however, the important task of appraising the beneficence or harmfulness of these central controls, and the extent to which the letter of the law constituted a fair picture of the inwardness of the situation.

At the outset it is necessary to draw a sharp distinction between the legal status of the governor and that of the assembly. The former, with or without his council, was the representative of the mother country or the proprietors, and hence comprised the autocratic element in any controls that might be exercised. The assembly, on the other hand, was made up of the representatives of

325

the colonists themselves, or rather of that fraction of them which was enfranchised. Thus, unless there were some clear cut economic or political cleavage between the residents of the cities and the majority of residents of the remainder of the colony, there would be (and was) a tendency for mutuality of interest to produce both cordiality and amenability to the city's requests and needs.

To speak of the governor and council as the autocratic element in the situation does not mean that this element was consequently not beneficent, but merely that it was juristically out of the control of the inhabitants. As a matter of fact, the prosperity and advancement of a city like New York or Charleston might be even more to the advantage of England or the personal fortunes of the governor than to the remainder of the colony.

To understand one aspect of this relationship it is necessary to recall that a large part of the compensation to a governor for his services was in the shape of the various perquisites attached to his office. Fees for incorporations or for additions to powers of instrumentalities already incorporated were or were expected to be among the most lucrative of such perquisites. Governor Montgomerie received £1,000 for the 1730 charter of New York City and Governor Dongan £300 for the 1686 charter.[1] Smaller cities, such as Wilmington (Del.), apparently paid proportionately.[2] Apart from such special favours, the patronage at the governor's disposal in New York City was considerable. The mayor, recorder, town

1. Peterson, A. E., and Edwards, G. W., *New York as an Eighteenth Century Municipality*, pp. 218ff. Cf. also *supra*, p. 62.
2. For Wilmington, cf. Minute Book, town meeting, Dec. 30, 1740. In cities other than New York the records of payments appear to be almost totally lacking, but probably payments were, in most instances, actually made.

clerk, and clerk of the market were all his appointees.[3] In the other colonies such local patronage was usually not so extensive.

The line between what was legitimate in the way of fees and what was not was blurred at best ; and many opportunities offered themselves for supplementary earnings from special favours granted to towns or 'rewards' from those appointed to office. The governor's own job was frequently royal patronage of the baser sort ; and retainers and favourites from England would be assigned a colonial province to 'farm.' Some few like Nicholson were 'career mèn' in colonial administration, but they were not the usual type. Many others, like Dongan, were able and well intentioned. The group as a whole was a mixture. Fletcher in New York apparently lost few opportunities to extort bribes, even to the extent of trading in on his 'nuisance value' — for example, in the instance already mentioned in which he ordered the gates of Albany closed.[4] He seems to have set out to make the assembly subservient to himself by means not dissimilar to those used in England — pocket boroughs, patronage, creation of numerous freemen, and the like.[5] Just what motives entered into his granting a charter to the tiny

3. In 1702 a combination was effected, and the mayor was also made coroner, clerk of the market, and water bailiff (Peterson and Edwards, op. cit., p. 32).

4. Cf. p. 131.

5. O'Callaghan, E. B. (Edit.), *Documents Relative to the Colonial History of New York*, vol. IV, pp. 128, 223, etc. Some doubt exists as to this, inasmuch as the reports were from hostile sources, such as the Earl of Bellomont in his report to the Board of Trade : 'I find by what unjust measures the former Governor procured pack'd corrupt Assemblies to gratifie his pride and avarice, but I shall alter the method and restore the blessing of an English Governt by a free and fair Election of Representatives altho' it will cost me much time and a great deal of trouble to purge corruptions that have taken such deep root here. (Ibid. vol. IV, p. 323.)

community of Westchester must be left largely to conjecture. Caleb Heathcote, its first mayor, was reputed to
be the wealthiest man in the colony and the borough
in general was fairly flourishing. The granting of the
charter also carried with it separate representation in the
assembly. Hence it doubtless fitted in with both the financial and the political aspirations of the governor, and was
the more easily obtained in that Heathcote was Fletcher's
friend and supporter. The borough levied a rate of £45
to cover the expenses.[6]

The personal factor was usually decisive in determining whether a governor's influence was good or bad. One
writer expresses it as follows in New York City :

> All the vices of a tyranny invaded the infant city.
> Sycophants who flattered and preyed upon the official :
> the faithful followers of the powerful who justified all
> their acts ; the lovers of rank and the rivals for prece-
> dence ; the persecuting churchmen, the corrupt
> lawyers and judges — all appear in the period of a
> Fletcher or a Cornbury.[7]

On the whole, the governors favoured or could be induced to favour the cities. In all the history of New York,
only Governor Cosby appears to have been hostile, and
with what motive is uncertain.[8] However, in one inci-

---

6. Wilson, J. G. (Edit.), *Memorial History of the City of New York*,
   New York, 1892-93, 2 vol., vol. II, p. 245. Heathcote had recently taken
   up residence in Westchester, and also had extensive land and other
   interests in the borough. The extant minutes record but one meeting
   of the corporation which he attended. He moved to New York City
   after a few years, but was annually elected mayor. (Westchester Records, MSS. in Bureau of Municipal Investigation and Statistics, N. Y.
   C. ; Fox, D. R., *Caleb Heathcote*, New York, 1926, pp. 18f., 54, 58, 59.)
7. Wilson, op. cit., vol. II, p. 212.
8. Peterson and Edwards, op. cit., p. 239f. ; Edwards, G. W., 'New York
   City Politics before the Revolution,' in *Pol. Sci. Quart.*, vol. XXXVI,
   pp. 586ff.

dent connected with Albany, such alleged hostility appears to have been with a view to securing justice for the Indians, and perhaps thereby making the frontier safer.[9]

9. In a letter of Dec. 15, 1733, to the Board of Trade, Governor Cosby reports that the sachems of the Mohawks had appealed to him 'for redress of a gross deceit and injury done them by the Corporation of Albany . . . the Mayor (John De Puyster) and some others . . . did about a year or two ago, insinuate to them that Gov[r] Montgomerie had in his lifetime an intention to take their lands from them, and that possibly some future Gov[r] might pursue the same intentions, that there was but one way to secure their lands to them from such attempts, which was to make them over to the Corporation in trust for them and that then the Corporation would withstand all such attempts, and preserve their lands to them . . . and they . . . executed a deed to that effect as they supposed and were told that the Corporation promised them a counterpart or copy of that deed but never gave it them ; that some time after the execution of that deed they were informed that it was not a deed of trust but an absolute conveyance of a thousand Acres of low or meadow Ground at a place called Tiononderoga being their best planting ground . . . I sent for the Mayor desireing him to bring the deed, he did so and it being read and interpreted to the Sachims, they cryed out with one voice that they were cheated, and that that deed was imposed upon them for a deed of trust . . . I enquired if the Corporation had paid or given the Mohocks any consideration in money or goods for it, whereby it may appear that there was an intention of a purchase, but not finding that they had given them anything . . . the fraud being but too evidint, I gave the deed into the hands of the Sachims, who first with great rage tore it in pieces and then threw it into the fire . . . The Corporation finding themselves deprived . . . talk . . . of applying to His Majesty for a confirmation of their charter, hoping thereby to attain their ends. . . . If the people of Albany think their Charter (1686) is void . . . I am willing . . . to grant them a new one . . . but as to the Thousand acres . . . it may be fatal to our frontier settlements to grant them . . . till they are first purchased.' (O'Callaghan, op. cit., vol. IV, p. 960f.) The Dongan Charter had granted the land in question, but Cosby claimed that only the right to purchase it was or could have been meant.

The recorded episodes in the *Albany City Minutes* (in Munsell, J., *Annals of Albany*, vol. IX) are as follows :

July 9, 1730 : The lodging of a *caveat* requested, inasmuch as certain persons are secretly trying to obtain the land from the Indians. The claim is made of 'his Majesties grant and licence to purchase . . . but haveing as yet not obtained a Purchase . . . thro' the evill insinuation of some of our people.' Terms of resale were agreed upon, but annulled at the meeting of Dec. 10. (cont. on p. 330)

This episode was also illuminating as to the methods and tone of the city corporation itself.

By virtue of their office, these governors held watching briefs for the British government or the proprietor — yet surveillance was normally exercised over the acts of the assembly rather than specifically in connection with the cities. The occasional disallowances in this latter connection, for which the governors were directly or indirectly responsible, apparently were confined to four spheres — prerogative, trade interests, revenue, and defence. Prerogative involved matters such as incorporation, the right of separate representation in the assembly,

Oct. 10, 1730 : 'Whereas the Moquas Indians having sent three Messengers on the 8th of this instant . . . that they where now full resolved to sign over' the land, a Committee was appointed 'to act and agree for the said land.'

Oct. 14, 1730 : The Committee returned with 'a deed executed by the s^d Indians to this Corporation, bearing date the 12th.'

Jan. 5, 1730/1 : Evert Wendell was given £15 for his services in the matter.

July 20, 1731 : 'Whereas an Express came down out of the name of Shaims of the Indian Castell of jenonderogo desired the Commonality to meet the Shaims . . . for that (they) where willing and desireus to make a gift . . . of the woodland joyning behynd the Low or Meddoland of Jenonderogo which they heretofore have given in trust.' A committee was named with full power 'and that they take up along with them four gallons Rum, two gallons Wine, four pounds Sugger, and six pounds Tobaco.'

Nov. 26, 1734 : The corporation asks for a legal opinion as to whether it can legally deed part of the land 'contained in the Indian deed which John De Peyster, Esq., late mayor of this city had in his custody . . . and which he says is destroyed.'

Nov. 29, 1734 : After favourable legal advice, the land was duly deeded, and legal opinion was asked whether the city could have an action against De Peyster for giving up the deed to the governor.

Aug. 30, 1736 : Litigation as to title.

Oct. 5, 1736 : Hearing to be called before governor and council. No record of this in minutes.

In 1773 the corporation signed an instrument restoring almost all the land to the Mohawks, in order to quiet them, 'so long as they shall continue a nation and be settled in said lands.' (Munsell, op. cit., vol. VII, p. 310.)

the designation of ports, and the establishment of markets and fairs. In only a few instances were any of these challenged. North Carolina's struggle lasting over many years has already been chronicled, as have Lord Baltimore's unsuccessful attempts to create 'port towns.'[10] A change of regime from one proprietor to another or to a royal province was apt to be followed by scant respect for the acts of the previous proprietor as regards chartering. The early charter of Philadelphia, the charters of Gorgeana and Newcastle — all were relegated to the limbo by subsequent unsympathetic governors. The early intentions of the proprietors concerning the independence of the port of Perth Amboy were equally vulnerable under an unfriendly Board of Trade.[11]

There were several ways in which a hostile governor could harass a city administration. In Philadelphia in 1704 there was evidently considerable friction and grasping at power, the causes of which were in part obscure. The city corporation had passed into the control of men opposed to the proprietor, but friendly to the majority of the assembly. Then, too, the city had offended or embarrassed the governor personally, by arresting the owner of an unsavoury resort at a time when the governor was alleged to have been himself a patron. In any event, the governor reversed the verdict of the mayor's court in the case ; and in more important matters harassed the city. He refused licences recommended by the city unless they

10. Cf. pp. 44ff.
11. Cf. pp. 359ff. The dispute dragged on for many years, and was finally settled in favour of the right of New Jersey to have free ports. The Earl of Bellomont, acting under an order from the Crown, had seized the ship *Hester* in 1698 to enforce the prerogative of the Port of New York. (*N. J. Archives,* 1st ser., vol. II, pp. 183, 200, 341 ; Tanner, E. P., *The Province of New Jersey, 1664-1738,* New York, 1908, p. 137.)

also had the recommendation of the county court. He granted exemption from serving their turn in the city watch to those who had enlisted in the militia.[12] While situations such as that of Philadelphia were exceptional, the particular instance illustrates the kind of power which a governor, if he desired, might exercise over a corporation.

Before its incorporation, the governor and council had played an exceedingly important role in the administration of Philadelphia. He had been authorized (in 1700) to appoint persons to regulate the streets, repair the landings, and levy the necessary special assessments.[13] He and his council had controlled the assize of bread and the regulation of the market.[14]

The requirement of the governor's approval for city ordinances and by-laws differed from colony to colony and even from city to city. Such approval was not required, for example, in Philadelphia and in Burlington, Elizabeth, and Trenton.[15] On the other hand, in Perth Amboy and New Brunswick, the duration of such local ordinances was limited to six months unless they had been submitted to the governor and council within six weeks of their passage.[16] Apparently such confirmation was needed, or at least valued, in St. Mary's, for records of such requests are still extant.[17] In New York City, by the

---

12. For the various incidents in the struggle, cf. *Minutes of the Provincial Council,* in *Penn. Colonial Records,* vol. II, p. 165f. ; Shepherd, W. R., *Proprietary Government in Pennsylvania,* p. 299 ; Keith, C. P., *Chronicles of Pennsylvania,* vol. I, p. 435.
13. McBain, H. L., 'Legal Status of the American Colonial City,' in *Pol. Sci. Quart.,* vol. XL, p. 195.
14. Scharf, J. T., and Westcott, T., *History of Philadelphia,* vol. I, p. 170.
15. Scott, A., *Early Cities of New Jersey,* in *N. J. Hist. Soc. Coll.,* 2nd ser., vol. IX, p. 156.
16. Ibid.
17. *Proceedings of Council,* Oct. 13, 1685, in *Md. Archives,* vol. XVII, p. 420.

1686 charter, such by-laws might remain operative three months only, and had to be re-enacted periodically. In 1730, the period was extended to one year ; and, if the governor and council approved, indefinitely. The city, however, chose rather to re-enact them each year in order to avoid this check.[18]

These requirements of approval of ordinances by the governor must not be confused with British control over detailed grants of power by the assemblies. These grants, as also all the other acts of the assemblies, required the concurrence of the appropriate English authorities, in the colonies and in London. During the period of over one hundred and fifty years, but few colonial acts involving towns and cities were actually disallowed under this category. Even in these few instances there was often considerable room for difference of opinion as to what the local will really was. This doubt was evident in the chartering of Charleston,[19] in the 'Bacon's Rebellion Laws' which included self-government for James City,[20] possibly in the law setting up a grant and assessment for the Savannah watch,[21] and in the various attempts in Virginia to foster the growth of towns by elaborate and impracticable legislation.[22] On the other hand, the reversals of the acts incorporating North Carolina boroughs involved questions of prerogative, and were apparently an exercise of autocratic power contrary to the wishes of the colonists. The same charters were almost immediately reissued as an evidence of royal favour. The dispute was over procedure, not subject matter.[23]

18. *Minutes of Common Council, passim.*
19. Cf. p. 193.
20. Cf. p. 90.
21. Cf. p. 252.
22. Cf. p. 159.
23. Cf. p. 45.

Surveying the entire colonial period, one is compelled to recognize that as a class the various governors — proprietary and royal — were at least not harmful to the best interests of the various towns and generally were definitely friendly and co-operative. In the light of the colonial administration of other nations of the period, these governors were distinctly in advance of their time in their policy and character. Here, again, is furnished one further illustration of the fact that it was not so much any day-to-day autocracy or maladministration on the part of the British that was primarily responsible for the American Revolution ; but rather deep, underlying forces of an economic and psychological nature which would not be denied. The cities had little cause to complain and much to praise in the British overlordship. Certainly they fared much better than did their sister incorporations in England itself.[24]

(B)

It was not the British-appointed executive but the colonially-elected legislature which concerned itself most intimately with its communities ; and which set up precedents which were ultimately to affect profoundly the evolution of American city government.

For a while during colonial days and after, it was customary but not universal to follow the English practice of according the incorporated boroughs separate represen-

24. Those interested in additional material concerning the position and role of the governor are referred to Labaree, L. W., *Royal Instructions to British Colonial Governors* ; ibid., *Royal Government in America*, New Haven, 1930, Chap. III, 'Captain General and Governor in Chief,' esp. pp. 131-33, and Chap. VIII, 'The Governor's Salary.' This latter often gave the assembly a powerful lever of control. Cf. also Haywood, M. D., *Governor William Tryon*, Raleigh, 1903 ; Keys, A. M., *Cadwallader Colden*, New York, 1906.

tation in the legislature. It will be remembered that, even in the close corporations, it was customary to allow qualified inhabitants to vote for their 'burgess.' This held true in Philadelphia, Williamsburg, Norfolk, and in the enfranchised towns of North Carolina, though these latter might still be governed by appointed commissioners for their local affairs. The charter of St. Mary's and the original charter of Annapolis provided that the council of the corporation should itself choose the members ; but the assembly declined to admit those so chosen from Annapolis, and forced an alteration in the charter itself whereby they were made popularly elective. A few cities, such as Wilmington (Del.), the Pennsylvania boroughs, and curiously Albany, did not have such separate representation ; although in Albany the city so dominated the county that the 'city and county of Albany' in practice was a rough equivalent of the city.[25] The proportionality of such representation was even more distorted than in most cases to-day. In certain instances — for example, Philadelphia and Norfolk — by 1775 there was under-representation. Philadelphia was granted but two representatives, the original counties not less than eight each. By 1771 the city paid one-quarter of the taxes of the province and still had a virtually impotent representation.[26] New York City fared somewhat better, having four members out of twenty-seven, but was even more grievously burdened with provincial taxes.[27] On the

25. In part this was because in practice the residents of the two manors and Schenectady did not exercise their right to vote for the county representative as well as for the one from their own district (O'Callaghan, E. B. (Edit.), Documents Relative to the Colonial History of New York, vol. VIII, p. 565). The 'township' of Schenectady had separate representation from 1718.
26. Scharf and Westcott, op. cit., vol. I, p. 265.
27. Cf. p. 343 ; also Edwards, G. W., 'New York City Politics before the Revolution,' in Pol. Sci. Quart., vol. XXXVI, pp. 598ff.

other hand, James City, which was mostly in ruins except for a few houses, still sent its burgess in 1775 ;[28] and Salem (N. J.), its two delegates, until in 1727 it was finally made one district with Greenwich.[29] In 1723, Salem was spoken of as a fishing village of twenty houses and seven or eight votes.[30] Annapolis with two representatives and Williamsburg with one were not grossly disproportionate. On the other hand, fair sized villages such as Edenton, New Bern, and Wilmington were given the same representation as tiny North Carolina hamlets such as Hillsborough, Brunswick, and Salisbury.

It will be remembered that colonial assemblies exercised the prerogative on occasion of passing upon the credentials of their members, those of Maryland and Delaware having refused admission to those of Annapolis and Newcastle on the ground that they were displeased with the circumstances of the incorporation and enfranchising of these cities.[31]

In New England the town was universally the unit of representation. Not only were the deputies elected at the town meetings, but a close connection was maintained thereafter. It was customary to 'instruct' a deputy, and

28. Spoken of in 1722 as 'an abundance of rubbish, with three or four inhabited houses' (quoted in Tyler, L. G., *Cradle of the Republic*, p. 83).
29. Representation was granted in West Jersey days to all towns. Salem's representation was retained in supplementary instructions to Governor Cornbury for constitution of general assembly in 1705 (Smith, S., *History of the Colony of Nova-Caesaria*, p. 234f.) ; it was lost in 1727 as part of a plan to retain equality between the two halves of the province (Smith, ibid. p. 497). It had been granted in the first instance to assure such equality, inasmuch as West Jersey had had one less county than East Jersey (Great Britain : *Journal of the Comnrs. for Trade and Plantations*, Apr. 13, 1705).
30. By Burnet, in Tanner, E. P., *Province of New Jersey*, p. 328.
31. For Annapolis, cf. p. 41 ; for Newcastle, cf. Keith, C. P., *Chronicles of Pennsylvania*, vol. II, p. 681f.

instances even occur of his recall. Boston had a 'committee on instruction' (of deputies) whose report was often the subject of several days' discussion in town meeting. The deputies themselves customarily reported back to their town meetings at the close of the legislative session. Rhode Island from 1647 to 1663 went even farther, and required that all laws be referred back to the towns for acceptance or rejection. Outside of New England such 'instructions' were far less common.[32] However, the New England precedent was largely responsible for the inclusion of the 'right to instruct' in a number of the state constitutions. The spirit of local self-government was at its maximum in these New England towns, and those that imitated them ; and they furnished, in colonial times and after, the very centre of the idea of the prescriptive rights of a locality over against legislation by the state.

The influence of the assembly was of great, perhaps decisive, importance to the communities when the question arose of choice of a capital city. The assembly killed St. Mary's ; it elevated Annapolis. It passed the death sentence of James City ; it made Williamsburg. It kept Perth Amboy alive. The question never was actually settled by the North Carolina assembly as to which of several petty communities was to be made the 'metropolis,' but a number of them strove mightily for the honour.

Perhaps of greater importance was the fact that the choice of a particular place as capital often made that place subsequently the object of a more detailed fostering care by the assembly itself. It was no accident that the assembly virtually usurped local government functions in Savannah, Charleston, Philadelphia, and to some

32. Colegrove, K., *New England Town Mandates*, in *Colon. Soc. of Mass. Publ.*, vol. XXI, pp. 411-424.

extent in Annapolis and Perth Amboy. The accessibility of the assembly, its lack of the kind of congestion of business which was to preoccupy its time in later periods, its usually sympathetic attitude — all tended in this direction.[33] It is significant in this connection that it was to the Pennsylvania assembly, not to the Philadelphia corporation, that petitions involving municipal matters customarily came to be addressed.[34]

How detailed such authorizations could be may be illustrated from several examples — for the most part chosen from the towns already mentioned. In Annapolis, 1696, when the townsfolk were empowered to purchase a common, details of even the gates and ditches of the town were incorporated in the Act.[35] The Edenton Act (1745) even prescribed the number of each kind of animal that might be kept by each person within the town bounds ; and empowered the commissioners to repair the town fence, as well as numerous other details.[36] The frequency as well as the extent of the details of the acts dealing with Charleston call for comment, as year after year minute regulations of this sort filled the books of the colonial legislature. One historian has described the situation in Savannah as follows :

Affairs of the town were administered by the provincial general assembly under the supervision of the governor and council. The legislation of this period had

33. e. g. in Williamsburg, 1747, where the mayor appeared before the house of burgesses in opposition to a bill, which the house then refused to commit (*Journal of the House of Burgesses*, 1747, p. 244f., cited in Pargellis, S. M., 'Procedure in the Virginia House of Burgesses,' in *Wm. and Mary Quart.*, ser. 2, vol. II, p. 150).
34. Cf. Scharf, J. T., and Westcott, T., *History of Philadelphia*, vol. I, pp. 245, 258.
35. Ridgely, D. (Edit.), *Annals of Annapolis*, p. 90.
36. *State Records of North Carolina*, vol. XXIII, p. 232f.

respect chiefly to the establishment and conduct of the market and the watch, — to the conservation of the common . . . to the construction and repair of public buildings and defenses — to the organization of a workhouse ; to the control of slaves and porters, to the care of churches and cemeteries, — to the maintenance of courts of justice, — to prescribing regulations for the control of sailors, pilots, powder receivers, lighthouse keepers, and retailers of spirituous liquors, — and to the cleanliness of the streets and squares. Subject to the sanctions of the governor and council, the government of this little quasi-municipality was assumed by the general assembly.[37]

Whatever may be said from the juristic standpoint about the extent of detail concerned with municipalities contained in colonial acts, it would be easy to gain a quite false impression as to its significance in practice. While, towards the capital cities mentioned, the concern of the assembly was doubtless real enough and may have extended to intimate discussions of the details included in the acts ; elsewhere it does not at all follow that because an act was detailed, the consideration thereof in practice was also detailed. For the most part acts that concerned the incorporated boroughs would to-day belong in the category of 'request' measures, their origin and framing being wholly local and the passage thereof verging on the automatic, once it was assured that the community itself wanted them. Except for certain requests from capital cities, I have not uncovered a single instance in which a request from a municipal corporation for further powers was denied by the assembly, during the entire period

37. Jones, C. C., Jr., *History of Savannah*, Syracuse, 1890, p. 310.

of over one hundred years.[38] On the other hand, the records of the legislatures are filled with general and detailed extensions of powers as and when requested. One example will suffice by way of illustration — the Lancaster (Pa.) Act of 1774, granted on petition of inhabitants. It contained, among other matters, a detailed code dealing with encroachments, streets, lamps, gunpowder, etc. A person reading it might charge the legislature with 'interference,' if he were not aware of the fact that it was practically to the last detail as requested by the borough itself.[39]

Such resort to the assembly for additional powers does not give the whole picture. A complete account must include the fact that additional powers were obtained by New York City under charters from Governors Cornbury and Montgomerie. Furthermore, the surrenders of the charters of Schenectady and Wilmington (N. C.) were accompanied by a request to the governor for ampler or at least altered jurisdiction. In other words, major extensions of power might still be sought from the Crown ; whereas minor details and alterations involving functions, not prerogatives, were (as in England) sought from the legislatures. The Crown could allow this with-

38. e. g. Williamsburg, denial of general taxing power (Gulick, L., and Pollard, J. G., *Modern Government in a Colonial City*, p. 31). Specific grants were readily forthcoming subsequently. The corporation of Philadelphia was denied the power to grant ferry rights (Scharf and Westcott, op. cit., vol. I, p. 199). The refusal to confirm certain North Carolina charters was complicated by the quarrel with the governor ; but, where really desired by the inhabitants, as in Wilmington, confirmation was eventually forthcoming. Cf. *supra*, p. 45f.

39. Chap. 1687, *Laws of Pennsylvania*, 1774. Another excellent example is found in Wilmington (Del.) in 1771, etc. The customary procedure was for the burgesses to draft a bill for improvements and present it to the legislature. The legislature would then hold an inquiry, possibly on the site in question. The borough would itself summon objectors. (Cf. Minutes of Burgesses and Assistants, Nov. 29, 1771.)

out impairment of prerogative, inasmuch as the right of disallowance was still retained.

There was but a negligible amount of what would be regarded to-day as 'interference' or 'ripper legislation.' The transfer to the assembly of the choice of the New York City excise commissioners in 1754 perhaps belongs in this category.[40] It is apparently necessary to go to New England for a second example. In Haverhill (1725, 1748) the general court of Massachusetts intervened in a local dispute concerning officers, and overruled the town meeting. In one instance, this was because it was alleged that ineligibles had voted.[41] In 1746, the restrictions on practicing in the New York City courts were altered by the assembly in defiance of the charter grant, but this was to break up a lawyer's ring.[42] On the whole, the picture of relations between assembly and city was one of utmost cordiality in the extension of powers to undertake new activities, to raise additional revenues, or to extend the bounds of self-government.

Much the same state of affairs ruled in the smaller 'towns' of the South, though in this instance perhaps the county commissioners might more properly be regarded as the supervisory body. Details in profusion might be included in the acts concerned ; but gradually, particu-larly in North Carolina and Virginia, the wording of the extensions became stereotyped, the grants identical, and in reality a 'general code' for small towns was evolved. Subsequent incorporations merely repeated word for

40. Peterson and Edwards, op. cit., p. 269.
41. Saltonstall, L., *Historical Sketch of Haverhill,* in *Mass. Hist. Soc. Coll.,* 2nd ser., vol. IV, p. 137.
42. For the reaction of the city council towards this, cf. *Minutes of the Common Council,* Jan. 7, 1745/6. The attempt was only partially suc-cessful (Morris, R. B. (Edit.), *Select Cases — New York City Mayor's Court,* p. 53).

word the previous acts for other towns.⁴³ In Charlestown
(Md.) the assembly went so far as to extend legal sanction to the local fair, after the inhabitants had 'proclaimed' it without authorization.⁴⁴ Curiously, it was
from the assembly that Bristol and Philadelphia sought
release from the 'obligation' in the charter of holding
fairs. The latter city was more successful than the
former, for Bristol did not obtain the desired release until 1796.⁴⁵

There were, however, a number of instances in which
duties were imposed upon municipalities. While at times
these laws appear to have been honoured more in the
breach than in the observance, yet at other times they
were real factors in inducing local action. For example,
Portland, in 1728, opened a school 'to keep the town
from being presented' under the Massachusetts law of
1647.⁴⁶ There were a moderate number of such instances
of coercion of New York City, at times re-enforced by
threat of fines. In 1695 and 1699, the appointment of
overseers of the poor and of public works and of buildings was made mandatory.⁴⁷ In 1706, New York City and
also Albany were required to levy a tax for fortifica-

43. e. g. Port Royal, Newcastle, Suffolk, 1745 (Hening's *Virginia Statutes,*
vol. V, pp. 387ff., etc.). For North Carolina, cf. the Beaufort Act of
1770, almost every clause of which Act was lifted bodily from other
charter acts (*State Records of North Carolina,* vol. XXIII, pp.
805ff.). The Massachusetts General Act of Incorporation [of towns]
was passed in 1635.
44. Andrews, M. P., *History of Maryland,* p. 270.
45. Note, however, the fact that the assembly took more drastic action
than was desired by Philadelphia, in that it abolished the fairs *permanently* in spite of the city's protest (*Minutes of Philadelphia Common Council,* Apr. 3, 1775). Cf. Scharf and Westcott, op. cit., vol. I,
p. 294 ; Bolles, op. cit., vol. II, p. 269f.
46. Dexter, E. G., *History of Education in the United States,* p. 53. Cf.
also *supra,* p. 281.
47. McBain, H. L., 'Legal Status of the American Colonial City,' in *Pol.
Sci. Quart.,* vol. XL, p. 193.

tions.[48] Later, occasional directions were given concerning the main highways.[49] Certain duties concerning trading with the Indians and maintenance of a military watch were imposed on Albany, in 1714 and 1746 respectively.[50] In 1771, the Baltimore town commissioners were directed to appoint numerous inspectors.[51] Yet even in instances such as these, there is little evidence to indicate strong objection to compliance on the part of the local authorities, on the ground that such action constituted central 'tyranny' or an undermining of a genuine local self-government.

Two or three times in the colonial period a deep-seated hostility arose between an assembly and a particular city. The pro-Catholic tendencies of St. Mary's had much to do with its undoing, once the Maryland assembly was in control and the proprietor out of the way. The country-city cleavage that was to loom so large in later history began fairly early to influence the attitudes of the Pennsylvania and New York legislatures towards Philadelphia and New York City. In each it tended towards the installation of fiscal systems which saddled the metropolis with what appeared to it to be an undue share in the provision of provincial revenues.[52] In New York the struggle was especially deep-seated, marking a clash between merchant and farmer which at times was the dominant colouring of the political behaviour of the

48. Ibid. p. 193f.
49. Peterson and Edwards, op. cit., p. 362.
50. McBain, op. cit., p. 194f.
51. Mereness, N. D., *Maryland as a Proprietary Province*, p. 419.
52. Cf. Spencer, C. W., 'Sectional Aspects of New York Provincial Politics,' in *Pol. Sci. Quart.*, vol. XXX, pp. 397-429 ; Peterson and Edwards, op. cit., pp. 235ff. ; Scharf and Westcott, op. cit., vol. I, p. 265. In New York, the clashes were latterly chiefly with the neighbouring counties. Albany and New York City tended to make common cause. Cf. also *supra*, p. 335.

assembly. As early as 1694 the interior succeeded in passing the so-called 'Bolting Act' aimed at breaking the
City's monopoly in packing flour. The City retaliated by
taxing the flour, but was forced to retract under extreme
pressure. Later, the issues were obscured somewhat by
numerous 'deals,' whereby (in a truly modern fashion)
the City representatives lined up certain counties on
their side. The tax issue usually appeared as a choice between duties and licence fees on the one hand and land
taxes on the other. Apportionment of representation
and quotas of militia furnished other sources of dispute.

(C)

Yet these instances of friction were so exceptional and
interfered so little with the spontaneous functioning of
local administration that they scarcely affect the general
picture of cordiality. Colonial municipalities when incorporated were for the most part free to grow functionally — provided only they asked for the necessary per-
missions. The real handicaps on such functional development were not those of central restraint but of local
financial stringency. The colonial period aided in establishing legal precedents for central tutelage — it did
nothing to render such tutelage an actuality. Even where
the assemblies themselves actually undertook the government of their capitals, the mainspring of action was
local need ; and the day-to-day association of the members of the assembly with the citizens of Charleston and
Savannah was so intimate that these communities felt apparently that they, too, were 'self-governing.'

Indeed, it was far more likely that these capital cities
dominated the legislatures, than the reverse. The commercial and social prestige of a deferential age assured

this. In due time, the controls by the English governor and the Board of Trade, perfunctory though they usually were, were to vanish and the legislature was to become all-powerful. If the legislatures in later periods had exercised one half the restraint or one half the beneficent interest of the colonial governor or their own predecessors in colonial times, the story of American cities would have been a far brighter one.

XIV

MUNICIPAL PUBLIC OPINION

THE term 'public opinion' is to be identified with those attitudes in significant portions of a community or state which affect governmental or collective behaviour. Such attitudes and their products and by-products may or may not be measureable, but any picture of government is incomplete without an attempt at their analysis.

The extent to which the colonial populace actually voted has already been discussed. It will be remembered that the actual percentage voting varied greatly from town to town, but in any event was small in comparison with the present-day percentage. Rarely were the majority of adult males even eligible to vote and still more rarely, if ever, did such a majority actually vote. Yet within the limited sphere of municipal government, what were the issues that divided the persons actually participating? How were these issues formulated? Were there emerging any major tides or cleavages or political parties as the cities grew, or as the Revolution approached?

It may be well at the outset to remind ourselves of the normal attitudes towards borough corporations. These ordinary attitudes differed considerably from those evidenced when issues were created by an emergency or crisis. In the smaller boroughs in the 'intimate' stage, the usual situation was quite similar to that in the New England towns. In these latter the selectmen were servants and leaders of the town meeting. In the smaller boroughs, even though the borough meeting was not always an integral part of the government, such meetings were none the less held in the majority of instances. An easy interchange of views between governors and governed was consequently normal. Where the borough meetings were not so held, as in Albany, community life was still so intimate that the aldermen and councillors in their ordinary walks of life could and did consult with the hundred or so 'fellow citizens' who made up the articulate voting list. It is possible that the aristocratic boroughs of Virginia constituted an exception, in so far as these were close corporations, and were still under the spell of deference to the landowners or merchants.

In Philadelphia, both the agencies of government and the vehicles for expression of public opinion were complex. The extent varied to which the close corporation which nominally governed the city was really near enough to the populace or active enough functionally to 'feel' or to be 'felt.' In its first few years of corporate existence, the city council probably had been indistinguishable in these respects from one popularly elected. Later it appeared not only to have lost touch with the needs of the community but to have deteriorated internally. Franklin galvanized it into a certain amount of life but even he could not save it from internal decay. However, the Philadelphians had other vehicles through which to make their opinions felt. Of these vehicles, the assembly was chief at the outset and remained powerful to the very end. After the separation of the Delaware counties, for many years the colony and Philadelphia seemed identical.[1] Of the numerous boards and commissions (the overseers, the street commissioners, the wardens, the assessors), all were at least in part elective and furnished a very considerable avenue for popular participation. Towards the middle of the century the grand jury

1. Scharf, J. T., and Westcott, T., *History of Philadelphia*, vol. I, p. 175.

revealed some potentialities in this direction, serving for several years as a focus of movements for reform and civic advance.[2] Finally, the citizens might always resort to direct action, if other devices failed. The Philadelphians apparently did not hesitate to resort even to violent means if the occasion offered — witness, for example, the tearing down of an unpopular market house. Hence, amidst all these divergent and somewhat abnormal vehicles of public opinion, it was not easy to gauge the views of the majority, or to analyse the various currents denied more normal expression.

In New York City the organization of government was much more simple, making possible the channelling of political opinion almost entirely through the single vehicle of the elected corporation. Here a real ebb and flow could be noted, and that clear translation of public opinion into responsible action which is the warp and woof of democracy. This being so, it was evidence of the relative 'acceptability' of a *status quo* to learn that for the most part existing aldermen and councillors would be returned term after term, not only without difficulty but even without opposition. Only occasionally would there be an overturn — yet it is on the study of the sharper discussion accompanying these overturns that we must largely rely to discover the elements of which the New York City electorate was composed.

In Boston, also — though this town is largely outside the scope of our study — the vehicles for expression of public opinion were clear cut through the town meeting, and the possibilities for selectivity and isolation of issues even greater than in New York. Here also were tides of opinion ; but here also overturns were infrequent, and

2. Cf. pp. 216ff.

on the whole, till the time of the Adamses, the decisions of the inner and influential group prevailed.

In general, one must approach the study of this period of one hundred odd years of civic existence not expecting too much by way of sharp expression of views or cleavage of issues. In the first place, men were preoccupied with making a living. Life was harder then than now ; the hours of work far longer ; the margin above the sub-sistence level even for the propertied classes too small to indulge in very many municipal luxuries. This in itself created the characteristic tone of opinion — 'spend not ; do not touch my business, except to help it.'

In the second place, the tempo of the time was far slower than to-day. Ten or twenty years might easily pass without a single alteration in municipal function or policy. In an age virtually devoid of those inventions which are the mainsprings of functional alterations, such alterations as did take place came about almost entirely through growth in size ; and then only after a conse-quent virtual collapse in the handling of some function would the new method be adopted. Any one introduced to a typical discussion concerning the municipal gov-ernment, if indeed a discussion could be found at all, would probably discover the conversation to be quite leisurely, rather grumbling, and mildly critical ; but con-cerned on the whole with small things discussed in a small way — perhaps with the peculiarities of a coun-cillor, with the fact that so and so did not take his turn on the watch or did not clean in front of his house, or with the inequalities of the latest assessment. A hard-working, man-power age resulted at one and the same time in a preoccupation with the day-to-day grind and in the slow tempo that seldom generated issues.

In the third place, relative to modern times, there were

not so many ways in which the municipality affected the individual — save only that in its capacity as a regulator of trade the city government might in this one respect affect the citizen at more points than to-day. Consequently a large percentage of the major issues arose out of this particular type of function. By way of contrast, while the enforcement of the limited sumptuary legislation of the day might be resented or defied, those opposed were not the conventional propertied classes who usually alone had the vote. In this connection, an exception may be made of the tavern keepers. Where democracy ruled, these tavern keepers often succeeded in having themselves elected to the council,[3] perhaps to ward off the passage or enforcement of the stricter liquor legislation.

Finally, there must be mentioned once more as a limiting factor on political divergencies that deference to social position which prevailed virtually unchallenged until well into the eighteenth century and which was still powerful thereafter.

These four factors then — the preoccupation with the day-to-day tasks, the slower tempo, the paucity of functions, the prevailing deference — severely limited the occasions on which sharply defined issues would emerge, and rendered the political life of the municipalities far less dramatic than in later and more complex ages.

(B)

It is basically a task for the social psychologist to analyse political issues. Some issues — a large number in fact — everywhere arise out of the psychological irritation accompanying all *new* proposals, quite apart from their actual effect on the individuals involved. The sceptical

3. e. g. Wilmington (Del.), Annapolis.

and the conservative oppose ; the innovators and the progressive support ; the flexibly minded and the realists finally decide the matter. Yet this conservative-progressive cleavage is definitely an over-simplification when applied to the majority of controversies. Over and above this division there is something else even more fundamental playing a part in issues that are felt emotionally. This is the element of heterogeneity that is present in all societies and communities save the very simplest. Out of this heterogeneity arises conflict. The conflict may be real in the sense of having an objective counterpart in actual divergence of interest ; or it may be imaginary — the product of unfamiliarity with and consequent suspicion of and hostility towards the 'ways' of other groups. If these 'ways' have assumed the importance of mores, the conflict can be very bitter indeed.

How far, then, did heterogeneity of this type reflect itself in the every-day political opinion of the colonial city ? As regards race, language, and religion, very considerably.

While it is true that in New York City there grew to be a surprising cosmopolitanism, none the less, racial and religious factors still played a substantial part. Not unnaturally, in the Dutch restoration of 1673, the English were removed from office. Military necessity may have demanded it. Over and above this, however, the groups of Dutch, English, French, and Germans had to be reckoned with politically ; and woe to him who antagonized one or more of them. By 1750 the Anglicans and Presbyterians had definitely attained an ascendency over the Reformed Dutch, while the Lutherans were steadily gaining.[4] The religious issue occasionally was openly

4. Peterson, A. E., and Edwards, G. W., *New York as an Eighteenth Century Municipality*, pp. 254ff.

urged in campaign manifestoes.[5] The mayors, appointees of the governor, were always Anglican ; the Dutch fared somewhat better in the common council.[6] Yet this very fact that there were so many large, fairly evenly balanced groups operated wholesomely also. It made fusion in political action a necessity, and thus year in and year out forced conciliation to win or hold office, and co-operation for government to function at all. This accounted in large measure for the cosmopolitan attitude that contrasted strongly with Boston, whose Puritan majority could for so long ride rough shod politically and socially over minorities.

In Albany, on the other hand, the Dutch were in an overwhelming majority and apparently did not hesitate to exploit the fact. It is difficult in these matters to separate mere suspicion from actuality, because the former is inevitable in situations of this sort. We quote, however, Sir William Johnson, to illustrate. He speaks of 'Albany justice' as follows :

> There never was anything more wanted than a change, as there is no justice to be expected by any Englishmen in this County, nor never will, whilst the Bench of Judges and Justices is composed entirely of Dutch, who pride themselves in the appellation, which alone, in my opinion should render them odious to everry Britton. I could give you, Sir, numberless Instances, supported by incontestable facts, of the partiality, cruelty, and oppression of those in authority here, who call themselves Dutch.[7]

5. Cf. in *N. Y. Gazette and Weekly Mercury*, Jan. 9, 1769. This was in connection with an alleged under-representation of the dissenters among the candidates nominated for the assembly.
6. Peterson and Edwards, op. cit., p. 259f.
7. In a letter to Lieut. Governor Colden, 1761 (*Cadwallader Colden Papers, Coll. of N. Y. Hist. Soc.*, vol. VI, p.13).

Whether or not this extreme picture is correct is not so much to the point as the attitudes herein revealed on both sides which inevitably affected political action.

In Philadelphia and Pennsylvania the situation was also complicated by racial and religious factors. The Germans represented one distinct group, the Quakers another; and there were all sorts of other less clearly defined groups — Welsh, Scotch-Irish, etc. — which had to be reckoned with politically. Apparently the Germans ordinarily held the balance of power and were reluctantly catered to by other groups — who divided on economic and governmental lines more than racially or religiously. On the other hand, many of the groups did not know quite what to make of the Quakers. Their professions were so different, their manners unfamiliar — and yet economically they were a success.[8]

Hence the Quakers became at one and the same time objects of suspicion and envy. As so often is true under similar circumstances, the particular aspect seized upon to make the political issue was actually of no great importance — but seemed to the people of the day to epitomize or symbolize the *difference*. This was the Quaker custom of substituting the affirmation for the oath. Yet this became a symbol or shibboleth to be fought over and to judge men by — though entirely unimportant in the realities of day-to-day government. Insistence upon the oath seemed to the non-Quakers an excellent way of ridding

8. Cf. Hershberger, G. F., 'The Pennsylvania Quaker Experiment in Politics, 1682-1756,' in *The Mennonite Quarterly Review*, Oct. 1936, pp. 187-221. This deals with the underlying situation from the standpoint of the Quakers themselves. The fundamental incompatibility between their religious beliefs and the exercise of any force in civil government is admirably set out. Ultimately this incompatibility led most of the group in the direction of a quietist non-participation. Previously the Quaker office holders had played their full part in the political factional quarrels of the city and province.

themselves of their political rivals. In 1709, for example, the assembly received a petition to bar a certain Thomas MacNamara from practising law as he openly in court 'did say . . . that it was inconsistent with the Queen to grant . . . an order allowing Quakers to take an affirmation instead of swearing.'[9] The charter of 1724 of Newcastle ran into this same obstacle (among others), inasmuch as Governor Keith, whether deliberately or otherwise, had included clauses requiring the taking of an oath to qualify for certain offices ; and this, together with the fact that he had appointed no Quakers as justices for Kent County, was exploited to secure the opposition of the Quakers to the charter and to the admission of the representatives to the Delaware assembly elected thereunder.[10] In Philadelphia itself no elections were held, for the actual corporation was self-perpetuating. None the less, the city council was the scene of a struggle for control between the two main 'parties' whose composition was only in part determined by racial and religious factors.[11]

In early Maryland the religious issue was one of the two decisive factors in the attitude and action of the house of delegates, which proved to be the death sentence of the city of St. Mary's. The latter was Catholic and on the side of the proprietor ; the former was predominantly Anglican and hostile to the proprietary administration.[12] How much of this attitude towards St. Mary's was emotional, engendered by group hostility, and how much

9. Minutes of Provincial Council, in *Pennsylvania Colonial Records*, vol. II, p. 457.
10. Keith, C. P., *Chronicles of Pennsylvania*, vol. II, p. 681f.
11. Cf. p. 370f.
12. In 1708, of the 2,974 Catholics in the province, 1,238 were in St. Mary's County (Seymour Papers, MS. in library of Maryland Historical Society. Census attached to a letter of Sept. 6, 1708 from Governor Seymour to the Lords of Trade).

was reasoned may be judged by the contemptuous way in which St. Mary's' protest against the transfer of the capital to Annapolis was received. The charter, the fact that the state-house and prison were already built, the ruin that would come upon its citizens — all were brushed aside. In reply, the comment was made that St. Mary's, 'like Pharaoh's lean kine, devoured everything and yet attained no size.'[13] There were arguments for Anne Arundel Town and against St. Mary's — legitimate arguments — but the decision to transfer the seat of government from the one to the other seems not to have been primarily traceable to these.

Those familiar with the history of New England will remember the dominant role played by religious belief in its political evolution, particularly in the seventeenth century. The various questions revolving around religious qualifications for voting or office-holding, the presence of persecuted groups outside the pale — all played their part on the agenda of the town meeting as well as of the legislatures. All illustrated the complicating and unfortunate effects of intolerance in the political realm, but were at least understandable in the light of the important place given to religion by these early settlers.

In the other colonies, racial and religious differences played somewhat less important roles. In the close corporation of Norfolk there was a certain amount of political rivalry between the English and the Scotch, but not enough apparently to distort materially the governmental decisions of a quite enlightened body corporate. In Charleston, differences between the French and English

13. Richardson, H. D., *Sidelights on Maryland History*, Baltimore, 1913, 2 vol., vol. I, p. 87 ; Sparks, F. E., *Causes of the Maryland Revolution of 1689*, pp. 77, etc. ; Andrews, M. P., *Founding of Maryland*, Baltimore, 1933.

may have influenced certain decisions ; but, if so, the differing economic status of the two groups in the earlier years was probably more responsible than race.[14]

At no point is there any intention of passing judgment upon the quality or attitudes of any one of the races or religions. It was not so much the question of which or what these were that mattered politically as it was the fact of the simultaneous presence of two or more groups that differed from each other in matters primarily outside the sphere of politics. Almost invariably these usually irrelevant differences, with their attendant dislikes and suspicions, were carried into the field of politics. There they were exploited, even in colonial times, by the manipulation of symbols and other appeals to prejudice, in order to attain the ends of those who were in office or sought to be.

Furthermore, it must be borne in mind that the influence of England came to be exercised (through the persons of the governors and council) almost wholly on the side of Anglicanism. There was, accordingly, as the struggles between the assemblies and the governors developed in certain colonies, some tendency to associate Anglicanism with what was earlier the court or king's or proprietor's party and later was to become the Tory group. The retainers and recipients of patronage naturally were of this ilk. Just how far this factor reflected itself politically in town elections it is difficult to say. By 1775, religious, racial, and economic factors had become almost hopelessly interlocked.

One word should be added concerning current attitudes towards those ordinances of municipalities which sprang from the religious creeds of the day. Among such

14. e. g. in the charter dispute of 1722, for which cf. p. 193 ; also McCrady, E., *History of South Carolina, 1719-1776*, pp. 40ff.

ordinances those concerned with Sabbath observance
were most frequent. To-day such laws would be openly
challenged in an organized way, and their vigorous enforcement would meet with opposition at the polls. It
was not so in colonial times. These ordinances were not
issues ; they were merely disobeyed. In part this was because convention and respectability would not think of
doing otherwise than to endorse them in principle ;
and convention and respectability were entrenched behind the property franchise ; and the unregenerate and
non-voting masses furnished the greater proportion of
the law-breakers. In part, however, it was because of that
well-known capacity of the individual to separate his
public conscience from his individual behaviour, which
at a later day, for example, was to aid in keeping traffic
or prohibition laws on the statute books, even if their
observance deteriorated to a farce.

Race, language, and religion, then as to-day, were
complicating rather than clarifying factors in political
action ; and, if they played the role they did in the simple
conditions of colonial times, one can gain a fair insight
thereby of the distortion they must create in the sphere
of political action of the present — when the really rele-
vant issues themselves are so many and so complicated as
to be for the most part seemingly beyond the wit of collective man to solve.

(C)

Of increasingly greater effectiveness in motivating political action in colonial towns were the economic factors.
Mention has already been made of a certain rising hostility between the country districts and the cities.[15] In part

15. Cf. p. 343f.

this hostility also can be explained sociologically in terms of the suspicions engendered by different ways of living ; but underlying it all, even this early, was the economic clash between agriculture and commerce. Curiously enough, at times the city of Philadelphia found itself allied with the 'country party,' but this was because mutual hostility towards the proprietary government for the time being overshadowed other matters.[16] In the choice of the popularly elected county sheriff, the issue was more sharply drawn between city and country.[17] That the plantation states also experienced this cleavage may be inferred from a letter published in the *Maryland Gazette* of December 21, 1758 : 'Should a merchant propose any Thing that might be of general advantage to the Country, this spirit of Aversion to the Merchant, and Opposition to every Scheme we apprehend to be Beneficial to Trade, make us conclude it of consequence ruinous to the Planter.'

A similar 'external' issue (external in the sense of being outside the sphere of political action wholly within one community) was the rivalry between city and city. This was overwhelmingly economic in its genesis, but was customarily even then surrounded with the aura of civic patriotism. Albany and Schenectady, New York City and Perth Amboy, Philadelphia and Baltimore, Annapolis and St. Mary's, Wilmington and Brunswick were the pairs of towns whose rivalry most obviously left its traces in political action. Ordinarily, but not always, this rivalry was associated with the custom of extending special trade privileges to port and other cities. In Albany and Schenectady, the privileged position of the former

16. Between 1704 (approx.) and 1741 (Keith, C. P., *Chronicles of Pennsylvania*, vol. I, p. 435 ; vol. II, p. 812).
17. Scharf, J. T., and Westcott, T., *History of Philadelphia*, vol. I, p. 246.

consisted in its exclusive right from Dutch days to the Indian trade, and the superior jurisdiction of its court.[18] Not unnaturally the Albany corporation sought to pre-serve both of these. Yet essentially the city was not always ungenerous when the more human or personal factors were involved, for it is recorded in the minutes that Albany granted permission to take up a collection towards the salary of the Schenectady minister, and doubtless the worthy aldermen themselves contributed.[19]

The struggle between Perth Amboy and New York (already noted) is worth recounting in further detail, not only as an indication of what agitated men's minds, but also as revealing the mechanisms by which 'ports' were created. The story begins with the granting to the then New Amsterdam of the 'staple right' for the entire colony. All cargoes were thereby required to clear through the one port. This was nominally confirmed when the English took control ; but the Duke of York almost im-mediately granted New Jersey to Berkeley and Carteret, 'in as full and ample manner.' In 1681, the twenty-four proprietors took over East Jersey from Berkeley and Carteret. At this time, the attorney general of New York informed the Earl of Bellomont, 'the purchasers send over Thomas Rudyard, Samuell Groom to be Gover-nours, they erect a town at Amboy, pretend to great priviledges, make some settlements there, but bring noe shipping further than Staten Island, where they were permitted to convey their household goods.'[20] However, Perth Amboy for the time being accepted a collector subsidiary to the New York City collector.[21] Neverthe-

18. Cf. p. 130.
19. Munsell, J., *Annals of Albany*, vol. IV, p. 118.
20. O'Callaghan, E. B. (Edit.), *Documents Relative to the Colonial His-tory of New York*, vol. IV, p. 382.
21. Ibid. p. 382f.

less, instructions from the proprietors to Governor Lawrie in 1683/4 concluded : 'care be taken that Goods be not exported to New York or other Places, but all be brought to Perth, as the chief Staple.'[22] Competitive underbidding of customs rates with a view to attracting commerce from New York soon followed. In 1687, an order in council was issued which, while it granted ships direct entry, insisted upon the same rates as New York.[23] In 1694, however, the Jersey assembly again took up the struggle, and declared Perth a port.[24] The governor of New Jersey later issued a proclamation declaring the town a free port, apparently after the surveyor general of the customs in America had received a letter to this effect from the commissioners of the customs in England.[25] Merchants prepared to leave New York for Perth. Bellomont, however, held up this order, pending further instructions, as it 'will be a destruction to the Trade of the City and province of New York, who have established laws, for Customs, by which a considerable revenue is raised to support the Government.' The protest was successful for the time being.[26] While loading and unloading were to be permitted at Amboy, the customs were still to be under the New York director. This state of affairs arose out of Bellomont's communications to the Board of Trade, who in turn took the matter up with the Lord Justices ; and in due course the latter's decision was confirmed by an order in council.[27] On the basis of this

22. *New Jersey Archives,* 1st ser., vol. I, p. 451.
23. Ibid. vol. I, pp. 537, 540. Order of Aug. 14, 1687.
24. Acts, 1694, Chap. III, in Leaming, A., and Spicer, J., *Grants, Concessions, etc., of New Jersey* (Reprint 1881), p. 342.
25. *New Jersey Archives,* 1st ser., vol. II, p. 178f.
26. O'Callaghan, op. cit., vol. IV, pp. 305, 314.
27. *New Jersey Archives,* 1st ser., vol. II, pp. 183, 200. Order of Nov. 25, 1697.

order, Bellomont seized the ship *Hester*.[28] Rather extended litigation followed, the final outcome of which was that Jersey won its right to free ports.[29] However, in the instructions to the New Jersey governor in 1702, it was stipulated that the New Jersey customs duties were to equal those of New York.[30] In 1718 the royal charter was granted to the city of Perth Amboy. Its preamble declared the city was to be 'for a place of trade and as a harbor for shipping preferable to those in the Province adjoining.' Yet all the legislation and 'rights' in the world could not contend with the underlying geographic factors favouring New York ; nor did the Jersey citizens themselves co-operate as they might, but continued to live up to their reputation as notorious smugglers.[31]

The rivalry between Philadelphia and Baltimore was later in its appearance, and its full fruition belongs to the nineteenth century. St. Mary's lost out hopelessly to Annapolis. Brunswick and Wilmington fought over smaller stakes, with the governor on the side of Wilmington — perhaps decisively so.[32]

But these disputes were external to a city's own political cleavages and debates. Inevitably, many ordinances and by-laws affected an individual's income. At best, cash was scarce and taxes were often paid in commodities. Except in the largest cities, a large part of the inhabitants usually eked out any non-agricultural trade or profession by gardens or live stock ; and in the smaller towns

28. Tanner, E. P., *Province of New Jersey, 1664-1738*, p. 136.
29. Ibid. p. 132 ; *N. J. Arch.*, 1st ser., vol. II, p. 341.
30. Labaree, L. W., *Royal Instructions to British Colonial Governors*, vol. II, p. 661.
31. Fisher, E. J., *New Jersey as a Royal Province, 1738-1776*, New York, 1911, p. 393.
32. *State Records of North Carolina*, vol. IV, p. 457f. ; Waddell, A. M., *History of New Hanover County*, p. 191.

the number of actual resident farmers was large. In this kind of economy, the marginal standard of living was the prevailing one ; the struggle to make a living was intense and unremitting ; and the reaction to any ordinance that would unfavourably affect that standard was apt to be violent. In another connection, there has already been traced the use to which the powers of the city were customarily put to secure to its 'freemen' one kind or another of monopoly. Noted also were the extreme difficulties experienced by the various assizes designed to fix price and quality.[33] Of a similar nature were the attempts to deal with the swine rooting in and along the streets. The privilege of such rooting doubtless appeared to the owners, and perhaps to the swine, as an inalienable right ; and in any event the deprivation of it required the owner to make other and more costly arrangements. Attempts in similar minute fashion to lessen the fire risks through prescription of better and more expensive chimneys and roofs met with similar passive resistance. In the 'intimate stage,' enforcement of this type of ordinance was often socially impracticable. The various economic pressures surrounding the processes of taxation and assessment have also been considered, and evidently played a very considerable role in municipal public opinion.[34] One of the best indications of this is to be found in the frequent alternation between paid and unpaid watch, or paid and unpaid paving and cleaning, that marked the ebb and flow of municipal 'extravagance.'

In fact, wherever a particular problem is discovered to have been settled in alternative ways in one or in various cities, it is fair to conjecture that here was a problem on the solution of which groups disagreed — in other words,

33. Cf. pp. 135, 144ff.
34. Cf. p. 319f.

an 'issue,' and political activity reflected the disagreement. Whether swine should be ringed or prohibited altogether from roaming ; whether or not owners of houses torn down in fire-fighting should be compensated ;[35] whether or not those serving in the militia should be exempted from watch duties ;[36] whether or not there should be a market and where ;[37] whether or not the excise should be farmed out ;[38] which streets, if any, should be paved ;[39] whether or not the mayor should be allowed to retain the fees obtained in his office ;[40] what should be the method of assessing taxes[41] — these and numerous other questions were the subject of many a discussion within and outside of the city council itself.

Even in the early Virginia 'boroughs,' an issue arose involving the municipal charters. This was the question of whether and how the artisans could be induced to follow their trades ; and hence 'urbanize' the community.[42] The tendency of the individual to go his own way economically, in spite of inducements and laws, had many an illustration in these early communities. The unsuccessful attempts of Maryland and Virginia to develop certain port towns ; Albany's difficulty with individuals taking Indians into their homes for trading ;[43] Phila-

35. e. g. Boston, 1652, no compensation allowed ; 1658, compensation allowed (Quincy, J., *Municipal History of Boston*, p. 46).

36. e. g. Philadelphia (Minutes of Provincial Council, in *Pa. Colon. Rec.*, vol. II, p. 165).

37. e. g. Philadelphia, 1773, cf. p. 152 ; Scharf and Westcott, op. cit., vol. I, p. 266.

38. e. g. New York City, 1752. Cf. *Independent Reflector*, Dec. 7, 1752.

39. e. g. Wilmington (Del.), 1773 ('Every Evening' (compil.) *History of Wilmington*, Wilmington, 1894, p. 23).

40. e. g. New York. Cf. p. 299.

41. e. g. Annapolis, where in 1760 there was great resistance to declaring horses and cattle for taxation purposes (Minutes of Annapolis Council, Feb. 3, 1760).

42. Cf. p. 93.

43. Cf. p. 131f.

delphia's yielding to the proprietors of slaughter houses, tan yards, and other nuisances (whose businesses the corporation had attempted to move to a more suitable location because of their unsavoury nature); the attempt to tax consumption of spirits in private families in Massachusetts — all represented this fundamental difficulty of implementing detailed laws of an economic nature. Of course, the individual did not usually argue the damage to his pocket book when resisting such edicts. In Philadelphia the ordinance was 'a daring attempt on the liberties,' that had been frustrated.[44] The townsmen of Newbury dubbed the taxation of spirits 'an infringement on the natural rights of Englishmen.'[45] The ability to penetrate beneath catchwords of this sort to the economic realities that lay back of them has been responsible for the rewriting of more than merely the municipal history of this and other periods.

Yet the issues thus far classed as 'economic' for the most part have had to do with special privileges or the incomes of small classes or individuals ; rather than with the more modern cleavage of 'class' v. 'mass,' or 'bourgeoisie' v. 'proletariat,' as the Marxians would have it. What evidence, if any, cropped out in connection with the internal politics of colonial cities which might point towards such a cleavage ? One must admit at the outset that only here and there were indications present of such factors operating. It has already been suggested that in most localities the 'masses' were unenfranchised and that traditional deference kept them so. The two opiates of drink and a religion otherworldly in its emphasis played their part, particularly as there was no irreconcilable incongruity felt at the time in the simultaneous excessive indulgence

44. Scharf and Westcott, op. cit., vol. I, p. 208.
45. Coffin, J., *History of Newbury*, Boston, 1845, p. 221.

in both. Quite apart from the influence of religion —
which at least in its Anglican variety certainly entrenched
'status' — the average man of the 'masses' in frontier trading towns, like Albany, or in the numerous port cities
led a more or less animal existence. He lived from spree
to spree, lawless, but neither articulate nor caring to be
so civically. He was not yet 'class conscious.' When he
was franchised, as occasionally in New York City, he was
an easy prey to bribery, particularly of the alcoholic
variety, and was thereby shamelessly exploited by the
less scrupulous.

In fact, only in those few towns in which apprenticeship was a way to 'freedom,' and which were at the same
time large enough to have considerable numbers of
artisans, could and did anything that approached a 'class
struggle' develop, which could express itself through the
medium of the ballot box or through other municipal
institutions, such as the town meeting or the petition.[46]
Extra-legal methods of rioting and the like occasionally
occurred in towns like Perth Amboy and Philadelphia,
where the masses found no adequate remedy in democratic institutions. In Perth Amboy, the proprietors' quit
rents and imprisonment for non-payment of the same
were sufficient to induce a mob to attack the gaol and
the mayor.[47] In Philadelphia, a large, disorderly, unassimilated mass was ready for trouble generally. In Wilmington (Del.), the rivalry between the relatively poorer
people of the 'lower town' and the Quaker group of the
'upper town' dominated much of the municipal life from

46. Perhaps it was fear of the 'masses' that led the 'classes' to seek an
   alteration in the liberal franchise of Campbelton, N. C. It was more
   likely, however, a dislike of the inhabitant Scottish Highlanders.
   (Cf. p. 206f.)
47. In 1747, the cause was obscure (*New Jersey Archives*, 1st ser., vol.
   VI, p. 464). In 1752 the issue was clearer (ibid. vol. XIX, p. 149).

1739 till the eve of the Revolution. In general, the latter group retained the control, but not unchallenged; and at times of indifference or slackness, representatives of the former would be elected.[48]

It was in New York and, to a less extent, in Boston that an underlying class antagonism cropped out most clearly. This class cleavage was already a factor in the Leisler episode in 1689;[49] and politically it forced sharp recognition by 1734. In 1684, the corporation had not hesitated to deprive virtually the entire carter's guild of their privileges when they went on a strike. In 1752, the *Independent Reflector,* a liberal weekly, pictures the city justices (aldermen) as men 'who stand in more Awe of a Band of Carmen than of an armed Host; because that proceeds not so much from natural Timidity, as a more political Reason.'[50]

In 1734, a revolt of the artisans resulted in the defeat of seven merchants for re-election, with ten out of the twelve members of the entering common council actually new men. These included three bakers, a painter, a bricklayer, a jeweler, and a bolter.[51] The new group consolidated its position, and the following year but one of the defeated former members regained his seat. The only actual resultant change in internal policy (but this was an important one) seems to have been in connection with the market. A petition of the butchers, which had been referred to a committee by the earlier council, was granted and the City assumed direct charge of the market, reduced the fees, and liberalized the regulations gen-

48. Wilmington Minute Book, var.
49. Cf. pp. 374ff.
50. Sept. 13, 1752.
51. Cf. Edwards, G. W., 'New York City Politics before the Revolution,' in *Pol. Sci. Quart.,* vol. XXXVI, pp. 586ff., for an excellent account of the episode and its aftermath.

erally. A new assize of bread raised the prices, perhaps to aid the bakers.[52] It is possible also that the magistrates may have 'liberalized' their justice to conform to their political supporters. However, the really acute issue was opposition to Governor Cosby, the supreme court, and the 'court party.' These were the stormy days of Zenger and his *New York Journal,* and intense class and partisan feeling generally. In 1741, an alleged 'Negro Conspiracy' revealed wholesale hysteria and instability of public opinion.[53] By 1750, and increasingly thereafter, the ambitious lawyer group sought and enlisted the support of the artisans against the merchants who had normally predominated. It was in this atmosphere that the artisans attained an articulateness which they never wholly lost — and which was largely responsible for making the internal political life of New York City the most stormy, the most striking, the most cosmopolitan, of any American city.

Mention of Boston must be incidental, but here also a radicalism, for the most part under the leadership of lawyers like John Adams, arose to challenge the long-continued sway of the Caucus Club and Merchant Club whose influence had hitherto been virtually omnipotent.[54]

In the period 1760-1775 evidences of such restlessness also crept into the records of Annapolis. Here again it was a young lawyer, Samuel Chase, who provided much

52. For the episode, cf. *Minutes of Common Council*, Sept. 29, 1733; Sept. 30, 1734; Oct. 3, 1734; Jan. 30, 1734/5; Sept. 16, 1735; Nov. 4, 1735; etc. Cf. also Peterson and Edwards, op. cit., p. 233, quoting the *Journal* of Oct. 7, 1734.

53. Peterson and Edwards, op. cit., p. 315f.; McKee, S., Jr., *Labor in Colonial New York*, New York, 1935, pp. 156ff.

54. Colegrove, K., *New England Town Mandates*, in *Colon. Soc. of Mass. Publ.*, vol. XXI, pp. 418ff.

of the leadership. His activity municipally commenced early in 1766 when he acted as scribe for the grand jury which had issued an attack on the city council for its inefficiency and disregard of popular rights.[55] His further activity in the riotous demonstrations of the 'Sons of Liberty' against the Stamp Act caused him to be denounced by the mayor and aldermen as a 'busy, restless incendiary, a ring leader of mobs, a foul-mouthed and inflaming son of discord.'[56] He in turn accused the members of the corporation of being creatures of the proprietor.[57] By the time of the municipal election in October his following was sufficient for him to be elected a councillor.

Disqualification of popularly elected but apparently propertyless councillors ; hostility to the city corporation, both as too slack and as too tyrannical ; a final culmination in the mass meetings just prior to the Revolution, with class pitted against class on the loyalty and

55. Cf. p. 219. The correspondence which followed the Grand Jury Remonstrance can be found in the files of the *Maryland Gazette*, Feb. 20, Mar. 13, Mar. 20, Mar. 27, May 1, May 8, June 19, July 17, 1766. It illuminated the moribund nature of the council, the bitterness with which the *status quo* greeted the rising radicalism, current practices of and attitudes towards municipal government. For the remonstrance, see *Md. Gazette*, Mar. 13, 1766.

56. *Md. Gazette*, June 19, 1766.

57. The broadside which Samuel Chase published in 1766 directed against the Annapolis city council was a masterpiece of vilification and vituperation. He accused the members individually and collectively of all kinds of vice and crime, becoming specific from time to time. The political implications, however, rest in his accusation that the corporation 'skulked in your homes,' while he burned the stamps. He claimed that the corporation members were generally sympathetic to the 'court party,' and that those who were accused of being 'mobs' were 'the people of this city,' who opposed the council members at the assembly elections. (Copy of the broadside is pasted in the back of the current volume of the *Maryland Gazette*, in the files of the Maryland State Library.) Cf. Sanderson, J., *Biography of Signers of the Declaration of Independence*, 2nd Edit., Philadelphia, 1820-27, 9 vol., vol. IX, 'Samuel Chase.'

law-and-order issues — all mark a subtle change from the age of deference.[58] It was in Wilmington (N. C.) that defiance of the Stamp Act was actually at its height. In part, at least, this was the issue which elected De Rosset mayor in 1766. He had already been a popular leader in the defiance, and immediately after his election he led the people in intercepting the boat sent to supply the beleaguered British troops and forced the captain and all other officers save only the governor to agree not to enforce the Act.[59] New issues and new forces were indeed showing themselves in the towns and cities, which were later to join with the radicalism of the Virginia Piedmont and the Regulators of the Carolinas in the ferment which in part forced on the American Revolution.

(D)

One other factor, fundamentally psychological, was primarily responsible for another group of issues well known as a fomenter of revolution since the days of Aristotle. These issues centred around the struggles of those in an inferior position against their superiors. The fact of inferiority itself may not have had any realistic results of an unfavourable nature or may even have been to the operative advantage of those placed in the inferior position, through the superior wisdom or benevolence of those in power. Revolts of the masses are always based

58. Minutes of Annapolis Corporation, Nov. 15, 1760; Jan. 29, 1765. *Maryland Gazette*, 1766, *passim*. Cf. Riley, E. S., *The Ancient City*, p. 166, for the Annapolis City mass meeting of May 27, 1774, which by vote of 47 to 31 carried a resolution against paying any personal debts to British. On May 30, a protest against the resolution bore 135 signatures; but the radicals were carrying things before them.
59. Sprunt, J., *Chronicles of the Cape Fear River*, Raleigh, 1916: Jan. 20, 1766; Feb. 5, 1766; *Letters and Documents re Lower Cape Fear, James Sprunt Hist. Monograph*, vol. IV, p. 78f.; Haywood, M. D., *Governor William Tryon*, Raleigh, 1903, pp. 44ff.

partly upon this factor rather than exclusively upon
actual economic cleavage. Even in colonial days, political
appeals to this type of prejudice crept into the elections
of certain cities.[60]

However, the most noticeable expression of this particular motivation in colonial municipalities was not so
much in municipal affairs as in the frequent cleavage
between the 'court' or 'proprietor's' party and that of the
assembly. To the former party attached prestige and
patronage ; the strength of the latter was in the very irritation at 'owing' the proprietor anything. Hostility of
this type fed on 'natural rights' ; it struck at even the
most benevolent of overlords. It resented William Penn
or Lord Baltimore, not because they were autocratic or
tyrannical, but because they were proprietors. Such resentment was of the essence of the political life of Philadelphia and Pennsylvania for many decades ;[61] and was
a definite factor even in the simple communities of North
Carolina or Georgia.[62] It furnished ultimately much of
the emotional symbolism which hurried on the outbreak

60. Particularly true of New York City, for which cf. Becker, C. L., *History of Political Parties in the Province of New York, 1760-1776* ;
but cf. also New Brunswick, 1755, where the 'country v. town' issue
was also a factor (*New Jersey Archives*, 1st. ser., vol. XIX, p. 473f.).
In general, the 'masses' began to show marked hostility to the 'classes'
from about 1750. Cf. Chitwood, O. P., *History of Colonial America*,
p. 583.

61. Cf. p. 331. This was true, even though first members of the corporation
were named by Penn in the charter, and were self-perpetuating.
The underlying attitude was changed to one of hostility to the proprietor within two or three years. For the political life of Philadelphia in the colonial period, cf. Scharf, J. T., and Westcott, T., *History of Philadelphia*, vol. I, p. 122, etc. ; Eshleman, H. F., *Struggle
and Rise of Popular Power in Pennsylvania, 1682-1701*, in *Pa. Mag.
of Hist.*, vol. XXXIV, pp. 29-61 ; Eshleman, H. F., *Political History
of Lancaster County's First Twenty Years*, in *Lancs. Co. Hist. Soc.
Papers*, vol. XX, pp. 37-68 ; Keith, C. P., *Chronicles of Pennsylvania*,
vol. I, p. 435, vol. II, p. 812.

62. Cf. pp. 44ff.

of the Revolution ; and which meanwhile led to spontaneous mass meetings of protest in cities and towns
alike.[63]

Over against the county or the colony, such jealousy
could be counted upon as a force on the side of local self-
government. Any share in control on the part of the
county irked alike a tiny community like Germantown
and a large town like Philadelphia. Such control was
responsible for protests or even defiance, and a constant
pressure upon governor and colonial assemblies for the
extension of exclusive local rights and privileges.[64] It
led New York City, albeit unsuccessfully, to press for the
right to choose its own mayor and recorder,[65] and Lancaster to ask for separate courts.[66] It was strongest in the
New England towns.[67]

Similarly, such an attitude would express itself over
against the position and modest special privileges enjoyed by even the local officials. In Germantown it forced
the members of the corporation to discontinue their
policy of exempting themselves from working on roads.[68]
In New York City it made for breaking down the distinction between great and small burghers.[69] Undoubtedly something of this sort was one of the factors leading Bostonians to prefer the atmosphere of equality of

63. One such meeting in New York City asked the assembly to erect a
    bust of William Pitt, for his services in securing the repeal of the
    Stamp Act (*Maryland Gazette,* July 10, 1766).
64. For Germantown, cf. Bolles, A. S., *Pennsylvania, Province and State,*
    vol. II, pp. 267ff. ; Scharf and Westcott, op. cit., vol. I, p. 170 ; *Hist. Soc.
    of Pa. Coll.,* vol. I, p. 257f. For Philadelphia, cf. *supra,* p. 110 ; Shep-
    herd, W. R., *Proprietary Government in Pennsylvania,* pp. 374, 426f.
65. Cf. p. 32f. This was at the time of the Montgomerie Charter of 1730.
    Cf. also Peterson and Edwards, op. cit., pp. 218ff.
66. Cf. p. 79.
67. Cf. p. 72.
68. Minutes of the Provincial Council, in *Penn. Colon. Rec.,* vol. I, p. 326.
69. Cf. p. 133.

the town meeting to the pomp and deference surrounding a city corporation, particularly a close one. Even Governor Winthrop used the incorporation of Agamenticus as one reason for excluding Maine from the Confederation of New England, 'because they ran a different course from us.'[70] Conversely, it made the officials themselves jealous of their prerogatives.

These issues, deriving from heterogeneity of race and religion, from economic interests, and from an antipathy to inferiority, made up most of what little ebb and flow there was in municipal politics. Such other issues as arose were for the most part peculiar to a specific situation. Towards the end of the period, the question was often mooted of abolition of the increasingly rowdy fairs. Incorporation itself, though usually eagerly sought, except in New England, was occasionally the subject of debate. The Albany corporation during the early 1760's was continually experiencing friction with the military quartered there, and with their commander, General Sir Jeffrey Amherst.[71] The motives and integrity of the city officials were occasionally called in question.[72]

These, then, were the issues that made up the picture of such 'public opinion' as existed in colonial days towards the municipal governments. Naturally the several elements seldom appeared in isolation, or as clearly expressed as in the foregoing analysis. Yet the raw material of public opinion was almost entirely composed of

70. Hosmer, J. K. (Edit.), *Winthrop's Journal,* New York, 1908, 2 vol., vol. II, p. 99.
71. This concerned the quartering of the soldiers, the zeal of the civic authorities in arresting them, the location of the barracks, etc. (*Cadwallader Colden Papers,* in *Coll. N. Y. Hist. Soc.,* vol. V, pp. 324, 386 ; vol. VI, pp. 168, 227, etc.).
72. e. g. New York City, in connection with the sale of water lots (Peterson and Edwards, op. cit., p. 351) ; Philadelphia, by petition in 1695 (Scharf and Westcott, op. cit., vol. I, p. 126).

the racial, religious, and psychological factors indicated. Of political parties in the modern sense there were none, even in a colony as a whole. Rather there existed factions, where there was division at all, known often by the name of the 'country party' or the 'court party.' Virginia and Maryland in 1689 had their 'Associations,' the colonial and Protestant counterpart of the advent of William and Mary ; but these had no municipal implication save as they hastened the fall of St. Mary's. Much the same appraisal applies to the 'Regulators' of the Carolina interior, though the resentment against the planter-merchant oligarchy may have affected the attitudes of the North Carolina boroughs in other matters as well.

Until about 1730 it was considered undignified for a man to campaign openly ; and even after that date the announcements of candidacy were most circumspect. Two of these will serve by way of illustration : The card addressed to the voters by Nicholas Saill, candidate for sheriff in the County of Philadelphia in 1744, read as follows :

> Though it has not till this time been customary to request your votes in print, yet that method being now introduced, I think myself obliged in this public manner to return to you my hearty thanks for the favors I have already received, and to acquaint you that I intend again to stand as a candidate for the sheriff's office, and request your interest at the next election to favor your real friend.[73]

And the customary formula in New York City newspaper advertisements read :

Whereas a great number of freeholders and freemen

73. Quoted in Scharf and Westcott, op. cit., vol. I, p. 211.

of the said city have agreed and resolved to choose the following persons to represent them : to wit . . . Your vote and interest are desired at the ensuing election.[74]

However, by the middle of the century in these two cities, the methods of the actual election were far less praiseworthy. Bribery, treating, intimidation — all were prevalent to the extent that the actual results in a time of an open ballot could by no stretch of the imagination be alleged as necessarily representing a 'public opinion' functioning in an ideal democracy.[75]

In the minutes of the Wilmington (N. C.) borough meeting of January 29, 1765, the following entry occurs :

That the following rule be observed by the Mayor, Recorder, Aldermen, and Freeholders in all debates : That the party speaking should not leave the subject in debate to fall upon the person of any member of the Common Council or other person.[76]

One wonders what background of factionalism evoked this.

One final illustration should be given of the complexity of the political situation when race and religion were inextricably interwoven with economic and other factors. This was the Leisler episode in New York in 1689.[77] This

74. Quoted in Becker, C. L., *History of Political Parties in the Province of New York, 1760-1776*, p. 18.
75. Cf. the appeal for the secret ballot quoted *supra*, p. 210. Note also that sharp practice in the form of a 'sprung' election was alleged in New Brunswick in 1749 (*New Jersey Archives*, 1st ser., vol. XII, pp. 529ff.).
76. Quoted in Waddell, A. M., *History of New Hanover County*, p. 197.
77. Reliance for material dealing with the Leisler episode is placed upon Col. Bayard's hostile narrative in O'Callaghan, E. G. (Edit.), *Documents Relative to the Colonial History of New York*, vol. III, p. 645 ; Leisler's defence in ibid. vol. IV, p. 213f. ; and the account in Fiske, J., *Dutch and Quaker Colonies in America*, vol. II, pp. 183-208. For

was the time of the flight of James II and the accession of William and Mary to the throne. Anti-Catholicism (or anti-Popery) had its colonial counterpart, and Jacob Leisler was of those fanatical on the subject. Not unnaturally he and others thought that Governor Dongan and Lieutenant Governor Nicholson (appointees of James) would favour the 'Jacobite' side, and in the overheated atmosphere of the day suspected that they might even deliver the colony to the King of France. Under this obsession, they refused to pay taxes and finally seized control in the name of William III. Leisler himself was a German, a wine merchant, but with an undisciplined mind. He formed an emergency committee of representatives from a portion only of the towns around New York. Albany took no part. Acting through this committee, elections for mayor, sheriff, and town clerk were held in the City — the appointments of whom had hitherto by charter been the prerogative of the governor. Peter De La Noy, one of the committee, thus had the distinction of being the first — and, for more than a century, the only — popularly elected mayor of New York. It is alleged, however, that only '70 or 80 ill affected persons' took part in the election. Leisler himself was chosen commander of the province by the assembly elected under the direction of the committee. There was delivered to him a letter addressed to Lieutenant Governor Nicholson 'and in his absence to such as for the time being take care for preserving the peace.' An attempt to exercise the taxing power brought trouble, and he found himself completely ignored in the list of new appointments issuing from England soon after. Under this stress, he insisted that the

the Earl of Bellomont's sympathy with the Leislerian faction and his alleged appointment of a Leislerian as mayor of Albany, cf. Fiske, op. cit., vol. II, p. 215, and O'Callaghan, op. cit., vol. IV, p. 621.

list was a mistake, and became more and more tyrannical. This lost him most of his popular support — for he had had a real appeal as a kind of champion against the 'court' group. When Governor Sloughter arrived, Leisler was thrown in prison and eventually hanged. He maintained his integrity to the end, and eventually the attainder was reversed. However, the damage was done ; and for years thereafter he was a kind of symbol politically. Parties formed themselves around the issue, Leislerians *v.* Aristocrats or Jacobites ; and even one of the governors, the Earl of Bellomont, apparently favoured the Leislerians. The episode and its aftermath thus revealed all the elements of political raw material in New York fanned into flame — race, religion, class, opposition to the English government ; and with these prejudices arose also their exploitation and the survival of the accompanying symbols as all-powerful factors, long after their original occasion had ceased to matter. Of such texture was, and is, public opinion.

The eve of the Revolution drew near, and new crosscurrents were felt. By 1765 the rising spirit of nationality had reached and largely dominated the town meetings of New England. Benjamin Franklin in Philadelphia had lashed a laggard municipal spirit into action. By 1770 or soon after, in Annapolis and Philadelphia and other cities, an incipient Americanism was burning halfsocial, half-serious incense at the shrine of St. Tammany, adopted patron saint of the Colonies. The Stamp Act and the Non-Importation Agreements and the Tea Tax crowded out the usual routine matters — not only in New England town meetings, but in spontaneous borough meetings in Elizabeth, in Annapolis, in Wilmington. Lancaster and Norfolk set up their committees of public safety to match those of Boston and Newport. The vague unrest was gathering force, and was finding leaders with much the same skill and political acumen in the cities of the Middle Colonies and the South as in the towns of New England. Local politics and issues were soon to be swept aside in the paramount and inescapable issues of revolt and freedom.

XV

THE QUALITY OF GOVERNMENT

THIS analysis of the issues in public opinion and the psychological and economic factors behind them may leave one somewhat cynical. Any such attempt to probe the factors governing human behaviour inevitably leads to a theoretical impasse — which almost forces an author to take sides in present-day psychological disputes. In the first place, full recognition must be extended to those basic elements which Pareto would call 'residuals' and Allport 'prepotent responses.' One must further acknowledge that the conditioning processes of society have distorted and combined these elements almost out of recognition. There is likewise room, ample room, in the particular approach to psychology tentatively held by the present author for 'freedom of choice,' 'conscious thought,' 'inspired motives,' and other humanistic and theistic concepts. Those who differ with such a point of view will be able to make the necessary allowances. The data at least are designed to be objective, however much the subjective element may have entered into their interpretation. With this introduction or general statement of approach, one may proceed to consider the quality of colonial city government.

Under the general term 'quality,' there is included both the motivation of the officials and the effectiveness of the administration in implementing the decisions made by the responsible authority.

When one treats of the problem of motivation in colonial times, one is concerned primarily with the actual members of the corporation — that is, with the mayor, recorder, aldermen, councillors, in whom ultimate responsibility was vested. This group was so all-powerful, its detailed oversight over such paid employees as there were was so constant, that the attitudes of its members towards their function were far more decisive for good or evil than at the present time, when the motives and ability of the key men of the appointive staff probably are more determinative. This difference represents one of the significant changes of recent decades.

In the first place, it will be recalled that throughout the period the services of these members of the corporation were ordinarily without direct financial remuneration. However, the mayor and the recorder, particularly in the larger towns, did receive certain perquisites in the form of fees. These sometimes amounted to fairly substantial sums.[1] This was most often true in those instances in which the mayor came to be somewhat of an actual administrator as well as a magistrate, and added to his titular position other posts such as clerk of the market or water-bailiff. Over against these fees must be placed the fact that custom decreed certain expenses as attaching themselves to the mayoralty — entertainments, ceremonial dress, contributions, etc. — which usually amounted to more than the fees he might receive. In addition, it must be remembered that for the conscientious these posts involved a very considerable expenditure of time away from their ordinary occupations.

Occasional instances of negligence in duty naturally occurred, as, for example, around 1750 when the mayor of New York was apparently seriously delinquent in his duties as water-bailiff.[2] The grand jury in Charleston

1. e. g. Philadelphia, where in 1748 the salary which had recently been granted the mayor was discontinued, on the ground that 'the business of the mayoralty had grown more profitable' (*Minutes, Common Council*, Oct. 3, 1749).
2. Peterson, A. E., and Edwards, G. W., *New York as an Eighteenth Century Municipality*, p. 225.

(S. C.) presented it as a grievance 'that the Laws for regulating the markets are not properly attended to by the Commissioners, but left principally to the Management of their Clerk.'[3] The deterioration in Annapolis in the early '60's has already been mentioned.[4]

The absence of formal remuneration did not mean that the ulterior-minded, or even those who accepted without question certain prevailing customs and privileges, did not use their office indirectly to enhance their private incomes. The manner in which this could be done will be discussed presently.

Full credit must be given to the strength of the religious motive in certain communities. While the modern version of the 'social gospel' was unknown, and while the emphasis of religion was still predominantly 'otherworldly,' yet the deep sincerity and disinterestedness of many who led these early migrations were reflected in a certain tone pervading the administration of their government. Leaving out of consideration a few of the New England towns, this tone was perhaps more marked in Germantown than in any of the other boroughs. Here especially, as one writer has indeed characterized all of the earlier settlers of Pennsylvania, 'one common principle attracted them to the spot, and that was the desire of religious liberty, the intense longing to escape . . . persecution . . . to which the chief tenet of their faith, non-resistance and submission to the civil authority, prevented them from offering any opposition. They were not of the church militant, like the Puritans and Huguenots and Anabaptists, and so it became them to join the church migratory and seek in uninhabited wilds the freedom of conscience denied them among the communities

3. *South Carolina Gazette,* Feb. 7, 1771.
4. Cf. p. 219.

of men.'[5] At the head of the records of the general court
of Germantown were scriptural quotations, put there by
the leader of the community and its first mayor, Pastorius.
The following will serve by way of illustration :

> There is no power but of God.
> And thou shalt take no gift : for the gift blindeth the
> ways, and perverteth the words of the righteous.
> Ye shall not afflict any widow, or fatherless child.
> Ye shall not respect persons in judgment ; but ye shall
> hear the small as well as the great.
> Take you wise men and understanding, and known
> among your tribes, and I will make them rule over
> you.
> And as ye would that men should do to you, do ye also
> to them likewise.

Elsewhere also the religious motive expressed itself
in a government of great beneficence. It was the inspiration of Oglethorpe in Georgia ; the keynote of
many of the Jersey proprietors, the seal of whose colony
was : Righteousness exalteth a nation. Its God giveth increase.' To cite these instances is not to confuse this
genuine attitude with the nominal adherence to those
creeds and coventionalisms which were the accepted
forms of the day, and which went hand in hand, even
among the clergy, with licentiousness of the person and
the most shameless acceptance of special privilege in
public life.

There was, however, also a very considerable 'carry
over' of the English 'squirearchy' tradition, under which
the county justices were called upon for and rendered an
enormous amount of unpaid service. People had ceased

---

5. Scharf, J. T., and Westcott, T., *History of Philadelphia*, vol. I, p.140.

to ask, if indeed they ever asked, 'Why ?' It was enough in
seventeenth and eighteenth century England and in certain, at least, of the colonial offspring that it was so.[6] It
was both the prerogative and the duty of the landed gentry in England to govern, as much a part of their life on
its political side as its counterpart of economic paternalism was on its agricultural, or the accompanying deference on the social. In Maryland, Virginia, and South
Carolina this English tradition came to be strongly entrenched ; and the governments of Annapolis, Williamsburg, Charleston, and many of the smaller towns were for
many decades conducted on this plane. Of petty graft
there was none ; of entrenched privilege, much — but entirely unconscious as far as motivation was concerned. In
this atmosphere the close corporation was entirely normal — but whatever the type, the same men would doubtless have governed and in the same way. The Annapolis
and Williamsburg corporations included in their membership a number of the influential men of their colonies.[7] For instance, the first mayor of Williamsburg
(Holloway) was also speaker of the house of burgesses
and the treasurer of Virginia. Outside of these three colonies, the same tradition was bound to operate as one of
the influences making for much fairly disinterested service of a high order. Perhaps exceptions should be made
of New York, and of Philadelphia in its later years —
cities where a restless cosmopolitanism militated against

6. The meteoric career of Cromwell and its colonial counterparts may
   be deemed exceptions.
7. Mayors of Williamsburg included John Blair, James Cocke, John Har-
   mer, George Gilmer, John Prentis, John Holt. In Annapolis a Calvert was mayor in 1732 (*South Carolina Gazette,* Feb. 17-24, 1733/4).
   Cf. also Davis, J. S., *Essays in the Earlier History of American Corporations,* vol. I, p. 53 ; Gulick, L., and Pollard, J. G., *Modern Government in a Colonial City,* p. 33.

THE QUALITY OF GOVERNMENT 383

such disinterestedness.[8] Similarly, the relatively primitive pioneer nature of the North Carolina boroughs lowered their tone somewhat, comparatively speaking.[9]

The close corporation of Norfolk was virtually in a class by itself. Here many of the same traditions of the 'governing class' held among its merchants who shared among themselves the government of the city unchecked by any necessity of catering to an electorate. 'The town was a thing apart from the rest of Virginia. Its people were Virginians, it is true, yet they had in many ways more in common with Boston or Philadelphia than with the planters of the James or the York. Although they rivaled the landed aristocracy in wealth, built substantial houses fitted with handsome furniture and costly plate, surrounded themselves with slaves, adhered to the Anglican Church and acquired a certain degree of breadth and culture, there were essential differences. They were first of all practical, keen business men, lacking the taste for political life, the urge for study, and the philosophical view which the plantation system fostered.'[10]

While it may be questioned just how far personal prestige was enhanced by the additional prestige of holding office in the tiny communities in their 'intimate' stage, in the larger ones undoubtedly the honour of position and its consequent deference were strong motives in seeking

8. Cf. *Independent Reflector*, Oct. 4, 1753: 'Our Corporation has for some years past, labour'd under a first-rate Grievance, by the audacious Attempt of some evil disposed Persons to introduce into the Common Council, men of sense and Distinction. Several Gentlemen of this Character, have actually been chosen.'
9. In North Carolina the county justices extorted exorbitant fees, and allowed themselves compensation from public funds for other purposes [Boyd, J. P., *The County Court in Colonial North Carolina, passim* (unpublished thesis, Duke University, 1926)]. Similar studies are needed of other colonies. It is possible that the 'squirearchy tradition' will be found to have been exceedingly lucrative.
10. Wertenbaker, T. J., *Norfolk*, p. 26.

or accepting office. We can sense just a bit of this when we note a New York City newspaper poking fun at the mayor and aldermen of Perth Amboy for 'using big words.'[11] Just how far the tailor who was mayor of Gorgeana responded with appropriate attitudes to the dignity of his 'sergants of ye white Rod,' history does not record ; but the idea back of such dignity was, for the age, and perhaps for any age, essentially sound.[12] 'Such things stand for perhaps the finest thing in British civic life — the feeling that there is a dignity involved and a responsibility as well, when one holds a place of rank in a city corporation.' They should remain — 'in spite of all their undemocratic character, at least till the time comes when democracy itself evolves through education an even higher concept — the simple dignity of being chosen by the people to serve them. Till the time — and that day has not yet arrived in the cities — when democracy shall recognize that there is much that was fine in the old order, all things which serve to enhance, even artificially, the respect with which official position is clothed should remain.'[13]

Over and above the dignity and the deference, what evidence, if any, was there of an essential 'civic-mindedness' springing from a sense of community obligation or from an inner urge to see things done better and more efficiently ? Not a great deal, as yet, for only here and there — most frequently in the larger New England towns

11. *New York Gazette,* Aug. 8, 1763 (quoted in *N. J. Archives,* 1st ser., vol. XXIV, p. 218f.).
12. In the Council Orders — Borough of Norfolk, June 26, 1755, it is recorded that certain persons, who had in derision named a negro slave mayor, were summoned before the mayor's court. The court, having resolved that this was a 'great indignity,' forced the 'criminals' to apologize.
13. Griffith, E. S., *Modern Development of City Government,* London, 1927, 2 vol., vol. II, p. 619f.

— did evidence of this kind of civic spirit crop out. The sense of trusteeship and responsibility for New York's exceedingly valuable water front varied. At times, 'water lots' seem to have been handed out with very little discrimination ; at other times, the common council showed a far-sighted solicitude for the public interest. Their petition of February 19, 1719/20, to the governor's council was a good example of the latter. The city council sought to strengthen the powers of the city over against private individuals who were endeavouring to extend wharves beyond the low-water mark uncontrolled by the city, and otherwise to encroach upon public property. As an example of the tone of the petition a few extracts will serve : 'the Landing and Shipping of Goods, Passing of Carts and Even Persons themselves would depend upon the Caprice of . . . those Proprietors' ; 'the front of this City which already makes a beautiful prospect . . . would be blinded by Warehouses . . . and other Paltry Buildings '; 'the Corporation will have A greater Regard to Common Utility than Private men will.'[14]

New York City also had occasional civic reformers who agitated for the secret ballot, and against the bribery and intimidations and privilege that had fastened themselves upon the municipality.[15] Livingston, through the instrumentality of his *Independent Reflector,* will serve as an example. To one who reads its columns even to-day, it is not surprising that it was suppressed. On the whole, however, the City's merchant-aldermen managed the city business with a fair amount of foresight.

In Albany, the Dutch traders who made up the corporation were intelligently responsive to the rather ele-

14. Petition in Original Records of Common Council ; cf. also *Minutes of Common Council,* vol. III, pp. 221f., 271ff.
15. Cf. p. 210, *supra.*

mentary needs of their community.[16] The small communities of New Jersey, Pennsylvania, and the two Wilmingtons were scarcely large enough to offer scope for much imaginative agitation or service ; but, particularly where the Quakers were in control, they experienced a modest, economical administration of a high order.

It remained for Philadelphia to furnish in the person of Benjamin Franklin perhaps the outstanding *citizen* of the Colonial Era, in the modern sense of the term 'citizen.' Almost from the time of his return from England in 1726, as a young man of twenty, he interested himself in the various functions of municipal administration — always from the standpoint of their greater efficiency. Quickly he attained the prestige of a man to be listened to. In 1748 he was chosen a councillor ; soon after, he was made an alderman.[17] The watch, the condition of the streets, better street lighting, all commanded his interest.

'Penn had founded a Quaker commonwealth. Franklin undertook to divest it of its sectarian garments, to modernize it ; to give it a place in contemporary politics, history, science, and art. He made war on the proprietary government and pulled it down ; he laughed and ridiculed the Quakers into a minority ; he united Quakers, churchmen, and German and Irish settlers in opposition to British pretensions and in sympathy with American ideas and principles. And, without enthusiasm, without ideality, without morality, or great command over or respect from men, he made Pennsylvania the foremost

16. Cf. Howell, G. R., and Tenney, J. (Edit.), *History of the County of Albany*, p. 465.
17. *Minutes of Common Council*, 1748-1755, *passim*. The truth of the matter is that, while he attended quite regularly as a councillor, after his election as an alderman his attendance was negligible at the common council. As a magistrate he may have been more regular.

American colony . . . by being himself the best public business man that ever lived.'[18]

He was also an excellent practical politician, allying himself at first with the artisans, building up a following, joining and using various social and literary clubs as sounding boards for his ideas. Perhaps his first instrument was the 'Junto,' which was originally formed for discussions 'on any point of morals, politics, or natural philosophy.'[19] It was a secret society of twelve members, but gave birth to five or six satellite clubs. Between them, they furnished an effective medium for discussion and agitation of Franklin's ideas. He was instrumental in the organization of a volunteer fire company, soon itself to become a political force to be reckoned with. In other words, he had an intuitive sense of the manner in which public opinion was formed ; he saw in a complex, heterogeneous city like Philadelphia, where the 'mass v. class' cleavage had appeared, that the old tradition of a governing class was not adequate to a situation in which the continuation of the tradition itself was perhaps the main political issue. New ways, new channels of expression, must be devised for civic progress — and if the close corporation could not alone serve as the vehicle, then resort must be had to the assembly, the grand jury, the special commission, and through them also must the needs of the city be served.

(B)

The old school book histories of colonial times would

18. Scharf and Westcott, op. cit., vol. I, p. 228. Cf. also Bruce, W. C., *Benjamin Franklin Self-Revealed*, New York, 1917, 2 vol. ; Morse, J. T., Jr., *Benjamin Franklin ; Autobiography of Benjamin Franklin.* Scharf has probably somewhat overstated Franklin's contribution.

19. *Autobiography of Benjamin Franklin,* (Bigelow, J., Edit.), pp. 150ff., 211f.

doubtless have ended the discussion of motivation at this point, but the complete picture of the colonial municipality must perforce include other and less pleasant factors. Chief among these were special privilege and vested interest. Of course, in most colonies, the boroughs formed a relatively minor aspect of the entire social and political situation in which certain customs — now seen to be essentially unfair and undemocratic — were accepted as part of the current folkways and mores. The privileged position of church membership in New England before 1692 and in certain other colonies ; a franchise restricted to property owners ; taxation and assessment systems introduced at the behest of a landed aristocracy entrenched in county courts and assemblies ; tithes and quit rents having their origin in proprietary grants of territory which were filched or purchased at nominal sums from the Indians after their award to royal favourites in another continent ; the whole court tradition of prerogative reflected in the position, patronage, and spoils associated with the office of governor and council — these and other like attitudes must be understood before their relatively trivial counterparts in the cities are appreciated. The appointment of a friend or relative to a position to-day is called 'spoils' or 'nepotism.' It was a recognized prerogative of office to a colonial governor. Contributions to political campaign funds to obtain favours in tariffs or taxation are called bribery to-day by many ; in colonial times the landed or the merchant classes preempted the municipal, county, and colonial offices and arranged the taxation and assessment to suit themselves. To-day we call certain appropriations a 'pork-barrel' ; in colonial times the incorporation of favoured spots as 'port towns' or the granting of borough charters was forthcoming in order to enhance the value of the land of the interested parties — and it was deemed desirable that this should be so.[20]

Only an occasional and belated voice was raised to question the easy sale of water lots by the New York City corporation to individual aldermen or their relatives,[21] or the award of printing contracts to partisans of the dominant faction.[22] The members of the close corporation of Philadelphia probably worked themselves around to a subconscious identification of the property they managed with the right to use it for their own ends — all the more so as their own tenure rested on no democratic base. It seemed 'right' to rent to themselves the wharves and market stalls, for they were the ones giving unpaid service to the management thereof. In most cities where the minutes survive, contracts were frequently let to certain of the council members, a practice which to-day would be deemed intolerable. If an innkeeper happened to be a member, perhaps the 'entertainment' would be ordered from him : market concessions, repair jobs, purchase of a fire engine, construction of a new market house, erection of a prison — all were frequently allocated to an alderman or councillor.[23] The Albany corporation was notorious in the utilization of its privileged position to enhance the profits of its trader group over against the relative *naïveté* of the Indians ; and only when it seemed wise from a military standpoint to placate the latter was

20. Cf. Griffith, T. W., *Annals of Baltimore*, p. 12 ; Riddle, W., *The Story of Lancaster*, p. 19 ; for Chester, cf. Ashmead, H. G., *Historical Sketch of Chester*, Chester, 1883, p. 22f.
21. *Independent Reflector*, Feb. 1, 1753 ; Peterson and Edwards, op. cit., p. 351.
22. Ibid. p. 391.
23. e. g. Norfolk prison (Council Orders — Norfolk Borough, Mar. 19, 1753) ; Philadelphia, *Minutes of Common Council*, Dec. 8, 1718 ; etc.

real justice usually done.[24] In Rhode Island for years the power of the landowners was sufficient to secure the total exemption of unimproved land from taxation, and thereafter its assessment was at a mere fraction of its value.[25] It is interesting to note in the *South Carolina Gazette* of April 19-26, 1740, the following : 'The Firemasters for Charles-Town hereby give notice that on Monday, the 5th of May next they intend to go about and examine the Inhabitants of the said Town, how they are provided with Buckets and Ladders. (N.B. Buckets to be had of John Laurens, Saddler).' Without attaching too much significance to the fact, it may be noted in passing that John Laurens was one of the firemasters. In Virginia and Maryland and the South generally, it was probably an unconscious expression of the same thing that made the polltax — not the property tax — the sheet anchor of the revenue system. In all fairness, however, it must be admitted that ease of collection was partly responsible for this ; and that a slave-owning aristocracy which had been anxious to dodge taxation could have devised a number of ways to lessen its burden other than what was virtually a tax on the number of its employees.

Yet the assumptions of special privilege in any given age must never be judged too harshly. Challenged they should and must be, but not in the mood of exorcising a personal devil. After all, these Virginia landowners and New York merchants took life more or less as they found

24. Cf. p. 329f. 'The Indians . . . Will on no occasion trust an Albany man . . . The Richest men among the Indian Traders are not in the least ashamed in having the basest cheating of the Indians discovered and this so far prevails that it has almost entirely destroy'd the morals of that part of the country so that they are become a proverb in other parts of the Country . . . No man has any confidence in an Albany Jury.' (*Cadwallader Colden Papers*, vol. II, p. 260f., *Coll. N. Y. Hist. Soc.*).

25. Cf. p. 318.

it, and must be credited at least with a conspicuous absence of deviations below the level of accepted custom, and with a very real amount of relatively unrequited service under the impetus of a sense of obligation which those who never feel it can never appreciate.

It must not be thought that corruption, even in the parlance of the time, was totally absent. Of outright peculation there appears to have been little, in spite of the almost total lack of effective auditing. Mayor Fishbourne of Philadelphia, who had already been the recipient of certain of the heretofore mentioned special favours, was, in 1731, found to be £2,000 short in the public funds which he was handling.[26] He alleged robbery, but was made ineligible to hold any further office. Two or three of the other members of the Philadelphia corporation who had been entrusted with the custody of certain monies or who had been given certain posts with attendant revenues had procrastinated so much with their accounting that the corporation had to sue their estates after their decease. In certain instances there may have been a real question as to whether the amounts might not have been legitimate fees.[27] In the grand jury presentments in Annapolis of March 7, 1766, complaints of misappropriation of lottery proceeds were lodged against the city corporation, but, judging by the published reply, were of at least doubtful validity. Apparently, however, this almost 'close' corporation had become lax in a number of ways — irregular attendance, obscurantism, failure to enforce by-laws, etc.[28] Some of the collectors in New

26. Scharf and Westcott, op. cit., vol. I, p. 205.
27. *Minutes of the Common Council*, Aug. 3, 1747. The sheriffs were the worst offenders ; but Thomas Griffiths, who withheld the subscription money for the fire engines, was among the 'defaulters.'
28. Cf. p. 219. *Maryland Gazette*, Mar. 13, 20, May 1, June 19, 1766. Personal venom was at least one factor in the accusations.

York after 1683 were found untrustworthy, but these were minor officials.[29] The *Independent Reflector* in its meteoric career in New York alleged a considerable number of abuses. Among these, the profits to the surveyor from the 2s. 6d. commutation fees were especially noteworthy as marking a decadence from the old householder obligation to work on the roads. Twice a year these fees (or the equivalent work) were due, and 4,000 people were under obligation to pay them.[30] The grand jury presentments in Charleston (S. C.) in 1772 advanced as grievances that the constables 'being in the execution of Persons of a mean low Character, whose poverty and ignorance subject them to take Bribes ; by which Villains do often escape justice ;' also the disorderly behaviour of the town watch, 'who beat and abuse Negroes sent on errands except those who can raise 10 shillings.'[31] The constables in New York City also abused their office at times. For example, in 1736, it is recorded that almost half of them were retailers of liquor, with results that may be imagined.[32] There were doubtless a number of other instances, particularly among the minor officials, both discovered and undiscovered ; but, among the major city officials, the doubtful instances of Mayor Fishbourne and one or two other Philadelphians were the only examples of theft in colonial times that I have happened upon.[33]

What did become regrettably prevalent in Philadelphia and New York particularly were widespread bribery

29. Schwab, J. C., *History of the New York Property Tax*, p. 54.
30. *Independent Reflector*, Dec. 14, 1752.
31. *South Carolina Gazette*, Jan. 25, 1772.
32. *N. Y. Weekly Journal*, Aug. 23, 1736.
33. It may be that the sheriffs were also occasional offenders. Their laxity at least in North Carolina counties was notorious. Cf. Boyd, Julian, *County Court in Colonial North Carolina* (unpublished thesis, Library of Duke University), pp. 121, 139, etc.

and fraud in connection with voting. In the preamble of the Pennsylvania Act of 1752 relating to corrupt practices in the election of sheriffs and coroners, one reads that it is 'too frequently their practice to engage persons to vote for them by giving them strong drink and using other means inconsistent with the design of voting freely at elections, by means whereof many unguarded persons are unwarily drawn in to engage their votes and rendered incapable of discharging their duty in that sober and weighty manner the occasion requires.'[34] A similar and perhaps worse state of affairs ruled in New York City. In the *Gazette*, February 15, 1768, there was a letter from a citizen to the effect that in a street in the West Ward a large and noisy crowd had collected at a small inn. There 'a dramshop was opened, and that every Freeholder or Freeman who was willing to part with his vote, might there meet with a purchaser.'[35] Complaints of widespread bribery by money as well as 'by the custom of intoxication' had begun at least as early as 1753.[36] By 1771, the complaints and abuses had become so numerous that substantial electoral reforms were introduced. The aldermen were no longer to be the returning officers for their respective wards; checks were established on repeating and false registration.[37] There had doubtless been some such practice even earlier — but more in connection with the elections to the assembly than to the city council. Perhaps the most conspicuous instance was that in which Governor Fletcher was alleged to have secured an assembly favourable to himself, in part by making a large num-

34. Quoted in Scharf and Westcott, op. cit., vol. I, p. 245f.
35. Quoted in Peterson and Edwards, op. cit., p. 248.
36. *Independent Reflector*, July 5, 1753. Cf. also Peterson and Edwards, op. cit., p. 249.
37. Ibid. pp. 244, 251.

ber of transient sailors 'freemen,' and then voting them for his candidates. During the whole Fletcher and Cornbury regimes the tone of public life was at a low level, set there by the example of the governors themselves.[38] That such devious ways were not unknown in smaller communities also may be judged from the allegations in Lancaster County (Pa.) in 1749, when it was claimed that more than double the number of votes were recorded than were actually voted.[39] Occasionally snap elections were alleged, made possible by the custom of *viva voce* voting ; and, in periods and situations in which the issues heretofore mentioned were strongly felt, such elections were doubtless rationalized by the perpetrators.[40]

Yet, when all is said, the verdict is unmistakable that for the most part municipal office was sufficiently attractive to induce the leading citizens to 'stand' (n.b. not 'run') for office where election was popular, and to accept it when it was the outgrowth of appointment or co-option. This applied equally to the Southern aristocracy and to the merchants of the port cities ; and was naturally most conspicuous in the office of mayor. Only in Philadelphia does there appear to have been any real difficulty in inducing men to accept this particular office ; and in Germantown with respect to the offices generally.[41]

38. Cf. p. 131 ; also O'Callaghan, E. B. (Edit.), *Documents Relative to the Colonial History of the State of New York*, vol. IV, pp. 128, 223, 323. For a somewhat more favourable estimate of the Fletcher regime, cf. Fox, D. R., *Caleb Heathcote*.

39. Eshleman, H. F., *Political History of Lancaster County's First Twenty Years*, in *Lancs. Co. Hist. Soc. Papers*, vol. XX, pp. 58ff., 67f.

40. e. g. New Brunswick, 1749 (*New Jersey Archives*, 1st ser., vol. XII, pp. 529ff.) ; Philadelphia, 1705 (Scharf and Westcott, op. cit., vol. I, p. 246).

41. For Germantown, cf. p. 433. The annoyance arising from the interference by the county in borough affairs may have been a factor. In Philadelphia, the first two mayors were (1691) Humphrey Morrey, a very wealthy man, and (1701) Edward Shippen, the president

The prestige involved, the deference attending it, the relative freedom from red tape that permitted accomplishments of considerable magnitude for the times, the tradition that it was the duty and the prerogative of their class to govern, and a not inconsiderable religious and civic motivation were ample, without too carping a search for perquisites or profitable privileges, to account for the cities' attracting to the higher offices the same substantial type which served the colony as a whole.[42]

This was in some ways the more remarkable because the population was notorious for its undisciplined elements. In Philadelphia in 1744 Scharf claims that about one building or house in every ten was an agency to sell liquor.[43] In New York City in 1772 there was one retail liquor outlet for every fifty-five inhabitants.[44] In Albany in 1706 there were forty-seven retailers of liquor, or about one to every twenty-five of the total population.[45] Governor Dongan described the people of New York City in 1689 as 'in short of all sorts of opinions there are some, and the most part of none at all.'[46] Riots in Philadelphia

of the council of the colony. After the corporation passed out of the control of the proprietor's party and again in the 1740's when the expense of the office had mounted greatly, it became more difficult to find suitable men who would accept the office. Cf. also Biddle, H. D., 'Colonial Mayors of Philadelphia,' in *Penn. Mag. of Hist.*, vol. XIX, var.

42. In writing this the author is conscious of one exceedingly important gap in the evidence. This is found in the absence of a study in detail of the cases tried before the city officials in their capacity of magistrates. It may be that such a study would show a misuse of power to safeguard vested interests or to grant immunities.

43. Scharf and Westcott, op. cit., vol. I, p. 211.

44. Peterson and Edwards, op. cit. p. 270.

45. Munsell, J., *Annals of Albany*, vol. V, pp. 130, 142.

46. Quoted in Gerard, J. W., 'Dongan Charter to the City of New York,' in *Mag. of Amer. Hist.*, vol. XVI, p. 35.

and Perth Amboy ;[47] canards resulting in a kind of mob rule as in the so-called 'negro conspiracy' in New York City in 1741 ;[48] smuggling ; a widespread disregard of any and all regulations and ordinances — were characteristic expressions of the unregenerate masses of the larger towns, and of many of the smaller ones.[49] The prevalence of serious crime characterized the Chester area as early as 1690.[50] Wilmington (Del.) is recorded as having sought incorporation in part because of the lawlessness of the transient seamen.[51] The Earl of Bellomont, admittedly a hostile critic, in characterizing the inhabitants of the borough of Westchester alleged that 'the major part . . . are felons upon record.'[52] Even in Virginia many of the earlier inhabitants were a lawless and independent lot, and created numerous difficulties for the early incorporations.[53] The trials to which the officials in that most placid community of Germantown were sometimes subjected can be appreciated by the following minute :

> Daniel Falkner coming into this court behaved himself very ill, like one that was last night drunk . . . The sheriff . . . telling him that he would not do so at Philadelphia, the said Falkner himself, answered, no, not for a hundred pounds ; and after abundance of foul language, when the Court bid the said Sheriff and the Constable bring him out, he went himself, crying you are all fools.[54]

47. Cf. p. 287.
48. Peterson and Edwards, op. cit. p. 315f.
49. Cf. pp. 261, 274.
50. Smith, G., *History of Delaware County*, Philadelphia, 1862, p. 179.
51. Scharf, J. T., *History of Delaware*, vol. II, p. 636.
52. Report to the Lords Commissioners for Trade, etc. (1698), in O'Callaghan, op. cit., vol. IV, p. 427.
53. Cf. p. 93.
54. *Hist. Soc. of Penn. Coll.*, vol. I, p. 256. On the other hand, there seems to have been a total absence of any serious crime during

It was almost of the ethics of the day to cheat strangers, particularly Indians, and to utilize the community trade powers to enforce monopolies against 'foreigners.'[55] The numerous ordinances and by-laws, by their very frequency and nature, illuminate the relatively low standards prevalent in ordinary trade, just as the story of other functions carried the conviction of widespread looseness and inefficiency.[56]

Yet in spite of all this, the 'tone' of the city administrations, whether at the 'intimate' or later stage of development, probably was higher than the commercial practice of the day. These administrations represented the attempt by the better element, not only to provide services, but also to establish some social standards of behaviour that would represent a distinct advance over the standards set by the majority of the individuals for themselves. Whether as much can be said of American cities in their later evolution is doubtful.

In the interest of completeness, it is worth while closing this discussion of the 'tone' of the communities with a quotation concerning New Haven. Unquestionably the quality of the population and the continuous exercise of the powers of self-government carried the civic sense of the average New England town, even the larger ones, higher than that prevailing among the rank and file in the Middle Colonies :

Organized action and organized responsibility and individual subordination were the keynote in colonial New Haven. This organized type of life expressed itself

the fifteen years of Germantown's corporate existence (Pennypacker, S. W., 'Settlement of Germantown,' in *Penn.-German Soc. Proc.,* vol. IX, *passim*).
55. Cf. pp. 133ff.
56. Cf. p. 290f.

in many ways ; there were the church communion and the ecclesiastical society, the freemen's meetings, those of the proprietors, those of the train bands (i.e., militia) and perhaps the most important of all, the periodic gatherings of the inhabitants of the town. An examination of each of those forms of social expression will show how necessarily submerged was the individuality of the average townsman and yet, on the other hand, how thorough was the schooling he received in serving public affairs as a mere instrument of community action.[57]

(C)

It is exceedingly difficult to know what criteria to apply in any discussion of the 'effectiveness' of the cities' functional provisions. If one were examining a modern city it would be relatively easy to discover the correct approach. To-day, administrative and financial practice have developed their norms ; functions have for the most part reached the stage at which objective measurement is possible within reasonable limits. It is easy enough to point to the accounting methods of colonial cities and call them inexcusably primitive ; or to comment upon the appalling inefficiency of the unpaid watch, or the dirty and disorderly streets. Yet this is not fair to the period, particularly as it leaves out many of the compensatory imponderables, such for instance as the amount of voluntary service, which helped make up the complete picture.

The administration of even the larger cities was or should have been a relatively simple problem — the functions were few and uncomplicated, the numbers to be dealt with, small. Yet public administration, even of

57. Gipson, L. H., *Jared Ingersoll*, p. 16.

simple situations, was a science not only undeveloped but unknown ; and in the light of this fact one must not judge too harshly practices and performances which to-day even the most corrupt of our cities would deem inexcusable.

In the first place, it must be appreciated that economy was the cardinal consideration in a period in which money was generally all too scarce. The inefficiency of 'service' taxes in road building at least left no one 'out of pocket' ; and much could and would be forgiven for this reason. The known standards of paving and hygienic cleaning of the streets were pitifully low even for a paid staff, in part because the householders themselves were not educated to the importance of the needful co-operation. Probably the corporations were ahead of, rather than behind, the majority of the inhabitants in this respect.

In the matter of concentration of responsibility, the majority of these colonial municipalities would, by any criterion, rate considerably higher than would be true of the majority of our present-day American cities. The council or court was all powerful — legislatively, administratively, and judicially. The electorate voted for council members ; the remaining officials were appointed by the council — simplicity itself. The complications of the Philadelphia local government were exceptional ; and the theoretically irresponsible close corporations were in a minority. A few of the smaller boroughs continued the town meeting practice of electing a multitude of minor officers, but these towns were so small as to make the intimate nature of the procedure a substitute for sounder administrative practice. Under the circumstances of concentrated responsibility and with an electorate primarily property-holding, an economical administration with a high standard of integrity might be expected and was ordinarily attained.

In a simple sort of way, a certain amount of 'integration' of functions occasionally took place. Mention has already been made of this in connection with the grouping of functions under certain boards, notably in Charleston and Philadelphia.[58] It was a rough and ready grouping — watch with street lighting, and paving with street cleaning ; but it served. However, this grouping was under 'boards' and there was little or no unification of control at the top. New York City adopted the doubtful expedient of making each alderman responsible for the majority of services in his particular ward.

There appears to have been no one method followed in the recruiting of the petty administrative officials. The data are not available to uncover the motives leading to particular appointments, and presumably a certain amount of favouritism entered in. This was more likely to have been eleemosynary than partisan in its nature. The original records of the New York City common council are full of petitions from individuals to be appointed to this job or that, with the arguments about evenly divided between the applicant's qualifications and his need. One applicant for keeper of the Bridewell points to his many years' experience as inmate thereof (as a debtor) as a qualification. He adds that he has a family consisting of a wife and eight small children 'and has nothing for their Support . . . but the Priviledge of Selling Liquor in Gaol, the Sale of which, at present, is so very Small.' He had also served as turnkey to the gaol.[59] Williamsburg was perhaps exceptional, in that it gave

58. Cf. pp. 249, 252ff.
59. MS., Petition of John Cox, Aug. 10, 1769, Original Records of Common Council.

notice through the columns of the *Virginia Gazette* that it proposed to appoint a watch 'of four sober and discreet persons' and applicants who answered the description were to 'give in their Names, with the necessary Certificates, to the Mayor, to be laid before the Common Hall' at its next meeting.[60] Here and there the election of the rank and file of administrative officials warrants theoretical criticism as being unsound practice ; but with civil service examinations unknown, perhaps the opinion of the general run of townsmen brought a result not too inefficient.

On one count, these colonial cities would stand high under any modern standard that emphasized security of tenure of appointive officials or continuity of service on the part of those elected. These factors made for continuity of policy, lessened materially the chances of peculation and in general added to the satisfactions and dignity attached to office holding. Perhaps the record in the larger towns was attained by William Sharpas, who served as city clerk for New York continuously from 1692 to 1739. Where the aldermen were selected by and from the councillors or assistants, the tenure was usually during 'good behaviour' or was automatically followed by repeated re-elections as long as the incumbent desired the office. Major overturns took place only twice in Philadelphia (1704, 1744) and only once in New York City (1734).[61] In New York City the average tenure for an assistant was four years ; for an alderman, seven years.[62] As opposition was infrequent, retirement was usually voluntary. In a fairly typical small borough, Wilmington (Del.), be-

60. *Virginia Gazette,* July 16, 1772.
61. Cf. p. 366f.
62. Peterson, A. E., and Edwards, G. W., *New York as an Eighteenth Century Municipality,* p. 249f.

tween 1740 and 1775, ten men served a total of fifty-eight
of the theoretically possible seventy years of service as
chief and second burgess. Many of these ten and of the
other burgesses also had records of service as assistants.[63]
In Albany, where the mayors were appointed by the governor, there were twenty-six in all between 1688-1770.
Peter Schuyler and Edward Holland held the office for
eight years each. Of the twenty-six, there were five Schuy-
lers, three Bleeckers, three Cuylers.[64]

Even in comparison with the notoriously lax conditions
of the present day, the actual enforcement of the various
by-laws and ordinances was ridiculously ineffective. Close
study of the minutes of a number of cities has led the
author to believe that probably the majority of the by-
laws in the majority of the towns were virtually unen-
forced after a year or two, except for occasional revivals.
Refuse was dumped in the streets in spite of by-laws ; price
'rackets' were ancient as well as modern ; chimneys continued to 'fire' and hogs to root ; the watch would drink
and not watch. Enforcement of law in the United States
has never, not even in the idealized colonial period, had
about it the quality of inexorableness that constitutes a
large part of its effectiveness in present-day England. The
pioneer, ultra-individualist tradition was bred into the
fibre of the nation in colonial times by the motives of the
immigrant colonists and their manner of living upon arrival. Part of the difficulty arose in the early stages from
the intimate nature of communal life. It was socially and
pychologically difficult to arrest your neighbour, or to
seize and impound his rooting hog. Later on, when the
population of the coast cities increased, the franchise was

63. Scharf, J. T., History of Delaware, vol. II, p. 637.
64. Howell, G. R., and Tenney, J. (Edit.), History of the County of
    Albany, p. 657.

not extended to the majority ; no training was theirs in the assumption of the responsibilities of citizenship ; the deference and respect for the law and its officers, if it had ever existed in their old country, eventually crumbled in the new ; fear, which might have been an efficient substitute, was lacking for the unpaid or ill-paid watch and constables with whom the need for economy had forced the community to content itself.

Financial controls on the whole were not needed, so strong were the forces on the side of economy and so effective the inner sanctions of conscience. An exception should perhaps be made in the case of the almost unbelievable procrastination, both as to paying to the city what was owed, and as to the city's paying its bills. Treasurers might conceivably turn over their funds two or three years late. Committees to audit accounts would report after three or four years. Frequently an individual would wait one or more years for his wages or the amount due him on a contract — and apparently not worry much about it.[65] Practices such as in Philadelphia, whereby the overseers were paid a percentage of their total expenditure, were as unusual as they were indefensible.[66] Some elementary reforms in financial procedure found their way into the accounting of the larger cities towards the end of the period, but they would have been totally inadequate had not the average administrator been honest ac-

---

65. Cf. p. 296. Philadelphia was a chief offender (*Minutes of Common Council*, Oct. 12, 1730 ; Nov. 25, 1734 ; Nov. 11, 1745 ; Aug. 3, 1747, etc.). Cf. also the Minutes of Annapolis, 1765, 1766, *passim* ; Norfolk, Sept. 5, 1766 (failure of mayor to take bond from a tax collector who subsequently defaulted), also Feb. 14, 1770. Seven years after Annapolis held a lottery the balance of over £100 still remained in private hands, until the grand jury goaded the corporation into action, at which time the custodian said that the city might have the money if 'called for as desired.' (*Maryland Gazette*, May 8, 1766.)

66. Cf. p. 296f.

cording to his lights. This same statement cannot be made as regards the elections, where abuses were all too prevalent.

Newport appears to have been exceptional in that in 1774 it advertised for *sealed bids* for the construction of a new market house.[67] However, competitive bidding as such was not infrequent in the latter part of the period. The street commissioners of Charleston in advertising for written bids for paving the footways also included the proviso : 'such owners . . . as chuse to lay pavements at their own expence will be at liberty to execute the same, under the inspection of the commissions.'[68] A good illustration, both of the current practice in letting contracts and of the policy of entrusting such matters to a special committee, may be found in the following notice which appeared in the *Virginia Gazette* of March 23, 1769 :

Williamsburg

The COMMON HALL having this day determined to build a commodious BRICK COURT-HOUSE, in this City, and having appointed us to agree with an undertaker to build the same ; we do hereby give notice that we will meet at Mr. Hay's on Tuesday the 4th of April, to let the building thereof. We are also appointed to dispose of the present Court-House and the ground on which the same stands.

JAMES COCKE
JAMES CARTER
JOHN CARTER
JOHN TAZEWELL

N. B. The plan of the above Court-House may be seen at Mr. Hay's at any time.

67. *Newport Mercury*, Jan. 31, 1774.
68. *South Carolina Gazette*, Oct. 29, 1764.

Over against the picture of relative inefficiency and failure in implementation must be put the nature and extent of voluntary service. In some communities virtually every freeholder took some part or other, without pay, in municipal activity — serving in the watch, on the roads, or in some petty office. At the upper level, the members of the city council were giving of their services, not for pay, but for other rewards and satisfactions, intangible as well as tangible. This was *local self-government* in the truest sense ; and, among the imponderables making for a responsible citizenry, it must rank high — so high, as to compensate in the mind of all but a martinet for much of the laxity and ineffectiveness with which such voluntary service was necessarily associated.

(D)

When one attempts to summarize the quality of city government in colonial days, it is apparent in the first place that the reality is something quite other than the idealized picture cherished by a certain brand of patriot and expounded from the platforms of certain societies genealogical in their interests. Where the spirit of public service did function, it was usually in a social *milieu* where special privilege was so prevalent that it would not knowingly be tolerated for a moment by any state or community in the modern United States. The English traditions of a governing class and of the spirit of public service were interlocked inextricably ; and, where one weakened, so also did the other — in America as well as in England. Only in the intimacy of the smaller communities, where the religious factor was strong, or under the exceptional stimulus of a Franklin, did a cosmopolitan community as yet evolve a spirit of public service which was divorced from social status. That achievement remained for a more modern and much maligned age. Corruption in the ballot and utilization of public position for personal gain had already tarnished New York and Philadelphia, at a time when greater issues and greater sacrifices were to challenge these more and more Americanized cities.

XVI

A SURVEY OF TRENDS AND CHANGES

HITHERTO, the present work has assumed the form more of a study of various aspects of the period than of its chronological history. The reason for this has been fairly obvious. The changes resulting from the growth in numbers on the whole were much more significant than those changes that were the outgrowth of new and altered ideas. The tempo of the age was such that there were fewer differences between either of the Wilmingtons in 1760 and New York in 1686 than between New York in 1760 and any of the many small towns of the same date. Developments were primarily functions of size rather than of the time element.

However, if the divisions adopted be not too minute, there is also significance in a recapitulation of these time trends, and such a survey will now be attempted. Broadly speaking, a pattern does appear, which is the product of changing ideas as well as of growth in size.

The story of American city government opens with 'paper' cities — Raleigh, Bermuda, James, and the rest. Expressed somewhat differently, the American city had its beginning in the imagination of those who undertook to settle a new land. The incorporations predated the settlements ; and originated in the proprietor's experience of what went to make up a civilized and prosperous state. Agriculturally, the method of tenure might have been conceived of as manorial (as in Maryland), or as of small holdings (as in Virginia) ; but port cities there had to be in either circumstance, with artisans and merchants and all the wealth that commerce could bring. For many decades — in fact at least until 1700 — this concept dominated municipal development outside of New England,

and Maine in New England. Assemblies and royal governors as well as proprietors vied with each other in establishing port towns, and in efforts to attract and keep an artisan and merchant class. Interest in customs revenues and in profits from landowning augmented the motivating forces.

Two other streams of urban development ran parallel to this. In the middle of the first half of the seventeenth century the Dutch also sent their people — a trading rather than a colonizing people at first, but gradually expanding to include colonizing groups of their own and other races. Drawing their inspiration from the vigour and prosperity and form of government of Amsterdam, they transplanted their municipal institutions to the new land — their schout, schepens, and burgomasters; their custom of double nomination; their burgher right. Their spirit was destined to survive their institutions.

Even earlier, the New England colonies were settled by a hardheaded independent people, deeply religious, to some extent democratically inclined in their church and communal life; and the 'town meeting' was the result. This institution influenced municipal development wherever New Englanders went — Long Island, New Jersey, and westward. Such a spread of the town meeting undoubtedly also checked the growth of *representative* self-government as expressed by a borough charter, while at the same time it stimulated its more direct counterpart. Devotion to the town meeting was responsible for the hybrid forms in Elizabeth, New Brunswick, Wilmington (Del.), and Wilmington (N. C.), in which borough and town forms joined — a borough 'court' of mayor and aldermen and a town meeting of the qualified inhabitants. In New England itself, loyalty to the town meeting was to be the decisive factor in a retarded development of municipal forms ; and the town meeting ideal was so powerful and so favoured by the Massachusetts overlords that it soon swept away the incipient city of Gorgeana and made it into the ordinary town of York.

Paralleling the general move on the part of the Colonies to create numerous port cities and towns, and outlasting it, was the attempt on the part of most of them to make at least their capital a true 'metropolis.' By implication a metropolis must be the seat of the government ; it must also be incorporated, with all the superior dignity of a city. To some extent care must be spent upon its planning, and its growth fostered. Perth Amboy, Burlington, Philadelphia, St. Mary's, Annapolis, Williamsburg — all were expressions of this motive ; and a similar fostering care, if not incorporation, was extended to Charleston and Savannah.

With the arrival of William Penn a new and powerful influence in the direction of urbanization appeared. His interest was not so much in the special privileges and revenues of favoured towns, but in the urban way of life — its aid to religion and education as well as its attendant prosperity. Because this attitude was coupled with liberal terms for settlement, and was aided by natural geographic conditions more favourable to urban development than in the provinces to the south, Philadelphia grew to be the largest city of the Colonies, and numerous other smaller communities sprang up in Pennsylvania and Delaware to attain at least an embryonic municipal life.

If one may speak in the broadest of generalizations, the desire to control and develop trade and craftsmanship was the strongest among the earlier motives of incorporation, and played perhaps the largest part in early city life. To exercise the staple right ; to attract the countryside to its markets and fairs ; to draw the attendant revenues ; to organize artisans into craft guilds ; to control the assizes of bread, lumber, meat ; to try violations of these and other regulations in one's own courts — these were the privileges that made up the bulk of the hold of incorporation on the imagination.

Other forces were operating also, forces destined to break down the paternalism of the proprietary forms in colony after colony. In almost all the proprietary colonies, the popular assemblies soon found themselves at variance with the aims of the proprietors. The psychology of an independent way of life, the resentment at any restraints, the economic drives which expressed themselves in resistance to quit rents, in smuggling and other means of dodging the 'perquisites' of proprietorship, the unwillingness to co-operate in a position of inferiority with an overlord, however benevolent — all these combined with other factors to bring down one after another of the proprietors ; and the government of a royal province followed. Virginia (1624), New York (1685), Maryland (1692), New Jersey (1702), South Carolina (1720),[1] North Carolina (1729), Georgia (1752), for one reason or another, forsook the proprietary type for the royal. Maine, 1652, signed its submission to Massachusetts. This left only Pennsylvania and Delaware under the old form, with Maryland also later reverting to its original status. Such changes were fatal to many of the incipient cities. The early Virginia incorporations became merely the orthodox counties. St. Mary's passed into oblivion, the incorporations of Burlington and Salem languished, Gorgeana became the

1. For the South and North Carolina dates, cf. Andrews, C. M., *Colonial Period of American History*, vol. III, New Haven, 1937, pp. 246, 266.

town of York ; and the grandiose paper constitution of John Locke and the South Carolina Palatine with its idealized 'cities' remained in the realm of political theory where it had started. It was not these surface changes in ephemeral cities that were the most significant ; rather it was the changing spirit which gave evidence that the Americans were thinking their own thoughts, and ultimately would go their own way — in spite of paternalistic proprietors or even the relatively light yoke of a British king.

The taking over of New Netherland was but one factor in a growing heterogeneity which was to reflect itself in the character of urban life. The Scotch-Irish were coming in great numbers, particularly to Virginia and southward. The French Huguenots formed an appreciable element in the population of New York and Charleston ; Swiss settled in New Bern and along the Georgia-South Carolina border. Pennsylvania welcomed to its lands and towns large numbers of Germans, Welsh, Irish, Swedes, Moravians, and Jews, all of whom contributed to what was for the age a polyglot population. Estimates are notoriously inaccurate and difficult to frame ; but it is probable that more than a quarter of the white population were non-English in New York, Pennsylvania, Delaware, Virginia, North Carolina, South Carolina, Georgia, and possibly New Jersey. While the initial result of such admixture might be intolerance, the ultimate effect was inevitably a broad cosmopolitanism which reached its climax in New York and Philadelphia.

This 'watering down' of the original small homogeneous groups meant a corresponding dilution of the powerful religious influence. Outside the sway of the Congregational, Dutch Reformed, and Anglican churches were unassimilated elements that remained relatively immune to the influence of any church, that made the enforcement of Sabbath legislation difficult, and that ultimately weakened seriously the union of religious and educational effort which had led in New England, New Netherland, Pennsylvania, and Virginia to the early foundation and fostering of schools.

With the growing population and the decline and fall of proprietary government came a change in the motivation of municipal incorporation. Instead of its being customary to foster such incorporation from above, it became more usual for the motivating force to be the expression of a natural growth of sentiment among the inhabitants themselves. From about 1710 on, the majority of the incorporations were of this type — more normal, more genuine, less ephemeral. The New Jersey towns, Bristol, Lancaster, Wilmington (Del.), Norfolk, the abortive attempt of Charleston, Wilmington (N. C.), — all belong more or less in this category, and represent a change from the fostered and impracticable earlier attempts at general development on the part of Virginia and Maryland.

Incorporation was at its height in these years ; and instead of such clauses as that of the Agamenticus charter which cited Bristol (England) as its model, or that of Westchester, instancing East Greenwich as the basis of its land tenure, the charters assumed a simpler form — one might almost say a more 'American' one. Schenectady copied and improved upon Westchester ; Pennsylvania and Delaware developed a 'borough type' ; the New Jersey towns consciously modelled their charters on their own and other American forms. Charleston, from what little we know of the Act incorporating it, seems to have adopted, and adapted, the New York City forms.

Except for Norfolk[2] and possibly Charleston, these later charters were all democratic in the sense that the council entirely or in part was to be chosen by the qualified inhabitants. This was to be expected when the motivating force was local and spontaneous, rather than proprietary or royal and fostered.

During the same period the popularly elected assemblies were revealing a growing articulateness and were becoming more conscious of their own potentialities. The precedent of obtaining additional powers from the assemblies rather than from the governors was formed during these years ; although the Cornbury and Montgomerie grants to New York City constituted exceptions. Nor did the assemblies stop with a merely acquiescent role, but began to impose duties upon their communities. In Philadelphia, Charleston, and Savannah, they took an intimate and increasing interest in local affairs in the absence of formally constituted city governments. Many of the assemblies insisted upon 'confirming' the charters granted by the governors ; and the North Carolina assembly in practice made this a condition of a charter's operation.

A genuine urbanization was in fact taking place in a number of these centres — an urbanization which was a product not merely of a growing population, but also of its diversity and of the growing trade and increase of wealth and culture. Chiefly it showed itself in Boston, New York, Philadelphia, and Charleston. Other centres — Salem, Newport, New Haven, Albany, Annapolis, Norfolk, Wilmington, Savannah — exhibited many of its symptoms.

Necessarily this growth and change meant changes in

2. It will be remembered that the close corporation was the type for all Virginia local units.

the functions of these communities. The more alert and mobile life, the expanding horizons, weakened the essentially narrowing monopolies of trade and craft. Assizes, which could be regulated in the intimate stage, atrophied administratively in the larger towns. Unpaid service for the watch and on the roads crumbled, as the sanctions of public opinion weakened and the needs of congestion increased. The numerous and disastrous conflagrations forced the substitution of the fire engine and the fire company for the old buckets. The urban imperatives of cleanliness and safety were doing their work. More elaborate docks and bridges, and even water works, appeared. Poor relief could no longer rely upon the benevolence of the churches for adequate resources, and turned to public authorities and public funds. The communal feeling which had introduced the school in the early days was weakened somewhat ; but commercial rivalry, the expression of a more materialistic age, was probably strengthened. All these factors meant a subtle change in the outlook of and towards the municipal corporations themselves. These corporations became much more administrative and governmental and less preoccupied with judicial matters — and the activities of New York City would have been almost recognizable by moderns.

This growth in population and function necessarily had its impact upon the governmental and financial structure. As in England, it brought to Philadelphia, Charleston, and Savannah the *ad hoc* commission or board — for watch, poor relief, paving, and other functions. This overlaid these communities with a web of authorities and jurisdictions, contrary to all modern standards of administrative practice.

Financially, such growth forced the various communities to seek powers from their respective assemblies to expand their revenues from the old reliance on fines, fees, and rentals. Chiefly this expansion took the form of property and poll taxes; and the former inevitably brought the problem of an adequate and fair assessment base. New and subtle issues were thus injected into colonial and municipal actions which were never thereafter to be absent. Class struggled against class to avoid the more extreme burdens. However, there was at least this crystallization of opinion — that whatever the tax basis ultimately chosen, at least it must conform roughly to a man's ability. Various were the experiments tried to approximate this and to reduce avoidance to a minimum. Unlike England, even unimproved land was brought within its orbit. Towards the end, the lottery came to be recognized as a form of revenue — apparently painless and not as yet seriously challenged on ethical grounds.

The growing population meant also a growing economic and social cleavage, and the phenomenon of incipient class revolt and resentment expressed itself with political effectiveness for perhaps the first time in American experience in the Zenger controversy and the election of 1734 in New York City. The success of the revolters was temporary, but the phenomenon recurred again and again thereafter. Franklin in Philadelphia sensed the power of the masses and used it to aid in gaining his ends. Lawyers in Boston, New York, and Annapolis came to exploit this power to advance their views and attain ends more radical than those of the entrenched merchants and landholders. To the heterogeneity of race was added the heterogeneity of class and occupation — both to remain as characteristics of American cities from then on. Deference as a factor yielded to the blows of class consciousness, and a new, more electric, but less honourable tone entered civic life. Below the artisan group were the masses of unskilled labour — seamen, indentured servants, and others — unfranchised, unassimilated, lawless — not yet politically minded, but presenting in their lawlessness and drunkenness serious problems for the city fathers.

With the rise of the masses and their advent to a share of political power came a deterioration in methods of campaigning. Bribery in various forms, partisanship, rioting, and sharp practices of one kind or another entered to win the votes of those who 'for the most part were of no opinion at all.' While these less savoury phenomena were confined to relatively few communities and to those of the more liberal franchise and diverse population, they were none the less symptomatic of a changing political life, an urbanization, an incipient radicalism. They were the visible signs of a breakdown of special privilege, of the traditional governing class, of vested interest — a breakdown which was to gain in strength and ultimately prevail in American municipal government generally.

Even metropolitan problems of built-up areas outside the actual city limits appeared in Philadelphia, where, more or less by accident, the original boundaries had been narrowly drawn. In the other cities, the cramping effects of limited areas had not been felt, for the original incorporations in conformity with English tradition had included large tracts of unbuilt common or assigned strips outside the little group of houses which made up the urban centre.

But this urbanization had its counter-force in the assemblies. A country-city cleavage, partly economic, partly social, began to express itself and foreshadow the day when with certain cities this cleavage was to prove an impasse to effective governmental progress. As yet it assumed the somewhat milder forms of under-representation and occasional overtaxation of the municipality, and in New York City it was evidenced in an hostility to the City's monopolies.

It is difficult to say, as certain writers have alleged, whether there was any falling off in the momentum of incorporation after 1750. A few incorporations did take place in these later years, and New Haven threatened to break the charterless character of New England. Apart from these instances, it is difficult to decide which towns might have incorporated that did not do so — possibly Baltimore or Newcastle or Kingston. Such failure to incorporate is rather meagre evidence on which to base a case for a deliberate cessation of incorporations. The town meeting tradition was strong and satisfying, even outside of New England, in the North. The assemblies were meeting the needs of other communities reasonably well. The incorporation 'urge' had perhaps lessened with the lessened possibility of special trade privileges, and towns were no longer artificially fostered. Otherwise developments were taking place quite naturally.

Towards the end the events which foreshadowed and brought on the Revolution undoubtedly occupied men's minds. A quickened and peculiarly American expression of views and ideals was precipitated in town and city alike. Moreover, incorporations themselves had for so long been completely local and American in their genesis that there was no incongruity between a move to incorporate and resentment at the governors of an English king — even though the actual charters might have to bear the king's name. The radicalism of the cities joined forces with the radicalism of the Piedmont and played its own part in an Americanism which ultimately severed all ties with the mother country.

(B)

One who draws a picture of the incorporated city in 1775 must be careful not to exaggerate its institutional importance. In this respect the city ranked below the town and county as well as the colony ; and was even rivalled by the village and vestry. In Pennsylvania the special district was very nearly as important. To be candid, the municipal incorporation had not yet found its sphere as an institutional type. A form which was applied at one and the same time to the hamlet of Westchester and the city of New York had scarcely crystallized. In North Carolina the borough was still primarily a mere unit of representation in the assembly. At no population level did the group of incorporated cities and boroughs include a majority of the communities, not even among the most populous. Of the four towns above 10,000, two, Boston and Charleston, were devoid of formalized municipal corporations, and Philadelphia was a hybrid. Only New York enjoyed full-fledged representative municipal government. Of the six communities between 5,000 and 10,000, only Norfolk had a municipal charter ; four of the others — Newport, New Haven, Salem, Gloucester — were New England towns ; Baltimore was still under its commissioners. Below 5,000 the proportion of New England and other towns and villages to the total increased faster than did that of the incorporated boroughs. In New Jersey, Newark and Woodbridge were certainly as large as the average of the four incorporated cities. The fact of the matter is that in all thirteen colonies, in 1775, there were apparently only fourteen communities still functioning under governments of the municipal type, unless the town commissioner type of North Carolina be included. In these fourteen, other institutions were more

prominent in at least Philadelphia and Elizabeth and possibly in two or three other New Jersey and Pennsylvania
communities. For one reason or another the charters of
Agamenticus, Schenectady, Trenton, Germantown, Chester, Newcastle, St. Mary's, Wilmington (N. C.), Charleston, had all lapsed — a number of them relatively recently.
Salem (N. J.) had lost most of its municipal privileges.

While these American charters were much simpler and
for the age more 'modern' than their English counterparts, they did still contain a certain number of clauses
that were scarcely suited to the times. The distinction
between freemen and non-freemen was still retained in a
number of cities ; but, even so, those cities with freemen
of the craft or trade possessed a larger electorate than
those which qualified voters on a property basis only.
In three towns, and those among the most important, the
close corporation still continued — even though its functions had become more governmental than managerial
and judicial.

However, the broad picture revealed an approaching
genuine urbanization, as witnessed by the use of committees, the grouping of functions, the incipient attempts at
financial control, and agitation (not without success)
for a more honest ballot. Improvement in the cleanliness
and paving of the streets and, above all, a certain cosmopolitan attitude were forcing forward the day when government by a state assembly, a close corporation, or even
a town meeting had inevitably to yield to a type more
suited to a triumphant urbanism. When that day was to
arrive, this rather neglected municipal corporate form
— basically representative — was to come into its own as
the inevitably favoured type for genuine city self-government.

The city frameworks in 1775 were still essentially English. The Dutch strain had dwindled away ; peculiarly American contributions to structure had not yet appeared. The cities were British in their defined rights and duties, in their legal basis. The royal prerogative had survived virtually intact as the ultimate chartering source. British the charters were in their variety ; in their mixture of open and close corporations ; in their terminology ; in their union of judicial, legislative, and administrative processes in one and the same agency. British they were in their absence of logically defined categories ; in the use of special boards and commissions for particular functions ; in the widely differing positions and powers of the mayors. Functionally the cities paralleled the British in the declining emphasis on control of trade, and the rising provision of municipal amenities ; and went beyond the British by making education in part a local responsibility. They were British in that they were usually units of representation in the legislative body.

Here the parallel ends. Seldom were they, like the British, manipulated by central authority for royal or partisan ends. Under the fostering care of governors and of their own assemblies, for the most part they blossomed into such activities as the age knew or their needs required. They did not decay as did so many of the British cities through inactivity, save as the incorporation in the first place was premature because of insufficient size. They were more clear of cluttering and complicating survivals. The guilds left no trace in their structure and played but little part in their life. If the earlier American incorporations had, by British precedent, been somewhat premature, that phase had passed and incorporations were more normal, more natural. While there were exceptions, the inhabitants of the American cities, as of the American towns, were generally more articulate than the British — not merely about local affairs alone, but in using their town and borough meetings with increasing zest and seriousness of purpose to agitate and discuss colonial and *national* questions as well. Their relationship with their assemblies was far closer than was that of the neglected English municipality with Parliament. Finally, this articulateness in a few of the larger communities had begun to express itself in a cosmopolitanism in which the Dutch played no small part. This was evidence of that peculiarly *American* point of view which marked the spiritual counterpart of the economic and geographic cleavage with the mother country, and which was destined ultimately to bring a political cleavage as well.

(C)

The elements of permanent significance to American urban development from the colonial period were actually not very many, but some were of very great importance. Of these, first place must be given to the 'rule of law,' to the theory that the city government was itself a corporation — with some peculiarities perhaps — but none the less a corporation with definite powers, continuity, and membership, and upon which duties could be, and were, imposed. It was of permanent significance that it was to the legislature and not to the governor that these communities looked for enhancement of their powers, particularly when the power of taxation was at stake. In spite of the fact that the cities claimed independence by virtue of their royal charters, it was significant that the assemblies treated the cities as subordinates — for the most part in all friendliness, but at times revealing that urban-rural cleavage which was in later years to complicate municipal affairs. It was significant that, none the less, these cities — and towns — developed a real spirit of local self-government, adding this also to the many really American traditions. The terminology largely remains to this day, though the mayoralty is profoundly altered, and the aldermen are no longer 'justices.' Regrettably, lawlessness also remains — but this and many other elements were far from exclusively urban products and were understandable only in the light of colonialism as a whole. The tradition of voluntary service did not survive ; nor did the institution of 'freedom,' or the property franchise. Elements in the taxation system did, however, remain ; to crystallize ultimately in the American property tax as we know it to-day — the most productive source of revenue for local government that the world has known.

These were not inconsiderable contributions from the colonial era, even though city charters were relatively few, and the largest community was scarcely 30,000. The story has its familiar and unfamiliar elements — the human factors of the economic drive, jealousy of prerogative, resentment at entrenched power — elements which are recognizable and understandable to-day. Other elements are less familiar — British, guild, rural, religious attitudes — long since withdrawn from the main political thought-stream. The bulk of peculiarly American tradition waited for a later, more independent age — when the forces of the frontier, the machine, and the 'alien' influx were to alter our municipal development out of all recognition. The forming of our municipal tradition was the task, not of the colonial age, but of the period from 1800 to 1870.

With the outbreak of the Revolution, ties were to be

severed which had hitherto largely determined American municipal development. The day of the English city outpost was to pass ; the American city was on the horizon.

APPENDIX A
DATES AND NATURE OF THE CHARTERS
A CATALOGUE

*(Together with a bibliographical note for each city, giving the principal
secondary sources. For primary sources,
cf. Appendix B.)*

A. VIRGINIA

  1. *Burmuda City, James City, Henrico, etc.* cf. pp. 91-
     7 *supra*.
  2. *Williamsburg.*[1] Town Act, 1698/9, Middle Plan-
     tation made the seat of government, ports laid out ;
     1705, incorporation as a 'city' authorized by the as-
     sembly — which incorporation by royal charter did
     not take place until 1722, in spite of a petition in
     1717.[2] Powers enhanced by acts of assembly subse-
     quently.
  3. *Norfolk.*[3] One of the towns included under the Act
     of 1705 — the town, a 'free burgh.' This Act was dis-
     allowed, but a start had been made. Royal charter,
     1736, with additional privileges extended from time
     to time later.

B. MAINE

  1. *Agamenticus, Gorgeana.*[4] Exceedingly liberal char-
     ters extended by Gorges (proprietor) as 'borough'
     (Apr. 10, 1641) and as 'city' (March 1, 1641/2).

---

1. Cf. Tyler, I. G., 'Williamsburg, the old Colonial Capital,' in *William and Mary Quarterly*, vol. XVI, pp. 1-65 ; Gulick, L., and Pollard, J. G., *Modern Government in a Colonial City*.
2. Gulick and Pollard, op. cit., p. 25.
3. Cf. Wertenbaker, T. J., *Norfolk* ; Burton, H. W., *History of Norfolk, Va.*, Norfolk, 1877.
4. Cf. Banks, C. E., *History of York, Maine*, Boston, 1931 ; Moody, E. C., *Agamenticus, Gorgeana, York* (Handbook History of the Town of York) ; Sylvester, H. M., *Old York*, Boston, 1906.

The charter was revoked in 1652 by the Massachusetts Bay Company, but there is some evidence that it may have survived in practice as late as 1676 under the vicissitudes of the numerous changes in government of the territory.[5]

C. New York

1. *New York City.*[6] In 1665 Governor Nichols confirmed (under the treaty agreements) the privileges of the old Dutch charter, making certain modifications to bring it more into accord with English practice. The Dutch type was resumed in 1673 ; the English again the following year. In 1686, charter from Governor Dongan, full privileges. In 1708, charter from Governor Cornbury concerning ferry rights. In 1730, charter from Governor Montgomerie, extended privileges.

2. *Albany.*[7] An example of a town which had acquired most of the rights of an incorporated borough by a succession of grants prior to the actual issuance of a royal charter.[8] As Beverwyck, under the Dutch it had been in receipt of numerous privileges, including a special court (a vice-director — later known as the schout — and commissarisen) which had appar-

5. Sylvester, op. cit., p. 91. Banks, op. cit., doubted this.
6. Cf. Peterson, A. E., and Edwards, G. W., *New York as an Eighteenth Century Municipality* ; Lamb, M. J., *History of the City of New York*, New York, 1896, 3 vol. ; Wilson, J. G. (Edit.), *Memorial History of the City of New York* ; Stokes, I. N. P., *Iconography of Manhattan Island*. For the Dutch incorporations, cf. Chap. IX, *supra*.
7. Cf. Munsell, J., *Annals of Albany* ; Weise, A. J., *History of the City of Albany* ; Howell, G. R., and Tenney, J. (Edit.), *History of the County of Albany*.
8. However, many of these earlier courts were more in the nature of district than town courts. Cf. p. 235 ; also Van Laer, A. J. F. (Trans. and Edit.), *Minutes of the Court of Fort Orange and Beverwyck* ; ibid. *Court of Albany, Rensselaerswyck, and Schenectady*.

ently been continued as 'commissioners' by agreement under the English.[9] The schout was even addressed as 'Mr. Mayor' by Governor Lovelace.[10] In 1673 under Dutch restoration, the town was made a *schepenen,* apparently of a higher order (four schepens), and given additional trade privileges.[11] These officers were again retained by the English as 'magistrates' or 'justices,' two of whom each year were to be members of the general court of assizes for the province.[12] Hence it is not surprising that when a royal charter was finally issued in 1686, it should declare : 'the town of Albany is an ancient town . . .' with 'divers and sundry rights . . . as well by prescription as by grants.'

3. *Westchester.* Royal charter, 1696, by Governor Fletcher. Continued in operation down to the Revolution, and functioned for a brief time in 1787. The extant records present considerable difficulties. The trustees' minutes are missing after 1730 except for records of deeds. The common council met with the court only occasionally. Ordinances were rare, or rarely recorded. There are recorded elections of aldermen or councillors prior to 1701.[13]

4. *Schenectady.*[14] Town court, governor's order, 1672.[15] Royal charter, 1765. No evidence of further

9. For its history under the Dutch, cf. Chap. IX.
10. Quoted in Munsell, J., *Annals of Albany,* vol. IV, p. 21.
11. O'Callaghan, E. B. (Edit.), *Documents Relative to the Colonial History of New York,* vol. II, pp. 653f., 675, etc.
12. Weise, A. J., *History of the City of Albany,* p. 160.
13. Westchester Town Minute Book, and other 'Libers.' Cf. p. 327f.
14. Cf. Monroe, J. H., *Schenectady, Ancient and Modern,* Geneva, 1914 ; Pearson, J., *et al., History of the Schenectady Patent.*
15. For petty cases only. Two to be named by the governor annually out of three chosen by the inhabitants. *Minutes of the Executive Council of the Province of New York,* vol. I, p. 146.

functioning subsequent to the choice of its first officers, except that its right to 'borough' representation in the assembly remained down to the Revolution. In 1766 its aldermen and assistants gave bond to qualify 'within Eight days after the governor grants a new and additional Charter for the said Borrough with the Alterations and Amendments to the Present Charter of the following Articles . . .' There follow a series of articles of a democratizing tendency dealing with more frequent elections, no licences for wagons, and reasonable fees for children of freemen to take out their own freedom. I have discovered no evidence of the granting of such alterations; and it might be conjectured that the original charter was allowed to lapse through dissatisfaction with its provisions.[16]

5. *Lansinghburgh* (Stone Arabia).[17] January 1, 1771, a compact, called at the time 'Proposals,' was agreed upon; and a committee of five persons and certain other officers (town clerk, pathmaster, fenceviewers) were chosen by inhabitants and freeholders to preside over 'the town and borough of Stone Arabia.' The only justification for mention in the list of boroughs is the fact that in 1771 the 'City of Lansinghburgh' was actually surveyed and for several years it was known as 'The New City' with every expectation of actual incorporation. Records are extant indicating that town meetings were fairly frequently held for the 'Borough of Stone Arabia,' eventually

16. Reprint from one of the Vrooman papers, in Munsell, J., *Annals of Albany*, vol. I, p. 368. More information is very definitely needed, before one can state with any authority the course of the apparently ephemeral borough government of Schenectady.

17. Cf. Weise, A. J., *History of Lansingburgh*, Troy, 1877.

called (after Jan. 4, 1774) the 'Town of Lansinghburgh.'[18]

D. Maryland

1. *St. Mary's.*[19] Proprietary charter, 1667 or 1670. The
   charter gradually lapsed through disuse with the
   decline of the city ; and the power of the corporation of separate representation in the assembly was
   abrogated by Act of the assembly in 1708.[20]

2. *Annapolis.*[21] 1696, incorporation, by Act of assembly, as a 'Porte and Town' with a separate court —
   also with power to hold a market and fairs.[22] On
   August 16, 1708, a charter was issued by the governor. Under challenge of the assembly after being in
   partial operation for a few months, this charter was
   withdrawn and a second and altered charter (November 22, 1708) was issued by the governor and
   confirmed by the assembly.[23]

E. New Jersey

1. *Burlington.*[24] Chosen in 1681 and reaffirmed by

18. Lansingburgh Town Record, 1771-1780, MS. in the Library of Con-
    gress.
19. Mereness, N. D., *Maryland as a Proprietary Province* ; Andrews, M.
    P., *Founding of Maryland.*
20. Scharf, J. T., *History of Maryland,* vol. I, p. 423.
21. Riley, E. S., *Annapolis, The Ancient City* ; Tilghman, O., *Annapolis,
    History of Ye Ancient City,* 2nd. edit., Annapolis, 1925 (?) ; Riley, E.
    S., *History of Anne Arundel County* ; Stevens, W. O., *Annapolis, Anne
    Arundel's Town,* New York, 1937 ; Jackson, E. M., Jr., *Annapolis,*
    Annapolis, 1936.
22. Mereness, op. cit., p. 417.
23. Cf. *Maryland Archives,* vol. XXVII, pp. 358ff. ; Mereness, op. cit., p.
    420 ; also p. 41f. *supra.*
24. Heston, A. M. (Edit.), *South Jersey — A History* ; Schermerhorn, W.
    E., *History of Burlington,* Burlington, 1927 ; Woodward, E. M., and
    Hegeman, J. F., *History of Burlington and Mercer Counties.* For an
    analysis of all the New Jersey charters, cf. Scott, Austin, *Early Cities
    of New Jersey,* in *N. J. Hist. Soc. Coll.,* 2nd ser., vol. IX.

assembly and governor in 1682 as 'the chief city and town' of West Jersey. Granted a market in 1682. Incorporated by Act of the assembly (according to power delegated by the Proprietors) in 1693 as a town and borough, with a town meeting, a burgess or chief magistrate, recorder, councillors, etc. Powers included a court, assize of bread, etc., full by-laws. These were extended by supplementary Act of 1695. These powers of a full incorporation were apparently exercised for many years, but some fell into disuse, and a full royal charter was requested and granted in 1733.[25]

2. *Salem.* Claimed, though never quite successfully, the same rights and privileges as Burlington. It was never quite sure of its ground in making such claims. In 1678 Governor Andros incorporated it as a town with six commissioners, four of whom constituted a court. The court was subordinate to the justices of Newcastle.[26] Salem was made a port town in 1682,[27] given a market,[28] and in 1695 was incorporated and endowed with the same type of government and powers as Burlington (q. v.), except that it was not the 'chief town or city.'[29] It never subsequently obtained a royal charter. It was even deprived of certain of its privileges — as a port by 1697,[30] separate representation by 1727,[31]

25. Cf. Burlington Town Book, MS. in custody of the clerk of the township.
26. O'Callaghan, E. B. (Edit.), *Documents Relative to the Colonial History of New York*, vol. XII, p. 610.
27. Laws of W. Jersey, 2nd session, Chap. VIII.
28. Ibid., Chap. IV.
29. Ibid. Chap. VII. Cf. Barber, J. W., and Howe, H., *Historical Collections of State of New Jersey*, p. 435.
30. *New Jersey Archives*, 1st ser., vol. II, p. 178f.
31. Smith, Samuel, *History of the Colony of Nova-Caesaria*, p. 497.

fairs in 1764.[32] Salem is a 'borderline' case, but should probably be included in a list of borough incorporations.

3. *Perth Amboy*.[33] An example of borough rights by accretion rather than by formal charter, though the latter was subsequently granted. It was erected as a town and 'city' by the proprietors about 1680,[34] and for many years thereafter engaged in a struggle with New York City to uphold its rights as a port town.[35] In 1683 it was declared to be the 'capital,' and instructions from the proprietors indicated that as soon as possible it should have markets and fairs, be the chief staple, and receive a charter.[36] In 1685 and 1686 the proprietors were largely concerned with the disposition of the land.[37] In 1686, markets and fairs were established by Act of the assembly, the officers to be chosen by the townsfolk ; and it was made the seat of a provincial court.[38] It also had separate representation in 1703 as the 'City of Perth Amboy' and in the earlier assemblies the usual town representatives.[39] However, in its local government,

32. *N. J. Arch.*, 1st ser., vol. XXIV, p. 332.
33. Whitehead, W. A., *History of Perth Amboy* ; Wall, J. P., and Pickersgill, H. E. (Edit.), *History of Middlesex County, N. J.*, New York, 1921, 3 vol.
34. O'Callaghan, E. B., *Documents Relative to the Colonial History of N. Y.*, vol. IV, p. 382.
35. Cf. pp. 359ff.   O'Callaghan,   op. cit., vol. IV, pp. 305, 382f. ;   *N. J. Archives*, 1st ser., vol. II, pp. 178f., 183, 341, 537.
36. *N. J. Archives*, 1st ser., vol. I, p. 451.
37. *Journal of the Proprietors of East Jersey, 1685-1708*, Mar. 11, 1685 ; May 13, 1686 ; Sept. 9, 1686 ; etc. (Cf. *New Jersey Archives*, vol. I, p. 451, etc.)
38. Whitehead, W. A., *East Jersey Under the Proprietary Governments*, New York, 1846, pp. 116, 167 ; Leaming, A., and Spicer, J., *Grants, Concessions, etc., of N. J.* (Reprint, 1881), p. 287.
39. Smith, Samuel, op. cit., p. 276.

it either drafted its by-laws in town meeting or remained under the county officers.[40] Certainly, in the Journal of the Proprietors, at least up to 1705, there is no evidence of any town or city government. I cannot find just how its representatives were chosen, but presumably in 'town meeting' as elsewhere in Jersey. The right to a ferry was granted in 1700 by the proprietors ;[41] in 1719 by the governor ;[42] in 1771 the rates were fixed by Act of assembly.[43] A full royal charter was granted by Governor Hunter in 1718.[44] Incidentally this was granted on the same day as a charter to St. Peter's Church, and the majority of the incorporators were the same. Later on, the church owned one of the ferries and ran a lottery for it. Second charter, 1753.

4. *New Brunswick*.[45] Royal charter, 1730. Second charter, 1763, but little modified.

5. *Elizabeth*.[46] A town with many corporate privileges, even before its royal charter of 1740. Additional privileges conferred in 1754.

40. The clerk for Perth Amboy joined with those of Newark and Elizabeth to send an address to the other towns in 1699. (*N. J. Hist. Soc. Coll.*, vol. I, p. 145.) See also Whitehead, W. A., *Contributions to the Early History of Perth Amboy*, p. 50.
41. *Journal of the Proprietors*, op. cit., Dec. 17, 1700.
42. Book B-2, p. 249, MS. in Secretary of State's Office. June 2, 1719; Nov. 14, 1719.
43. Chap. DXLIX, Laws of New Jersey.
44. In the charter there is continual reference to 'the present' mayor, assistants, etc., which may have no significance or may possibly indicate an actual functioning of a city government predating the charter. It will be recalled that Governor Dongan arranged for such functioning in New York City two years before the formal charter. References to it as a 'city,' in laws and elsewhere, were frequent after 1700. e. g., *Laws of New Jersey*, 1713, p. 66.
45. Cf. Wall, J. P., *Chronicles of New Brunswick*, New Brunswick, 1931; Benedict, W. H., *New Brunswick in History*, New Brunswick, 1925.
46. Cf. Hatfield, E. F., *History of Elizabeth*.

APPENDIX A 433

6. *Trenton.*[47] Shire town, 1719. Royal charter, 1745 ; surrendered as unsuitable, 1750.

F. PENNSYLVANIA[48]

1. *Germantown.*[49] Proprietor's charter, as borough, 1689, in operation, 1691 ; forfeited for failure to function, 1707. Petition from inhabitants for reinstatement apparently not granted.[50]

2. *Philadelphia.*[51] Some evidence of a borough charter as early as 1684. In the Charter of 1691, Penn refers in the past tense, 'I have . . . erected the said Town into a Burrough,' whereas the incorporation into a city was, 'I . . . do erect,' etc. In the minutes of the provincial council and the acts of the assembly prior to 1691, it is constantly referred to as a 'city.' Acrelius speaks of it as having been chartered in 1682.[52] In 1684 on the records of the provincial council, 'Thos. Lloyd, Thos. Holme, Wm. Haigne appointed to draw up a charter of Philadelphia, to be made a Borough, consisting of a Mayor and six Aldermen, and to call to ye assistance any of ye Council.'[53] Chartered as a city, 1691, by the proprietor. This charter apparently lapsed when Penn was superseded in 1692. New charter issued in 1701,

47. Cf. Lee, F. B., *History of Trenton, N. J.,* Trenton, 1895.
48. Cf. Holcombe, W. P., *Pennsylvania Boroughs,* J. H. U. Series, vol. IV, No. 4.
49. Cf. Pennypacker, S. W., 'Settlement of Germantown,' in *Proc., Penn.-German Society,* vol. IX, 1898.
50. Undated petition, bearing forty-two signatures, addressed to Thomas Penn. (MS., Collections of Pennsylvania Historical Society.)
51. Cf. Allinson, E. P., and Penrose, B., *Philadelphia, 1681-1887,* Baltimore, 1887 ; Scharf, J. T., and Westcott, T., *History of Philadelphia* ; Oberholzer, E. P., *Philadelphia; a History of the City and its People,* Philadelphia, 1912, 4 vol.
52. Cf. Acrelius, p. 112.
53. July 26, 1684.

by Penn. Functioned continuously thereafter, but from 1750 on, increasingly divorced from the citizens ; many functions of municipal government were placed in the hands of commissioners, etc.[54]

3. *Chester.*[55] Court at Upland, from Dutch and possibly from Swedish days. Borough charter issued by proprietor in 1701, several 'rights,' such as markets and fairs, having come down from earlier grants. Evidence of operation thereunder lacking, except that its 'chief burgess' sat with the county justices and also performed certain magisterial functions, such as signing indentures, etc.[56]

4. *Bristol.*[57] Market town, 1697. Borough charter granted by proprietor, 1720. Increased powers, by Act, 1745.[58]

5. *Lancaster.*[59] Borough charter, 1742, by proprietor.

G. Delaware

1. *Newcastle.*[60] (Swedish, Christenehamn.[61] Dutch,

---

54. Cf. pp. 252ff.
55. Cf. Ashmead, H. G., *Historical Sketch of Chester* ; Ashmead, H. G., *History of Delaware County.*
56. Enough of these deeds and indentures are extant in the possession of Chester Baker (Chester, Pa.), and elsewhere, to warrant this statement. The probabilities are that the 'chief burgess' was elected at town meeting annually ; and that, apart from magisterial functions, the borough as such soon became moribund and 'government' remained a matter for the town and its officers. However, the important records are lost and this is but a conjecture. The commissions issued to justices of the peace by the governor's council of Nov. 22, 1738, May 25, 1752, and other dates (for Chester County) included 'The Chief Burgess of the Town of Chester for the Time being.'
57. Green, Doron, *History of Bristol, Pa.,* Camden, 1911 ; ibid. *History of Bristol Town Council,* privately printed, 1928.
58. Ch. 367, Laws of Pennsylvania.
59. Cf. Riddle, W., *The Story of Lancaster.*
60. Cf. Scharf, J. T., *History of Delaware* ; Conrad, H. C., *History of the State of Delaware.*
61. Cf. p. 53 ; Johnson, A., *Swedish Settlements on the Delaware.*

New Amstel.[62]) With the British occupation, the Dutch corporation was continued for a time with English names.[63] It was in 1672 made a 'balywick' by the governor's council in New York, with jurisdiction over the entire Delaware district. Superseded in 1673 by the Dutch, who presumably reestablished their governmental forms. On reoccupation by the English, the county courts apparently resumed control, the 'balywick' not being continued.[64] It became a part of Pennsylvania and seems to have been endowed with certain privileges of a shire town, such as markets and fairs.[65] The court set up for the Newcastle area passed a number of by-laws applying only to the village.[66]

For administrative and legislative purposes, Delaware separated from Pennsylvania in 1704, but retained the same governor. In 1724, Governor Keith issued a charter of doubtful validity constituting it a city, only to have this annulled by Governor Gordon in 1726 (?).[67] We read that 'popular clamor' was responsible for this demotion in status. Why is conjectural, but the question of Quaker predominance was involved, and also Newcastle's potential rivalry to Philadelphia. The charter itself had in part been granted to quiet the fears of the inhabitants that the

62. Cf. p. 238.
63. *Duke of Yorke's Book of Laws: Charter and Laws of the Province of Pennsylvania* (Reprint, 1879), pp. 446, 451.
64. Cf. Conrad, H. C., *History of Delaware*, vol. II, p. 512.
65. Thomas, Gabriel, *Account of Pennsylvania and West New Jersey*, 1698, p. 6 (Reprint, Cleveland, 1903).
66. Cf. de Valinger, L., Jr., *Development of Local Government in Delaware* (unpublished thesis, University of Delaware, 1935), var., for this episode.
67. Cf. Shepherd, W. R., *Proprietary Government in Pennsylvania*, p. 349f. ; Keith, C. P., *Chronicles of Pennsylvania*, vol. II, p. 681f.

'three lower counties' were about to be granted to Lord Sutherland. It had not been favourably received even in Delaware. Thereafter it remained a 'shire town.'

2. *Wilmington.*[68] Proprietory charter as borough, 1739.

H. NORTH CAROLINA[69]

1. *Bath.* Town, 1705.[70] Borough town by Act of assembly, 1715. Seaport town, 1716, by proprietor.

2. *New Bern.* Town, 1715. Borough town, 1723. Royal patent, 1760. This latter appears not to have operated, as the assembly withheld confirmation.

3. *Edenton.* Borough town and metropolis, 1722. Royal patent, 1760. This latter appears not to have operated, as the assembly withheld confirmation.

4. *Wilmington.*[71] Town (Newtown), 1735. Borough town, 1739. Royal patent, 1760. Royal charter, 1763. Powers confirmed and increased by Act of assembly, 1764.[72] Charter surrendered, 1766 or 1767. The 1760 charter was denied confirmation by the assembly and hence appears to have been inoperative until 1764, when a reissue in 1763 was confirmed by the assembly the following year. It functioned for only about

68. Cf. Scharf, J. T., *History of Delaware* ; Conrad, H. C., *History of the State of Delaware* ; Ferris, B., *History of the Settlements on the Delaware,* Wilmington, 1846.

69. An excellent account of the checkered career of the North Carolina boroughs may be found in McKinley, A. E., *Suffrage in the Thirteen Colonies,* pp. 109-117. Cf. also *supra,* pp. 44ff., and Nash, F., *The Borough Towns of North Carolina* (*N. C. Booklet,* VI, 1906).

70. According to Cooper, F. H., *Some Colonial History of Beaufort County,* N. C., Chapel Hill, 1916 (U. of N. C., *James Sprunt History Publ.,* XIV). The original Act is lost.

71. Cf. Waddell, A. M., *History of New Hanover County* ; Sprunt, J., *Chronicles of the Cape Fear River,* 2nd edit., Raleigh, 1916.

72. *State Records of North Carolina,* vol. XVIII, pp. 654ff. (Ch. VII).

three years and was surrendered in 1766 or 1767. Apparently, a petition for a new charter either accompanied the surrender or was forthcoming later. Whether it was finally granted is not clear from available evidence. It was under consideration by Governor Martin in 1774.[73]

5. *Brunswick.* Town, 1745. Borough town, 1754. Charter repealed and reissued by the governor about 1755.

6. *Halifax.* Borough town, 1757. Royal patent or charter, 1760 and 1764.[74] The 1760 charter appears not to have operated as the assembly withheld confirmation, although admitting to its body a representative elected under the Bath Laws of 1715 which enfranchised towns reaching a certain size. The governor protested vigorously.[75] The 1764 charter may merely have granted right of representation.

7. *Salisbury.* Governor's charter, 1765 or 1766.

8. *Hillsborough.* Governor's charter, 1770.

9. *Campbelton.* Governor's charter, 1772. Abolished about 1774.[76]

10. *Tarborough.* Governor's charter, 1772.

These last four charters apparently, as far as the governor as custodian of the royal prerogative was concerned, merely gave (or confirmed) the right to send borough representatives to the assembly. 'Town' incorporation under commissioners had previously been granted by the assembly.[77]

---

73. Cf. p. 340 ; ibid. vol. IX, p. 818.
74. Nash, F., *Borough Towns of North Carolina,* p. 93 (*N. C. Booklet,* VI, 1906).
75. *State Records of N. C.,* vol. VI, pp. 245, 365, 538-H, 598, 752-3, 983-9.
76. Information from Dr. Robert D. W. Connor, U. S. Archivist.
77. Cf. MS., Minutes of the Commissioners of Tarborough, 1760-1793, custody of State Archivist, Raleigh, N. C.

I. South Carolina

1. *Charleston* (Charles-Town).[78] 1722, charter by assembly and governor. Disallowed by Lords Justices, 1723, after hearing.[79]
2. *Georgetown.* Doubtful, 1732. *The South Carolina Gazette* hears that it has been made a 'free port.'[80]

J. Georgia

1. *Savannah.*[81] Doubtful, 1733. As late as 1764 the 'Town of Savannah enjoyed separate representation in the Georgia legislature.'[82]
2. *Frederica.*[83] Doubtful, 1735.

These municipalities apparently complete the list of incorporated municipalities, although it is entirely possible that the discovery of lost records may reveal others — perhaps Gloucester (N. J.) under the proprietors ; or the continuation and confirmation of certain Dutch incorporations ; or Beaufort and Georgetown, South Carolina.

78. Cf. Pringle-Smith, J. J., *History of Charleston,* in *Charleston Year Book,* 1880.
79. Cf. pp. 192ff.
80. All town records have been burned.
81. Cf. p. 83 ; also Gamble, T., Jr., *History of Savannah* (in the *City Report* for 1900) ; Jones, C. C., Jr., *History of Savannah.*
82. *South Carolina Gazette,* October 29, 1764.
83. Cf. p. 83.

APPENDIX B

BIBLIOGRAPHICAL NOTE ON
CHARTERS AND MINUTES

A. CHARTERS.

These are printed or available as follows :

Agamenticus, 1641 : Hazard, Ebenezer, *Historical Collections,* Philadelphia, 1792-94, 2 vol., vol. I, pp. 470-4.

Gorgeana, 1642 : Moody, E. C., *Handbook History of the Town of York,* Augusta, 1914, pp. 7-10.

New York, 1686 : O'Callaghan, E. B., *Documents Relative to the Colonial History of New York,* Albany, 1853-87, 15 vol., vol. III, pp. 218, 331-4.

New York, 1730 : *Colonial Laws of New York,* vol. II, pp. 575-639.

Albany, 1686 : Howell, G. R., and Tenney, J., *History of the County of Albany,* New York, 1886, p. 461f.

Westchester, 1696 : Bolton, R., Jr., *History of the County of Westchester,* New York, 1848, 2 vol., vol. II, pp. 184-195.

Schenectady, 1765 : *Cadwallader Colden Papers,* vol. VII, pp. 13ff., in *Coll. N. Y. Hist. Soc.,* vol. 50-56.

Burlington, 1693 : by Statute, q. v.

Burlington, 1733 : Woodward, E. M., and Hageman, J. F., *History of Burlington and Mercer Counties,* Philadelphia, 1883, p. 128f. Liber AAA of Commissions, Office of Secretary of State, Trenton.

Salem, 1693, 1695 : by Statutes, q. v.

Perth Amboy, 1718 : Book C-2, Deeds of East New Jersey, Office of Secretary of State, Trenton.

Perth Amboy, 1753 : Missing ?

New Brunswick, 1734 : Scott, A., *Charter and Early*

439

Ordinances of New Brunswick, New Brunswick, 1913, pp. 7-23 (*N. Bruns. Hist. Club Public.*).

New Brunswick, 1763 : Book C-2, Deeds of East New Jersey, Office of Secretary of State, Trenton.

Elizabeth, 1740 : Murray, N., *Notes Concerning Elizabethtown*, Elizabethtown, 1844, pp. 28-44 (abridged).

Trenton, 1746 : Liber AAA of Commissions, Office of Secretary of State, Trenton.

Philadelphia, 1691 : Allinson, E. P., and Penrose, B., *Philadelphia, 1681-1887*, Baltimore, 1887, pp. xlvii-lii.

Philadelphia, 1701 : *Laws of Pennsylvania* (1803 edit.), vol. VI, Appendix pp. 15ff.

Germantown, 1691 : *Pennsylvania Archives,* vol. I, 1852, pp. 111-115.

Chester, 1701 : *Laws of Pennsylvania* (1803 edit.), vol. VI, Appendix pp. 20-23.

Bristol, 1720 : ibid. pp. 23-27.

Lancaster, 1742 : ibid. pp. 27-30.

Newcastle, 1672 : Scharf, J. T., *History of Delaware,* Philadelphia, 1888, 2 vol., vol. II, pp. 859ff.

Newcastle, 1724 : Missing.

Wilmington (Del.), 1739 : *Ordinances of the City of Wilmington,* 1872 Edition.

Annapolis, 1708, first charter : Missing.

Annapolis, 1708, second charter : Riley, E. S., *The Ancient City,* Annapolis, 1887, pp. 87ff.

St. Mary's, 1667-70 : Missing.

Bermuda City, etc. : Missing.

Williamsburg, 1722 : *William and Mary Quarterly,* 1st ser., vol. X, pp. 84-91.

Norfolk, 1733 : Hening's *Virginia Statutes,* vol. IV, pp. 541ff.

Wilmington (N. C.), 1763 : *State Records of North Carolina,* vol. XXXIII, p. 654f.

Charleston (S. C.), 1722 : Missing.

B. MINUTES.

Original manuscripts or reprints of the minutes of the colonial municipalities are extant in a number of instances. To the extent to which they have come to the attention of the author, they are located as follows : —

Agamenticus, Gorgeana : Missing.

Albany : Under the Dutch, as Beverwyck, Van Laer, A. J. F. (Edit. and Trans.), *Minutes of the Court of Fort Orange and Beverwyck,* Albany, 1920-23, 2 vol.

Under the English, prior to 1686, Van Laer, A. J. F. (Edit. and Trans.), *Minutes of the Court of Albany, Rensselaerswyck, and Schenectady,* Albany, 1926-32, 2 vol.

Under the Dongan Charter, 1686-1753, printed in a slightly abridged form in Munsell, J., *Annals of Albany,* Albany, 1850-59, 10 vol.

After 1753, in Munsell, J., *Collections on the History of Albany,* Albany, 1865-71, 4 vol., vol. I.

New York City : Under the Dutch, *Records of New Amsterdam, 1653-1674,* (Fernow, B., Edit.), New York, 1897, complete and printed in seven volumes.

Under the English, *Minutes of the Common Council,* 1675-1776, New York, 1905 (H. L. Osgood, Ch. of Edit.), are complete, and printed in nine volumes.

In addition, the complete records of the Mayor's Court from 1674 are in manuscript in the Hall of

Records in New York City. Prior to 1674 they were included in the Council Minutes (q. v.).

Kingston : Oppenheim, S. (Trans.), *Dutch Records of Kingston,* New York, 1912, 2 vol.

Westchester : Certain of the minutes and other records are in manuscript in the Bureau of Municipal Investigation and Statistics, New York City. Extant are the Trustees' Minutes, including the town meetings for election of officers, 1665-1730 ; an undated codification of the By-laws of the Church Wardens ; and numerous deeds, etc. The Mayor's Court Minutes, 1696-1706, 1717-1775, with certain gaps are in the Library of the New York Historical Society. Two or three scattered entries of the Mayor's Court (1721, 1724) are found among the Minutes of the Trustees.

Schenectady : Missing.

Stone Arabia : Lansinghburgh Town Record, 1771-1780, in the manuscript division in the Library of Congress.

Perth Amboy : Missing. They may have been destroyed in 190 ?, when $200 was paid to clean out and burn all the old papers and records in the City Hall.

Elizabeth : Except for fragments in the office of the city clerk, the borough minutes are missing. A town book with a few entries of town meetings in borough days is in the possession of Princeton University Library.

New Brunswick : Minutes of the Common Council between 1730-1750 were printed in 1913 by the New Brunswick Historical Club, which has the manuscript. The remainder are missing.

Trenton : Missing.

Burlington : The township minute book, covering the records of the town meetings during its city days and earlier, is in the custody of the clerk of the township, who resides at present at the Masonic Home near Burlington. The minutes of the city corporation are missing.

Salem : Fragments only of the minutes during its borough days are in the Library of Rutgers University. The township minutes after 1758 are in the State Record Office at Trenton.

Bristol : The manuscript of minutes of the council after 1730 is in the office of the city clerk. Earlier minutes are missing ; also minutes 1734-1742.

Germantown : The *Rathbuch* (proceedings and court records of the burgesses) is in the Library of the Historical Society of Pennsylvania. The Society also has an English translation.

Philadelphia : The *Minutes of the Common Council, 1704-1776,* were printed in Philadelphia, 1847. They are missing prior to 1704. The minutes of the Street Commissioners, 1762-1768, are in the possession of the Library Society of Philadelphia ; of the Commissioners and Assessors, 1771-1774, in the possession of the Historical Society of Pennsylvania. Fragments of the records of the Mayor's Court are also in their possession. The docket of the Mayor's Court, 1759-1764, is in the office of the Clerk of Quarter Sessions.

Chester : Missing.

Lancaster : The minutes of the council are in the city clerk's office. Internal evidence indicates that the entries are not complete, particularly between 1746-50 and 1753-65.

Wilmington (Del.) : The minutes of the borough meetings, with incidental entries of meetings of the burgesses and assistants, are in the Library of the Historical Society of Delaware at Wilmington. The minutes of the burgesses and assistants, 1771-1777, are in the Hall of Records at Dover. Prior to 1771, they are either missing or were never kept — the town meeting records being deemed sufficient.

Newcastle : City and bailiwick records missing. The records of the county court have been published.

St. Mary's : Missing.

Annapolis : The Mayor's Court Proceedings 1720-1726 are in the Land Office in the Hall of Records at Annapolis. The volume is labeled 1720-1784, but after 1726 the entries are rare indeed. A book of the minutes of the Corporation, 1757-1767, is also in the Hall of Records. This also contains the records of the Mayor's Court in these years. Apart from these two books, and an account book, the records are missing. Fragments dealing with the Mayor's Court may be found in the Rainbow Papers, Black Book 3, nos. 25, 27, in the Maryland Hall of Records, Annapolis.

Williamsburg : Missing — perhaps burned at the time of the Civil War.

Norfolk : Minutes of Council (Council Orders), 1736-1798, in the city clerk's office, Borough Court records missing, probably burned at the time of the Revolution.

North Carolina boroughs : The records are almost entirely missing. The minutes of the Commissioners of Tarborough are in the custody of the North Carolina Historical Commission at Raleigh. The Town Record Book of New Bern, 1753-79, is in the vault of the Clerk of City Court, New Bern. Samuel Ashe (Battle, K. P. (Edit.), *Letters and Documents of Lower Cape Fear,* 1903) mentioned and used a Town Book of Wilmington, but I have not been able to locate this.

Charleston (S. C.): Minutes of St. Philips Parish,
1732-1755, and after 1762, are in the church vestry.
Prior to 1732 they were burned by the wife of the
clerk, when possession was demanded. Minutes of
the city and of its various commissions are all missing.

C. STATE RECORDS, ETC., CITED.

Massachusetts : —

Massachusetts Historical Society Collections, 1st-
7th series and continuous thereafter (from vol. 7),
Cambridge, 1792 — .

*Publications of the Colonial Society of Massachu-
setts,* Boston, 1892 — .

Boston Town Records, in *Reports of the Boston
Record Commissioners,* Boston, 1876 — , W. H.
Whitmore and W. S. Appleton (Commrs.), volumes
2, 7, 8, 12, 14, 16, 18.

Rhode Island : —

Rhode Island Colonial Records, Providence, 1856-
65, J. R. Bartlett (Edit.), 10 vol.

Proceedings of the First General Assembly, Providence, 1847, W. R. Staples (Edit.).

Town Records (Portsmouth, Warwick, etc.) were
published by the Rhode Island Historical Society,
with various editors.

Rhode Island Historical Tracts, Providence ; 1st
series, 1877-1895, 20 numbers ; 2nd series, 1889-97,
5 numbers.

Connecticut : —

Papers of the New Haven Colony Historical Society,
New Haven, 1865 — .

New York : —

Documents Relative to the Colonial History of the State of New York, Albany, 1853-87, E. B. O'Callaghan (Edit.), 15 vol.

Collections of the New York Historical Society, 1st series, New York 1809-30 ; 2nd series, 1811-59, 10 vol. ; 1868 — (no series number).

Colonial Records, Albany, 1899, G. R. Howell (Archiv.), (State Library bulletin ; history, no. 2).

Colonial Laws of New York, Albany, 1894, 5 vol.

New Jersey : —

Documents relating to the Colonial History of New Jersey (Archives of the State of New Jersey), Newark, 1880 — , Editors, vol. 1-8, W. A. Whitehead ; vol. 9-29, F. W. Ricord and/or W. Nelson ; vol. 29, W. Nelson and A. V. Honeyman ; vol. 30 — , A. V. Honeyman.

Collections of the New Jersey Historical Society, Newark, 1846-1900, 9 vol.

New Brunswick Historical Club Publications, New Brunswick, 1887 — .

Pennsylvania : —

Colonial Records of Pennsylvania, Harrisburg, 1851-53, S. Hazard (Edit.), 16 vol.

Collections of the Historical Society of Pennsylvania, Philadelphia, 1853, 1 vol.

Memoirs of the Historical Society of Pennsylvania, Philadelphia, 1826-95, 14 vol.

Pennsylvania-German Society, *Proceedings and Addresses,* Lancaster, 1891 — .

Lancaster County Historical Society Papers, Lancaster, 1896/7 — .

Delaware : —

Maryland : —

Archives of Maryland, Baltimore, 1883 — . Editors :
1883-1912, W. H. Brown ; 1913-15, C. C. Hall ;
1916-28, B. S. Steiner ; 1929 — , J. H. Pleasants.

Virginia : —

Hening, W. W., *Statutes at Large,* Richmond, Philadelphia, New York, 1810-23, 13 vol.

North Carolina : —

Colonial Records of North Carolina (continued
from vol. 11 as *State Records of North Carolina*),
Raleigh, 1886 — ; Editors : vol. 1-10, W. H. Saund-
ers ; vol. 11-26, W. Clark.
James Sprunt Historical Publications (Univ. of N.
C.), Chapel Hill, 1900 — .

South Carolina : —

Laws of the Province of South Carolina, Charles-
Town, 1736, N. Trott (Compil.).
Statutes at Large of South Carolina, J. D. McCord
(Compil.).

Georgia : —

Colonial Records of Georgia, Atlanta, 1904-06, A.
D. Candler (Edit.), 26 vol.

APPENDIX C
ESTIMATES OF POPULATION OF COLONIAL CITIES

AVAILABLE estimates are notoriously inaccurate, and are valuable only in a general way in aiding the reader in determining the approximate size of a community at various stages of its governmental development. In many instances the following estimates are the author's own, calculated from available information as to the number of tithables, houses, etc. Inhabitants are calculated at an average of six to the house in the North and seven or slightly more in the South. Numbers of tithables are approximately doubled (a little less) to obtain an estimate of towns whose population is calculated on this basis. Where a (?) is put after a population estimate, the estimate is but little more than a guess. The population is of the juridical area, usually much more than the actual built-up portion.[1]

CITY	DATE	ESTIMATED POPULATION
Gorgeana	1642	300
New York	1652	800
	1675	7,000
	1756	13,040
	1775	23,000
Albany	1697	700
	1775	2,500 (?)
Westchester	1700	160
Schenectady	1775	1,500
Perth Amboy	1760	1,200
Burlington	1750	1,750 (?)
Elizabeth	1750	1,500 (?)

1. Cf. also Sutherland, S. H., *Population Distribution in Colonial America*, New York, 1936.

City	Date	Estimated Population
New Brunswick	1740	1,300
Trenton	1750	800
Philadelphia	1700	10,000
	1775	28,000
Germantown	1700	500 (?)
Bristol	1750	750
Chester	1750	600 (?)
Lancaster	1775	4,000
Newcastle	1725	1,000 (?)
Wilmington, Del.	1739	600
	1775	1,229
St. Mary's	1665	480
Annapolis	1775	3,700
Jamestown	1625	175
Williamsburg	1759	1,000
	1775	2,000
Norfolk	1740	1,000
	1775	6,250
Edenton	1775	550
New Bern	1775	550
Wilmington, N. C.	1775	900
Charleston, S. C.	1722	1,500
	1770	10,863
Savannah	1741	1,000

Non-incorporated towns

Boston	1775	17,000
New Port (R. I.)	1774	9,209
Baltimore	1775	5,934
New Haven	1775	8,000
Providence	1774	4,321
Salem	1776	5,337

APPENDIX D

A COMPARISON OF ORDINANCES OF NEW YORK AND ALBANY AT DIFFERENT DATES

A. *New York City*

The titles for New York City in 1701 were :

(1) For the observation of the Lord's Day
(2) Concerning strangers
(3) Concerning freemen
(4) Concerning keeping the streets clean
(5) Concerning retailers of liquor
(6) Surveyors of the Citty
(7) To prevent fire
(8) Concerning negroes
(9) Concerning Engrossers and Forestallers of the Markett
(10) Assize of Bread
(11) No timber, etc., to lye in the streets
(12) Concerning Swine
(13) Regulations Concerning Carmen
(14) Officers to be observant in the Execution of these Laws
(15) Concerning Negroes and Indian Slaves
(16) Common Council not to be absent on summons
(17) Gaugers, Packers, and Cullers
(18) Weights and Measures to be sealed
(19) Masters of Vessels to give an account of their passengers
(20) Concerning Bucketts
(21) Packers Marke on beef and porke
(22) Freemen to be Inrolled
(23) Apprentices to be bound before the Mayor, etc.
(24) Ordinances for paving. etc.

(25) Laws for the Dock and Slips, etc.
(26) Oath of freemen
(27) Regulation for the Markett
(28) Against Firing Guns
(29) Relating to Apprentices
(30) Who are deemed Freemen
(31) Freemen to be made by Mayor and Aldermen
(32) To prevent Fire
(33) Against Hawkers
(34) Against Emptying Odours in the Streets
(35) About Carmen
(36) Killing cattle in slaughter house only
(37) Keeping the Streets Clean
(38) Swine prohibited in the Out Ward

By 1775 the following changes are noted : (Cf. pp. 118ff.) Numbers (1) (2) (6) (7) (9) (10) (13) (15) (17) (25) (31) (33) (36) were retained without substantial change. The regulations concerning paving and cleaning were somewhat strengthened, and the city's responsibility enhanced as compared with that of the individual. The various ordinances concerned with fire prevention followed a similar trend, and the fire engine appeared. The swine seem to have disappeared from the streets. The market code had become more elaborate in some respects, in so far as the weights and measures of more articles were safeguarded. The ordinances concerned with apprentices and licensing had disappeared, perhaps as the city's role lessened and the province's increased — or as court procedure became standardized. New objects of regulation appeared in fences, midwives, gunpowder, unripe fruit and oysters, raffling, sale of liquor to the 'centinels.'

All in all the changes were exceedingly moderate, and almost all of them were accounted for by the growth of the city from approximately 8,000 to about two and a half times that number. To a very limited extent an actual rise in urban amenities can be observed. (Data from *Minutes of the Common Council,* var., esp. Dec. 23, 1701; Feb. 4, 1749/50; Jan. 12, 1775.)

B. *Albany*

A similar comparison of subjects of municipal concern in Albany between the years 1686 and 1774 shows but little change, save as the town grew in population from probably under 1,000 to something over 2,000.

1686 : oath to officials, trial of a negro for theft, rules for election of assessors, Sabbath observance, fine for non-attendance at council, regulation of Indian trade, repairing of wells, rating, sale of lots, purchase of land by corporation, swearing in of porters, inspection for fire risks, no rinsing of clothes near wells, no carrying of sand from cemetery, rules for liquor licenses, resistance to fire master, erection of a pound, licensing of carmen, commanding services of citizens in building stockade and serving on the watch.

1774 : ferries, streets, nuisances, docks and wharves, carts and carmen, public markets, Sabbath observance, danger of gunpowder, fire prevention, prevention of accidents by fast riding, taverns, treasurer's duties, midwives.

There is little difference 'in kind' between the two years, save that the corporation in the meanwhile had acquired ferries and certain other public properties. [Munsell, J., *Annals of Albany* and *Collections on the History of Albany,* var. ; Howell, G. R., and Tenney, J. (Edit.), *History of the County of Albany,* p. 468.]